dream lovers

dreamlovers

The magnificent
shattered lives
of Bobby Darin
and Sandra Dee
by their son
DODD DARIN
and Maxine Paetro

WARNER BOOKS

A Time Warner Company

Grateful acknowledgment is given to quote from the following:

"Beyond the Sea." Written by Charles Trenet and Jack Lawrence. Copyright © 1945 PolyGram International Publishing, Inc. On behalf of itself, France Music Corp. and Edition Raoul Breton (and as designated by co-publisher). Used by permission. All rights reserved.

"Beyond the Sea" (*La Mer*). English lyric by Jack Lawrence. Music and French lyric by Charles Trenet. © 1945 (Renewed) Edition Raoul Breton. English version © 1947 T.B. Harms. © Renewed 1975 MPL Communications, Inc. All rights reserved. Used by permission.

"The Curtain Falls" by Sol Weinstein. Used by permission of Sol Weinstein.

"Dream Lover"—Bobby Darin. © 1959—Alley Music Corp. and Trio Music Co., Inc. Copyright renewed. Used by permission. All rights reserved.

"Long Line Rider"—Bobby Darin. © 1968—Alley Music Corp. and Trio Music Co., Inc. Used by permission. All rights reserved.

"Song for a Dollar"—Bobby Darin. © 1969—Alley Music Corp. and Trio Music Co., Inc. Used by permission. All rights reserved.

Grateful acknowledgment is also made to Barry Gray
to reprint portions of his interview
with Bobby Darin, July 1960.

Warner Books, Inc., 1271 Avenue of the Americas, New York, NY 10020

W A Time Warner Company

Printed in the United States of America
First Printing: September 1994
10 9 8 7 6 5 4 3 2 1

Library of Congress Cataloging-in-Publication Data

Darin, Dodd.
    Dream lovers : the magnificent shattered lives of Bobby Darin and Sandra Dee / by their son Dodd Darin and Maxine Paetro.
      p.   cm.
    ISBN 0-446-51768-2
    1. Darin, Bobby.   2. Singers—United States—Biography.   3. Dee, Sandra.   4. Motion picture actors and actresses—United States—Biography.   5. Darin, Dodd.   I. Paetro, Maxine.   II. Title.
ML420.D155D37   1994
791.43'028'092273—dc20
[B]   94-10203
                                                  CIP
                                                  MN

Book design by Giorgetta Bell McRee

*This book is dedicated to my parents:
two very special human beings
in all the ways that really count.*

ACKNOWLEDGMENTS

First and foremost I want to thank my mother, Sandra Dee, who gave me her blessing to do this book. She answered all of my questions, sacrificed her privacy, and exposed herself to whatever facts and feelings I turned up in the course of this journey. I am eternally grateful to her for her generosity and her support.

An undertaking of this magnitude required the selfless contributions of the many people who were part of the lives of the principals of this story. In particular I wish to thank my aunt Vee Walden, who gave unstintingly of her emotions as she told me about her relationship with my father and about his effect on their family. She and my grandfather, Charlie Maffia, are brave and decent people who loved my father deeply, warts and all. I am indebted to Dick Lord and Dick Behrke, two of my father's lifelong friends. Dick Lord not only told me the most wonderful stories, but he was willing to put his vulnerability on the page. Dick Behrke added tremendously to my understanding of my father's background, and together, Dick Lord and Dick Behrke provided context for the narration of Bobby Darin's life. My father's dear friend, the irrepressible Harriet Wasser, not only offered valuable insight into his personality, but helped us connect the dots as we pieced together this story. Thank you, Hesh.

A heartfelt expression of love goes out to Steve Blauner, who had a special relationship with my father. It began as manager and artist and evolved into a loving friendship. Over the past seven years he has become a most important person in my life, and I, too, have had a special relationship with him. He has been the individual most responsible for my understanding who my father was and what he was really all about—the good and the bad. It is through him that my father's voice still resonates. For that I will always love him and be forever grateful.

My deep gratitude and respect go out to the following people for their help in bringing this book to life: Rona Barrett; Mickey Behrke; George Burns; Andrea Burton; Dick Clark; Rudy Clark; Jackie Cooper; Troy Donahue; my aunt, Olga Duda; Ahmet Ertegun; Barry Gray; Peggy Lee; Carol Lynley; the late John J. Miller; Dr. Philip Oderberg; Artie Resnick; John Saxon; and the late George Scheck. Ross Hunter and Jack Freeman, who cherished the child star who was my mother, told us a part of her story that would have been lost without them. I am indebted to them both. I am also grateful to a terrific writer and journalist, Peter Greenberg, who interviewed friends of my father back in 1975 and gave us the use of his invaluable work.

My sincere thanks to Dr. Josh Fields for his friendship to my father and for all he did to prolong my father's life. If there are any mistakes in my translation of his descriptions of my father's heart disease, I want to say that the errors are completely mine. I would like to express my love and appreciation to two people who were dear friends with my father during his lifetime and absolutely loyal to his memory since his passing: David Gershenson and Wayne Newton. David Gershenson has become a dear and loving friend of mine and in my father's last days was there when it really mattered. Wayne Newton also proved that a friend in need is a friend indeed. He came through for my dad when the chips were down, out, and gone, and he never asked for thanks. Both Wayne and David have helped keep my father's spirit alive. I also wish to acknowledge Andy DiDia, who was with my father heart and soul since his first performing days, and the Masterantonio family of Pueblo, Colorado, who were the core of my father's fan club. My mom and I consider them all Darin family members.

My thanks go to Barbara, Nick, and Arthur Friedman. Arthur Friedman has been a tremendous help in encouraging me to bring this book into being and to take the risks to explore new opportunities for my creative energies.

My love goes to my in-laws, Barbara and Thomas Tannenbaum,

ACKNOWLEDGMENTS

Eric and Lillah Tannenbaum, and Madelyn and Carey Waggoner for welcoming me into their family. And I wish to also express my love and friendship for Rick Ward of San Diego; he is the brother I never had.

On the professional side, I would like to thank the incredible Nanscy Neiman, my editor and publisher of Warner Books, for believing in me and for giving us her total support during this project. What started out as simply a book about my parents has resulted in much more—a valuable and enriching learning experience for me. My gratitude to Harvey-Jane Kowal, managing editor at Warner Books, for her patience and professionalism and for keeping her sense of humor at deadline time.

I want to thank Thelma Seto, our transcriber, for the devotion she gave to this book. My thanks, too, to Ana Crespo for keeping the pieces together and Madeline Paetro for her excellent assistance as a researcher. We did much of our research at the Library for Motion Picture Arts and Sciences, and we also thank the staff members for their help. Thanks to Sona Vogel for having a sharp mind as well as a sharp red pencil.

Last, my deepest appreciation and respect go to my co-writer, Maxine Paetro. Part psychologist, detective, diplomat, and, of course, talented writer, this bright and perceptive woman was very patient working with the difficult, temperamental personality that I possess. Max constantly helped me strive for the truth even when it was painful to do so. For that I cannot thank her enough. Quite simply, this book would not be what it is without her.

dream lovers

INTRODUCTION

It's been said that sometime between the ages of six and puberty, a boy comes up against an urgent and unavoidable conflict. His father is the most powerful being on the earth: bigger, stronger, and smarter than he is in every way. One day the little boy understands that he's going to have to defeat this giant, bring him down to human size, so that he can have his own life as a man. This battle is a normal passage for fathers and sons, but for sons of men who are larger than life, the battle is harder fought and not always won.

In my case, I am the only child of two celebrities: Bobby Darin and Sandra Dee, both superstars in the late 1950s and early 1960s. My mother is alive, but her story is a painful one to tell. Her problems are deep and crippling, and our conflict is ongoing—my intense desire for my mother to have a healthy life, against her inability to do so. We fight often.

My father, however, died at a young age. If he hadn't, I'm sure I'd look at him and say, "There's a human being. He made some records. He's talented, but he's rude. He's got warts," and I would know him as a man. But because he died when I was twelve, before I had won my fight with him, he's been frozen in my mind. I adulated him and was so much in awe of him when he was alive, I cannot help but compare myself to him now—and I come up short. When my father died, he left me with awe and myth, his face and name, and a sense that I am Bobby Darin's living remains.

1

In Beverly Hills, California, there are many celebrities and celebrity sons. During my early life, John Clark Gable, Clark Gable's son, was my best friend. He and I went to the same school, lived just two miles apart. We didn't need our parents to drive us around because we rode our bikes everywhere. In fact, it was our normal routine to go bicycle riding after school and then hang out together. One night in December of 1973, we ate dinner at John's house, watched TV, and I spent the night.

When we got up the next morning, we noticed that the radio and TV were gone from John's room. We had watched the TV the night before, so we looked at each other, said, "What the hell is this?" and went to find Mrs. Gable. Kay Gable was a sweet lady, and I liked her very much. We asked her about the mysterious TV disappearance, and she gave us a nonsensical response, something about an electrical problem. It never occurred to me that there might be something on the news I wasn't supposed to know. She said, "I'm going to drive you home, Dodd, because your mom wants to see you right away."

I said, "I'll go home, but let me ride my bike. There's no need for you to drive me."

"No," she insisted. "I'll drive you home."

I argued some more, but it was useless. So John, Mrs. Gable, and I got into the car with my bike, and we traveled the two miles to my house. I found my maternal grandmother, Mary Douvan, sitting in the living room with a couple of her friends.

My grandmother said, "Your mom wants to see you. She's in her room."

I'll never forget the way my mother's bedroom looked that morning. The drapes were closed across the sliding glass doors and windows, the TV was on, and it was very dark in there. My mom was in bed. Beside the bed was a big, green chair. I plopped down on that, and she said, "I have something to tell you. Your father died last night."

I sat quietly for a second. Then I asked her some questions, talked to her a little bit. I remember my first thought was to ask her how she was doing. She had obviously been crying. Although I have no idea where these words came from, I said to her, "Well, I expected this to happen. We're gonna be okay, don't worry, Mom." In looking back, I realize it's kind of a strange statement. But that's what came out of my mouth. "We're gonna be fine."

Ten minutes later I was out skateboarding with my friend John, and if I knew then my life had changed irrevocably, it was an idea that I buried very deep. I recognize now that I made quite a statement that morning. In a couple of sentences I took on the responsibility for my mother's happiness and denied the pain of losing my father. Twenty years later I find I'm still feeling responsible for my mother and still denying in large part the reality of my father's life and death.

During my father's last years, while he was ill and not always rational, he acquired a valise. It was an ordinary vinyl suitcase, medium size and tan, with a zipper all the way around, but it was very important to my father. Whenever he would go on a trip, he'd leave the valise with my mother with instructions that she was not to open it until after his death. The case was unlocked, but neither of us dared to look inside, although we often wondered what my father valued so much that made the suitcase so dear.

A few weeks after my dad died, my mom and I opened the valise. I've completely blocked out the memory of that moment, but in the years that followed, I examined the few artifacts my father left behind and began to understand something of what my father prized most. Still, the contents of the suitcase didn't answer all the questions that gnawed at me as I got older and started struggling with the larger issues of my life.

A year ago, when I turned thirty, I found myself telling a woman I deeply loved that if I didn't find a way to be happy with myself, I wouldn't be able to be with her. I told her that my parents were legends, and I was not, and that my chances of matching their success was very low. As I considered her dismay and the thought that I might give up this important love, I realized how much work I had to do. It became clear to me that I needed to understand the events that made my parents who they were so that I could better comprehend their legacies and myself. And I hoped that in the end I might set myself free.

My father's beginnings were mysterious. He didn't learn who his real mother was until he was thirty-two years old, and he never knew his father's name. Because of his childhood bouts with rheumatic fever, my father also knew that his life span would be short. He was a man in a hurry. He could be rough and he could be ruthless. For years I'd heard that my father wasn't the heroic figure I imagined him to be.

3

I'd respond, "Yeah, my father was a prick, but . . ." and I'd smile. I rather enjoyed his salty reputation and his aggressive ways without realizing that by excusing his faults and gilding them, I was perpetuating the myth that has kept me in his shadow.

My mother's childhood was a horror story made more unbelievable by the contrast between the public's image of Sandra Dee—a golden teenage princess—and the truth. She suffered wretched abuse as a child. Today she is still quite beautiful, but she is reclusive, alcoholic, anorectic, and dependent entirely upon me for emotional support. I love my mother, but I'm angry at her. She has usurped my childhood, and she's wasting her life. For the sake of my sanity, I've asked her to tell me about the damage that was done to her, and I find that I've had to delve into the darkest parts of her existence. In the process, I've come to a new and unwelcome understanding of my maternal grandmother, whom I deeply loved.

Recently I came across a box of interviews transcribed from tapes of my father's friends and associates only two years after his death. This box of interviews, like my dad's valise, revealed intriguing slices of my parents' lives and made me want to know everything there was to know. I dug deeper and found many people alive today who had known my parents well and were anxious to tell me about them. There were people who considered Bobby Darin the centerpiece of their own lives, and they still choked up with emotion talking about him two decades after his death. In setting down these stories, I've sometimes used the storytellers' own words. In some cases, like my mom's, the conversations took place over long periods of time, so I've condensed the material to a reasonable length. In all cases, I've been true to the context and content of the information I've been given.

I've called the book *Dream Lovers*—in part after my dad's hit single, and also because of the images the words evoke, images we understand and love of the scrappy kid from the Bronx and the fresh-faced girl next door. Together, my parents embodied a dream of what one could be, or have, or marry. But the stories of Bobby Darin and Sandra Dee are shockingly different from the public's perception of them. *Dream Lovers* is about two people whose childhoods were cruelly twisted by forces they could not control and whose extraordinary spirits emerged brilliantly on the stage, screen, and in recorded sound. This book is about their attraction to one another, their marriage, the emotions that broke them apart, and the aftermath of the breakup of their marriage.

Dream Lovers is not the definitive history of my parents' music and movie careers. It is the record of my search for the truth about my parents as people so that I can accept them, separate from them, have my own life as Dodd Darin, not Dodd-Darin-son-of-Bobby-Darin-and-Sandra-Dee. To do this I've had to examine everything I know about myself and my parents. This book will reveal what it was that made Sandy and Bobby different from ordinary people, people like you and me.

1

Bobby, 1936-1952

No one can write the true story of Bobby Darin unless they take it from the beginning. You had to understand about his illness. If you didn't, you weren't seeing him.

—HARRIET (HESH) WASSER
Bobby's friend and secretary

———

My earliest memory of Bobby as a child was about his rheumatic fever. We couldn't walk on the floor because just walking across the floor would put him in agony. I remember Bobby crying and screaming and my father having to pick him up and carry him to the bathroom, he was in so much pain. I remember being told all my life, "Bobby's sickly. You have to be careful, and you have to protect him." So that's what I did, and that's what my family did. And it was a mistake.

I'm not saying he shouldn't have been protected or carried to the bathroom. I'm saying we should have also made him into a human being, and that we didn't do.

—VIVIENNE WALDEN
Bobby's sister

The year was 1936, and Vanina Cassotto was pregnant.

She was a lusty seventeen-year-old, unwed and living with her mother in a cramped apartment in Harlem. The two women were making do on "home relief" when a welfare worker paid them a surprise visit one afternoon and mistakenly thought that no one was home. In fact, mother and daughter were sleeping and never heard the knock at the door. But the social worker reported that the Cassotto women were now employed, and abruptly, payments to the tiny household stopped.

Nina, as the young woman was called, was looking forward to the birth of her child. It's likely she had reservations about the boy who got her pregnant, because she never told him the big news. It's odd that she didn't tell him. One would imagine she could have used some emotional and financial support, if not a wedding ring, but she never said a word to this boy, and she kept his identity a secret her entire life. We'll never know the real reasons Nina Cassotto was willing to bear and raise a fatherless child, but of the many theories advanced over the years, this is the one most consistent with her personality: The baby was *hers*, and she wanted to keep it. As far as she was concerned, the baby's father was irrelevant. Nina's mother supported her daughter's decision, knowing full well that if her husband had been alive, he would have made Nina give up the child. But Nina's father, Saverio (Big Sam Curly) Cassotto, had died at Sing Sing prison a year before.

We can't find Sam's name in the *"Who's Who* of American Crime," but he was a colorful character nonetheless. Those who knew him say he was a minor league racketeer, a friend of Mafia chief Frank Costello, a likable fellow, and a bit of a screwup. He was a cabinetmaker by trade, and he also invented a nonsensical thing or two. The pop-up doll game that can still be found at carnivals and shooting galleries was one of Sam's better creations. As for his criminal activities, Sam was into the small-time stuff—picking pockets and con artistry. He was arrested many times for these offenses and usually got off, but the last time he got caught with his hand inside someone else's jacket, the judge really nailed him. Unfortunately for Sam, he was addicted to heroin and morphine. When he got sent off to prison, he was unable to conceal enough dope in the hollow heel of his shoe to carry him through his sentence. The care and treatment of drug addicts wasn't very refined in the thirties, and Sam died from heroin withdrawal.

Sam's widow was someone special. Her full name was Vivian Fern Walden Cassotto, but she called herself Polly. Everyone loved Polly. She was a retired show girl with a gift for making people feel really good about themselves. She was intelligent, lovely to look at, and not your everyday grandmother type at all. For one thing, she was a polygamist. For another, she, too, was addicted to morphine. But she wasn't a junkie in today's sense of the word. Morphine was legal in Polly's time. She had suffered pain from a dental problem, borrowed some of Sam's drugs, and found herself hooked. Although Polly kept her habit hidden, sadly, it was with her for life. It's harder to explain the polygamy. Sam Cassotto was Polly's third husband, and I've been told that Polly never divorced husbands numbers one and two. No one now living knows why, but from what I've heard, it seems that she considered divorce a petty formality that she'd just as soon forgo.

Polly's life story is not what one would expect of a blue-blooded girl. Her roots went back to the *Mayflower* by way of Pascoag, Rhode Island. Both parents were of English descent, and Polly's dad was a well-to-do mill owner; her parents divorced when she was in her teens. Polly went to college, then dropped out and went into vaudeville. I don't know what in her background caused her to be such a nonconformist, but she must have had an interesting upbringing.

At the time of Sam's death and Nina's pregnancy, Polly was still petite and beautiful, and she was her daughter's best friend. Abortions were available in 1936 if you knew how to get them, and Polly knew how. She'd had more than one herself, and this wasn't Nina's first pregnancy, either. But there would be no abortion this time. Of course, it was scandalous to have an illegitimate child anywhere in America, but it was especially true in this particularly religious Italian community in Harlem. So, in deference to the values of their neighbors, Polly and Nina cooked up a scheme. Nina was a large girl, able to hide her condition easily. Just before her due date, daughter and mother disappeared and resurfaced a short while later in a different neighborhood a few blocks south of the old one. When they moved into their new apartment, they brought with them a baby boy and told everyone he was the son of Polly and Big Sam Curly, deceased. The baby's name was Walden Robert Cassotto, and as soon as he could understand, he was told that his father had died taking a fall for a Mafia chief, that his sister, Nina, was eighteen years older than he, and that his mother was the incandescent Polly—who gave birth to him when she was close to fifty years old. This lie would remain unchallenged for the next thirty-two years.

But to continue the story, Nina and Polly Cassotto's new address was 125th Street and Second Avenue. Two blocks away, on 126th and Third, lived a cheerful young man named Carmine (Charlie) Maffia. There was a social club in the neighborhood, and Charlie used to go there to listen to records and dance. That's where he met Nina. When he met Nina is disputable, but that they became lovers is fact. Shortly after Bobby was born on May 14, 1936, Charlie came to live with Nina and Polly. He had a good job with the New York City Sanitation Department, took on an additional job repairing refrigerators, and brought in a decent income so he could support the family of four—one of whom had an expensive morphine addiction. Because of hard-working Charlie the bleak years were over for Polly and Nina. In 1942, when Bobby was six years old, Nina and Charlie got married.

The identity of Bobby's father is and always has been in dispute. Perhaps it was the mystery boy, perhaps it was Charlie; Nina died in 1983 without divulging her secret. But one thing everyone agrees with is that if Charlie was not Bobby's actual father, he was his father in every other way. He worried about him, nursed him, worked like a dog to keep food on the table. And Bobby was a sickly child from the moment he was born. It's been said that he was so frail, neighbors expected the scrawny thing to die in the cardboard box that served as his crib. Charlie scraped up the money for medical bills and to buy goat's milk imported from Albania, because for a long time it was the only food Bobby could digest. Bobby had problems with his eyes. He broke a leg when he fell from a chair at the age of three.

Then, in his eighth year, Bobby got *really* sick.

Rheumatic fever is caused by a streptococcus infection that attacks the heart muscle. A common complication from the infection is valve damage, and that's what happened to my father. Today rheumatic fever is rare; children who get strep are treated with antibiotics before irreversible damage is done. During the early 1940s, rheumatic fever was life-threatening, and Bobby was ravaged four times between the ages of eight and thirteen. The disease racked his body and left him with the ruined heart that would both inspire his success and kill him.

Bobby Cassotto grew up in a railroad flat at the corners of "Walk and Don't Walk." The apartment was always filled with the smells of cooking food and the sounds of yelling and singing and ragtime on the Victrola. Charlie remembers that Bobby was talented almost from the time he was born; that he sang and played toy instruments and wrote jingles that rhymed when he was only six. But the kid had his limitations. He didn't go to school for long months when he was sick. He couldn't climb stairs or play rough with other boys. And because of his bad heart, he couldn't exert himself in any way. He spent a year in a sanatorium in the mountains, a place for victims of TB and heart disease. The members of his family always watched him like hawks.

Today Charlie lives in New York in an attached brick row house not far from JFK Airport. He's got a couple of dogs, a cat, and a parrot living with him, and pictures of his kids are pasted on the walls. There's even a picture of me taped to the refrigerator. Charlie is seventy-nine years old, but he has no trouble with his memory. "Bobby was in such pain he couldn't walk," he recalls. "I used to carry him everywhere and even picking him up, he's screaming. When he had his last attack, the doctor said, 'I don't want to say this, but even with good care, this boy is not going to live to see sixteen years.' It was a really sad thing."

Bobby overheard what the doctor said, and learning you're going to die is a hell of a burden for a little boy to bear. But even without a death sentence, his frailty affected him daily. To make up for what other kids enjoyed, Bobby created his own world of books and music. Charlie was a big band nut. He entertained Bobby with records and says that Bobby loved the sound of swing. Polly tutored him at home when he was confined to bed, and she told him great and glorious stories about her career in show business. Bobby was the focus of the family, and they dearly loved him. They called him "the king."

Charlie remembers how he'd stagger in after a hard day's work and get barely a nod of recognition, but Polly and Nina would fight over who would get to feed Bobby his dinner. In fact, Charlie was pretty much used as the family mule, but he didn't seem to mind. He took

Bobby for rides in his garbage truck and took such obvious pleasure in the little boy's charm that it doesn't seem farfetched to suppose he thought, "Wouldn't it be great if this boy really were my son?"

While Nina convinced herself that she was content with the role of Bobby's sister, Polly took on the job of Bobby's mother with a passion. Bobby thrived under her care; she was his lucky star and his inspiration. She saw Bobby through the pain and taught him that he was special. She played him Al Jolson's records, got him a piano, and encouraged his love of performing. She was also very protective of him. It was not unusual for her to lean out the window and yell down to another kid, "Ronny, take off your jacket and give it to Bobby. He's cold."

Polly was also strict, and Bobby respected her. In 1971 he told a reporter this story about his relationship with Polly:

☞ *One day when I was six or seven, a few of my young friends and I were playfully dropping rocks off a trestle onto moving traffic. Well, that was better than throwing ashcans at poor drunken people who were sleeping near the train station, which the older guys did, and which did intrigue me, I admit. And there were quite a few rumbles in our little melting pot. But anyhow, I dropped this rock and maybe hit a truck, and everybody was laughing. Next thing I knew, I felt that I'd been grabbed by the nape of my neck. The grabber whipped me back to my apartment, and he was mad. He said to my mother, "This spoiled brat could have killed someone."*

I didn't blame him for being mad. I remember looking up at my mom, who wasn't particularly tall, so that's how young I was, listening as this tirade went on. And my mother listened sweetly to what the man had to say, and then she said, "Sir, I guarantee you with all that I have in me that he will never drop rocks again."

She needed to do no more. I never had the desire to do it again, nor certainly did I ever do it again. Her words, her ability to control any situation just verbally, was enough to intimidate me totally. And I didn't even have to say "I'm sorry." She knew it. So that contradiction in terms of the neighborhood and upbringing always has existed, and it still does to this degree—that I am a street fighter who would much rather talk my way out of it.

By the time my father was dropping rocks on trucks, the kazoo, the harmonica, and the imitation Woody Herman clarinet that Charlie had given him as toys had been replaced with a set of drums. Soon after that, Nina and Charlie Maffia brought two daughters into the world. Vivienne (Vee) came along in 1943 and Vanina (Vanna) came along four years later. Brother Gary followed in 1956, after Bobby was out of the house, but Vee and Vanna, who grew up with Bobby, were clearly affected by Bobby's death sentence. While I tend to romanticize my father's story a bit, they do not. The younger girls adored the charming side of "Uncle Bobby," but they also had to have felt resentment. Bobby was clearly a pain-in-the-ass pampered kid.

Recently I spoke with Bobby's oldest sister, my aunt Vee. She is a solidly built woman whom many describe as formidable. She emotes fearlessly—cries, laughs, uses profanity, and has an almost poetic cadence in her speaking voice. Vee lives by the truth and is not afraid to fight with her hands. She works with teenagers who've been in trouble, and they hold her in high regard. At the age of fifty, Vee wears a long, blond braid down her back. She owns a trailer home on an acre in New York State that backs up against a rushing trout stream. She bought the property with her own money, and she has no debts. Her independence is important to her. For most of Vee's life she believed herself to be my father's niece, seven years his junior. When she learned Bobby was her brother, she felt it was something she'd always known. Vee grew up with Bobby and refuses to sugarcoat her memories. I thank her for telling her story honestly:

Bobby was wonderful, but he thought the sun rose when he got up in the morning. He thought that everything existed for his pleasure or his need or his wants. This is the result of spoiling a sickly child. You give them the best of everything, and the best is not good enough. Bobby flat out stated on many occasions that he didn't get what he should have gotten.

The truth is he got better than I got. He got better than my sister got. When we all ate hamburgers, he ate steak. When

13

my sister and I had our tonsils out, we went to a clinic. It cost my mother twenty dollars for the two of us. Bobby was sickly, so Bobby went to a specialist for his tonsils, and it cost sixty-five dollars. Today sixty-five dollars is peanuts, but in the forties it was a whole lot of money. My father didn't make sixty-five dollars a week. We didn't have much, but Bobby got the best we had. It became a way of life. And as a child, I didn't think, This isn't right. I should be getting the steak. I wasn't sickly. I was as healthy as a horse.

I loved my brother dearly. He was seven years older than I and skinny. He was always funny. He was hilarious. No way I thought he'd be a singer. I thought he'd be a comic. He had a tremendous sense of humor. As a kid, he did crazy things. He did crazy things because he couldn't do the normal things. He couldn't ride a bicycle normally, but he did ride downhill so he wouldn't have to pump. We lived across the street from the Triborough Bridge, and there was a ramp to the bridge on this one-way street. Bobby would walk the bike up this ramp, and then he would ride down the ramp. And he would do tricks. Like standing on the seat of the bicycle with a cane in one hand, twirling a hat in the other, singing at the top of his lungs, just crazy!

Bobby was well liked. When the kids played stickball, he couldn't run the bases, so there was somebody to run the bases for him. All he had to do was hit the ball. We lived in a city where you sometimes had to prove you were a man whether you wanted to or not. On a few occasions, Bobby got into fistfights that he couldn't talk his way out of. I was a fighter. When somebody would jump on him, I'd jump on them.

Bobby could con you in a heartbeat. Bobby could make you love him. It was a thing with him. When he first got into show business, it was very exciting. When he played the Copacabana, the gangsters would come there on a Saturday night with their girlfriends. Sunday night was the night they took their wives. And Sunday night performances were off-the-wall, they were so good, because Bobby had to make those people stand up and cheer. He had a cold audience. They'd already seen the show the night before. It became his obsession to make sure that they got more than they paid for, that they stood up and screamed. And they did. He did that. That's who he was from the time we were little.

When Bobby was an adult, his attitude toward my family was, "You took care of me your whole lives, now take care of yourselves." He could be very mean, and it was because he was brought up to believe that he was the center of the universe. I'd like to say it was all his fault, but it wasn't. My mother used to talk about people who had an affliction, who had polio when they were little and had a limp. She said they were very bitter people. And she said you always had to be careful around them. I can remember being horrified. How could you say that about someone who has to limp for the rest of his life or someone who's blind in one eye? But when I got older, I could see her point. There's a bitterness that sets in if you are disabled, and very few people can overcome it. Very few people even try.

Bobby was like that, except that the limp was on the inside. He felt bitter because he couldn't do and didn't have what he thought he was entitled to, and he carried these feelings until the day he died.

Something I just find hysterical is how Bobby always said how poor we were. It's funny, and it's sad. There were times when my mother and I sat in front of the television and laughed. We'd watch Bobby saying, "We were so poor that—" and we'd look at each other and say, "Do you remember being that poor?" And we weren't. We lived in a very poor neighborhood. We had six bicycles. Everybody in my family had a bicycle. When I went roller-skating, I took three or four of my friends with me. I had that many pairs of skates. I had more clothes than you could imagine. Bobby wanted to see us as that kind of poor. "I pulled myself up from the dregs," et cetera. That wasn't true.

His first few years, before my father married my mother, the family was poor. They were on welfare, and they didn't have any choice in the matter. But my father was a good provider, and when he moved in, things improved dramatically. My mother didn't want to live in Harlem, so we moved to the Bronx. We didn't have a brand-new vehicle, but we had five cars, two trucks. You'd have to push one car to start another, but that was all right with us. We had a telephone before anybody, and we had the first television, too. It wasn't Hollywood, but it wasn't poverty.

But that was Bobby. He thought we were poverty-stricken because nothing was ever good enough. He wanted to compose great music, music that would last throughout the ages. He wanted to be Beethoven. He wanted to be Bach. Bobby resented that he wasn't a brain surgeon or a heart specialist. That he wasn't Van Cliburn, that he couldn't play. I'm not making up that I think that he felt that way. These are things he stated. But Bobby would never have gone through all the schooling you have to go through to become a brain surgeon or a concert pianist. Never. Even if he had been in good health. And, had he been in good health, he probably would not have achieved what he did achieve. His illness was the driving force in his life.

Bobby could sing. He was a singer's singer. He could do things with his voice that no one else could do. You could hear ten of his records and think they were sung by ten different people, he had that much range. He was immensely talented, but because that came easily to him, it was not important. It was not good enough for what he should have been, *and he felt this his whole life. And that's the crux of the matter. If you set your sights on being Van Cliburn and you play the piano by ear, you've got a problem.*

Bobby was never truly happy. He was always trying to live up to his idea of what he was supposed to be, and that's the God's honest truth.

Young Bobby Cassotto felt he was living in poverty, even if his sisters did not. He was treated as royalty, but he wore Charlie's secondhand underwear stitched down the back to fit him—a difficult disparity to absorb. Compounding his uncertain fix on his identity was an aversion to the way he looked. I remember him telling me about an insult that convinced him he was ugly. He was eight or ten years old, and he was shining shoes. A customer gave him five dollars for a twenty-five-cent shoe shine and said, "Keep the change." That was a lot of change for anyone during the war, let alone a kid. My father was shocked, and he asked, "Why the big tip?" The guy responded, "So you can save up to get your face fixed."

Bobby left his face alone but capitalized on his personality and his talent. He saw an opportunity to advance himself and grabbed for it. The opportunity was the Bronx High School of Science, a school for gifted kids and one of the best high schools in the country. It was hard to get into this school; it required passing a stiff exam and a recommendation from the principal of the student's junior high. My father's academic record was excellent, and he got in. Having gotten in, he had the pins knocked out from under him almost immediately. At Science "the king" wasn't the king. He was one bright kid among hundreds, and he wasn't the brightest one at that.

Ten years later, when my father had become known for his music and his attitude, he said this to the *Saturday Evening Post*.

☞ *All the arrogance you read about stems from those days in high school: a desire never to be anyone's fool again. All the kids were smarter than me—scientifically, academically, and semantically. They were better versed in Schopenhauer and Chopin, Bach and Berlioz. They'd throw lines at me and poke fun, and I'd take it because I felt unequipped to answer back. And then one day, I realized that creatively—in sensitivity, in my soul, I buried them all. I looked at myself as into a mirror, and I knew what I had.*

One of the things my father had was a chip on his shoulder, and I say thank God for that! Without that chip, the Bronx would have had Walden Robert Cassotto, butcher or baker or numbers runner, but the world would not have had Bobby Darin.

While at Science, my father made a lifelong friend, Dick Behrke. Dickie was tallish and thin, with refined features and ways. He was known as a serious fellow, perhaps a bit fastidious, certainly more grown up than the kids my dad knew from the old neighborhood. So with complementary characteristics and common goals of getting into the entertainment world, Dick and Bobby began their long friendship. While at Bronx High School of Science, Bobby and Dick joined a couple of other boys and formed a band. In the summer between their junior and senior years, they took their act to the resort capital of the eastern seaboard, the Catskill Mountains. Later Dick Behrke would forge an impressive career in music as a musician, a conductor, and award-winning creator of music for commercials. Today Dick lives in New York City and on Shelter Island with Mickey, his wonderful wife of thirty years. But it all began with a high school band. Says Dick Behrke:

☞ *Our first band was made up of myself and Bobby, a guitar player named Walter Raim, a saxophone player named Steve Karmen, who afterward made his career in commercial music as I did. The fifth member of the band was a piano player named Eddie O'Casio, who became a doctor. So four of us were very heavy into music later in our lives, and the fifth, the leader, was a doctor. We called the band the Eddie O'Casio Orchestra. The first job was at school, an after-school dance, for which we got paid five dollars for all of us and a pack of gum. The year was 1951, and the money wasn't taxed, so in retrospect it becomes a better bargain every year.*

Our junior year ended, and we all went away to the Catskills and got a job at a place called the Sunnyland Farms Hotel. This was a ten-dollar-a-week job: nonunion, no gum, we had to run the snack concession. When it was busy, we had to carry the bags. It was a tiny little mountain hotel, probably didn't have more than eighty or ninety people at a time, and we had a terrific summer. The owners stocked the concession stand for us, because we didn't have any money. We sold candy, sodas, frozen Milky Way bars with special sticks we would put inside for prizes. Bobby was going to summer school that year. So every morning he would get up at about six-thirty and hitchhike into town, come back in midafternoon, and work at night.

In those days all small bands played the same kind of music. I suppose it was derivative of the big bands. We used to work from things called "combo work," works that were like old standard songs arranged for four or five pieces, or else we'd play by ear. We were not terrific readers, not that organized. We were halfway in between. We played not bad Dixieland, as I recall.

I remember we played a lot of baseball up in the country, and Bobby was quite good. There was no outward sign of his illness except that he would pace himself periodically. He would withdraw from something when he was tired, but it was not that obvious. His family would have seen much more of it when he was younger. And then when he became older, it reasserted itself. But at that period, it didn't really cramp his style.

While playing at Sunnyland, my father met and became friends with another guy named Dick. Dick Loeb was also thin and dark haired. He was a year younger than Dick Behrke and Bobby, had a wide smile, a noticeable nose, altogether an expressive face. Dick was also a terrific storyteller. Later he changed his name from Loeb to Lord and became a comedian. He's a successful comedian today performing in clubs and resorts across the country, but at the time my father first met him, he was a teenager playing drums.

Dick Lord tells this story of meeting my father for the first time:

☞ *I first met Bobby when a girl wanted to jerk me off at a resort in the Catskills. I was working in a band at the Melody Country Club. I don't remember the name of our band. Whatever kid bought the music stands, that's the kid who put his initials on it. We played our music in a recreation hall. When it was time to take a break, we went outside and had a cigarette. Fifteen minutes later, we'd go back in and go on again. So, at this time, I was on break, sitting on this swing, and a blond-haired girl named Susan came over and put her hands on my pants, and I got scared. I thought people might walk out back there, and I was scared anyway. I was like fourteen or fifteen.*

I said, "What are you doing!? What are you doing!?"

She said, "Well, I thought I'd take it out."

I said, "Not here! I have to go to work."

She said, "That's okay. I'll go to Sunnyland Farms. There's a drummer there, he doesn't care. He'd let the whole town watch."

So I said, "What's his name?"

"Bobby Cassotto."

I went back inside, and we played the set, and then I said to the guys, "Let's go hear the band at Sunnyland Farms." So we went over and met all the guys. Behrke was playing trumpet. There was a piano player named Eddie O'Casio, and Bobby was playing the drums. They only knew three songs. It was amazing. They kept playing the same three songs over and over again. The guys were very nice, and I was impressed with Bobby. He told me about getting up at dawn and hitching into town to make up the course he'd flunked, and I realized then that Bobby was a very intense guy. That there was a lot more to him than a blonde named Susan.

Here's what I imagine there was to my father at sixteen—a snapshot, if you will. Bobby Cassotto stands not too tall, barechested, his rib cage so narrow you can span it with one hand. He's flexing a muscle, wearing a smirk, posing on the stoop of the housing project where he lived. The project is a big step up from the railroad flat where he was born. According to Charlie, the apartment was open and bright, and you could see the planes coming in over the water. But Bobby Cassotto doesn't see it the way Charlie sees it. He sees the house crowded with crude, limited people who remind him of what he doesn't want to be.

He hates his slummy life and everything in it.

He thinks about the future, and he wants one. His death sentence has an incremental quality. If he lives until twelve, maybe he'll make it to sixteen. If he lives to sixteen, thirty is possible. He has exceeded the first leg of his life expectancy. He's in one of the best schools in the country. He's learned big words, and he uses them. Desperately. He's become a self-taught drummer, and he's working for pay. He sees that music is going to be his way out.

In a conversation with a journalist from the *Los Angeles Times* about a year before he died, my father stripped away the reporter's glamorous notions about his career: "I didn't see my music as anything but a way to get me the fuck out of that ghetto. Of a way to get me out of the city, of a way to get me out of the crap of being poor, the garbage of being oppressed because of poverty. And when I say poverty, I mean poverty. No poorer than any man's ever been, but just as poor as any man's ever been. And that's what I saw in music—something I could create that would enable me to get out, period. 'Cause that's what was instilled in me. 'Get out via that which makes you different, Bobby.'"

Nearly half his life was gone, and he had no time to waste. Dick Lord says of that summer, "Bobby's the only guy I ever knew who failed the test to get into the musicians' union. He was a good drummer, too. He had a terrific sense of rhythm and all of that, he just didn't want to take the time to read the music, which you have to do on the test. So he failed it. It was a scream because it was so easy."

He was in a hurry, my dad. He was working hard, and he was wanting. Wanting! He came home to the apartment one day unexpectedly, and a door opened both literally and figuratively. Bobby caught Charlie in bed with a woman.

Charlie remembers it this way:

> *I was married at the time, but the family was away for the summer at a bungalow colony in Staten Island. I was home and had a woman in bed with me. I was cheating. Bobby had a key and walked in on us, so I told the woman, "It's about time he got fixed up."*
>
> *She said, "All right."*
>
> *So I went out of the room. I figured I'd let Bobby have her, too, so he'd keep his mouth shut and not get me in trouble with Nina. I left them alone, and then after a while, the broad came back to the kitchen.*

She said about Bobby, "He's pretty good."
I said, "Well, he's green, you know. I think you took his
cherry."
She said, "Yeah."
And then Bobby came out. I said, "How was it?"
He said, "Boy, what I've been missing! Is it really this
good?"
I said, "Yes, Bobby. But you gotta go easy, because you're
not strong like me. Believe it or not, as good as it is, in your
condition, it takes a lot out of you."
And Bobby says, "What a way to die."

If Bobby heard Charlie's advice, he didn't heed it. He was not a cautious guy, and he never seemed to get sex off his mind from that point on. In the summer after high school graduation, Bobby and the guys made a return engagement to the Catskills. Bobby had a full-time girlfriend then, and friends remember that my dad used to boast about his virility.

At this point in the story, Bobby was seventeen. He was doing well with girls, and he had discovered acting. His heart was giving him trouble, but not enough to stop him from doing what he wanted to do. He had applied to Hunter College before leaving Science, and when summer ended he began his first and last days of higher education. By this time he had formed a personality as the loudest, most crass, most outspoken kid around, which I interpret as defensiveness and his antidote for a deep-seated insecurity. But a lot of kids liked him, and surprisingly, he was popular with the parents of the girls he dated. But popularity wasn't enough. It was time to decide what he was going to be when he grew up.

Bobby naturally gravitated to the drama department, and the first semester he was in school he read for everything, got the leading roles in all the plays. In his second semester the drama professors asked him not to read because other students needed a chance to get parts and experience.

They said, "Why don't you work on lighting or paint scenery or something?"

He said, "I'm not into that. I'm here for a purpose. I really just want the chance to read. If I get the part, fine; if I don't, fine—but please don't exclude me."

And they said, "I'm sorry, we can't do it your way."

My father told me that that was when he realized he wanted to act, and he would not achieve that goal through academics. Shortly thereafter he quit school and began building the rocket that would launch him up and out—far away from the Bronx. Interestingly, just before his death he had an urgent need to return to the scene of his early years and to bring me with him.

It was 1972. I was eleven, and he took me on a trip to New York. It was a father-son trip, the two of us on a guided tour of his old stomping grounds. We went by limo, which Charlie Maffia drove. My dad took me to the places where he was raised; Clark Junior High; the Bronx High School of Science; and next stop, the Catskills. After the Catskills we went out and saw where Nina lived in a small trailer in New Jersey.

It was a really important trip to me because it gave me a tangible sense of what my father was about. Truly, I had grown up in a different world. I was born and raised in California with all the comforts and material things that my dad could provide. He wanted me to go with him to his birthplace so that I would know him better. And I believe he understood this would be his last chance to show me.

I was and am in love with my father, so this tour of his beginnings was an emotional experience. He said, "This is where I played stickball. Here is where I took music lessons." And I remember one instance in particular, which wasn't planned, but it turned out to be the point of the trip. We were driving through the Bronx in the limo, and while stopped at a light we saw a boy of about eight shining shoes. My father said to me, "Look at that. What do you think of that kid?"

And I said, "Not much." The scene had no effect on me. My father saw this, and his face flooded with disappointment.

He said, "You don't even get that, do you? If it weren't for me, that could be you."

I could see that my dad was upset, and that upset me, but I couldn't understand what I'd done wrong. I was a kid from Beverly Hills. I went to private school. What was I supposed to make of a kid shining shoes in New York?

So my dad sat beside me, as good as saying "This is what I had to do," and when I didn't get it instantly, it made him think I didn't appreciate what I had been given or what he had gone through to give it to me. Even worse, he saw that I didn't understand that having *been* that boy shining shoes was what made him fight every minute of his life for power and acceptance and freedom from want.

To him, that kid was the essence of what made Bobby Cassotto turn himself into Bobby Darin.

2

Sandy, 1944-1956

*My mother fed me with a spoon until I was six years old.
I only knew how to eat out of a bowl. I was like a cave child.*

—SANDRA DEE

———

*"I married you just to get Sandy," Douvan used to tease
his young bride. Says Sandra, who worshiped her stepfather,
"I always said, 'When we married Daddy . . .' "*

—*The* American Weekly *magazine*
November 1959

There is no way to talk about my mom without calling up the image of her mother, Mary Douvan. The two were never apart, and they were often mistaken for sisters—one blond, one brunette. My grandmother was as much a part of my mother's life as air or gravity. My mother has often said that Mary was the best girlfriend in the world. And that she was the worst mother.

In the last few years there has been a spate of celebrity revelations about childhood sexual abuse—almost a trend. And because of the

25

amount of recent exposure, there's a tendency to be cynical, to disbelieve what might be talk-show hype. But I think there's a deeper reason for our unwillingness to believe victims of abuse who suddenly come forward. Sexual abuse is hard to prove, and more than that, most of us just can't stand to believe that bad things happen to little children.

I say "we" and "us," but I'm comfortable speaking for myself. My grandmother died in 1987. A few years before her death, my mother told her that she'd been sexually abused by her stepfather, Eugene Douvan. My mother had been drinking, and my grandmother barked, "What the hell are you talking about?" It was a rhetorical question and the extent of her curiosity. This alleged molestation came up a few more times when my mother and grandmother fought, and I remember talking with my grandmother once after my mother had left the room.

"Is there any substance to this?" I asked her.

And her answer was, "Absolutely not. I can't believe that it ever could have happened without my knowing it. I would have killed him with my own bare hands. Sandy is making it up. She's full of shit."

I loved my grandmother with all my heart. She was a wonderful, vibrant, attractive person in every way. After my father died, she held the family together. She took care of my mother and was the core of the family. Let me put it another way: I could not have loved anyone more than I loved Mary Douvan. So I was in terrible conflict when she and my mom denied each other's words. I heard what my mother was saying, but to believe her meant believing that my grandmother had either turned her eyes away or had actively known that my mother was being harmed. And if I had to accept that, I knew, my love for her would be destroyed; I would have to see her as evil.

Having admitted that I emotionally reject the idea that my mom was abused repeatedly and continuously throughout her early life, let me now say that her assertion is nonetheless persuasive. First, my grandmother was married to a wealthy man, and she would not have let anything jeopardize her marriage. Second, she had a long history of denial. Third, later in life Mary Douvan showed that she was all too capable of lies and deceit—particularly with respect to issues such as the suicide of her young lover and my mother's alcoholism. Fourth, her mothering techniques were so unusual, that is to say bizarre, that one more layer of aberration seems to fit with her personality.

I want also to add that although my mother is no stranger to denial herself, she does not lie. She does, however, drink, have severe problems with food, have an absence of real friends, and has not, to my knowledge, been with another man since my father's death in 1973. These circumstances are extreme and lead one to an unescapable conclusion.

Bad things happened to little Sandra Dee.

We've become accustomed to the notion that where there is abuse, predictably, the abuser was abused. My mom feels that her mother knew Eugene was having sex with her and, by letting it go on, was complicit. Even putting aside the abuse, one cannot help but wonder how my grandmother formed her style of mothering, which was at once both overprotective and neglectful. Had she simply used the *Ladies' Home Journal* as her bible, she would have done far better by my mother than she did. I wish I had been more persistent with my questions when my grandmother was alive, because when I look into Mary Douvan's history, I turn up very little in the way of enlightenment. Not only is she gone, but so are her parents and her infamous husband, Eugene. But Mary had a younger sister, Olga, who is very much alive and well.

My great-aunt Olga is a small, tidy woman with tightly curled blond hair. She is nearly seventy, still attractive, and goes by the name of Ollie, her nickname since childhood. Ollie lives with her husband, Peter, in a nicely decorated, squeaky-clean, brick row house on a good street in Bayonne, New Jersey. She is fiercely protective of her family, so any skeletons in the Cymboliak closet are still there after talking to Ollie.

What I did learn from my aunt Ollie is that she and Mary were first-generation daughters of a working-class Russian Orthodox couple. The two girls were born in the 1920s and raised in one of Bayonne's blue-collar neighborhoods. The Cymboliak's were religious people. What they lacked in money they made up for in the richness of their community life. When pressed for information, Ollie remembers that Mary was happy as a child:

☞ *Mary was three years older than me. Growing up, we lived a very simple life. My mother and father really didn't have money. They tried to give us whatever they could, but we didn't have luxuries. There was one place where we splurged. Easter and Christmas we would dress to the hilt, even if Mom and Dad had to deprive themselves of something they really needed.*

Mary and I were very close, but I was the tomboy in the family and she was the lady. Mom and Dad wanted me to be like her, but we were each individuals. I'll never forget one time when Mary was going to secretarial school. I had this beautiful little outfit that Mom got me for Easter. I would hang it up a certain way, and one day I noticed it was hung up differently. I knew that Mary had worn that suit. That got me angry. I accused her of wearing it, and she denied it. I said, "You did *wear my suit."*

Mary was always the prim and proper missy, but that was not my style. As the years went by, we grew up and got closer and closer. I got married, and we have lived together in Bayonne for forty-three years. I wouldn't change a minute of my life. I was the little housewife and mommy, that was me. It was Mary who was worldly and clever. She was the sophisticated one. She knew everything, and she did everything right. My sister painted everything so peachy rosy. Everything was always great, even if it wasn't.

Mary Cymboliak's first marriage, to John Zuck, was one of the things that wasn't so peachy rosy. She got pregnant right away and on April 23, 1944, gave birth to a baby girl, Alexandria: my mother. Her date of birth will take on meaning as this story unfolds.

Although I've been told that his family was wealthy, John Zuck was a bus driver, and he lived on his wages. Perhaps his parents were trying to discipline a young man who apparently drank, gambled seriously, and swung his fists around. After five years of marriage Mary divorced John and got a secretarial job working for real estate entrepreneur Eugene Douvan. Douvan was a great deal older than Mary, somewhere between thirty and forty years older. My mom says no one knew how old Eugene Douvan really was, but she was told that he left Russia when the czar was overthrown. Regardless of this difference in age, when Eugene and Mary found each other, they fell in love. Ollie says,

☞ *Eugene was a lot older than Mary. She looked up to him, and he treated her like a little princess, which was very refreshing after seeing how she was treated by her first husband. Gene really idolized her. They got married, and they had a very happy life together. They lived on Long Island, and Gene used to pick up my mother and me after work on Fridays, and we'd go to my sister's house for the weekends. During the week, Mary and Gene stayed at the Olcott Hotel in New York because Gene was so involved in his business and worked late at night.*

Mary always dressed Sandy like a little doll. She always put her in flouncy skirts, and I would knit Sandy outfits, like a skirt with an Eisenhower jacket and a little hat. When Sandy came into church, everybody would admire her. Mary dressed her beautifully, and she was an excellent mother to her. And Sandy was a beautiful, beautiful baby. Mary did everything for that girl. Sandy herself has said, "Mom would be there to wake me up in the morning. She'd be right there to give me whatever I wanted." Sandy didn't have to do anything for herself. We all used to say to Mary, "Sandy is a big girl now. Let her do something for herself. Let her grow up a little." Mary would say, "Oh, no, what am I here for if not to take care of my daughter?" She really catered to her. And I did tell Mary she was wrong. I don't think she realized she was harming Sandy rather than helping her.

Mary always made everything sound so great, but maybe if she had talked to Sandy about the pros and cons of life, that bad things could happen, or at least taught her about reality, Sandy would be better off today. But Mary cushioned her all her life. Sandy loved her mother desperately, even though all those things happened that we didn't know about. Now, when we talk, Sandy will say, "Oh, Mom. She did this to me." But I say, "Your mother was like an ostrich. When it came to the bad things, she'd bury her head in the sand."

When Sandy told me a few years ago that Eugene had abused her, I was shocked. I told her she should tell the truth and not be ashamed. But I had no idea at the time. All I knew was that the three of them were always very happy together.

When Mary married Eugene, John Zuck essentially disappeared from my mother's life. My mom recalls getting on a bus with Mary when she was eleven and noticing the startled look on her mother's face. "Oooh, Sandy, that's your father," Mary said of the bus driver. But no conversations among the three of them ensued. In 1960 a fan magazine came out with a scrapbook pictorial of my mother's life. There is one photo of Zuck in a T-shirt and casual pants, holding an infant Sandy in his arms. He is an unsmiling man, thin, with combed-back dark hair. The reporter from the fan magazine asked Zuck if he had seen any of Sandra's films, and he apparently replied, "No. I have memories of my beautiful daughter, and that's all I need." According to the same article, Zuck remarried and had a son named Kenny in the late fifties, but my mother knows nothing of her father's whereabouts after 1948. I have been told he passed away sometime in the late 1960s.

My mother is a lovely looking woman. She is still blond, still has a great figure. She still has the liquid-brown eyes she was known for and the flawless complexion she had as a teenager. She could easily be taken for a woman in her midthirties. She smokes too much, eats too little, reads voraciously, and has deep psychological problems that started when she was very young. For the inside story of her life, I now turn the page over to my mom.

☞ *I was always a ham as a kid. We belonged to a Russian Orthodox church, and there was dancing at the social events. The older kids did kind of a Cossack dance with their knees up and kicking, and they had a routine. They were twelve.*

I was four, but I wanted to join in. I remember begging the priest to let me dance, and my mother was trying to pull me off him, she was so embarrassed. But the priest said, "Let her dance," and I did. Obviously I couldn't keep up with the older kids, but I did my own version of what they were doing. At one point I looked up and saw that everybody was laughing. I knew they were laughing at me, but I loved it.

We lived in a small apartment, and I remember knowing that my father drank and gambled our money away. I remember him coming home from work in the afternoon and playing cards with his friends. And he would send me out to the local bar to bring him back big tankards of beer. I also remember sitting with my mother in front of a gas stove in winter because it was freezing outside and my father hadn't paid the heat or the rent. Because he didn't bring home his paycheck when there was one, my mother had to work. She lied about my age so she could put me in school and get a job. When I was four, I went into the second grade. The authorities found out I was underage and wouldn't let me go to school there. Then I took a test to get into a different school, and I passed it with flying colors.

I remember the night my mother had to leave my real father. I was just under five years old when this happened. Once a year, my mother would get a terrible virus. At this time, she was really sick. I was sitting in the kitchen playing by myself when I heard my father coming up the stairs outside. I could tell he was loaded. He went into the bedroom and yelled something loud and crude at my mother. She started crying, so I went over to the phone and called my grandfather. He spoke Russian mostly, and it was always hard to communicate with him. But I got him on the phone, and he could tell that I was very upset. He said "Where's your mama?" I spelled out "s-i-c-k" so he would be sure to understand. Then my father came into the room and swatted me with a wire hanger. He knew my grandfather would be coming over soon. It wasn't

*the first time my father hit me, but it would be the last. We
left my father soon after that and went to live with my
grandparents until we got a place of our own.*

*My grandparents lived in a great big house with lots
of rooms. Many family members lived there from different
generations on both sides of the family. I slept in a room with
my mother, and there were other kids in the house. There
was always someone around. My grandparents' names were
Alexander and Anna, but I called my grandfather Didi and
my grandmother Bobke. Bobke worked in a brassiere factory
her whole life, and Didi was a watchman in the city park.
He used to come home in the middle of the afternoon, and
that's when my mother went off to the second of her two jobs.
Didi used to baby-sit for me until Bobke got home. Or sometimes my aunt Ollie would do it. My aunt Ollie was my
heroine. She was like Nancy Drew to me, a real tomboy,
while my mother was more the "Eeek, a mouse!" kind of
woman. When I was growing up, Ollie was everything my
mom wasn't. She was caring. She was a fighter and a rebel.
She was the one who answered back to Bobke.*

*My mother wrote her own book on child raising. She nursed
me until I was old enough to unbutton her blouse. Then when
I was two, someone told her to cut it out, that milk wasn't
enough for a child my age. I never had a bottle. I went from
the breast to the cup. Then my mom decided that if milk
wasn't enough, I ought to have an egg in the milk, and that
was the beginning of the battle of the food.*

*My mother fed me with a spoon until I was six years old.
She would make me a bowl of oatmeal. Not a little bowl—
a huge bowl. She'd crack an egg into it, raw, and forget what
it tasted like, cold and lumps and streaks, I had to eat it all.
And then she decided, if you put the meat, potatoes, and peas
in a bowl of soup, it was just one bowl. And if it took me
three hours to eat it, that's how long it would take. If I
finished at twelve-thirty and that was time for the next meal,
here it would come, and I would have to eat that, too. She*

32

would sit there with that spoon until I finished. It was like a religion. People would say, "She's not hungry. Leave her alone." Oh, no. She had her way.

The woman was a little bit off her rocker in this area, and I've tried to understand what was going on. It's been suggested that this all-the-food-in-one-bowl thing was ethnic, but my grandparents did not eat this way. My mother invented her own method. I believe she put the solids into the soup because the liquid made the food go down fast, and she didn't want to wait for me to chew and then swallow. No little airplane games for us. She wanted to get the food in me, and she just shoveled it in. No one could stand being around my mother's house at mealtime with me. I'd scream and cry and hold my breath. When my aunt Ollie would baby-sit, my mother would say, "Olga, don't forget the e-g-g." I knew what it meant, and I'd flatten my lip.

"I don't want it," I'd say. And no one else would really make me eat this way but my mother. My aunt would say, "I don't blame you. Lousy, eh?" And I would gag.

It's interesting that I liked all kinds of food when I could get it. Didi would make me sandwiches of black pumpernickel bread, butter, onions, and salt, and those I couldn't get enough of. And I clearly remember sitting in a high chair slurping steamed mussels that he cooked up for us both. They had a very strange texture, but I loved them. Then my mother would come home and scream and yell because I reeked of garlic. I was always comfortable with my grandparents when I was a kid. I never needed friends. There was a little brown shelf in the living room where I used to keep my dolls, and I played with them all the time. Didi used to tell my mother, "She doesn't need anybody."

I'll never forget the first time my mother and I went out with Eugene Douvan, the man who would become my stepfather. And I did love him. From the beginning he always made me feel welcome, a part of the family. I remember going to this nice restaurant for this first meal together and being filled with trepidation because I knew there was going to be a scene. I sat on my chair at the restaurant and I waited. The only way I knew how to eat at this point was out of a bowl with everything in it. Like a cave woman or cave child. Imagine my delight when the waiter came out with a clear cup of consommé! There was nothing in it. When they brought the second course, I said, "No, I'm finished. I've had my soup."

And my stepfather-to-be said, "Honey, you're not finished. Don't you want a hamburger?"

I said, "No! I'm finished!"

At this point he couldn't understand the food war, and my mother was so much in love with him, she didn't dare open her trap. And I realized then that I had the upper hand. I was never going to eat at home again.

Before Eugene was my father, my mother put me in velvet dresses with lace collars and Mary-Jane patent-leather shoes. I looked like I belonged in Windsor Castle. When she took me for the first day at my new school, the kids were in gym clothes and they started laughing. They just took one look at me and thought Miss Fauntleroy. I really wasn't that bad. I couldn't help the way I had to dress, so I made some friends. The next year, out came the velvet dresses, and I was totally humiliated again.

School was never simple for me. I was always the tallest one in my class. Also the youngest and the most developed. It was a paradoxic fit, and I just couldn't stand it. My mother didn't want me to go to school, anyway. The first days of school, she'd stand outside the classroom door and peer into the little window that's cut into the door and she'd cry until my teacher put a curtain across the glass and made her go home. Sometimes she'd say, "Sandy, you can't go to school today because it's raining." She'd close the drapes so I couldn't see outside, and I'd stay home with her. The next day the teacher would say, "That's funny. It didn't rain here yesterday." Of course it didn't rain. My mother just wanted me to keep her company. She loved to spend the day curling my hair.

My mother and Eugene dated from the time I was five until I was eight. Gene had a big commercial real estate business. He owned a dozen buildings in New York, and he had an apartment on the East Side. My mom would bring me into the city with her on the weekends so that she could spend the night with him. For entertainment, they would take me to see Jerry Lewis. At night they would put me in the bed between them. Gene started molesting me when I was five. I didn't know exactly what it was that he was doing, but I did know that something was wrong. After a couple of years, I refused to go with my mom to New York. I caused a big stink between her and Gene, and I remember Bobke saying, "What's wrong? You used to love to go."

"I don't want to."

And my mother said, "But we'll see Jerry Lewis."

"No." I just knew instinctively, no. When something of this sort happens, you just know it's not supposed to be. No one at five, six, or seven could say "This is sex." I didn't know what the hell it was. If I'd been asked, I don't think I could have told anyone because the words were not in my vocabulary. But for a year, from the time I was seven, I did not go into New York with my mother. I think I held out for that long.

Then my mom and Gene made their plans to get married. My mother told me to apologize to Gene for being such a brat. She said, "You want me to be happy? We're getting married." I wanted her to be happy. I didn't say to my mother "I don't want to be near him." I didn't say anything. I don't know what I apologized for, but I did apologize, and they were married. Then, forget it. It was no holds barred.

I barely remember the wedding. I know that I danced on Gene's shoes and that now he was my daddy. The newlyweds took me along on the honeymoon, and I slept between them. That became our routine. Eugene always said he was marrying both me and Mary. It sounded nice because I was included but later I saw that he'd married two children. One of them was me and I became his pet girl. My mother became an outsider. I was eight, and now, when my mother wasn't there, "Daddy" started having sexual intercourse with me. I still didn't know what was happening exactly, but I knew it was different. His breathing changed. It was scary. I thought he was having a heart attack because I knew he was always on nitroglycerine for his heart. I didn't tell my mother. After all those years of sleeping between them, I thought she knew.

My eighth year was momentous. My parents got married, and I got my period. It was way too early, but I was physically mature, if not mentally mature. I've been told that the sexual activity may have had a role in hastening the onset of puberty. At any rate, my mother handed me a Kotex and said, "Wear it." She didn't say "Wear it for a few days, and then next month . . ." I thought I was to wear it for life. I believe my mother never prepared me for menstruation because she never wanted me to grow up at all. If I grew up, she would get old. When I got my period my breasts developed and my mother decided to flatten them down with T-shirts. I didn't want breasts, either. Who could blame me? I was only eight!

Mary and Gene had been married about six months when I started getting huge welts on my body. The welts coincided with something else. I had gone to Macy's and had seen a dog in the pet department that I wanted to have. When I broke out with these huge rashes, my father insisted that my mother take me to a doctor. The doctor thought I must be having an allergic reaction to some kind of food, and we altered my diet. But the welts kept coming, and the skin patch tests revealed nothing. I itched and scratched until I bled through my clothes. I remember that my mother painted some sort of tincture on me, slopped it on with a paintbrush every night. When the welts didn't go away, the doctor suggested I go to a psychiatrist. That must have scared my parents to death.

I overheard them talking one night, and they decided I was upset because I didn't get that dog. They gave me the dog for Christmas, and I also got a prescription for tranquilizers. I was the hit of the school for a year. I had to take my tranquilizers three times a day. The welts disappeared. But the sexual abuse was constant.

Gene didn't molest me only in the mornings, but during the day, at night, whenever he wanted to and there was an opportunity. He'd say, "Let's snuggle." And I never fought back. I was too small. Too young. Gene was head of the house, and what he said went. I reasoned that if I protested, that would dignify what was happening and make it real. It was better not to do that. On the face of it, I had a very kind, very generous daddy. The truth was I didn't really have a father at all. I thought I did for an hour, but it was a real short hour. Very early on I was juggling things, hiding things. I grew up, and nothing was ever that nice anymore. God forbid I should ever run into the room and put my arms around him, no matter what the time of day.

Emotionally, this is how I handled what was happening to me: I separated. I just pushed all of my feelings down. I told myself this wasn't my real daddy who was having sex with me. It was some monster. At breakfast, things were back to normal as far as talking to him. And I was so happy to have my daddy back. I could look at him straight in the face. But I couldn't be spontaneously affectionate. At the time, I saw him as two people, and I see him that way even now. At night and in the morning, during that twelve-hour period, it was as if he weren't there and I weren't there. I would shut off my brain. Then, after breakfast, he would come back and I came back.

Soon after my parents were married, we moved to Long Island for a time and I had a normal life. My stepfather said to my mother, "I'm taking her shopping this year." And he did. He bought me gym clothes and saddle shoes. He bought me a skirt with a poodle on it. I was overjoyed.

When my mother saw the clothes he bought me, she cried as though I had died. She carried on, screamed, cursed him. He was laughing, it was so ludicrous. And she kept saying, "My daughter's died. You son of a bitch, my daughter's gone." As far as she was concerned, I really was dead, yet my father was only trying to help me fit in. He wanted me to belong. I remember what my mother said—"You don't belong with any of these people." My stepfather was pretty sick, but at least he made me feel like a person.

When I went back to school, I got along great with the other kids, but Eugene wasn't happy. I often heard him complaining to my mother, "This isn't my life!" He didn't want to live in the suburbs, so we moved into Manhattan.

Eugene worked from eleven in the morning until seven at night. He stayed in bed after I'd gone to school, and I would have to go into his bedroom to say good-bye before I left in the morning. My mother would be in another part of the house, and I would say to her, "I don't want to say good-bye to him! I don't want to!" But she always made me do it. She would've had to be deaf and blind not to know something was wrong when I'd come out of the bedroom forty minutes later, unbuttoned, saying, "Button me up, Mom." And I went to her quite deliberately. I was quite old enough to button my own clothes. But I couldn't just tell her what was happening. In this way I was like my mother. Don't say it and it won't be true. My mother was as bright as a whip, but she was blind about what was happening to me right under her nose. My dad was having extramarital affairs. I'm sure my mother knew. Not the details, but she knew. Turning a blind eye was her way of surviving.

With all of the many painful episodes, I loved Gene. He was the first person to say to me "You may not wear makeup. No dates with boys. You don't have to eat that." I had good sense, but I wanted somebody to say "no" to me. I wanted boundaries. Later in life, my mother would say to me, "I'm your friend." And I'd say, "Oh, Christ. All my life I've wanted a mother. Be my mother, okay?" I think it wasn't until I had Dodd that I saw what it was to be a child. And I didn't hate Gene as much as I hated my mother at that time. I didn't expect much from him. I expected more from my mother.

Thirty years after Gene's death, I told my mother what had happened at last. She was ranting on into the night about what a saint Gene was, and I finally couldn't stand it. I said, "He wasn't a saint. He had sex with me."

She said, "You're crazy and you're drunk. Go to bed."

I went to bed, and the next day I said to her, "Now I'm sober. And it happened." She didn't say anything. She had nothing to come back with.

My mother tells me that she never had a family life. When the Douvans moved to New York City, they didn't get an apartment, they lived in a suite in a hotel. Eugene and Mary were working together in his business, and often they wouldn't return to the hotel until late at night. After school my mom would go home, but no one was waiting for her there. And there was no place for her to go. Mary's family lived far away in New Jersey, so Sandy had to amuse herself.

Sometimes Gene took my mom with him on overnight excursions. She loved the traveling but she trembled from dread knowing she would have to have sex with her stepfather. Sometimes both her parents went on these business trips taking their daughter with them. All in all, my mom was traveling too much to attend a regular school so she was admitted to a school for professional children. Attendance could be irregular at this school. The kids, mostly actors and models, could sign in and out and take their tests by mail. With so little to do after class, my mom started hanging out with her school chums, other little girls of about the same age who were working as models. Her three closest friends were Lorna, Carol, and Tuesday. My mom lost track of Lorna Gilliam, but Carol Lynley and Tuesday Weld became film stars around the same time my mother did.

My mother was eight years old, passing for ten, when she remembers going to a tryout for a Girl Scout fashion show. She wasn't a model, but her friends talked her into coming along with them. After protesting a bit, she did. While sitting by herself backstage, one of the dressers coaxed my mother into a brown corduroy uniform, and a little later my mom was signed up for her first modeling job. She was reluctant to tell her strict father the news, but Mary was delighted, and she helped Sandy convince Eugene that modeling for the Girl Scouts was a proper activity. At last he agreed.

Of course, my mother had no training as a model. When the day came, she was scared, but she followed the girl in front of her out onto the runway and apparently distinguished herself. The powers-that-be in the Girl Scout world were taken with her charms and wanted her to be the cover girl for their *American Girl* magazine. It was a twelve month contract, and my mom wanted the job. She and Mary went to Eugene and again sold him on the virtuosity of the endeavor. Needless to say, his hypocrisy of wanting to protect his darling girl from the big bad world makes me want to gag, but at any rate, he agreed. And once he had agreed, he became a convert. He bought a hundred copies of my mother's first cover and bragged about her to his friends. He was the first to predict a big career for Sandy, but as my mother says, "It was a day he would never live to see."

Carol Lynley is lovely, still blond and with the same engaging personality in "real life" that has always endeared her to her fans. When I met with her recently, she was on her way to a studio to shoot a pilot for a new TV series and was excited about her future. Still, it only took a little prompting for Carol to flash back to the 1950s and her past. Carol was ten years old when she was in the Girl Scout fashion show, but she has clear recollections of it and of the years she went to school with Sandra Dee and Tuesday Weld. Carol tells me that she remembers thinking Tuesday's personality was so different from my mom's that no friendship between them was possible. But Carol spent some time with Sandy during this period of her life:

☞ *Sandy and I were never close friends, but we hung out to a fair degree. Sandy and Mary used to invite me over to the hotel to have dinner sometimes, and I was very impressed with her hotel existence. I loved the constant room service, and I remember being impressed by Gene. He was tall, good-looking, courtly, and elegant. I didn't have a father figure of my own to compare him with, so I thought he was pretty neat. He took Sandy and me to my first Broadway play, and he used to take us to great restaurants. Gene used to say, "My God, look at that girl eat, Sandy." And I would scarf up the food. He clearly wanted to use me as kind of an example to Sandy.*

Mary and Sandy were very much the same type of woman. Mary was bouncy and vivacious and very pleasant. No bad news at all. Mary's face was not as classic as Sandy's, put pretty. They both had full skirts and coiffed hair, and my best friend, Tuesday, and I didn't get this at all. Tuesday had a switchblade knife when she was ten, to give you some idea. Sandy and her mother had an unusual relationship. Sandy was an extension of Mary, and Mary had some kind of strange identification with Sandy. Mary used to love to tag along with Sandy on her modeling jobs. To this day, I have never seen a relationship quite like theirs. Adolescence is a time when you try to break away from your parents, and Sandy was just so tied to her mother. But I also remember feeling that Sandy didn't have a mean bone in her body. She was very good natured. She was a happy person, and I think she wanted to please. She wasn't a rebel the way Tuesday and I were. She was very nice, jolly, bubbly, very pleasant.

I remember once Sandy and I had a modeling job in Boston, and my grandparents lived right outside the town. Sandy and I stayed at a hotel and shared a room, which we had done before. So it was cool. I loved the feeling of being on my own, but Sandy spent the whole night on the phone with her mother.

I said, "Come on, we'll go see my grandparents." But she couldn't wait to get back to her mother. Theirs was a tremendously mutually dependent relationship. I liked Mary, but I saw that she was raising Sandy as an emotional cripple. I don't like to talk about someone who's not here to defend herself, but I admit that even at a very young age I knew something was very wrong.

After the covers my mother did for the Girl Scout magazine, she got a call from Harry Conover, who had a prestigious model agency. My mom took the first letter of the name "Douvan" and converted Sandra Douvan to "Sandra Dee." Then she signed on with Conover's agency. According to accounts of her at this time, she was a solemn little girl, quite professional, who took her modeling very seriously. She did print and catalog work as well as a few TV commercials and TV programs. She found herself becoming quite independent. Her parents were hardly around, and she was working. So she made do for herself. She bought herself a broiler with her modeling money and cooked her own food. For the next three years, from the ages of eight to eleven, she got on subways and went to her assignments alone. No mother dear, just Sandy and the photographers and the ad people. Scares me now thinking about it.

My mother remembers what happened one day at breakfast when she was around ten years old:

☞ *Eugene put his hand on my tummy and said, "Whoops, someone's had too many pancakes." That remark hit hard. He was just kidding with me but I wanted to be perfect in my parents' eyes. I decided then that fat was bad and that I wanted to be thin. From that time on, I did everything I could to destroy my body. I found it easy to restrict my food to almost nothing. A year after that, my period stopped. I was nearly eleven, and by then I had some idea about how a person got a baby. No one was hiding anything from me, and it never occurred to them that I might take the lesson about the egg and sperm to heart. When my period stopped, I figured I was pregnant. I wasn't smart enough to know that you could have a miscarriage. Had I known, I probably would have thrown myself down the stairs.*

I made my mother take me to the doctor. I didn't tell her I thought I was pregnant, I just told her I had pains. And she didn't want to take me. This was one of her stranger things. She never used to call the doctor until after I was well. If I was sick, she'd keep me out of school with whatever I had, and when I was better, she'd have the doctor come over. And he'd say, "What was wrong?"

And she'd say, "Oh, she had a fever."

I wonder if she thought that having a sick kid made her look like a bad mother. She didn't know if I had measles or chicken pox, but by the time she called the doctor, the spots would be gone. But this time, I said something. I got to the doctor and he examined me. And he explained that my periods would come every twenty-eight or thirty-one days and that I should write down the dates, tell my gym teacher, and that my periods might be sporadic at my age. Now, I think that not eating caused my periods to stop because after three months of not having them, I got them again. Thank God it was anorexia, not pregnancy. Really. When I was older and thought about why I didn't get pregnant, the only reason I could come up with was that Gene must have been sterile.

Eugene set up a charge account for his stepdaughter at the Russian Tea Room, one of the poshest restaurants in New York City. It's a red, plush-lined establishment near the theater district, a place where famous people indulge their cravings for wonderfully prepared, full-fat, Russian food. But my mom didn't eat the Tea Room's famous blinis with sour cream and caviar. She'd eat an egg or a plain lettuce salad. When I look over magazine clippings, interviews with my mother as a child, the references to her eating disorder are very much in evidence. There are mentions of her six-shrimp-a-day diet, her vitamin pill diets, bribes by makeup men: a new lipstick if Sandy would just drink a malted milk.

Carol Lynley remembers that all of the girls were trying to keep their weight down and were very impressed with Sandy's discipline. She remembers thinking my mom's head-of-lettuce-a-day diet was just great. She tried it herself but found she couldn't stick with it for ten minutes. In the 1950s anorexia nervosa was not part of our everyday vocabulary. The signs were all there, but nobody recognized it or knew how serious this type of self-abuse was.

Meanwhile, my mother was becoming one of the best-paid models in the business. After two years with Conover she switched to Huntington Hartford's agency. At the age of eleven she owned a champagne-colored fur coat and was making $78,000 a year. And finally, thank God, the sexual abuse stopped. These days Sandy was working very hard. She came home late and took her dinner into her room. I wonder what made Douvan leave her alone at last. My mom suggests that as a full-fledged member of the work force, she was tired at the end of the day and this was reason enough for him to leave her alone. Maybe she was right. Or maybe he was worried about his health.

Soon after Douvan stopped touching her, his heart went seriously on the blink. He had oxygen in his bedroom and he was due to have an operation. It was in September of 1956. Douvan was in his sixties (or perhaps seventies), and Sandy was left alone with him one evening. Mary's relatives were in town and Mary went with them to the theater. Douvan was on a restricted diet and before Mary left, she gave her eleven-year-old strict instructions not to give her stepfather anything that he wasn't supposed to have. The door had hardly closed when Douvan called out to Sandy, begging her to let him have some strawberry ice cream. "Just a taste," he pleaded. "Just a teaspoon." Sandy relented and no sooner had he had the ice cream than he had an allergic attack. My mother was terrified, but she didn't panic. She was unable to locate Mary, but she did get through to doctors, who responded to the emergency. By the time Mary got home, Gene was stuck all over with needles and tubes. My mom was afraid to go into his room to look at him even though he was calling out to her.

She says, "He was trying to tell me not to blame myself; that if I hadn't gotten him the ice cream, he would have gotten it himself. But in my little head, I was guilty." Guilty of making him sick? Or guilty of wanting him to *be* sick? I doubt my mother analyzed her emotions. Douvan was taken to a local hospital that night and in the morning he was transferred to a hospital in Washington, D.C. There was a surgeon there who had pioneered a new development in heart surgery and this experimental procedure was all the hope Douvan had.

My mom went to D.C. to stay with her stepfather during his surgery. She remembers,

> *I had a modeling job coming up in New York and Gene overheard me on the phone trying to get out of it. I hated modeling by this time and wanted to quit anyway. Gene made me hang up the phone, and then he gave me a stern lecture. He said, "When you started modeling, I told you if you make a commitment, you keep it. I'm delighted you want to quit, but you can't break your promise. You can't help me here. Go*

44

back to New York and after you do that modeling assignment you can quit and I'll be happy. But first keep your promise."

I went back to New York and did the job; a TV commercial for Harry Winston diamonds. I called my mother from the studio and she told me that Gene was doing fine, that he was going into the recovery room. Later, as I was getting dressed, there was a knock at the door. It was one of my father's friends. I could tell from the expression on his face that the news was bad. "Your father is dead," he said.

My mother came back to New York alone and went off the deep end. She was completely hysterical, and it never stopped. She was wailing and wandering from room to room. You'd have thought God died. She stopped eating. She couldn't say hello. She didn't know who I was. I was constantly watching her to see if she was standing up. It was just awful. When it was time for the funeral, she threw herself on the coffin and wouldn't let the men from the funeral home take it outside. Finally I said, "Mom, you've got to come with me." I took her to a coffee shop. I said, "You've got to get a hold of yourself. You're making everyone a wreck." And she listened to me. I couldn't believe it. And I remember feeling that if someone is worse off than you, it makes you feel strong. This is when I took over from her.

I went to the funeral, but I hardly remember it. My mother cried her eyes out, but I had decided that I wasn't supposed to cry, so I didn't. I was taking care of my mother because I was the only one who knew what the hell was going on. When I went past the coffin, however, I fainted. I guess that was when I realized his death was real.

If I close my eyes and try to imagine my mother at that time, I see her as a little girl of twelve working like an adult. She's weary and longs for a normal family life. Her mother disappoints her horribly, yet she protects her mother from the awful truth. The most important man in her life is both cruel and kind. He has done terrible things to her at night and at the same time has given her the only measure of normalcy she knows. She has loved him, and now he has done the most unforgivable thing yet: he has died. And he died intestate. Mary, ever afraid of reality, kept putting Eugene off whenever he wanted to discuss rewriting his will. After his death there was a complication that interfered with the normal distribution of the estate. Eugene had a son from a previous marriage who was mentally disabled and living in a state-run institution. The way I understand the story, Eugene's estate was essentially impounded and put in trust for the care of his son. Mary worked for Eugene at the time of his death. So suddenly she was both widowed and unemployed. My mom was now the family provider.

Weeks before Douvan died, my mother had promised her agent she would meet with a producer who was with Universal International. She didn't feel like auditioning for anything, but Eugene had told her to keep her promise. And Mary was so off the wall with grief that Sandy needed to get out of the house for a few hours. So my mom kept a date with a man who would change her life.

Ross Hunter was at Universal's offices in New York. He was in town looking for a girl to star opposite actor John Saxon in a film to be called *The Restless Years*. Dressed completely in black, depressed and in mourning, my mother waited for eight hours for a chance to read some lines for Ross Hunter. When she met him at last, she couldn't believe this youthful-looking man was a movie producer and had a thought that she was being put on. Ross Hunter told the *Saturday Evening Post* that Sandy's face was "so white it looked like it had been dipped in flour. All except the black circles under her eyes." He wore horn-rimmed glasses, preppy clothes, and a bow tie, but he wasn't the twenty-year-old my mom thought he was. He was on his second career, having once been an actor. Now, he was producing films and well on his way to enormous success.

But Sandy really didn't care who or what Ross Hunter was. She was exhausted and enraged by the time it was her turn to read for him, and her emotions finally overwhelmed her. Today Ross Hunter is as animated as the kid Sandy thought he was in 1956, and he looks very much the same as he did then. He talked to me in the screening room of his home in Beverly Hills. Nearly forty years after meeting my mom for the first time, Ross still remembers her.

Here was this tiny, lovely sophisticated little girl who was crying. I just flipped out when I saw her. And I said, "Why are you crying?"

And she said, "My daddy just died."

I said, "Well, my name is Ross Hunter and I'm a producer, and I think you're just a darling girl and I'd like you to think about coming under contract with Universal."

Sandra said, "Oh, sure."

I guess she thought I was kidding her. I gave her my card and told her to call me. Two days later her mom called. She said, "I'm Mary Douvan. I'm Sandra Dee's mother, and what is this all about?"

I said, "Well, I think your daughter is just a sophisticated, darling little girl, and how old is she?"

And she said, "Fourteen."

Then I told her that I thought Sandy was the kind of girl I could develop into something really big, because I felt very strongly the minute I saw her that moms all over the world would say, "Gee, if my daughter could be like little Sandra Dee, maybe it would be wonderful."

Wonderful indeed.

3

Bobby, 1953-1958

I was sitting in Hansen's one night and this guy walked in. He said, "You're John J. Miller?"

And I said, "Yes."

He said, "I'm Bobby Darin, and I'm going to be a star. I think you should know me. I think you should write about me. I think you should pay attention to me."

And I said, "I have no interest in you whatsoever, Mr. Darin. None."

And that's how our friendship began. We were both seventeen and cocky. Sacrilege was ordinary, everyday stuff.

—JOHN J. MILLER
Journalist and friend

———

Bobby was going to stay at my house for the weekend. I was broke, and Bobby had already spent his last money on a cab.

I said, "For twenty cents, we can get to my house by train."

But Bobby hated to take the subways. He used to say, "Think big. I want nothing to do with trains." But this time he said "Okay. It doesn't matter that we're taking the train today."

I said, "How come not today?"

He said, "Because ten years from now, I'm gonna win a fucking Academy Award."

Ten years later he was nominated for an Academy Award.

—DICK LORD
Comedian and friend

———

There is a difference between conceit and egotism. Conceit is thinking you're great; egotism is knowing it.

—BOBBY DARIN
Saturday Evening Post

The early 1950s marked the beginnings of the public awareness of rhythm and blues because this was the foundation of what would shortly become rock and roll. In 1953, when my dad and his friends were hanging around the after-hours bars and clubs in New York City, music fell roughly into three main categories. There was classical, which doesn't come into this story. There was what was known as "race music," performed by Black groups and listened to mostly by Black audiences. And there was popular music, or "pop."

The audience for pop music was both Black and White, and it had no age or gender boundaries. Sinatra was Sinatra to young and old. Patti Page was Patti Page, and tunes that were recorded decades apart were played back to back on the same radio programs. Big band music prevailed. Race music had a different origin from the music the White groups played. It was based on gospel and on jazz, which inspired a different sound. Music at the time was incredibly diverse, and these dual markets were represented in separate sections in the record store. Pop music was alphabetized in one place, race records in another. Then Jerry Wexler at Atlantic Records coined the phrase "rhythm and blues," and it stuck.

Bill Haley and the Comets changed the form of music, not just the name, when they recorded "Rock Around the Clock" in 1955. Elvis Presley followed and turned the world upside down with his rendition of "You Ain't Nothin' but a Hound Dog" in 1956. It was then that rock 'n' roll was born, and from that time until the next decade, you could listen to one radio station and hear everything: Tony Bennett, the Four Aces, Frank Sinatra, and the Cadillacs. Music would cross all lines until the 1960s, when specialty music would come back in style.

In 1953 my father was going on seventeen. While still at Hunter College, he and his pal Dick Behrke got a bachelor apartment together. Behrke and my dad's other close friend, Dick Lord, remember a great deal about my father and about the five years that were a passionate struggle toward success for them all. Dick Behrke remembers that he and my dad lived in a one-room apartment on Seventy-first Street and Broadway. It was quite a nice building, but Behrke suggests that they were the most disreputable things in it. They had secondhand furniture, and Behrke had managed to get his piano installed. The two teenagers had very little money. Dick was working in a bakery for "a hot $40" a week, and my dad was in and out of town with a children's acting company. Both had dropped out of college, and Behrke's dad was giving them a little financial assistance. Their rent was only $80 a month, but even that amount was usually beyond their means.

Behrke told me that he and Bobby kept wild hours, hanging around clubs until early morning and consorting with waitresses at their tender ages. Not that they were winning too many women over: they were not only young, they had no money for fancy wining and dining. In fact, they barely had enough to feed themselves. One time, Behrke recalls, he took advantage of the fact that the commercial bakeries used to deposit their goods outside the small grocery stores late at night for the morning trade. That night when Bobby came home, he found fourteen dozen purloined bagels strung across the room, courtesy of his roommate! And they lived on those bagels for months. As Behrke tells it:

☞ *We used to take turns doing the dishes. One night we had an argument about whose turn it was to wash them, and we were both very stubborn about it. Neither one of us would admit that it was his turn, so we just stopped doing them. We discovered penicillin during that time. The bugs grew four feet long. We kept using whatever dishes were left until finally there was nothing left in the house and they just piled up. I think, by actual count, it was six or seven months before we dealt with them. They just lay there on the counter, covered with green. We put a sheet over them, and life went on as usual. We used paper plates, ate off the floor.*

Finally one day we decided it was ridiculous, but we didn't know what to do with this horrible mess. So we picked the dishes up, Dick Lord opened a pillowcase, and we dumped them in. Then we dropped the whole thing out the window in the vague direction of the garbage area, closed the window, and didn't look back.

Other parts of our life were more problematic. I suspect neither of us really wanted to be out on our own yet, but we each had our reasons for forcing ourselves to do it. Bobby's was to get out of the environment he'd come from. He wanted to get out of the slum desperately. But with all the fun and games that that entailed, maybe we were a little too young. We were sad and a little lonely. We weren't old enough to really get the swinging bachelor life, and it didn't exist that much in those days anyway.

As for our futures, I would have been satisfied to be a good trumpet player. Later, I would be satisfied to be a good piano player, then a good nightclub conductor, and so on. I would wait until the next step came upon me, then I would become frustrated within each step. Bobby had the desire to be a star in some area. It wasn't that locked in which area. His first love was acting. He would try singing, try acting for a while, try being partners with a dance team. It just happened to click for Bobby that he was a singer. It could have clicked someplace else. If it had clicked in acting, I think he would have been happier.

We lived in that apartment for about two years. In those early days, we got a special on white tuxedos for five dollars

*a piece. They were giant shawl-collared, double-breasted
things that were all the wrong sizes because they were secondhand. And we were resplendent in these rags we were wearing.
We would travel to jobs on the subway, and we were noisy,
yelling and singing and playing the instruments and being
generally rowdy, but not to harass other people. We were
sweet, all of us. We were loud, but we would make people
smile. And I admit that our carrying-on was self-conscious
because I remember being aware that we were doing it. I
never had total abandon, although maybe it was different for
Bobby.*

    *We had to grow up quickly. The world we wanted to belong
to was fairly sordid. Cheap show biz is not really terrific.
There were clubs and various questionable-type people. Bobby
was doing sometime work in the Catskills and then played the
bongos for a girl dancer. I was working crummy places playing
piano and trumpet. Baltimore. Eastern Pennsylania. We
moved out of the apartment, and I was living with my sister
and brother-in-law by 1955 or so. One day Bobby showed
up and came to live with us. He was working in some sort of
munitions factory or steel works. He would come home every
night incredibly greasy and miserable. We started working
little jobs around town with various pickup bands. And he
was starting to sing now. But he was very unhappy with
what he was doing. Very depressed.*

A lot of the depression had to do with that girl dancer Dick Behrke
mentions in passing. My dad was working in the Catskills when he
got a call: Bongo drummer needed on an emergency basis. Could
Bobby play bongos? Sure. Or more truthfully, he'd figure out how.
The woman's name was Bernice. She was a blond-haired, older woman
of thirty-one, and I've been told by many that she was nuts and lied
about everything. My dad was still relatively innocent and spent the
rest of the summer rehearsing with her for what she claimed would be
their South American tour. There was no such tour, but before my
father realized this was not going to be his big break into show
business, but rather was Bernice's ruse to have an affair with him, he

was hooked. It's been said that my dad helped Bernice perform an abortion on herself and twice prevented her from committing suicide. She did, in fact, succeed in killing herself a few years later. My father said of this lady, "Before I met her, I was just like any kid in the Bronx. Afterward I was the most disillusioned human being in the world. But I was no kid."

It took my father almost two years to heal from this relationship, but during that time he didn't lose his determination to make it in show business. He got photos made, put a portfolio together, and started hanging around the entrance doors to music studios on Broadway. He still wanted to be an actor, but the country was on the verge of rock and roll, and my father felt that singing was his best shot. He reasoned that his voice might be the battering ram he needed to get to do pictures.

While my dad was pounding the pavement, he was doing small band jobs with Dick Behrke. He sang and played the cocktail drums, there was a bass player, and Behrke was on the trumpet. They would do rent-raising parties and gigs downtown at New York University. They never got paid for work at clubs, but played for free at a place called Club 78, which was just off Broadway at Seventy-eighth Street.

Behrke remembers that they would go to Club 78 night after night. Bobby would sing and Behrke would play the piano or the trumpet. Many nights there was a blind, Black guitar player named Chuck who took the kids under his wing. Every time they'd come in, he'd call them up and the two friends would perform with Chuck, who was a pro. They must have been in heaven.

One time Dick Behrke got an actual paying job for the group, but two days before they were to play, he recalls, Bobby disappeared. Behrke was worried, called Bobby's family, and in a veiled way tried to find out where Bobby was. No one knew. When he turned up again, my father just said, "Oh, I had to get away for a while." I mention this because sudden disappearances were a trait of my father's throughout his life.

Behrke also remembers an innocent love, the object of which was a beautiful, red-haired waitress with lovely skin. Her name was Lorraine, and she worked in a place across from Club 78. Both Behrke and my father fell in love with her. The two friends would stay and drink coffee for an extra two or three hours after they had finished playing, waiting for Lorraine to get off work. Then they would take turns walking her home, just so they could talk to her. Behrke says, "Nothing ever happened. We were just children." But years later Bobby called him in the middle of the night, a hushed tone in his voice. "Guess who's in my dressing room?" he asked. It was Lorraine.

Dick Lord remembers staying up all night so that Bobby could walk Lorraine home. She worked from twelve midnight until six in the morning, and Dick wanted to go home to bed. Sensible idea, but he didn't want to leave Bobby alone. He tells me that they used to walk through Central Park and lie in the grass near the Seventy-ninth Street Boat Basin. Bobby, he says, was a learning experience for him. Through Bobby he saw his first junkie and his first drag queen, and that they used to go to all-night movies. Bobby would yell things out in the theater and break everyone up. He says that he knows a lot of funny people but that Bobby was the funniest person he's ever known. Dick Lord remembers a time when he and Behrke and my dad were in Klein's Department Store on Fourteenth and Broadway:

☞ *We were stealing uniforms for the bands we worked in because we didn't have any money. I discovered the tan jackets and linen slacks we needed, and we had put them on, over and under our clothes. We had tucked in the tags and draped jackets casually over our arms as if they were ours. We were about to slip out of the store when Bobby noticed a closed pink-and-white-striped umbrella leaning against the radiator at the entrance to the store.*

Bobby handed me a jacket, opened the umbrella, and burst out onto sunny Fourteenth Street, twirling, leaping, singing, bowing, jumping, spinning the umbrella. He reached the corner, turned, curtsied, closed the umbrella, and entered an occupied taxi. All while the people were sitting there. He said, "Pardon me," climbed over the people, got out the other side of the taxi, opened the umbrella again, and jumped onto the hood of a car. People were going berserk. Traffic was snarled. Pedestrians were spellbound. He jumped off the car, twirled the umbrella over his shoulder, minced his way through the cars, and finally climbed into the cab of a big truck. He dropped the umbrella to the ground. The light changed. He disappeared, and I didn't see him for three days. That's what it was like to be with Bobby.

We walked out with enough uniforms to outfit the band. That was a lot of stuff. I had a new size forty jacket. I tried it on the next time I saw him. I said, "Does it look nice?" He said, "Oh, it's lovely. Makes you look like Gene Krupa."

Bobby Darin was a shock a day. I'll never forget this story. It was quintessential Bobby.

The Brooklyn Dodgers had won the World Series. Dick Behrke and Bobby lived with Dick Behrke's sister and brother-in-law in a mixed neighborhood, Black and White. They had a terrific apartment, but at this time the three of us were walking down the street in a very bad neighborhood when we saw a sign in a bar window that said "Jam Session Tonight." Behrke said, "Let's come back here later and we'll play."

Bobby said, "Yeah, yeah, that'll be good."

I said, "I don't think so."

"What do you mean, you don't think so?"

"Well, it's scary here." Cars were triple-parked. It was New Year's Eve. Grown-ups were staggering out of doorways and retching in the street. People were leaning out of windows, throwing things. It was pandemonium. I made an observation: "We're the only White people here."

Bobby said, "What! You said a thing like that! I never heard you speak like that." He turned to Behrke. "Do you believe that? Did you hear what he just said? What's wrong with you?"

I said, "Well, bottles are crashing around our heads."

"What do you mean? What are you talking about?"

So we went back to Behrke's sister's house, and I was hoping they were going to forget about this jam session because I didn't want to be accused of being a racist again. But they didn't forget, and we went back to the bar. Inside, there was a front room and a back room with a little stage. It was about ten o'clock at night, and everybody was really drunk, wearing

*party hats, and we walked in, three little White schmucks.
There was an amazed hush that I remember in retrospect. I
don't think we noticed it at the time. We walked up to the
bar and Behrke said, "Hi, so can we sit in?"*

*The bartender couldn't even speak. He just pointed to the
back room. Suddenly I thought, Maybe I was wrong. It was
going to be okay. I was holding drumsticks in my hand.
Bobby said to me, "Wait here a minute." Okay. So they went
into the back and I was left standing at the bar, trying to be
cool. I don't even think I'd ever ordered a drink in my life.
So I ordered a beer. I was just looking around, and suddenly
a guy next to me said, "So who'd you bet on?"*

I said, "I don't bet."

"Yeah, but if you did bet, who would you bet on?"

I said, "Brooklyn. Brooklyn Dodgers."

*He said, "That's too bad." He took a Yankee pennant out
of his pocket and unzipped his fly and put the pennant in his
fly, and then he zipped up so the pennant was just hanging
out there. He said, "Kiss the flag."*

*Now, I knew I wasn't going to do this, and I now know
that I was right all along: I was going to die. A circle of
people formed around me, and I could see this was going to be
good sport for everyone. The guy said it again: "Kiss the flag."
And the circle was getting smaller and my back was against
the bar, and I was holding the drumsticks for dear life. I
said, "Naw, this is a joke, right?"*

*Suddenly Bobby came from the back room, leaped on the
bar, grabbed the sticks out of my hand, and started to play
on the beer bottles. Then he took a napkin. He opened his fly
and stuck the napkin in his fly, and he did a perfect impression
of that guy. Just perfect. I don't really think Bobby knew
what had gone on exactly, he just sized up the situation and
jumped in. I was struck dumb, but pretty soon everyone started
to laugh.*

Then Bobby said to me, "Run! Run! Let's run!"

And we ran out. That was really something.

Something everyone knew about Bobby was that he bore no racial prejudice at all. In fact, he insisted on working with Black comedians when he was a big-name performer, and if he was refused, he wouldn't perform. When we were kids it was just as clear. As outspoken and as rude as Bobby could be, his compassion for the underdog was always there. If you were Black, if you were in trouble, if you were poor, if you were disfigured, his heart went out to you, really. I remember we were in Coney Island and he gave a shoe shine kid a dollar. We had thirty cents left. That Black kid who shined the shoes got the dollar. We got thirty cents. He said nothing and I said nothing. The kid looked at Bobby as though he were made of gold.

Around 1955, my father—still using his own name, Bobby Cassotto—started to write songs. He used to go into a studio and make demo records, and then he and Dick Lord would take the demos around to music producers. Once one of these gentlemen commented in front of my father that he liked the song but not the singer. From then on Dick Lord went on his rounds alone. He'd knock on a door and ask if he could play the demo, and lots of times the answer would be yes, because no one ever knew where a hit song might come from next. But while Dick Lord got opportunities, he was never successful getting any of those early tunes sold.

Hansen's was a drugstore on Fifty-first Street and Broadway, just blocks away from the three TV network studios. It attracted performers and music publishers and was the center of life for a group of people, including a newspaperman named John Miller and my father. Miller had fair hair and wore glasses, and no one I've spoken with remembers him wearing anything but a suit, even when he was seventeen years old. He was a columnist for the *National Enquirer* when he met my dad and worked for many other publications before he died. When he was interviewed two years after my father's death, John Miller had vivid memories of all of the goings-on in the nightclub and music worlds:

"Hansen's was called the 'little store,' and the 'big store' was Lindy's across the way on Broadway," he recalled. "The little store was where the people who couldn't make the big store went, and I used to hold court there when I was seventeen. It was just a dopey drugstore with a few tables in the back and a fountain up front, but all the comics would come in. Everybody from Gene Baylos to Milton Berle, who was a big star. Berle would go to the big store, but before he went he'd stop at the little store and say hello to all the other guys. You could run into almost anybody at Hansen's. And it stayed open all night, so at six in the morning, when there was no place to go, that's where all the people were."

It is in this setting that I imagine my father when he was in his late teens. I can see Dick Behrke and Dick Lord and John J. Miller sitting at one of those tables in the back, and the comics and musicians coming in. My father recognized all of the groups and would do whatever schtick was appropriate to them. And they would greet Bobby by name and with a friendly word. I can picture my father doing his best to make people laugh, which did not at all contradict his feeling of imminent death.

According to Dick Lord, "Charlie used to come and pick Bobby up."

☞ *We'd be hanging out in front of Hansen's and he'd go to make a phone call. I'd say, "Who are you calling?"*

"Charlie. Charlie will come and get me. I'm not supposed to walk but several steps."

He told me, "I have to make it very fast, because I'm going to die."

"What?"

"Yeah. I had rheumatic fever when I was a kid. I'm not going to live long."

He was sixteen years old. Who talks like that? And so matter-of-factly. I didn't believe him. I believed that he believed, but I couldn't believe it. I said, "That's ridiculous. They must be wrong. Look at you. You're jumping on tables."

No one would believe him. Toward the end, when he was really sick and had oxygen with him backstage, Behrke and I would say, "There he goes with that oxygen shit."

John Miller had an irreverent relationship with my dad. They were always needling each other and talking for hours about "zillions of things" (as John used to say), and neither of them knew what they were talking about. "Bobby thought he was going to die any minute," John said. "He was very fatalistic about it. He accepted it. He felt he had to live the way he did because he had a very short time. And we had a deal—a very strange one. The deal was that whichever of us died first, the ghost and the spirit of the person who died would come back and fuck the other one's girlfriend. We mapped this out one night in Hansen's in all seriousness because he liked some of the girls I was seeing and I liked the girls he was seeing, so we made this pact. And I told that to a girl that I was seeing, and she was scared to death.

"Bobby said his death was inevitable and was going to come one day fast. He did not eliminate the possibility of being assassinated. He thought that there might be a crank someday who might wipe him out onstage. He thought it would be terrific if he got hit in the middle of doing a show. He didn't want it done on Fifty-third and Sixth. He wanted it done in front of an audience."

In 1955 my dad was introduced to Don Kirshner, who would one day become a music publisher, writer, and promoter extraordinaire. Don was a little older than Bobby, and he, too, was struggling. He decided to become Bobby's co-writer and manager. Early on they wrote little jingles, the first one a commercial for a German airline. They copyrighted their first song in January of 1956. At the same time they were constantly making demo records, trying to break through.

Kirshner and my dad used to hang out at 1650 Broadway. It was a very busy show business building, and Donny had an office there. Dick Lord remembers that Donny really loved my father and was proud of him. But all the pride and work and knocking on doors wasn't doing the trick. They were getting nowhere.

Dick Lord remembers Bobby delivering some bad news "at a place called Duffey's. Bobby told Donny Kirshner that he couldn't be his manager any longer. And Donny started to cry, right there at the table. We weren't embarrassed or anything. Donny was so sad that he hadn't made Bobby a star yet. Tears came from his eyes as Bobby was telling him, 'You can't be my manager,' and Donny was saying, 'I'm sorry.' He wasn't angry. He was just so sad that he couldn't be

Bobby's manager any longer. I remember we were having spare ribs. He started to cry into the spare ribs. Today Don would first say, 'Don Kirshner presents tears,' but at the time it was all spontaneous and genuine and from love."

Sad as Don Kirshner was, he took the news well, and the two met a man who would influence them greatly. George Scheck was a real TV producer. He was a gruff sort of gentleman, with a balding head and thick-rimmed eyeglasses. He was well dressed and at five feet nine inches, my teenage dad towered a full head over this gent. But what George Scheck lacked in height, he made up for in heart. He had a soft spot for talented kids, and for a while he became like a father to Bobby and Don. George Scheck was known for a show called *Star Time* on NBC, which was sort of a variety show for a cast of child performers who appeared every week. The show ran for eight years. George Scheck told an interviewer of the time Kirshner brought Bobby up to the office and introduced him. Scheck thought they looked like two nice kids, but he realized that they didn't know how to write songs. He told them he had no time for them, but Bobby pleaded for a chance.

Before he passed away, George Scheck reminisced about knowing my father: "Bobby charmed me right away. He immediately sat down at the piano, and he couldn't play but with two fingers. But I saw this kid had a flare for singing and playing and that Kirshner was a promoter. I said, 'You want me to teach you how to write songs? If you two guys will listen to me, I'll show you how to become important songwriters.' "

With this, George Scheck sent the two to the library to get songs that were in the public domain. He showed them how to come up with new arrangements, and this they did. Before long they were working for Scheck, helping him with his acts and his shows, doing whatever he needed done. They kept bringing him music, and Scheck says they "conned" him at every opportunity. Scheck was on to them, of course, but he helped them write their first four or five songs— which he got published for them immediately. The songs went nowhere, but my dad's dream was materializing at last. He was in the game.

And he knew he hadn't gotten into the game by himself. He often said to his inner circle of friends, "When I get some cents, I'll never forget you people." Even though he was still in his teens, his friends knew he meant what he said.

Around this time, Scheck introduced Bobby to a young Italian girl with a beautiful voice. She didn't like Bobby at first, but Mr. Scheck prevailed upon her to give Bobby a chance. Bobby and Don wrote a song called "My First True Love" for the up-and-coming singing star Connie Francis, and she and my dad fell hard for each other.

Connie says in her autobiography, *Who's Sorry Now?*, that when she met Bobby she entered "the most bittersweet period of my life. My whole world revolved only around Bobby—everything he did, everything he said, every dream he dreamed for him and for me. . . . Life took on all sorts of delicious new dimensions now that Bobby was in it. Ours was a world of starry-eyed romance, hand-holding over shared egg salad sandwiches in Hansen's drugstore, and dreaming the most stupendous dreams of a future together."

My dad told his friends that he loved Connie because she was a good girl, pure and innocent. Their love was the real thing, and despite the antagonistic force of Connie's tyrannical father, the two saw each other as often as they could. However, Dick Lord remembers that in the end, Connie's father broke it up:

☞ *George Franconero was all right, but he was a strict Italian father. We were all bums to him. I was a drummer. Bobby was a halfway singer. Behrke was a trumpet player. In a way, I don't really blame him. We never had any money, and we didn't have any jobs. On the other hand, Bobby was articulate, bright, perceptive, and capable of great compassion. Why was he a bum? Because he was in show business? So was Connie.*

Bobby and Connie and my wife-to-be, Ellen, and I would double-date all the time. Connie was shocked that Ellen and I would neck on the couch. I remember we used to take three trains to go to Connie's house. We didn't have a car yet. I would go from Brooklyn to Manhattan. Then we'd go somewhere and take a bus to New Jersey. Then we'd take some other kind of local transportation to Connie's house. We'd be there like a half hour and Franconero would come home, and we'd be thrown out. I wanted to kill Bobby because of what I went through for him. It took all night to get there, and thirty minutes later we were on the street again.

I said to him, "You've got to stop taking this girl out. This is ridiculous."

He said, "No, no. She's very innocent." That would always get him. That's what he said about Sandy, too. When he called me from Rome to tell me about her, he said, "She never kissed anybody."

I said, "What are you talking about?"

He said, "She never kissed anybody."

I want to pause for a moment to describe my father's social life at eighteen and nineteen because it foreshadows the choices he made when he grew older. He was passionately in love with Connie Francis, a good girl who was watched constantly by her overprotective father. While he was seeing Connie, my father was having sexual relations with other women. Bobby told her that he had to have sex to keep his skin clear, and Connie not only believed him but has said that she was not threatened by these other girls. Her and Bobby's love was pure. Pure with Lorraine. Pure with Connie. And later, pure with Sandra Dee.

There were stories going around that my father would swing with couples, and that his occasional disappearances had to do with sexual adventures. He seemed to separate his relationships with good girls and have a secret world that involved sex and pleasure. I'm sure he never forgot for a moment that he was going to die. There was no time for prudery. Everything was forward motion for my dad. And of course, nothing was more important to Bobby than his career.

There came a day that George Scheck remembered well:

☞ *I said, "Bobby, take this song and have someone do a demo on it."*

They went upstairs and couldn't find the girl I wanted to do the recording, so Bobby decided to do the song himself. Now, at this time he had never sung for an audience, but he did the demo and came down to my office. He said, "Don't get angry."

I said, "What's the matter?"

He said, "I'll play the record," and he did.

I said, "Whose voice is that?"

Bob looked up and said, "Don't get mad at me. It's me."

I said, "Play that again. Play that again." I was listening. And he looked at me, nervous, and I said, "Bobby, I'm going to put you on records. How would you like that?"

He laughed in my face. He said, "I'm not a singer. I'm a writer."

I said, "Start picking out a new name. You're going to need it for your recording contract." And four days later I put him on Decca Records.

There are two stories regarding the choice of the name Darin. My father has often said that he liked the letter *D*, turned to the *D*'s in the phone book, and found Darrin there. He dropped one of the *r*'s and had a name he liked. The other story is that he saw a neon Chinese restaurant sign with the "Man" burned out of "Mandarin," and he took "Darin" from that. Either way, "Bobby Darin" sounded good to my father's ear, and the name Big Sam Curly gave him posthumously was left behind.

Now my dad had a stage name and manager. He was excited. Scheck had told Bobby to keep a book of his expenses, so Bobby went to the five-and-ten and bought a small notebook. In it he wrote, "First expense, notebook, 99 cents." He and his friends thought this whole thing was just wonderful.

The song my dad recorded that George Scheck placed with Decca was called "Rock Island Line." In his book, *That's All: Bobby Darin on Record, Stage, and Screen*, Jeff Bleiel describes the song as "an ill-advised, unnatural choice for Darin. Opening with a spoken-word introduction, the record featured only a strumming acoustic guitar and drumming as accompaniment. Darin's off-key impression of a train whistle drove a nail into the record's coffin."

Four days after my dad recorded "Rock Island Line," George Scheck got Bobby his first TV appearance. It was on a series called *Stage Show*, produced by Jackie Gleason and hosted by the Dorsey brothers. Bobby begged George not to make him perform. He said he'd rather cut his arm off rather than sing in front of an audience, but George wasn't having it. He told my father to write the key lyrics to the song on the palm of his hand so he wouldn't forget them, and my father did it. Then he sweated the lyrics off. He lost his place in a song he'd sung a hundred times and afterward critiqued his own performance in two words—"I bombed."

Even knowing what I know of my father's will to live, I'm sure that after the Dorsey brothers' show, he wanted to die. In truth, even if he'd been ten times as good as he was, he wouldn't have impressed anyone that month. A week before his TV debut, a handsome young fella from Memphis performed and broke a king-size hole through the world of music as it was then defined. He was immediately booked for a return visit, so it turned out that Bobby Darin was sandwiched between Elvis and Elvis. Poor Dad.

But George Scheck cleaned him up, bound his wounds, and sent him on the road to the first of hundreds of small-time club dates my dad would play in those early years. You can't win success if you cave in to failure, but I think because of his embarrassing first performance, my father tried to give himself a safety net. And he didn't tell Mr. Scheck what he'd decided to do.

One day, not long after this, my dad was on a club date in Detroit. Scheck flew down without telling him, meaning to watch Bobby's performance and perhaps see him after the show. To Scheck's amazement, Bobby and his friend Steve Karmen were doing a duet. Karmen was supposed to be backing my dad on the guitar, not singing. Scheck grabbed them both by their ears and let them have it. He told Karmen to go back to New York, and he told my dad to do his single. "Why did you do this?" Scheck asked Bobby. And my dad, who would be known in the future as a world-class entertainer, said that he was afraid.

"Everybody thought he was so sure and cocky," George Scheck recalled:

☞ *But Bobby was never sure and cocky inwardly. He learned, though, to enjoy himself.*
I remember his first professional appearance for a big benefit.

There were all big names on the show. He had some records now on Decca. He'd been on television, and the house was loaded with names. I said, "Bobby, I'm going to put you on this benefit, but there's one thing that I'm going to insist. Watch me. When I tell you to get off, don't you dare do another number."

He rehearsed three or four numbers when I wasn't looking. I said, "Rehearse only two. I would rather you do one or two numbers and then get off. I want you to kill them and get off." There were about ten acts on this benefit show, and Bobby followed Jackie Gleason. I introduced him: "Ladies and gentlemen, here's another big talent. In fact, he's got a record out called, 'Rock Island Line,' and he was a hit on Stage Show. *And here he is, Bobby Darin."*

One number and he killed the people. Two numbers and they were applauding. Bobby knew I had said "Look at me," but he wouldn't do it. He went and took bows and was standing so he wouldn't look, and he did the third number. And died. Afterward I said, "Bobby, that was a terrible thing. Why didn't you look?" He said, "Because I knew you were going to make me stop, and I loved it out there."

It seems appropriate at this time to introduce Harriet Wasser. Harriet was a tiny woman with thick, curly hair and a personality that makes the word *outgoing* seem like an understatement. She was energetic and devoted and had a great eye for talent. Harriet was working as a secretary for entertainers Eydie Gorme and Steve Lawrence when she met Bobby. It was 1956, and he had just made those records for Decca, which were indisputably dogs. It didn't matter. Harriet saw something in Bobby that others would see later, but she can lay claim to being one of the first. She met my father at Hansen's drugstore, and from that first meeting Bobby was the focus of Harriet Wasser's life. He called her "Hesh," and she called him daily. Her love for my father was not of the usual type. They never had an affair. She simply believed in him beyond the limit and wasn't afraid to tell what she saw.

"Harriet would corner you and give you three hours on Bobby

Darin," Dick Lord recounts. "People would run the other way. Not because they didn't like Harriet, but because she was so completely obsessed with Bobby. She would talk to plastic, wood, a chair. Anybody, anything that would be standing still, she would tell about how great Bobby Darin was. People would tease him about it. He had more publicity on the street from Harriet than if he had the highest-priced PR agency at the time. This was a woman whose life was devoted to talking about him."

But while she was talking about him, sending out hundreds of notes and records, Hesh was learning about Bobby. Today she still lives in New York and is still a dynamic publicist. When I met with her recently, I was knocked out by her continuing vigilance and her undying love for my father. It came as no surprise to learn that she's still promoting his music and his legacy. Hesh remembers that it wasn't only my father's heart that was making him a nervous wreck; it was his hair:

> *Bobby was very worried about his hair. It had a tremendous affect on his life because he started to lose his hair very young. By the time he was on the stage performing, he was already wearing a toupee. I remember him going into this barber shop on Fifty-fourth Street one day, and he was so unhappy. The barber's name was Joe, and Joe said to him, "Look at me. I lost my hair when I was very young and you don't see me worrying about it."*
>
> *Bobby said, "Yeah, but you're not going to be a star. You're a barber, so naturally it doesn't matter."*
>
> *But Bobby knew he was going to be a star. I remember him saying to me, "I'm wonderful. I'm a great actor."*
>
> *And I'd say, "How do you know?"*
>
> *He'd say, "I can feel it."*
>
> *And I never would deny it because I felt that he was a natural-born actor. If he had lived and kept making movies, I think today he would be a monster star. He had a natural gift, and that's why I fell for him.*
>
> *There are tons of people out on the street who are looking to*

make it and want to make it. And what makes one person make it and another not is just an intangible thing. But we're not talking now about hit records. We're talking about someone who goes into a club in Brooklyn and literally floors the audience before he ever has a hit. Bobby could talk. He had the whole audience like magic. He was just a natural.

Hesh had a friend named Rona Bernstein who was a dumpling of a girl with a prominent nose and a crooked leg. Like Hesh, Rona was enamored of the entertainment world. When I met with her recently in her gracious home in Los Angeles, she referred to the child she was as "little Rona." This was to distinguish the ugly duckling she'd been from "big Rona," the premier Hollywood reporter she became. Today, Rona Barrett is blond, slender, and a wonderfully colorful speaker. Her business now is film production, and she had a million projects going at once when I met with her in her office at home. Still, she took time out to recall for me the details of her early days in New York.

Rona told me that she and Bobby used to see each other around the Brill Building, the center of music publishing and music, before Hesh formally introduced them in 1959. Bobby was there trying to sell his music, while Rona was a fan club mover and shaker. She handled Eddie Fisher's fan clubs, then went with Steve Lawrence, which is how she met Hesh. She says that she developed a reputation as a teenage music maven and knew Connie Francis. She told me that my dad's romance with Connie was very intense, more so than other teenage loves she'd seen.

For Rona Barrett, that first meeting with Bobby is memorable:

☞ *We had dinner at a drugstore up the street close to Fifty-seventh Street. I remember we sat in a booth and it was a late lunch—early dinner kind of thing, but it was very dark by the time we left. From that moment on we were just always in touch. I always knew that when I was with Bobby, I was in the company of somebody extraordinarily rare and gifted. I recognized this even as a kid. And I just loved him. And he knew a lot about me. I had been born crippled, so he empathized with that and admired my spunk and my ability to pull myself up by the boot straps, which is what all of us did. None of us in that crowd were born with silver spoons in our mouths. We all had to rise above where we were born, and I think that was the bond that brought us all so close together.*

The "intense romance" my father was having with Connie Francis was doomed. They continued to see each other, but Connie was constantly torn between obeying her parents and obeying her heart. In her autobiography Connie tells of coming home one night from a date with my father and finding her two pieces of luggage outside the front door of her house. The door was locked. Connie was stunned, and so was my father, but he recovered first. Connie remembers that he dropped to one knee and proposed to her, saying, "I would like you to be my wife, my friend, my partner for life, and the mother of my children. . . . Get in the car, C.F."

They got in the car and drove. Connie said her heart was breaking, and that while Bobby was seeing a white house with a picket fence, she was seeing a funeral—theirs. My dad asked her to have faith in him, that things would turn out all right, but she was so afraid, she made my father drive her home. He told her that in that case they couldn't be together anymore.

But they did see each other again later, when they taped a television show. There was nothing to going on between them at this time, but Mr. Franconero believed otherwise and took matters into his own hands.

George Scheck recalled that someone told him Connie's father was coming and had a gun.

☞ *So I got rid of him somehow. Bobby ran out through the back exit. Later I said to Bobby, "From now on, don't call me, I'll call you. Because Mr. Franconero is going to shoot you or he's going to beat you up."*

And Bobby said, "You only care about Connie. What about me?"

Well, Franconero had told me I had to make a choice

*between and Connie and Bobby; I couldn't manage them both.
So I had my hands full. I said, "Bobby, things aren't working
out too well. I know you're going to make it, Bobby, any day.
But I have a problem."*

*And he said to me, "What are you going to do? I have no
father. You're like my father."*

*I felt very bad, but I said, "I'll always look after you,
Bobby. I'll always give you advice." And he tried to get hold
of Connie, and she wouldn't talk to him. And then Bobby
went on Barry Gray's radio show and said, "I went up to
my manager's office and he said, 'I'm not your manager
anymore.' " He said this on the radio.*

*It hurt me, but I had a great love for Bobby, always.
Years later we talked the whole thing out. And he felt that
I was always on the father's side. That hurt him. But he did
tell everybody that the two people responsible for his success
were George Scheck and George Burns.*

George Scheck stuck with Connie Francis, who in time made thirty-seven gold records and, because she sang her songs in many languages, is probably the greatest-selling female recording star of all time. Connie had been Scheck's client before Bobby, and I guess he made his decision based on that. At the same time, Decca Records, having patiently produced half a dozen of my father's unsuccessful records, dropped Bobby Darin from their label. Bobby left Mr. Scheck's office in tears.

It was a dark day for my dad. He'd lost his manager, he'd lost his recording contract, and he'd lost his girl. But better luck was around the corner. Joe Csida and Ed Burton were a talent management and song publishing team. They set up a meeting with my father, and it's been said that Bobby's strategy was to behave as if he were auditioning the managers, not the other way around. That's why I'm sure my dad was as cool and reserved as he always was.

Ed Burton, who has since passed away, was once quoted as saying, "Bobby jumped up on the piano, stuck a cigar in his mouth, and ran around the room imitating Groucho. I suppose he did his Chinese waiter routine as well. Our reaction was, This kid is nutty, but he's right. We figured him for a real big rock and roller. To be honest, though, we never saw the ultimate in him. He saw it in himself all along."

Ahmet Ertegun is and always was an elegant man with a legendary talent for finding music at the cutting edge. In the fifties Atlantic Records was a small independent company producing mostly rhythm and blues for the Black market. Ahmet had two partners—his brother, Neshui, and producer Herb Abramson—and their company was starting to expand. Ahmet says that Herb had some ideas about what he wanted to record, so a new label, called Atco, was created under his aegis.

Ahmet remembers my dad and Don Kirshner coming into the offices one day. Bobby had recorded an old Billy Rose song called "I Found My Million Dollar Baby," and Ertegun dug it in a big way. Bobby signed with Atco and reported to Herb, but there was a piano in the room next to Ahmet's office, and he said that Bobby would bang away on it all day. He said that my father had an irresistible energy and talent and a great understanding of the blues idiom, and Ahmet found him a very enticing artist.

Ahmet's enthusiasm and Csida and Burton's connections led to better nightclub gigs and more media notice for my father, but still no hit record. More songs flopped, and after a year Neshui and Herb Abramson were ready to drop Bobby Darin. Time, as usual for my dad, was running out.

But something going on in the background was about to change Bobby Darin's future. While promoting his records for Atco, my dad had become friendly with a local rock and roll DJ and promoter. His name was Murray Kaufman, known commonly as "Murray the K." Apart from his radio show, Kaufman also produced shows at Harlem's Apollo Theatre. The Apollo audiences were Black and notorious for chewing up White artists who were "not real." But my dad not only found acceptance there, he was held over.

One day, at Murray Kaufman's apartment, Bobby overheard Kaufman's telephone conversation with his mother, Jean. Apparently Jean Kaufman wanted to be a songwriter and believed her son could make it happen. She wished! Murry got a big laugh out of this latest idea of hers. "She's got a crazy idea for a song. Splish splash, take a bath," Kaufman said.

Bobby bet Kaufman that he could write a song about it. Laughing, Kaufman went off to take a shower and change his clothes, emerging twenty minutes later to the sounds of Bobby Darin wailing away on the piano.

Ahmet Ertegun remembers what happened next:

☞ *Bobby was running around town a great deal at this time. He was superenergetic and nervous, not the kind of guy who would be sitting at home. I liked him very much personally from the very beginning. I think that he wanted to work with me, and somehow, the way it fell, he was working with Herb. Herb was a great recording producer, but the chemistry wasn't there, and as our contract with Bobby was about to expire, Herb wasn't anxious to keep things going with him.*

But I wanted to give it a real good last chance. I decided I would make a session because I felt there was something really groovy there that somehow I didn't hear on the records we'd released previously. What Bobby was doing was creating a completely different kind of music. And I also thought that he needed a much funkier backing than he'd been getting. He'd been getting straight studio kinds of arrangements, rock and rollish but also popish and sort of lackluster. I thought we should get into a much more feeling groove.

So I decided to go in and do a split date, because I also had just made a deal with Morgana King. We had our own studios then on Fifty-sixth Street, right above Patsy's Restaurant. The place had been our old office, but we turned it into pure studio. We put in a little control room and made lots of hits there. So on this occasion I got together a little rhythm section of the currently good R and B players. They were people Bobby also knew and liked, and Bobby and I got together and decided what we would use.

I was going to try to cut two or three sides with Bobby in an hour and a half and two or three sides with Morgana King. I insisted on Bobby playing piano because that was really one of the things that got me about him—the basic rhythm that he put into his songs. I think Panama Francis played the drums. We had a couple of good guitar players, maybe Al Caiola and Carl Lynch, and a saxophone player we used all the time. It was a good tight little rhythm section, and we got "Splish Splash," "Queen of the Hop," and another song in an hour and a half. We got "Splish Splash" in only three or four takes.

Morgana King didn't fare as well during that session. Ahmet says he was trying to put her in a commercial groove and misread her talent. He realized later that as a great jazz artist, she wasn't right for singles, but really I think it simply wasn't Morgana King's day. It was Bobby's.

That was April 10, 1958. There was a hopeful celebration at Hansen's that night. Don Kirshner, Dick and Ellen Lord, Dick Behrke, Steve Karmen, Neil Sedaka, and Hesh Wasser were all waiting for Bobby at the drugstore. Hesh stood him in front of the jukebox and took a picture of him in a soulful pose. "This may be the last time we see you in here," she said. After the candid photo, Hesh took Bobby to a recording session of a top-notch performer, which is how my dad met Sammy Davis Jr. for the first time.

Meeting Sammy was frosting on the cake. "Splish Splash" became one of those incredibly memorable events: everyone who knew Bobby can remember something that bonded their own lives to that song. Ahmet Ertegun must have felt like handing out cigars. He said, "When I cut the record, I thought it was going to go to the top. You can tell. It was undeniable. It was a cute novelty lyric, and everybody dug it. Everything worked for it. Without the lyric it would have been a hit because of the music of the song and the track. It was just there."

Rona Barrett hated it. Neil Sedaka marveled at its "Fats Domino–ish sound" and knew it was going to be a hit. Dick Lord remembers that he'd been working in the mailroom of the William Morris Agency, and for some time he'd tried to get his bosses to come see Bobby. Finally he succeeded. They went out to Long Island, where

Bobby was booked at a club called the Safari. Unfortunately the owners of the Safari forgot Bobby was playing there and didn't arrange time for him to rehearse. Bobby sang, and the agents were unimpressed. They told Dick Lord that my dad couldn't sustain the high notes, which incensed him. Dick said, "He's going to be the greatest performer in the world! Fuck the high notes."

Time passed. "One night Bobby and I met at 1650 Broadway," recalls Dick Lord.

☞ *It was cold for April, but Bobby was in a sweat. He had two demos under his arm. He dragged me to the Colony Record Store to listen to them. One was called "Splish Splash," and the other was "Queen of the Hop." The artist sounded Black, but I knew it was Bobby. He had paid his dues on the streets for all those years. Now he says, "This is the one. This is the hit."*

And boom, that was it. He was on the way.

I took the first copy of "Splish Splash" to one of the agents at William Morris.

He said, "If this guy is White, it's all over." In this man's defense, I must say it wasn't a prejudiced remark. It was the late fifties. There would be one rock and roll show for Blacks, one for Whites. It was a business remark.

I said, "He's White. It's my friend, Bobby, the guy you didn't care for at the Safari."

George Scheck still loved Bobby and would no matter how many years passed. Back in 1975, after my dad died, he recalled the day Bobby brought in his breakthrough record:

☞ *Once Bobby and I were in Atlantic City. It was in the summertime, and Black people were singing on the rooftops like it was New Orleans. I said, "Bobby, you're a great mimic. You can do anyone. You'll be different. You want to sing, and 'blackie' is gonna be in for a long time." And Black people were just starting to make it mainstream. I said, "You ought to sing like these people."*

He hits me on the back and says, "You know, I've been thinking about that." Later, when he did "Splish Splash," he came into my office with the demo in his hands. He was shaking when he put the record on my turntable. And he played it, and I says, "Bobby. Atlantic City!"
And he says, "Yes. Atlantic City."

Dick Clark had a show called *American Bandstand*, which was a showcase for rock and roll performers and was one of the biggest television sensations of the day. My dad had been on Clark's show before but hadn't caused any notable reaction. This time, with some confidence infused with bravado, my dad played "Splish Splash" for Dick Clark, and a spark caught. Clark responded, "Well, Robert, I think this time you've got it." He remembers putting Bobby on *American Bandstand* at Berwyn's Skating Rink in Philadelphia. When he introduced Bobby, my dad only got a smattering of applause. But when he finished singing, the audience was his.

Dick Clark has an enviable life. He's a five-time Emmy Award winner and continues to be one of the most recognizable television personalities around. His production company takes up the whole of a great three-story building in Burbank, his wife, Kari, is terrific, and their dogs come to work with them every day. There are photos lining his walls edge to edge, and although the people he is standing with have aged, Dick Clark looks much the same as he did in 1958.

I was pleased that Dick could still clearly remember my dad "coming down the aisle with his finger-snapping routine. He gave them a performance that no one had ever seen. 'Splish Splash' is not the most extraordinary piece of music that was ever written or sung, but it just turned them on, and they responded incredibly."

Dick Behrke was driving back from Las Vegas in spring 1958. He had a new Hillman car, he recalls, "and I'd driven [it] right to the studio where Dick Clark was doing his show, this time in New York. Bobby was singing 'Splish Splash.' His record was just starting to make it, and I surprised him at the studio.

"That night we went down to where Dick Lord was playing in a band. I sat in and played with them, and Bobby sang. We all hung around, and it was a great reunion. This was the first real glimmer that Bobby was going to be a star. It was the first serious talk of it. We knew that something was going to happen."

Dick Behrke, Dick Lord, George Scheck, Connie Francis, Ahmet Ertegun, Dick Clark, Hesh Wasser, Don Kirshner, John Miller, Rona Barrett, Charlie and Nina and Polly—all the faithful—had long believed in the skinny kid with the big ego. They knew he was talented, and they knew that beneath the bravado that had become his signal personality trait was his fear of dying without leaving his mark.

Now they watched as "Splish Splash" hit the market running. It sold more than one hundred thousand copies in three weeks, charted at U.S. number three, and held there for sixteen weeks, later selling over a million singles. Bobby's family, who had seen him through the terrible, painful years, told each other, "We've made it." His friends were elated. They twisted the radio dial in anticipation of hearing their friend's voice, and they shouted when each day brought a climb in the charts.

Naturally I wonder how his hard-won success felt to my father.

He was twenty-two years old. After five years of beating on doors, suffering humiliation, honing his craft in hundreds of small clubs around the country, his work paid off. The world was no longer so hard and cruel. He earned $40,000 that year. His days of poverty were over, and he'd developed a performing style.

In order to get a sense of my father's feelings, I have to reach a couple of years into the future. Barry Gray was a well-known radio talk show host who had been approached repeatedly and mercilessly by Harriet Wasser on behalf of my father. Gray hated "Splish Splash" but when he finally played my dad's first album, he played it a hundred times. He credited Harriet with turning him on to my dad and had Bobby on his show in 1960. By then Polly Cassotto had died.

My dad's feelings were close to the surface that night on Barry Gray's show. He talked first about the woman he thought was his mother:

☞ *My mom was a very powerful influence because, when I was born, I was born different than anybody else, as far as she was concerned. I was a very sickly individual, and because it was hours and hours without sleep to take care of me, she just accepted the fact that God wouldn't do that to her or to me without making up for it later. So she just brought me up to try to think for myself, try to understand.*

That was the key to her entire existence—the word under-standing. *In other words, that I should understand myself, and then I can understand everybody. I enjoyed just a smattering of success before she passed away. And even in that time she never got so excited that she would go around saying "Did you see what my son has done?" She didn't have to. She accepted it from the time I was born. Like it was supposed to happen.*

And the rest of my family pretty much accepted it on that basis. I am not inflated with "Look what I can do that nobody else can do." I'm dragged that I can't do it better than I do it. I am as grateful for the things that happened to me in the short four years that I'm in the business as I am for God's gift for breath in my body. But this is the way I'm constructed. There's no other way for me to think.

I am two years behind myself.

I should have been twenty when the first thing happened instead of twenty-two.

4

Sandy, 1956-1960

I've never had any friends, but it's like strawberry short-cake. If you've never had it, how can you miss it.

—SANDRA DEE
Newsweek, *June 1959*

———

TEENER ZOOMS TO STARDOM UNFETTERED
BY FRIENDS OR FUN

She may be another Elizabeth Taylor. When you look at her you get the same feeling of drowning in a pair of magnifi-cent eyes. You sense her possession of that super-femininity some call sex appeal. You observe her complete absorption in movie making. And you wonder how things will be with Sandra Dee ten years from now. . . .

—MURIEL BARNETT
Mirror-News, *April 30, 1957*

Several themes show up over and over again in the magazine articles about my mother during the late fifties. Her beauty and sophistication

79

were always mentioned, but other subjects came up so often that they would be red flags to us today. Sandra's starvation diets were frequently cited. Eugene's coy brag that he married both Sandy and Mary is noted often. And another theme, which seemed less sinister but just as telling, frequently came up: Sandra Dee had no friends.

From the article in the *Mirror-News*: "She has no friends her own age. No time for the ice-skating and horseback riding she used to enjoy. No time for much of anything but being an actress. Day after day, her lunch is a hard-boiled egg and half a head of lettuce—with a teaspoon of vinegar when she feels reckless. . . ."

I'm looking at this article about my mother. It appeared in April of 1957, only days after her birthday, and the photograph is of a girl so young and innocent looking, she could be nine. The caption reads, "This Is Sandra Dee, Barely Fifteen Years Old." But she was nowhere near fifteen. The lie her mother told, advancing her age by two years, had been set in concrete. Alexandria Zuck was not born in 1942, as all her biographical notes say. My mom was born in 1944—you heard it first here. And that would make her thirteen in this picture. Thirteen and one week.

I asked my mom to look at this picture with me. She said, "Oh, isn't that gross? See how swollen my eyes and nose were?" referring to what she had done to her body. She'd been subsisting largely on lettuce for nearly a year when the picture was taken, and because of the lack of protein in her diet, her flesh is bloated with fluid, and it shows on her face.

But I want to back up six months, to what followed right after Eugene Douvan's death in September of 1956.

The Douvans had bought an apartment they had planned to move into, a permanent home at last. But now that Eugene had died, neither Mary nor Sandy had the heart to move there. My mom remembers that Mary became dependent on her twelve-year-old daughter, and it was okay with Sandy. Douvan's money was gone, but Sandy was doing so well as a model, she and her mother would have been fine financially. Emotionally, though, things were different. Douvan had set himself up as a father to them both, so the loss was surely great.

My mom had forgotten about her audition with Ross Hunter, which had taken place the month before, but then the phones started ringing.

Girlfriends were calling. "Have you seen the *Post?* Louella Parsons says you're going to Hollywood!" But my mom hadn't seen the *Post*. Suddenly there were plane tickets in hand, New York to Los Angeles, and a screen test was scheduled.

Sandy and Mary flew.

The purpose of the screen test was to see how Sandra Dee would play opposite handsome, twenty-year-old John Saxon, who was cast to star in Universal's upcoming film *The Restless Years*. My mom remembers that the script called for her and John to walk down a path, and when they got to a certain tree, John was to kiss her. She remembers that every time they got to the tree, she urgently had to go to the bathroom. After three such misfires, a woman in the crew asked her if she had a urinary tract infection, and Sandy confessed that she'd never been kissed before. The woman immediately told the entire crew, which broke the tension, and the test went off without further snags. John Saxon remembers feeling that Sandy seemed young to him, and I imagine he would have been shocked had he known she was only twelve.

Sandy's grandmother saw the film clip later on, and Bobke was horrified. "Wherever did you learn to kiss a boy?" she was widely reportedly as having asked. And my mother said she just threw herself into it, and that kissing Johnny Saxon was easy. She said in interviews she was only sorry they had done that kiss right on the first take and hadn't had to do it again.

With all due respect to John Saxon, according to my mom the truth was that, thanks to the hell she went through with Eugene, John Saxon's kiss had no effect on her at all; she merely told the papers what they wanted to hear. I know, because she has told me that kissing a man was like kissing a wall. Her acting must have been great, though, because Ross Hunter arranged to have Mary and Sandy moved out to California for good.

My mother and grandmother made the move to Hollywood in early 1957. My mom says she thought if she didn't get her mother away from New York, Mary would surely have died of grief. So she was surprised at how quickly Mary recovered. My mom notes that my grandmother flourished from her first day in the California sunshine. But unbeknownst to them, Ross Hunter was having problems selling his vision of Sandra Dee, future star, to Universal. The heads of the studio didn't like Sandy as much as Ross did.

Ross Hunter picks up the story:

☞ *The studio heads complained that Sandy hadn't developed yet, physically. They didn't want to put her under contract, and they wouldn't do it. I thought they were a bunch of asses. I said that I would personally hold her contract for a year. Sandy never knew this. I wanted her to think she was under contract with Universal because that was the glory, being under contract to a studio, not to a particular producer. So Sandy came out, and we got her and her mother a little house, and I didn't really know what I was going to do with her right away.*

One evening I was at a party and Piper Laurie was there and Paul Newman, and they were looking for a little girl to play Paul Newman's sister. And I said, "I think I have the perfect girl. She's the most natural. She's lovely. She's sophisticated. She's just a terrific girl, and I'm absolutely nuts about her." And so they met her, and they took one look at her and, of course, fell in love, too.

No one explained to Sandy that Ross Hunter had loaned her out to MGM. The limo came and picked her up, and she was given a script, not the one she'd rehearsed and been tested for. The picture she was hired to do was called *Until They Sail*, and it was about four New Zealand sisters during World War II after the marines had landed. It starred Paul Newman, Piper Laurie, Jean Simmons, and Joan Fontaine. The character my mom played was the youngest sister, and she was supposed to age from twelve to eighteen in this film. She says that with her height (then five feet four inches) and what would have been her normal bustline, she could have played the entire age range unaided. But because she was starving herself, an inflatable rubber suit was made for her, and it was pumped up according to the required age of the day's shooting.

The first time she saw it, my mom was very excited. She leaned out of her dressing room and yelled: "Mr. Newman, Mr. Newman! Want to see my body?" One can only imagine the surprised look on Paul Newman's face as he pondered my mother's offer. Hammers stopped hammering, and a hush came over the set as young Sandra Dee went back inside her dressing room, zipped herself into her body, then modeled it for all. My mom said she was proud of that rubber body, but even though she loved it, she loved taking it off even more.

My mother's acting experience at this point had been limited to TV commercials, and there was some consternation on her part as she learned her craft on the job. She rehearsed her opening line, "Hello," endlessly. Someone asked her what she was going to do after "Hello," and she said, "Don't cloud my mind." She figured if she got the first word right, the rest would follow. And it did. Ross Hunter says that MGM liked my mom so much in *Until They Sail* that Universal put her in the film she had originally tested for, *The Restless Years*. It was directed by a German director named Helmut Kautner and starred Margaret Lindsay, John Saxon, and Sandra Dee.

John Saxon is an actor who has never stopped working. He has made eighty films and countless television shows, and when he talked with me from his home in Los Angeles, he was leaving for Russia the next day to costar in a film, *Jonathan of the Bears*, which was being shot outside Moscow. John remembered costarring opposite my mom back in 1958:

☞ The Restless Years *was about a sensitive girl, sensitive because she is illegitimate. I played the son of a typical American family. My "father" was a salesman, and my "mother" wants to find one place to live because the family is always moving around the country. And in my role, I'm an extremely sensitive boy.*

When Sandra and I meet as characters, there is an immediate recognition that we are both outsiders. The truth of the matter was that in a way, we both were. I was from Brooklyn, had come to Los Angeles about five years before, and I was in the movies playing the American boy next door. This seemed to me a huge leap as an actor. I was assuming the kind of identity that I had never known in Brooklyn. I had been born

Carmine Orrico. My parents were immigrants, and there was an Old World kind of darkness and suspicion attached to things.

I think I quickly perceived that Sandra was also a fish out of water in this respect. She had been a model in New York, I discovered. But I could sense that she was young. She clearly had a facility about acting; she had a great knack, a technique of acting. She knew timing. She knew changes. She knew where all the points were, but now I have a feeling that she didn't actually know where they were in a sense. She assumed. What I think is that both of us were making an approximation of what it was all about, this American boy and girl next door. In some respects, we shared something. It was an uncanny sense of what was desired of us more than what we really understood.

I remember one scene, probably the first kissing scene, where I felt a little awkward. She seemed young and kind of delicate and perhaps inexperienced. And I remember the director saying, "I know I made you too old for this part." Maybe I was actually too old for the part. Maybe I should have been seventeen, not twenty. But I was certainly too old in comparison with Sandra.

The Restless Years was a success. Ross Hunter told John that the film did better than a Cary Grant–Sophia Loren film in some markets, and John felt good about that. He remembers that he and my mother were young stars, and they were interviewed constantly. They would occasionally see one another at Ross Hunter's house, but there wasn't a great deal that went on between them. Then a movie called *The Reluctant Debutante* came up. *Debutante* was about two British parents who were to present their Americanized daughter to society. Directed by Vincente Minnelli, it starred Kate Kendall and Rex Harrison. The film was shot in Paris.

John Saxon recalls that shooting in Paris "was one of life's great experiences. I was twenty-two. And I wanted to do everything that I couldn't do at home in L.A. The first day came, and I was taken to

A boy from the Bronx and his "big sister," Nina Cassotto, Easter, 1943. Bobby is seven years old.

A living doll. Alexandria Zuck, age six, Bayonne, New Jersey.

Sandra (age eleven) with her stepfather, Eugene Douvan. Douvan said he married Mary to get Sandy. (*Copyright 1955 by V. L. Sladon*)

Three members of the Eddie O'Casio band. From left to right, Steve Karmen, Dick Behrke, and Bobby Cassotto on drums, 1952. (*Photo by Larry Blumenthal*)

As one of New York's top teen models, my mom earned over $75,000 a year. This photo was taken in 1954 when she was ten years old.

My dad, a future teen idol, age sixteen. He said that music was his way out of the ghetto.

My mom's early days with Universal. Here, at the Russian Tea Room with her tutor, Gladys Hoene (*left*), her dog Pom-Pom, and her mother, Mary Douvan (*center*). Sandy is about thirteen years old.

Harriet (Hesh) Wasser. This was taken after my dad sang "Splish Splash" for the first time on Dick Clark's show. (*From the personal collection of Harriet Wasser*)

Friends from the neighborhood. My dad said he would never forget them when he got famous. And he didn't. From left to right, Dick Behrke, Dick Lord, Bobby, Steve Karmen, and Ellen Lord.

Producer Ross Hunter
aptly described his
little star-to-be as "a
sophisticated baby." This
is Sandy in 1957 when she
was thirteen.

My dad with legendary TV
host Ed Sullivan and a true
love, Connie Francis.
Connie's father came after
Bobby with a gun and broke
up their romance.

Night work on the set of Universal's *Teach Me How to Cry*. From left to right, Sandra, Ross Hunter, his dog Archie, and actor John Saxon. (*Copyright © 1957 by Universal City Studios, Inc. Courtesy of MCA Publishing Rights, a Division of MCA, Inc.*)

A family portrait: Bobby with his "brother-in-law" Charlie Maffia and his "sister" Nina. My dad wouldn't find out that Nina was his mother for another ten years, and he never learned the identity of his father. (*From the personal collection of Harriet Wasser*)

Sandra Dee and Troy Donahue in *A Summer Place*, 1959. It was a film about teenage love and passion and was a huge box office hit. Donahue was surprised at how well my mom could kiss.

My dad had his first taste of big success with Atlantic Records and he had his most significant label relationship with them. The Atlantic brain trust, from left to right: Jerry Wexler, Neshui Ertegun, Bobby, and a man my dad thought the world of, Ahmet Ertegun. (*Photo by William "Popsie" Randolfph. From the personal collection of Harriet Wasser*)

Bobby with the man he considered his brother, 1960. Steve Blauner was "a manager who drew blood."

My dad said if he could have picked a father, he would have picked George Burns. Mr. Burns says he felt the same way. But Bobby was too young to be his father. *(Photo by Elmer Holloway. Copyright NBC Photo. Courtesy of the National Broadcasting Company, Inc.)*

the hotel. I took a bath. Someone brought me my per diem, which was an enormous amount of francs, I realized. I took a taxi to the Left Bank, and I didn't come back to the hotel for two days. Throughout the making of this film, I had a grand time. Paris. A different restaurant every day. Sandra, by contrast, never left the hotel."

A word here about the life of a contract actor, because the studio system was ending as my mother came on board with Universal. She and John Saxon and a handful of others were the last of the contract players, meaning that they were, in fact, employees. They earned salaries. Saxon remembers he was making about $150 a week at this time. My mother was making a bit more but still much less than she had made as a model. The actors worked with many of the same people from picture to picture and were sometimes loaned out to other studios.

There were classes in fencing, dancing, diction, whatever was required, and contract players were subject to studio rules and regulations. Their publicity was choreographed by the studio, and the way they looked, behaved, and led their social lives was scrutinized and often created by their employers. Movie star life in the fifties was quite a world apart from today's free agent system, where often the star produces and develops his or her own film properties and might get a piece of the action as well.

For my teenage mother, things were even more different than for others. The studio believed her to be sixteen when she made this film in Paris. She was still protected by the child labor laws and was required to take classes in math and biology, the same as any other American kid. But there were no other kids on the set with Sandy, so as usual she had a tutor all to herself.

Back in Hollywood, my mom would be the lone kid in a classroom with twenty-nine empty chairs. Sometimes she had a teacher who would let her smoke a cigarette in the open. Sometimes she had a strict disciplinarian who would shut down the shooting of a scene moments away from completion in order to get her young charge into the classroom the moment the second hand ruled the time had come. Never mind what it cost to set up the scene the next day.

As *Debutante* was being shot in France and John Saxon was having the time of his life, my mother remembers working nonstop on the set, then being sequestered with a tutor. Her restaurant experiences also differed from John's. She remembers going to a fancy restaurant and ordering a single egg. The chef rushed out of the kitchen to see for himself the source of this insult.

John Saxon remembers that my mother was always concerned about her weight, and that she was "always slightly sucking in her cheeks." He remembers doing a scene that called for him to dance with her. He put his hands around her waist and said, "Sandra, I could strangle your waist." That's how thin she was. When I see this film now, I see that my mother's shoulder blades and vertebrae were painfully obvious. No wonder everyone was trying so hard to get her to eat.

Ross Hunter was concerned for my mother's health. He says that her diet was ridiculous, that she'd eat a slice of cucumber or half an egg. "Sandy felt her face was awfully full. She was of a mind to be thin, thin, thin. She was a little topheavy, but not noticeably so. We were very concerned that she was just eating nothing. Our whole little group just loved this little girl, and we nurtured her. In the meantime, someone was telling her she was getting fat, that she was getting out of proportion, and that her face was fat. We never knew for sure who it was, but we all guessed that it was Mary. There was nothing we could do to get Sandy to eat because she would say, 'I'm not hungry.' "

Last week, while going through a box of papers, I found an astonishing document. It's a diary that my mother more or less kept while she was making this film. I say more or less, because although my mother started to write in it, within three days my grandmother was correcting her spelling and adding entries in Sandy's voice. By the end of the first week, all the entries were Mary's—writing as if she were her daughter. Here's my mother speaking, when just short of fourteen:

> *My goodness, I don't know what it is, but I just can't seem to get enough sleep. Today I got up around 3 P.M., had breakfast, then met my tutor, hairdresser, and makeup man from MGM. Boy are the French friendly. They talk to you on the street, which at first seemed rather strange, but now I realize they are warm and friendly.*

DREAM LOVERS

Here's an entry in my grandmother' hand:

☞ *Today, made many new friends. There are a lot of Russian people working here. And they found out I was of Russian parents and so Mother had fun speaking Russian. I'm sorry to say I don't speak fluently at all, but understand it all. My first performance age twenty-one months was in a Russian play at church.*

I find it scary that my grandmother was taking over my mother's diary, and I have no comfortable explanation for it. It says a great deal on its own without any interpretation from me. But reading my mother's entries, I wonder if she was having any fun with her grown-up schedule. I know she worshiped actress Kay Kendall, and she was fascinated that Rex Harrison spent two hours with the director discussing how he would pick up a piece of paper. She commented on how hard it was to get her hairstyle right, and my grandmother wrote of their sight-seeing trips, shopping, and many pastries consumed in cafes. My mom turned in a terrific performance in *Debutante*. The "sophisticated baby" easily looks eighteen, and Ross Hunter remembers that her star quality "was so unusual in that she was so natural. You never felt that she was acting. She really was above the average girl, and yet she was very down-to-earth with it all. And of course we created the monster, if the truth be known. We wouldn't let her out of her house unless her hair was done and unless she wore a beautiful dress and unless her makeup was lovely.

"After those first few pictures she was really on her way. So I decided I would start putting her in sort of teenage-type movies so that the kids could really get to know her. We did quite a few pictures with her, and then we loaned her out to Columbia to do *Gidget*, which added a completely new dimension to Sandy. She was one of the kids then. No matter how sophisticated she may have been in some of the other pictures, she was one of the kids, and they fell in love with her and with *Gidget*, then with *A Summer Place*."

Troy Donahue played opposite Sandra Dee in this dramatic film about teenage love and unwanted pregnancy. Again my mom and her costar played all-American kids, clean cut and as innocent as lambs. At the time, Troy was twenty-two, a blond-haired heartthrob; there was hardly a girl alive who didn't have a crush on him. Today Troy Donahue does films and entertains on cruise ships. I would describe him as a tall, good-looking guy who wears his hair in a ponytail. I found him open and very helpful.

Troy had this to say about meeting my mother for the first time:

When I found out I was going to do A Summer Place *and that Sandra was going to do it, too, I was very excited. I met her for the first time outside of makeup. Her mother was with her. Her mother was always with her. Sandra was wearing a Connie Stevens dress with a lot of petticoats. And she was so polite. It was as if she were always wearing white gloves. But she wasn't. I had the feeling she had Mary-Janes on. But she didn't.*

At this first introduction, Sandra said she was very eager to work with me. I couldn't even figure out how she would know who I might be. But it was a nice line and gave me a sense of security and a feeling that everything was going to be okay. And it was.

Sandra and I loved working together. She was professional. And sometimes you think if you do a film with someone and it's a love story, something romantic might happen off camera. I found Sandra attractive, but I knew for some reason that nothing was going to get me to make a move on her. It was out of the question, and I can't explain why, other than to say I felt that she would have broken. When she did the love scenes, she surprised me that she knew how to kiss. She knew how to act these things.

I found Sandra Dee a paradox. She was very fragile, but she had a kind of tenacity. And she was funny in a kind of quiet way. She would say things. There was a scene in the garden with fireflies all around, and a rosebush catches her dress. In the scene I kneel down to unsnag her dress, and Sandra astonished me with a joke. Like, "While you're down there . . ." But it was done as a joke, not as a sexy come-

on. There was no sense that later on there might be something else.

But we did feel great warmth toward one another.

I thought Mary was living her fantasy through Sandra, the way many stage mothers do. Mary was very lovely, a sexy lady, and very protective of Sandra, and Sandra deferred to her. Not that Sandra didn't have her own feet under her, but her mother sometimes charged out in front. I never posed any kind of threat to Sandra because I knew the situation was too breakable. She wasn't allowed to be alone with me much, anyway. She was with her hairdresser and makeup people.

As for me, I was full of myself at that time. I thought I was indestructible. I had this glorious career that would never end. And I would do all the films that Robert Redford and Warren Beatty did. I had several girlfriends. I was smoking and dropping and drinking in front of the camera, off the camera, wherever. But I never showed up drunk, and I never showed up late. I just did what I did to take the edge off so I could do my job. It enabled me to function. I was fearful. I lacked confidence.

And I had a feeling sometimes that Sandra would rather have been somewhere else. That she wasn't as enthusiastic about her career as other people were, and that she had become a commodity. That she had become too important to let go of.

One of the things my mother was feeling was that her mother's constant presence was strangling her. As she puts it:

I was like a parent in New York. I was on my own. I was taking care of myself, but when we came out to Hollywood, the law required my mother to be with me, and she felt needed again as a mother. So she took over. She loved it. I just wanted to stand on my own, and my mother would always be on the set. She loved to hear people say "You can't be her mother. You must be her sister." I loved my mother, and I miss her, but she was stifling.

I would say, "Kay, can I have a Coke?" Or "Jack, can I have a cigarette?" But my mother would always get what I needed. I didn't want my mother to bring me the Coke. The people who worked for the studio were paid to do that work, and it was wrong for her to do it. Once she wrote me a pathetic letter, along the lines of "All I want to do is be with you and help you." It was a sick letter. I didn't want things to be on a level of "Hey, buddy," with my mother. She deserved more than that. And I tried to explain things to her, but she just cried.

My mom told me she felt like property—Mary's property and Universal's property. After *A Summer Place*, Sandra Dee's name was everywhere, so her value was rising with every picture. The next film Ross Hunter cast her in was called *Imitation of Life*. Lana Turner was starring, and Ross says he knew that if the picture was a success, Sandy would become one of the big box office stars in the country.

Imitation of Life was, in his words, a picture that people were afraid of. The story was about a Black mother and a White mother and their two daughters. The daughter of the Black woman (played by Susan Kohner) was passing for White, and all kinds of people told Ross the picture couldn't be done because it would bomb in the South. This was highly risky in the fifties.

Ross says, "The reaction was marvelous. The South just took the film into their arms, and it was probably one of the biggest hits that ever played for Universal. Sandra Dee then became every mother's dream. In the picture, Sandra's character graduates from high school, and we had designer Jean-Louis do a marvelous graduation dress for her. Then we announced to the world, via the publicity racket, that any mother who wanted the pattern could get it for nothing. All they had to do was show two tickets to *Imitation of Life*. In the first month we gave out fifteen thousand patterns, and then we had to stop because it became almost ridiculous. After that I realized that Sandy could really hold a picture on her own."

John Saxon remembers working with my mother on the next film. He and Sandy were starring with Lana Turner and Anthony Quinn in a thriller called *Portrait in Black*. It was 1959, and by then John says he was doing several character roles—my mother's star had risen higher than his, and after this film they would not work together again for more than thirty years. But back then, he recalls, "there was a makeup man and a hairdresser following her wherever she went. She couldn't have been more than eighteen, and she had an entourage. And I thought that all of this added to this hothouse experience of Sandra's life. She went from a child playing all kinds of things that she'd never known, and now she was ensconced in the Hollywood glass bubble."

Which brings us backstage to my grandmother, Mary Douvan. Most people recall that Mary doted on my mother, that she loved being on the set, and that she and my mother were inseparable. Aunt Ollie came to visit Hollywood and brought her husband and oldest child with her.

Ollie remembers how exciting it was to actually watch her niece perform: "It was all so new to us. Just to watch her. We admired her because she was so great in whatever part she played. We'd say, 'That's our Sandy. That's our Sandy.' And we'd go down to the studio and watch her every day. We'd have lunch in the commissary and then go back to the studio. She'd have certain scheduled hours, and she had a little house, her dressing room, which was like a little bungalow with her name on it. It was Sandy's little house. So cute. And she was so good. And they all adored her on the set. She got along so well with everybody. And her mother was so proud of her. Sandy could do no wrong. That was her little idol, Sandy, and Mary was always with her. Sandy didn't have to do anything for herself."

My mom remembers what her aunt remembers, but her take on it is different:

☞ *My mother wanted a cripple. She didn't want me to fly. Before a camera she was fine. She would never butt in there, but otherwise she would just glom onto me. She hated Jack, and she hated Kay, because they were important to me. She wanted to live her life through me, and she wanted to make me a part of her.*

I readily concede that my mother was miserable in her first marriage. When I was born, she made me the object of her attention. She took me over to the point where even the most skeptical person would see why I became anorectic. She was obsessed with having this perfect child.

Then she met Eugene Douvan, and she saw a whole new world. When they got married, she took him over. He was her new wonderment, and he interested her more than me. It was real easy to phase me out a little bit, and I didn't mind. I started to choose what I ate. I started to model. I got around by myself and kept myself company. Then Gene died, and for a few months I took over, but then things changed again. My mother needed a substitute for Eugene. Sandra Dee, movie star, became that substitute. First and foremost, Mary was Eugene's wife. Then, first and foremost, she was a movie star's mother.

And by this time Sandra Dee was a genuine top-drawer box office smash. She was getting more fan mail than Rock Hudson. Ross Hunter says they couldn't open a movie starring Sandra Dee, no matter how bad it was, and not make money.

But my mom was having a very weird life.

She associated entirely with adults. If she was doing a beach movie, the kids for the beach scene would work one day and then they'd be gone. She didn't date. The studio fabricated publicity dates for her with Johnny Wilder, Sal Mineo, Jimmy Darren. But in real life she wasn't romantically interested in them, and truly, they weren't interested in her. She said at the time that boys her own age were too young for her and the older boys found her too young. And there was a tight circle of guards around this little movie star. Mother never left her side. Ross Hunter screened Sandy's would-be "dates" and escorted her to public functions himself. My mom's hairdresser, Kaye Reid, and makeup man, Jack Freeman, were her best friends and constant companions.

The word *dapper* describes Jack well—impeccably groomed, neatly styled salt-and-pepper hair, pleasant and thoughtful. Jack Freeman says he got started in films rather late. He may have been in his thirties in 1958 when he started doing my mother's makeup. With Sandy Jack used a light touch. He said her face was so perfect that she needed almost no cosmetics, certainly not the heavy makeup that was the style of the day.

☞ *I loved Mary very much. She was a perfectionist. She wanted Sandra to have perfect manners. She always wanted her to look perfect, and Sandra always did. It became second nature to her. She was the best-groomed young lady I've ever known. Even if she had only two hours' sleep, she never arrived for makeup or to go somewhere without being absolutely fresh, with her hair done and her makeup just lovely.*

Sandra, in my mind, was always two people. There was the public Sandra Dee. That Sandra was the perfectly poised young lady who knew how to say just the right things on interviews. Then she'd go back to the dressing room and be a different person. This was the Sandra who was with her closest friends: Ross Hunter, Kay Reid, and myself. With us she was confiding, very responsive, very concerned that you had everything you needed.

Now, Mary was perhaps excessive in her mother love. She liked to be included. She liked to see the wardrobe and say if she liked it or not. I think she was very good at that. And no one could do things for Sandra the way Mary could, because Mary knew her completely. And Mary indulged her completely. And I thought whatever she did was for her daughter's welfare and happiness. I just knew that to be true.

I loved Sandra, but I have to say I thought that sometimes she treated her mother very cruelly. If Sandra feels that her mother ruined her life, that was not true. Sandra Dee, from the time I knew her, called the shots. Mary had a certain power because she was of a certain age, but Sandra had a will of iron. If she decided it was "no," it was "no." And then she would change her mind at the last moment.

Mary would never provoke a confrontation in front of people, so what went on behind closed doors, I don't know. Mary had to give in constantly in front of people so there wouldn't be a scene. But Mary's nature was really devoted and loving. She may have made some mistakes, but they were the kind that would come with raising a willful daughter who had a great deal of power.

Although Jack's description makes me feel suffocated on my mother's behalf, I understand why he disapproved of how Sandy treated Mary. I understand, because I once felt exactly the same way. I saw that my grandmother had essentially donated her life to supporting and cleaning up after my mother, and I didn't like my mother for this. But neither Jack nor I knew the "back story"—the history between mother and daughter before Gidget went Hollywood.

Had Jack Freeman known, I think he might have found it a relief— as I do now—to realize that my mother was fighting back against the person she was angry at. It seems like normal adolescent rebellion when compared with the way Sandy generally expressed her rage. From the moment she was served that first clear cup of consommé, my mom most often vented her anger through food. And the object of her attack was her own body.

While doing her first picture, my mom had a horrific experience. She had overdone the lettuce diet to the point that her renal system shut down from lack of protein. She could no longer urinate the toxins from her body, and the fluids backed up. Her body became, in a matter of moments, so swollen that the seams of her pants literally split.

Sandra, who was working at the time, called her mother. Understandably, Mary couldn't recognize the seriousness of the swelling. "We'll soak your feet in Epsom salts," she said. But when she saw Sandra, she phoned Eugene's former doctor, who took the red-eye from the East Coast to Los Angeles. (Grandma! They had doctors in Los Angeles!)

When Gene Douvan's former doctor saw Sandy, he said, "It looks so bad, it just can't be what it seems." Sandy describes herself then as an "eighty-pound child who looked like an elephant from the waist down." It was called acute edema. Protein was added to Sandy's diet, and my mother recovered, but soon after that, Epsom salts would play a new role in my mother's life.

Some months later, my mother went with several older actresses to get a massage. While at this salon, she overheard someone telling Kim

Novak about Epsom salts. When combined with water and drunk, Epsom salts were a powerful laxative that "cleansed the system," sometimes used as a method of losing weight. Sandy told her mother what she'd heard, and Mary was horrified, but Sandy knew she was going to try it.

My mother had a habit of closeting herself on Saturdays. After a week of school and work, she took one day a week for herself. No fancy clothes, no makeup, just herself in her room with books and magazines. When she first tried the Epsom salts, my mother put a tablespoon of the stuff in a glass of water and drank it. When that didn't work as she hoped, she doubled the dosage. And then she doubled that. Finally she was drinking eight ounces of salt barely moistened with water. She figured if she could drink milk with a raw egg, salt was no worse.

And why was she doing this to herself? Because on Saturday, on her day off, my mother would eat walnuts. That was her treat. And then, having eaten the walnuts, she had to get rid of them.

"I wanted to punish myself for being bad," she says. "The food was bad. I punished myself, and then I felt good."

Mary had gotten accustomed to Sandy's solitary Saturdays. Since her schedule revolved around Sandy's, Saturday was a good day for her, too. She would spend time with her sister and have her friends over for a swim at their cute house in Benedict Canyon. On one particular day, after the sun had gone down, Mary noticed that she hadn't seen Sandy for twelve hours. When she called to Sandy through the locked bedroom door and received no reply, Mary forced it open— and found her daughter comatose on the floor.

No time to fly in the doctor from New Jersey this time. My mother said it was apparent to my grandmother that if she didn't get her to a hospital, she wasn't going to make it. Her eyes were open and unfocused. UCLA was the nearest hospital with an emergency room. Sandy's stomach was pumped, and all the while the doctors were questioning Mary: "Does she have a boyfriend?" They thought Sandy had tried to commit suicide.

"No, no!" said Mary. "She takes Epsom salts and eats walnuts!"

The doctors may not have been enlightened by this, but tests showed that Sandy's blood was depleted of potassium, which they corrected intravenously. Soon my mother was talking her head off. The doctor in charge said to my mom, "Shut up. Why are you talking so much?"

And she said, "Because I thought I'd never talk again."

The doctor "thought I was a little snot," my mother says.

☞ *He didn't realize I wasn't being bad. I was taking care of the bad I did with the walnuts.*

He said, "You're never going to do this again."

I said, "No, no." And I didn't drink Epsom salts for a while, but Saturday would always come around again. I would never do anything that would interfere with work. I would never take any chances on Monday. Monday was work. Saturday was "be sick." I'll never forget this. My mother was at her desk writing checks. I drank the Epsom salts. I knew the minute it went down that I was in trouble. I gagged and I could feel this heat going through my body. I came out of my room, said, "Ma? I did it again."

"Oh, no."

This time it was different. This time we didn't call an ambulance. She didn't want anyone to see me. She called one of her friends to drive me, and I heard that when I arrived at UCLA, my feet were out the window. But this time I wasn't unconscious. This time I was awake enough to tell her, "I gotta go in." I was awake when they pumped my stomach, and no one would ever want to be conscious for that. I never took Epsom salts again.

My mother notes that when she was in the hospital this second time, there was a newspaper story of another blond actress who had committed suicide. The photograph showed the actress covered entirely by a sheet except for her blond hair. My mom says that Mary saw the picture and was horrified because she thought it was Sandy. My mom insists that Mary was less concerned that her daughter was dead than that having a daughter who had committed suicide would reflect badly on her.

My mom was just a kid: she must have gotten this wrong because it can't possibly be true. Yet it wasn't light-years away from the truth to say that Mary was more concerned with appearances than with reality. The evidence is everywhere you look, and in researching all these articles, talking with people I'd never spoken with before, and really hearing my mother's words head on, I've come to realize that I believe my mom's story of her wretched childhood.

Some people would say "That was then, this is now. The past is the past. Tell your mom to get a grip." To these people I would reply "It didn't happen to me, yet just *believing* that it happened to someone I love simply undoes me. How do I get a grip on that scum Douvan? How do I reconcile my love and extreme distaste for my grandmother? How do I say 'Mom, get a life' when she never had the foundation to build one?" And that doesn't mean I'm not angry at my mother. Sometimes the word *anger* can't begin to describe the enormity of my feelings as I watch her destroy herself with alcohol. But these are my problems. I leave the reader to draw his or her own conclusions.

Sandy was fifteen when in June of 1959 *Newsweek* quoted the "public" Sandy: "I love acting. I love the glamour. I love the premiers. I love getting dressed up and living in California and having a white Thunderbird and getting my first ticket. I love performing. I'm in my biggest glory when visitors come to the set. I get the biggest kick when people are around me even though I might be stinking in the scene. I guess I'm a ham."

In real life my mom has told me that after the first picture, acting was just work. The car was critical to her well-being. She needed to be able to get from the set to school and to leave her mother at the set, "because I was getting crazy with my mother twenty-four hours a day. I was like a prisoner."

Ross Hunter concludes, "Mary was around so much, if I'd been Sandy, I would have done anything possible to get her out of my life. I don't think Sandy was rough on Mary. I think Sandy was trying to have an existence of her own. Sandy was also surrounded by pretty awful things to have to face as a young girl. I'm sure there were times when she just went into a corner and cried her eyes out. This was a young kid who was thrown into stardom so fast that she didn't know which end was up. I think she handled it beautifully, I really do. I also thought she handled Mary beautifully. I'm not saying that Mary was a complete villain. I'm just saying that Mary, who lived vicariously through Sandy, did not present to her the best a family could present to a young girl growing up."

Not to say that my mother never had a moment of fun. People would not have so often described my mother's nature as "sunny" and "good-natured" if she were always depressed. But from what she's told me, I think what Sandra Dee loved best about being a movie star was the sense of having a family around her. She had a stable life for the first time, the most normal life she'd ever known. For years she knew where she was going to be day after day. When working on a picture, she'd be on the set. When not making a picture, she'd be in school from nine to twelve. And there were fathers and mothers and uncles everywhere who focused their attention on her. She could take a math problem to the president of Universal!

I started this chapter by talking about Sandy, a teenager without friends, and now I can see where that came from and where it goes. As a child, she played alone with her dolls. Her grandfather said, "She doesn't need anybody." I think he was wrong. Mary said she loved her daughter but dressed her in velvet outfits that made her look like a jackass. My mom was always taller than her classmates, more developed, and at the same time younger. Kids don't like kids who are different. "You don't belong with any of them," said Mary.

My mom treasures the memory of the one year she rode her bike with her schoolmates, wearing the ordinary clothes her stepfather got her. She loved her stepfather, but she couldn't trust him. She was working professionally from the age of eight. Her only kisses were bought and paid for. I listen to her contemporaries: Carol Lynley, John Saxon, Troy Donahue. They liked her. They respected her. But they didn't touch her. Sandy was too different. Too frail. Too other.

I've read recently that psychologists are beginning to study childhood friendships and are finding that they build fundamental self-esteem and are models for subsequent long-term relationships and marriage. I'm ashamed to admit that dozens of times I've shouted, "Ma, forget being Sandra Dee. I just want you to be a housewife somewhere on Long Island. I just want you to be happy." I wonder how I thought my mother could bring off something like that. She doesn't date. She hardly goes out. She has barely worked in the last twenty years. She's a sweet person, but she finds it impossible to relate to people. She was Sandra Dee. Who is she now?

I picture my mother at fifteen. She is sitting in her dressing room at Universal, staring at the mirror. She is sucking in her cheeks and wondering how to make that baby fat go away. She's already read the script through once and knows her lines. Learning lines is no sweat. Jack and Kay are chatting happily around her, dusting her face with powder, combing her pale, cotton-candy hair. Mary hands Sandy a Coke through the bars of her gilded cage.

I wonder what my mother's life would have been if she hadn't been so pretty. If she hadn't been so attractive to a dirty old man. If her mother hadn't been so mesmerized by her beauty that she used her as a mirror and turned her into a doll. I wonder what would have happened to my mother if Mary hadn't been able to use Sandy as currency and a ticket out of Bayonne. If Sandy hadn't had those melting brown eyes that told a Hollywood studio they were looking at a movie star. I wonder what would have happened to my mother if she hadn't been so appealing to angels with hollow canine teeth. If my mother had been plain, would her life have turned out better or worse?

I quote now from an article in *Movie Screen*, June 1959. The headline has type two inches high: I HAVE NO FRIENDS: SANDRA DEE. We pick up at the end of this six-page article as it summarizes:

> Sandra Dee is different from the average teen-age girl in more than her career. The fact of her luxury-centered childhood makes her more poised, more socially assured than most girls; she has no worries about which fork to use, how to speak to a waiter, what to wear where, how to talk to adults.
>
> Both her indulgent mother and autocratic stepfather contributed to her social maturity. On the other hand, in specifically teen-age affairs, she knows less than most girls do, has dated less and has shared in almost no teen-age girl life. This makes her present life lonely and difficult and makes her work assume even greater importance than her natural ambition would give it.
>
> She is a forceful, confident, able person. In a strange way, the tragedy of her beloved father's death probably had its good side for Sandy. As she grew older, she could scarcely avoid clashes with him over the very things that made her

adore him previously. His firm-handed running of everyone's life. His insistence upon his own way in everything.
Under the circumstances, her memory of him is unspoiled.

Now both she and her mother are centered upon Sandy's
career, and it is Sandy who runs the house to some extent,
plans the meals, does in fact whatever she wants to and finds
interesting. They are tremendously conscious of her mother's
need to remarry because Sandy will be leaving her one day.
It is not, as you might expect, centered on Mary marrying
and leaving *her*.

This reporter feels that Sandy's career is the *result* of her
basic difference from most girls and not the *cause* of it.

Of course in many ways she is like other girls. She is self-
conscious about her appearance, nervous and hopeful about
boys and will probably sooner or later feel strongly the fact
that she had no one to lean on, but is being leaned on
instead. I couldn't make a case for this girl as the average
teen-ager plunged into the glorious upheaval of Hollywood,
because it just ain't so.

In the autumn of 1960, my mom was sixteen. She had been in
Hollywood for three and a half years and had made more than a half
dozen films when she was picked to do a film called *Come September*.
The picture would star this teenager who would soon become my
mom, and it would feature a young actor who had written the music
for the title song.

His name was Bobby Darin.

5

Bobby, 1958 - 1960

*A great voice, he ain't got. An actor he don't seem to be.
A matinee idol he certainly ain't. A happy kid he's not either,
they tell me. But you put all the ain'ts and nots together, and
you got the hottest talent to walk across a stage in over twenty
years.*

—ANONYMOUS "SHOW BIZ OLD-TIMER"
Cosmopolitan *magazine, November 1960*

———

*Some people would say to me, "You found Bobby Darin."
I had as much to do with finding Bobby Darin as the man
in the moon. You find nobody, 'cause they're on the stage
for twenty minutes by themselves. They're on their own feet.
It would be impossible to stop Bobby Darin from being a
star because he had nothing to do with it. The audience
made him. He was good. He was great. He sang great,
he danced great, he moved good, he was a good actor, he
had a great sense of humor, he told things funny. And it*

*would be impossible for Bobby Darin to be anything differ-
ent than a star.*

—GEORGE BURNS
Actor and friend

When "Splish Splash" was born, my father's life changed fast. He may have claimed he was two years behind himself, but to all but his closest friends and family, Bobby Darin came out of nowhere and arrived at the summit having broken all kinds of land speed records along the way.

"I know there are people who would take a bullet for me, but I wouldn't take a bullet for anyone," my dad said to more than one friend. Endearing? No. But, interestingly, his attitude didn't stop his friends from flanking him on all sides. Bobby Cassotto, AKA Bobby Darin, had more loyal, lifelong friends sitting around him in Hansen's than most people have strung out over a lifetime.

They said they were moths drawn to a flame.

A typical story of the time has my father sitting in a dressing room between sets. The room is crowded with fans and friends and influential people. My father picks his guitar. He doesn't talk to anyone. He's thinking about his heart, or his performance, or more likely the next step in his career. Suddenly he says, "Okay, that's enough. Everybody out." A stunned silence follows, but no one moves.

Hesh Wasser turns to Bobby and says quietly, "Bobby, you can't talk to people that way. If you're tired, just excuse yourself politely."

Bobby snaps, "Did you hear me? Everyone out." He stalks away.

Hesh Wasser knew my dad before he made it, and she knew him after:

☞ *People used to say to me, "He put you on a pedestal. Every word you say, he hangs on to." It was true, until he became a star. And then he wanted me to hang on to every word he said. I think Bobby was so damned anxious to make it that he would do anything for anybody at a certain point in life. But once he did make it, he didn't have to be so pleasing anymore. And my feeling is that since he knew he wasn't going to live long, it was more important to him to make his statement as an artist than as a diplomat.*

There was a time when I would see Bobby four or five times a week. When he made it, I hoped I might see him four or five times every two years—but those few times would have meant something to me. And the reason I say that is because anybody who came in contact with Bobby was changed by him. You could not forget the experience. You could not forget that this was someone who was going to remain in your mind forever. "He's nice" was not the kind of thing that you would say about him. You would either say "He's the cat's meow" or "He's a bastard." But your opinion would have conviction because his personality was so strong.

When my dad recorded "Splish Splash" in that split session with Morgana King, he had every reason to expect Atco was going to drop him, so he had a backup plan. He recorded "Early in the Morning" without telling anyone at Atco, and Murray the K sold the master to Brunswick Records. Brunswick called Bobby and his backup singers "the Ding Dongs" and released the single right after "Splish Splash" hit. But Ahmet Ertegun wasn't fooled. He knew Bobby's voice and sound. He reined in his star-to-be, who was still under contract to Atlantic, and put the song out again, this time calling Bobby's group "the Rinky Dinks." A small war broke out as "Early in the Morning" was released yet again, this time sung by Buddy Holly. Now two non-Atlantic releases were cutting into profits that should have been Atco's. But Bobby was forgiven his clandestine recording. His Atco version of the song reached number twenty-four on the charts, while Holly's only got as far as number thirty-two. And Ahmet, fully understanding why Bobby had gone rogue, signed him up with a new contract.

Now my dad's career began in earnest. Atco released his first album, *Bobby Darin*, the LP that Hesh Wasser then pushed on Barry Gray. A single, "Queen of the Hop," was fast off the mark when it was released in October 1958, finding its way into the top ten. Then my dad wrote and sang "Plain Jane," which made the charts and stuck at number thirty-eight. At this point Bobby Darin could do no wrong.

While his records were breaking, Csida-Crean, my dad's managers, were getting Bobby Darin out on the road. He toured with the best: Buddy Holly, Dion DiMucci, Clyde McPhatter. On tour he met a petite blond singer whom promoter Alan Freed had labeled "the Blonde Bombshell." She hated the nickname, but she loved Bobby and he loved her—so much so that for a couple of years the movie magazines were full of stories about the doomed love affair between Bobby Darin and beautiful Jo-Ann Campbell. WHY BOBBY CAN'T LOVE was a typical headline. WHAT BOBBY DARIN DOESN'T KNOW ABOUT LOVE was another. And what was the problem with Bobby? He wanted Jo-Ann to quit singing, and she wouldn't. He wanted everything in his life to be focused on his career.

When my dad recorded a tune called "Dream Lover," it shot to number two and became his third gold record. With that, there was no getting around it and no saying no to it. He was enthroned as a "teen idol." He wailed, "With rock 'n' roll, I'm like a thousand other guys. Now, I've got to prove I can sing." Honestly, I think he'd be the first to say that while he liked the music, he saw his hits as a step toward bigger and better things.

Says Dick Clark, "Nobody looked like him. Nobody performed like him. He had a maturity that most teen idols didn't have. He didn't want to be called a teen idol, but he fell into that batch. He was at the moment idolized by little girls, and that makes you a teen idol. The Beatles were teen idols. And Presley and Rudolph Valentino. There was nothing wrong with that tag."

But it wasn't okay with Bobby Darin.

Without even waiting for the dew to dry on the glistening dawn of his rock 'n' roll career, my dad went to Ahmet Ertegun and said, "This is not really what I'm about. I want to record an album of standards." My dad was twenty-three years old. He had hit records, he was working, he was doing it, but he wasn't satisfied. He looked at his contemporaries and saw that they were jamming in buses, going on rock 'n' roll tours. Half of them were so busy making money, so poorly managed by their inexperienced young managers, they'd forget to go back into the studios to record!

My dad wanted to play the Copacabana. He wanted to perform on Vegas stages. He wanted to do Frank Sinatra music and Sammy Davis Jr. performances. He thought rock 'n' roll was a fad, and he wanted to do music adults would listen to. When he told Ahmet Ertegun that he wanted to record an album of standards, Ahmet's mouth must have dropped open. Bobby Darin was Atlantic's first White star, and now he was going to screw it up. Ahmet said, "What are you talking about? You'll ruin your career."

My dad was insistent. He pointed out that Atlantic owed him royalties from "Splish Splash" and some of his other hits, and he rolled over his money to pay for a recording session at his own expense. Brave fellow—and of course his elders were shocked. They were sure he would lose his teenage following, and their fear was understandable. Never before had anyone crossed that bridge.

Sometime in 1958 my dad saw a production of Brecht-Weill's *Threepenny Opera* in a theater in Greenwich Village. It was a remake of a turn-of-the-century play called *Moritat* and had a grisly theme of murder and mayhem. Not the usual background for a pop standard. But one song in the play piqued my dad's interest: "Mack the Knife." My dad had heard Louis Armstrong's rendering of this song, and he liked it, so he started singing "Mack" on tour from June 1958 on. The audience didn't go wild for the song at the time, but "Mack" had gotten under Bobby's skin.

Through Hesh Wasser Bobby met a young arranger named Richard Wess, and he introduced Wess to Ahmet Ertegun. Ahmet liked Wess, described him as working "in the tradition of the big band. Semijazz. Semipop. What we would come to think of as a Las Vegas–type background." Some discussions ensued, plans were made, and Ahmet went along with Bobby to record an album of standards. In December 1958 *That's All* was recorded in one of the big orchestra-size studios on Fortieth Street. The standout song was "Mack the Knife."

Ahmet picks up the story: "As we were cutting 'Mack the Knife' on the first date, there was no doubt in anybody's mind. Everyone knew that this was going to be a number one record. Then I realized that having done the rock thing, Bobby was now going to have a big pop hit. He's going to become a major, major star, which eventually happened. But we knew as we were cutting it. We were jumping up and down. After the first take, I said, 'You've got it! That's it.' "

My dad was in a recording session in February 1959 when he got a call from his "sister," Nina. The news was bad: Polly had had a stroke and wasn't expected to live. By the time, Bobby arrived at her bedside, she was gone. He attended her funeral, stood at the back of the room as hundreds of people, some clutching autograph books, filed past Polly's coffin. When the room was empty at last, Bobby said his good-byes alone to the woman he believed to be his mother. She hadn't lived to hear the songs that he believed would take him from teen idol to star, but he felt a need to leave with her a token of their mutual love and faith. He had with him one of the acetates of his new album, which he placed inside her coffin.

If Bobby had doted on his mother, he sorely missed having a father. He still thought that Sam Cassotto was his father, and although Charlie Maffia was filling in gamely, he was never given the respect or the title—not in his home or on the road in his role as Bobby's valet and baggage handler. In the first half of 1959 my dad would find a mentor he loved as a father, but first he would land himself a big brother named Steve Blauner. My dad often said that Blauner was a genius, but that he was even more of a genius for recognizing that Steve was one. My dad's cockiness was showing, but in truth he was right. Steve was a diamond in the rough.

Steve remembers that the beginnings of his relationship with Bobby began years before they ever met. He was in the air force, on leave in New York, and he'd gone to the Copacabana to hear Sammy Davis Jr., who was performing there. He walked up to Sammy Davis and shook his hand. Then Steve said, "My name is Steve Blauner, and the way you feel about Frank Sinatra is the way I feel about you."

A friendship began that Steve says lasted until Sammy's death. Steve took a trip to California, stayed at Sammy Davis's house, and was given an entrée to Hollywood beyond his dreams. When he got out of the service, Steve found a job as a "go-fer" at a talent agency, General Artists Corporation (GAC), in New York. For technical clari-fication, talent agents, or "bookers," made dates for their clients, negotiated fees, and collected a cut. Talent managers, by contrast, directed the course of their clients' careers. Steve's job at GAC was to assist various talent bookers. He shared an inside, no-window office with another young agent-wannabe whose name has long since been forgotten. Steve was twenty-five years old, six feet three, three hundred pounds, and was already balding. And his personality was . . . well, loud. GAC was a huge organization, but although Steve was also huge, he was no agent.

Steve recalls that Pat Boone was one of GAC's clients and that Sammy Davis Jr. was in town to do the *Pat Boone–Chevy Showroom*. Steve decided to pay a call on Sammy's agents at the William Morris Agency to assure them that although he planned to be with Sammy Davis twenty-four hours a day, they had nothing to fear. He wasn't trying to steal Davis away for GAC. He was just a friend. Apparently the William Morris people didn't believe Steve, because he started to hear some backwash that he was attempting piracy. It pissed him off.

Blauner says, "I was really mad. Then I heard that William Morris was about to sign some guy named Bobby Darin, who was a rock 'n' roll singer. I hated rock 'n' roll. Never listened to it and didn't know who Bobby Darin was. But I remembered a young lady named Harriet Wasser. I didn't know what she did exactly, but she was always around saying, 'Oh, this kid, Bobby Darin.' I hadn't been interested, but when I heard his name this time, I called her up and said, 'I'd like to meet him. I want to sign him.' So Bobby and I made an appointment. I borrowed someone's outside office with windows, pretended I was a big man, and out of spite to the William Morris office, I got Bobby to sign with GAC. And then, of course, I felt terribly guilty because I was in no position to help him."

Steve toughed out his audacious act. My dad's managers had booked him into a rock 'n' roll show in Bridgeport, Connecticut. The first half of the show featured three rock 'n' roll acts, then Eydie Gorme and Steve Lawrence were going to close the show. Dick Clark was the emcee. Blauner got his friend Steve Karmen to give him a lift, and he went to Bridgeport to watch Bobby open the show.

"Bobby hit the stage and my mouth dropped open," Blauner says.

☞ *I didn't know what he was singing, and I didn't care. There was just something about him that put me into orbit. The next day I went back to the office and went up and down the aisles screaming about how if this kid could sing one note, he'd get to be one of the biggest stars of all time, and basically, nobody paid attention to me. I wasn't booking talent at this point, but I was Bobby's champion.*

Shortly after that, I was transferred to California because

*GAC was expanding, and when Bobby came out occasionally,
he would sleep on the couch in the living room. One day we
were driving down Sunset Boulevard and he asked me to
manage him. I almost crashed the car. And I said, "No."*

And he said, "Why not?"

*I had three reasons. One was that he was going to be a big
star and I'd been in the business a minute and a half. Two,
it was unethical because I was with GAC. And the third
was the real reason: I was scared.*

Not long after this conversation, my dad handed Steve a brand-new
acetate of the soon-to-be released album *That's All*. Steve loved it,
because in his words "now Bobby was into the kind of music that I
liked." Steve had heard that George Burns was going to play his first
engagement without Gracie Allen, who had retired. George Burns had
never before played in a nightclub. He'd done vaudeville, but not Las
Vegas. Burns's plan was to go to Lake Tahoe for two weeks, break in
the act, and then do four weeks at the Sahara Hotel.

Steve had heard that George Burns was looking for a boy singer to
take with him.

It's interesting that although Blauner was not working for my
father, he was working for him anyway. He just wasn't being paid for
it. Recently Hesh Wasser found this letter Steve wrote to her on
February 20, 1959.

Dear Harriet,

This may ramble, but I'll write as things come into my
head. Thanks for remembering me on Valentine's Day. It
was very sweet of you. Also thanks for the note about my
being a good friend of Bobby. I felt so inadequate as I
couldn't be with him throughout his time in New York.
I'd have blown my job if I had to, but this wasn't the main
factor. It was a simple thing as the buck. I am busted and
deep in debt. I just couldn't get all the money. You don't
have to thank me for anything, as it is impossible. The
thanks come from my friendship, which is so deep that I
won't even let him know—so I won't leave myself open to

being hurt as I have in the past by other people. All I can say is, and this may sound immature—if my giving up a finger would make him a bigger star, I would.

I am now going to tell you a few things that you must not tell anyone, especially Joe [Csida] or anyone in the office. In fact, you must not mention this to anyone whosoever, including Bobby, even though he knows about it. The following are things that are in the works. They may all fall through, but in each case there is sincere interest on the part of other people. When I finish you won't believe this could be happening, but they are all true.

1. A kinescope for his own half hour TV show.

2. His singing the title song for the movie "Blue Denim." Also an appearance in the picture.

3. A lead part in the movie that Columbia is doing called "The Gene Krupa Story."

4. A picture deal with Columbia similar to the one that Boone has at 20th.

5. Pictures and TV with Dick Clark.

6. Two deals in Vegas. One that the office is working on for Bob to go into the Dunes with Pinky Lee. The other that I'm working on and if it happens will be the biggest break we could get. His going into Vegas in June with George Burns. This is Burns' first trip, and it will be seen by every big person in Hollywood.

Once again I must tell you not to say one word to a soul, even your mother. I cannot tell you why in this letter, but I will explain when I see you next month.

As you can see from the above, I have spent almost all my time on Bobby. In fact, just today someone threw a line at me that if I spent more time on my job and less on Bobby, I would be better off. I told this person that if they didn't like the way I was conducting myself, they could fire me. I don't give a damn if they do, as I am sure that Bobby will become one of the biggest stars in the history of this business. And I am going to help even if I'm not working for GAC.

Love, Steve

And there's the clue to the big mystery. On his own, Steve Blauner got in to see George Burns as though he were managing Bobby. Steve knew George Burns was being represented by the giant talent agency MCA, and he knew that MCA had a million "boy singers" in their stables. For his meeting with Burns, Steve had brought with him the acetate of *That's All*, and he proceeded to play George Burns three songs from the album.

After seventy-five years in show business, George Burns needs no introduction from me. I'll only say that he's as funny and as sharp as always, and it's easy to see why my father would have done anything for this man. Today, in his offices in Los Angeles, Mr. Burns remembers that time in 1959 when he received his copy of "Splish Splash." And he remembers that he loved it. But he thought it was Bobby Darin who had sent it and had someone set up an appointment to meet him.

"I wanted to meet Bobby Darin," Mr. Burns recalls. "When Blauner came in, I thought he was Bobby Darin. I was terribly disappointed. I said to myself, Jesus. He's a big, fat kid. I don't want to take him to Vegas. Finally Blauner told me who he was, that he was his agent, and I took Bobby to Vegas. And he didn't come cheap for a kid who never did Vegas before."

Blauner got Bobby $1,000 a week for the two weeks in Tahoe and $1,500 for the four weeks in Vegas. He says he was triumphant, had beaten out a million-to-one odds in getting Bobby a spot with George Burns:

☞ *I walked into the office, went to the head of the nightclubs department, and said to him, "Well, I took care of Darin for the summer."*

And he said, "What the hell are you talking about? Bobby's going to England in a rock 'n' roll show."

And I said, "For Christ's sake, Bobby Darin can go to England for a rock 'n' roll show anytime."

Then he said, "You know, opening acts in Vegas get more money than you got for Darin with Burns."

I said, "If I were Bobby Darin's manager, I'd pay George Burns ten times that to take him, because for Bobby to survive, he has to make the transition from rock 'n' roll."

*The man said, "Will you stop interfering in the nightclub
department?"*

*I said, "Yes. I will never interfere in the nightclub depart-
ment again. Because I quit."*

*And I got up and left with no place to go. I still didn't
have the guts to manage Bobby. And I ended up taking a job
in the movie business for two hundred and fifty a week, more
than I'd ever made in my life. And I had nothing to do.*

It was said of my dad, by an anonymous source, that he not only
wanted his managers to get results, "he wanted them to leave a trail
of blood. He wanted the manager to smack the desk and leave the
booking agent bleeding on the floor." When my dad went to his
manager, Ed Burton, and told him he wanted to go to Vegas with
George Burns, Burton said it was impossible. He said that Bobby was
already committed to the rock 'n' roll tour. Bobby said flatly, "Get
me uncommitted." Ed Burton was a gentleman. He dealt with people
in a civilized way and hoped Bobby would do the same. Of course he
didn't realize that my dad thought he had seven years left to live and
being a gentleman was not a priority.

In May 1959 Bobby opened at Harrah's in Lake Tahoe for George
Burns, and then they went on to Las Vegas. It was during this engagement that the two developed a father/son relationship. "You know,
Mr. Burns," I said to him this year, "my dad always said if he could
have picked a father, he would have picked you."

Mr. Burns nodded his head solemnly. "And I would have picked
Bobby." There was a beat as he took a puff of his cigar. He added,
"Of course Bobby was too young to be my father."

I wish I could have seen them perform together. The closest I can
come to being with my dad on that momentous occasion is to listen
to the interview he did in July 1960 with Barry Gray. By then *That's
All* had been released, and "Mack the Knife" was Bobby's crowning
achievement. The disk jockeys didn't care that the song was on an LP,
they played the "Mack" cut and the country went crazy. Tune in to
Bobby Darin and Barry Gray now:

BG: I think Vegas is where the real breakthrough started.
BD: I had a choice. I could either go to England for

nineteen hundred a week or I could go to Las Vegas for a considerable amount less, and my choice was to go to Las Vegas. The people who were handling me, whom I love and get along with fine, thought I should go to England.

BG: Well, they were wrong. We both know guys that go to England and they line the streets waiting for them, but they can't get arrested in the United States.

BD: Exactly. And of course they were partially right. Because at the time, Mr. Burns said, "What's a Bobby Darin?" With respect, he was perfectly right. He's the most lovable, most beautiful man in the world. But he didn't know me. Steve Blauner, who was working in California for GAC at the time, piled it on thick. And Mr. Burns said, "I'd like to see the kid out here." And I flew out. I met him and I sang a couple of songs for him, and he went, "Kid's great. I want him."

And the next thing I knew, we had signed the contract and played two weeks in Tahoe and four weeks in Las Vegas, and the roof fell in. It was the beginning. He is to me the closest thing I've ever had to a father. He has a kind of warmth that just comes out at you. He's the most beautiful man in the world. And Mr. Burns, going into Vegas, was as nervous and as excited as I was going into the Copa last week. And he's been in the business, as he says, for a thousand years. It was the first time he'd ever been in a nightclub, and he regarded it as the most important thing in the world at that time. That's the way he treated it. So he was very careful to make sure that the show was well rounded. When the show opened, there was nervousness on everybody's part. Of course, Mr. Burns has sixty-four years of controlled nervousness. But he was nervous inside. After a few days when the routine settled down, my nervousness was gone. His was certainly gone. We would study each other. There was such a rapport on that stage, which we have even when we talk over dinner. That rapport is what created that excitement, Barry.

I have to be fair about it. I'm not going to say that I walked out and did twenty solid minutes because I didn't.

I walked out and did eight fair minutes. I did three or four songs, and not until the time I walked out to do a number with Mr. Burns did it all happen. At the end of the fourth song, Mr. Burns walked out and said, "Bobby, you were just wonderful," and I'd start to talk to him. At that time electricity happened.

Before that I was frightened. The Sahara is a very, very big club. It's like a barn. And I couldn't see faces except for two or three people immediately down front. As far as I knew, I was playing to a void. But as soon as Mr. Burns came on the stage and we started to talk, you could feel everybody mentally go, "Oh, isn't that nice. . . ." So, it wasn't me. They know Mr. Burns is great. They accept him, but here was something new for people to talk about pro or con. Now I'm sure that a lot of them walked out and said "Well, Darin's not as much as everybody says."

BG: Bobby, in all honesty, I have not talked to one person who has seen you perform who hasn't said the same thing: that it's one of the greatest performances. That it's like an old, old pro pushed into a twenty-four-year-old body. They don't know where the great experience and the show business savvy comes from, but they say onstage Bobby Darin works like a guy who's been in the Palace thirty times. That's a great compliment.

BD: Well, I make sure that I keep two feet planted firmly on the ladder to keep it in balance. As a person, as a learning performer. Somebody said today I've been on the stage like a guy who's been on thirty years, then five years from now I'd like them to say he's been on the stage as if he's been on it for forty years or for sixty years. I want to constantly improve. And that is my shortcoming, a major one.

BG: I don't think it's a major shortcoming. You talk to people who feel you have a great deal of assurance for one so young. I don't find this a sign of assurance at all. I find this as an indication of doing well, and wanting to do better.

BD: My assurance lasts from the time I walk on the floor to the time I walk out. I don't know of anybody who works as assuredly as I work. With those lights off and that music out, I'm a different person.

BG: Bobby, I'm certainly older than you and a little more experienced about people in the business. Everybody in this business is secure when they're working and insecure when they're not. This is par for the course. Why should you be any different from anybody else? I'm sure you're advised properly.

BD: Well, managerially I am. I have a twenty-six-year-old genius for a manager. And anything that's happened to me in the past year, Steve Blauner is definitely responsible for.

I love this interview with my dad. His sweetness is palpable, and it was probably the last time my dad spoke with such modesty. A year after this interview, he was interviewed by a reporter from the *Saturday Evening Post* who, in raising the issue of my father's well-known brashness, may have been suggesting that humility might be appropriate in one so young.

"Humility," said Bobby. "Humbleness? The biggest thing between you and God is death. The biggest success in the world walks around with the knowledge that he is going to die like everyone else. That's the only source of my humility—the only source. As for my talent, it has been given to me to use while I can. I will use it the way I think best, and I will never apologize for it."

But while my dad was working with George Burns, he was as close to humble as anyone would ever see him. He had a father, and this father didn't cater to him. This father appreciated him, loved him, but wasn't beyond giving him a good smack when he deserved it.

I'll let Mr. Burns tell it in his own way:

Bobby was a tremendous talent. He sang, he danced, he played the guitar, the drums, the piano, and I think he played some brass instruments. He was twenty-two years old when we first worked together, and they were nuts about Bobby. And the girls were nuts about Elvis Presley, too. Elvis and Bobby met in Vegas and were friends. They were standing together, and the people were knocking down the doors. The girls were screaming, "Elvis!" "Bobby!" Those who couldn't get Presley wanted Darin. So, just to be funny, I went over to where they were standing and said, "Kids, just in case you run short on broads, let me know and I'll fix you up."

And Presley said, "Thank you, Mr. Burns."

He thought I was on the level. Here I was thinking it was a very funny line, and he said, "Thank you, Mr. Burns." I couldn't fix myself up with my sister.

In between shows is about two and a half hours, and the wonderful thing about Bobby is that he'd stay backstage during that time and work. He'd play the piano, the guitar, the drums. He wrote the words, the music, the whole job. He was not a dancer, but he looked as though he could dance as good as Sammy Davis. He couldn't make a wrong move when the music played. He had that quality.

When we were in Vegas, Bobby was getting $1,500 a week. And Bobby won $1,500 on the tables. I liked Bobby. I was like a father to him, so I went over to him, and I said, "You won $1,500. Give $1,300 to me to hold and you'll have $200 to gamble with." I said, "That's cash. That's good money."

Bobby always called me "Mr. Burns" even until he passed away. He said, "Mr. Burns, I got a system. I know how to win."

I said, "Bobby, nobody knows how to win when you're shooting craps." So, he didn't give me the $1,300.

The next day, he comes to my dressing room and tells me he's lost the fifteen hundred. So I slapped him across the face. And at the beginning of the show, he used to come out and we'd talk together for a minute or two, and then Bobby would do his stuff. This night I was so mad at him, I wouldn't talk to him when I introduced him. I just made an introduction at the next show, and I walked off the stage.

And Bobby ran after me and said, "If you don't talk to me, I won't be able to work." Because he did like me. Loved me, really.

So I told the audience the story. I said. "Look, this little punk won and lost fifteen hundred dollars gambling, and I think that's too much at his age and I'm very mad at him. And I'm leaving it up to you. Should I talk to him?"

And the audience said, "Sure. Talk to him." So I did, and we made up on the stage.

Bobby played with me twice. The first time was the four weeks at the Sahara. Then "Mack the Knife" came out, and it got to be a terribly big hit. He just went through the roof, and then he played the Sands Hotel by himself. He was headlining, and he was twenty-three years old. He was there for three or four weeks, and he didn't do well. Bobby would get very temperamental when people talked in the audience, and sometimes I would tell him, "Bobby, don't get mad at people who talk in the audience. In the first place, they all paid to see you, and anyway, they may be saying to one another, 'Jesus, isn't he marvelous. I love that kid. I wouldn't miss him.' "

I had dinner with Bobby, and I said, "Bobby, how did you do at the Sands?"

He said, "I'm heartbroken. I didn't do very well."

I said, "What do they pay you at the Sands?"

He said, "Seven thousand."

I said, "I'm going into the Sahara in two weeks. I'll pay you seventy-five hundred if you come in with me." So I gave him a five-hundred-dollar raise for being a flop. He went in it with me, and he was a riot. And of course from then on, he was a smash.

The legendary singer and performing artist Peggy Lee met Bobby while he was with George Burns. When I met with her in her home in Bel Air, I was impressed by her sweetness and her gentility. She wasn't feeling very well that day, but nevertheless she was eager to share her memories of my father.

Miss Lee says that when she met Bobby, "it was like instant love."

☞ *And he felt that way, too. Had I been younger, who knows what would have happened. It was as though we'd known each other forever. And he used to ask me about things that were troubling him. I remember once there was a Shriners convention, and these conventions used to get pretty rowdy. Bobby asked me between acts, "Shall I walk off?"*

And I said, "No, Bobby, never walk off. Stay there and brave it out, and don't let them know they are even bothering you." And that's what he did. Thank God, because people misunderstood that part of Bobby. He had a feeling about the dignity of his profession, and he knew the depth of his talent and that it was going to develop and develop.

I remember when he was headlining at the Sands, there was one thing that they did with the lighting. A spot came down from the top, a red shaft of light, and Bobby did "Mack the Knife." And he was totally captivating.

Between those engagements at the Sahara and the Sands, Steve Blauner's wheels were turning. He was working for a division of Columbia Pictures run by director Sam Katzman, who was making down-and-dirty B movies faster than anyone. But as Blauner says, "B movies were going out of style." Every afternoon Sam would stop by the office, pick Steve up, and take him to the track. Steve knew that even though he was making money, this job had gone on long enough. It was no way for him to get ahead in life. He called my dad and said:

☞ *"If you want me to manage you, okay, but it's got to be now. I can't stay here any longer." Now here's the guts of Bobby Darin. This was a man who by no means had any money. The year before, he'd made forty grand. His managers were big-time music publishers, and he had four years left on his contract. Bobby went to them and said very amicably that he wanted out of his contract and asked what would it cost him. And they said a hundred thousand dollars, which was a lot of money in 1959—but even still they shortchanged themselves.*

Bobby made a deal with Csida and Burton that he would pay them the one hundred thousand dollars the following way. Anything he wrote as a songwriter, that he would record, he would give them the publishing rights until they made their hundred thousand. Once they hit that figure, he would no longer be bound to that publishing deal, but they would still own the copyrights to the songs they had already published. And those might be worth millions.

He made this deal so that I could manage him, when I'd been in the business a minute and a half. And then—I have no idea where I got the balls to do this—I looked him in the face and said, "Look, you sing and dance. That's yours. I'll be all over you suggesting, recommending, pestering, but in the final analysis that's yours. Now, I need my own thing. I don't want to ever have to come to you and ask your permission for anything. I want to have total power to manage your career."

Today, I can't even assimilate this. How could I, who had said "no" because I don't know how to manage him, weeks or months later say, "Give me your life"? And Bobby said, "Okay." And we had a handshake deal. We never had a piece of paper. I was getting fifteen percent, and I insisted on power of attorney, which he gave me. I signed all his contracts, and I carried the checkbook with me. I took over this man's life, which he gave me. And Bobby was the last person in the world you would think would let anyone else run his life.

But as my dad said, he was a genius for recognizing Blauner's genius. Blauner ate and slept Bobby Darin. He had no women, no other life. He suggested strongly to Ahmet Ertegun that he break "Mack the Knife" out of the album and issue it as a single. Bobby thought Blauner was crazy. So did Ahmet, but Blauner convinced them both, and the single was produced.

Dick Clark told Bobby it was going to be a turkey. "I said to

Bobby, 'I don't know what you think you're doing, but you're trying to be something you aren't, and you're probably going to die with this thing. What kid is going to buy something from the *Threepenny Opera?*' I knew him well enough so that I could jump on him and I did. It gave me great pleasure, years later to say, 'I wasn't as smart as I thought I was.' Obviously, it was his biggest-selling record ever."

"Mack," the single, went to number one in October of that year and stayed there for nine weeks. It hung in in the top ten for an entire fifty-two weeks and was gold record number four for Bobby Darin. It eventually sold over two million singles. While "Mack" was soaring, Blauner was also working the movie part of Bobby's dream. He found a script he thought would be right for my dad. The film was to be called *Cry for Happy*. It was to star Glenn Ford, and Blauner saw that Bobby could realize a film presence in this picture.

But my dad had already commited to George Burns for a return date at the Sahara for $7,500 a week. Blauner went to Mr. Burns and told him he had an opportunity he'd like Bobby to take. In fact, the contract with Burns had an "out" clause for instances like this, and there was plenty of time for Mr. Burns to replace Bobby in his act. So Blauner asked Burns if they could back out on the Las Vegas commitment, and Mr. Burns said no unequivocally.

Mr. Burns called Bobby and told him that he would get nowhere by breaking promises to people. He said, "If I were still paying you peanuts and you had a chance to better yourself, I wouldn't think twice about it. But I have a responsibility toward the club, and for the kind of money you're getting, you have a responsibility toward me." Without knowing the scope of the opportunity, or the amount of money involved, Mr. Burns scolded my dad but good. Hardly blinking, Bobby said no to the film and yes to Mr. Burns. "I love the man," my father said simply. Blauner was incensed. The next time he saw George Burns, he refused to shake his hand.

Along with making pictures, my dad had long wanted to play the Copacabana, which was unquestionably the most prestigious nightclub in the country. The Copa came through with an offer for Bobby to do an engagement that coming January of 1960. This time it was Blauner who said no. He wanted Bobby to do the Copa only when huge success would be assured. He didn't think the time was right, so the Copa date was postponed. Instead my dad went on a nightclub tour far different from the earlier tours of unknown bars in his days with George Scheck. This time my father was hot. He called his old friend Dick Behrke, who remembers the incident:

☞ *I was working little jazz trios around town, and in late 1959 Bobby said, "Come out to the Coast with me. He was starting to work clubs, and we had always talked about how I was going to conduct the band. Finally he was in a position to take someone—not pay them, just take someone. So from then and through the first half of 1960, Bobby would just take care of me. Pay my food and rent. I stayed with him at Steve Blauner's house in the hills above Sunset Boulevard. Then we started to go out on the road very heavily. The first job was Blunstrum's in Boston, then the Chez Paree in Chicago. We went all the way back east, then started to work our way across the country. We did some clubs in the middle, then we opened at the Cloisters in L.A., which was just shy of the Copa in prestige and renown.*

The Cloisters was major excitement. I hadn't started writing arrangements. I was still playing the piano and conducting at the smaller clubs. But now we were at a big, important club. Dick Wess came out and wrote the arrangements and conducted the first week at the Cloisters, then he left and I took over the second week. I was petrified, but somehow we managed. That was very, very exciting. It was big time.

Everything was terrific. We got great reviews, and it was a terrific show. Bobby Darin was the new man in town, no doubt about it. Then the next big opening was the Copa.

During this tour, Blauner, working his own particular blend of ferocity and love, arranged TV appearances for the man he thought of as his brother; Bobby guested with Jimmy Durante, Ed Sullivan, Perry Como, George Burns, and Dick Clark and appeared on two NBC spectaculars. Then Blauner cut an unprecedented deal for Bobby: Paramount signed him to a seven-year, multimillion-dollar nonexclusive contract—the biggest ever for someone who'd never been in a movie before.

To cap off 1959, my dad won two coveted prizes: a Grammy for Best Record for "Mack the Knife" and one as Best New Artist for Bobby Darin. He was twenty-three, and he thought he was two years behind himself. Perhaps he was comparing himself, as he often did, to Frank Sinatra. Upon receiving his Grammys, he said something to UPI reporter Vernon Scott that would haunt him for the rest of his career. Apparently, Scott asked Bobby how he thought he stacked up to Frank Sinatra, and according to Scott, my dad said, "I hope to pass Frank in everything he does."

My dad claimed later that he told Scott he didn't want to be compared with anyone, he just wanted to be the best Bobby Darin he could be, but regardless, the quote stuck to him and caused some animosity between him and Frank Sinatra, whom he did truly revere.

Not that the publicity hurt. John Miller, the reporter and friend from early Hansen's days, recalled that Bobby heard that Frank Sinatra made up stories about himself that would make him seem exciting. So Bobby exhorted his friend to make up stories about *him*. "Good for the image," my dad would say. "You've got to make *me* exciting. Why don't you do a story where I punch the waiter who brought me a hamburger that wasn't cooked right." And John Miller would run the story.

In the background, foreground, and midground, Steve Blauner was proving himself the personal manager of the decade. He says now and said then that Bobby was unstoppable and would have made it without him. He says he knew that he was riding a comet, and he was loving it. Steve said he lived through Bobby, that if Bobby got a standing ovation—which was uncommon in those days—he'd be in the back of the room with tears in his eyes. He used to walk down Fifth Avenue with Bobby's album in clear view under his arm. He'd walk into records stores in whatever city they were in, and when no one was looking, he'd move Bobby's records up to the front of the rack. He sent albums to singers, promoters, and TV and radio personalities. Sometimes he'd bring records to important people's houses, put Bobby's record on, and say, "You're going to die when you hear this." Inevitably he got the reaction he was looking for. Blauner says managing Bobby was an incredible experience and one that he took very seriously.

One day when Blauner was bemoaning his own looks, my dad said,

"When I wake up in the morning, you know what I see in the mirror? I see an ugly, short, balding, double-chinned Italian with a big nose and puffy eyes. But when I go out the door, I put my game face on. I look like Rock Hudson." To tell the truth, he's said this same thing to me, and I never liked to hear him say it. I *do* look like him. But whatever he looked like in the morning, he looked sexy as hell on the stage. And it translated offstage as well. Women were all over him.

Reporter and musicologist Gene Lees told his readers in *Down Beat* that my dad had to "literally sweep the girls off the doorstep. They write mash notes, some of which are pretty torrid. They haunt the corridors of hotels where he's staying. They knock timidly at his door, sounding a little like mice in the woodwork. If he answers, they have fits of titters and then, after recovering from the traumatic joy of his speaking to them, thrust autograph books at him."

Charlie Maffia was working for my dad by then. He was acting as a cross between road manager and valet, and this drove Blauner crazy. He said that Charlie didn't know how to do the job, but at the same time he understood that Charlie had carried my dad in his arms when he was young and that this was Bobby's payback. Charlie and my dad also had had that first-time sex experience between them, and these little "scenes" didn't stop when my dad was sixteen. Now that the kid was in demand, Charlie was quite happy to sample Bobby's leftovers—although my dad seemed to really like someone, in this case Charlie, to open his act for him, so to speak. Charlie tells how many times, when he'd have a woman in his bed, Bobby would be in the next room listening. When he deemed the time was right, Bobby would strip down and enter Charlie's room, naked. He'd say, "Honey, how about this?" Then he'd join in.

Sometimes the female attention got to be so much, Blauner would unclench a female hand from Bobby's arm and, without saying a word, peel her off and shove her back into the crowd. Blauner says that my dad's sex life "was more active than anyone knew. Everything he did, he did in a hurry, because he didn't think he had long to live."

Which is the story behind the story of Bobby Darin as reported by Shana Alexander in *Life* magazine. The headline read I WANT TO BE A LEGEND BY 25. These eight words joined the remark my father may have made about outdoing Frank Sinatra. Both satisfied the public need to understand Bobby Darin. But although the article was a glowing tribute to this young performer, one point got lost. Bobby needed to become a legend by twenty-five because he expected to be dead by thirty.

I WANT TO BE A LEGEND BY 25

In his dressing room before a performance, Bobby Darin is nothing special to look at. He is a slight, sleepy-eyed, rather worn young man of 23 whose face suggests a putty mask of Perry Como. As he gets into his ruffle-front shirt and inserts the diamond-and-sapphire cufflinks, he says, "I want to make it faster than anyone has ever made it before. I'd like to be the biggest thing in show business by the time I'm 25 years old." In the dressing room this seems like a forlorn hope.

A moment later Bobby steps onstage, and suddenly it becomes clear why he has been one of the fastest-rising singers in recent years and has earned the right to dream big. . . .

And now the dreams were all coming true. Walter Winchell, who had seen Bobby at the Cloisters, had become a fan. "He has a zing to him," Winchell said, "both on the stage and off." Today it's hard to imagine the power of Walter Winchell, Louella Parsons, and Hedda Hopper, but these columnists had tremendous influence with the public. Winchell trumpeted Bobby in his columns and followed him on tour.

Gene Lees best described my dad's performing style:

Darin is probably the most fascinating singer to watch on this side of the Atlantic. When he breaks in a new tune, he talks about working out the "choreography" for it. And he does indeed move like a dancer. He has a loose-limbed agility that permits him to intermix shuffles, kicks, and countless eccentric steps the semantics of which probably died with vaudeville. With his combination of excellent movement and intense driving singing, Darin's one of the most stimulating and vital acts in show business today.

And now the day my dad had dreamed about for years was upon him. Blauner had turned down that first Copa date, but, suddenly, it was June. Dick Behrke tells me it's impossible to imagine what the Copa was like at that time except to say it was "the epitome, the premier club. It was big-time, and big-time Mafia. Julie [Jules] Podell was running the place. It was like a Sinatra movie. It was vastly exciting."

The Copa date went off as Blauner had hoped. My dad's dressing room was flooded with telegrams from friends and well-wishers: George Scheck, Eddie Fisher and Elizabeth Taylor, Paul Anka, Keeley Smith and Louis Prima, and Tony Bennett all sent their love and best wishes. "Come on swingin' and go out the same way. What you do in between is your business. Have a good night," wired Pat Boone. "Knock 'em dead. Best wishes on this very big night for you," from Bobby Rydell. And this from my dad's beloved George and Gracie: "Just go out there and do it. You are too young to be nervous."

And then the fun began. Blauner says, "Bobby went into the Copa at prom time, and it was the most incredible engagement ever. There was a night when they couldn't get all the prom kids in for the late show and I said, 'That's okay. Keep putting them in.' And it ended up with Bobby doing the last show on a Saturday night at two or four in the morning, sitting on the piano because there was no place for him to work."

Blauner and Bobby were a wonderful team. But with all stars a kind of competition develops in the circle that surrounds them. Old friends versus new. Everyone hoping to be the favorite one. Dick Lord remembers being inspired by Bobby. They were friends. He figured Bobby had made it and so could he. He wanted Bobby to give him a chance doing comedy on the same bill. Lord says, "Bobby used to tell me, 'You're going to be a star. You're a great actor.' Yet every time jobs came up, he would give them to Black comedians. 'I don't use White comedians,' he'd say. The man was living in my house. I was driving him everywhere."

I'm sure Dick Lord understood even if he didn't want to that my dad was trying to spare his feelings. He didn't think Dick Lord was a good enough comedian, at least not yet. Dick Lord observes that Behrke was a very intelligent and perceptive man. "He was also a guy who doesn't really like people and so whomever Bobby liked, Behrke didn't like, automatically." Add Blauner to the mix and you can imagine the hostile possibilities. Blauner was not a subtle person, and the only person he cared about was Bobby. Lord recalls a time when he and Bobby and Blauner and Behrke were all in the same car together, and Behrke and Blauner got into a fight. Behrke told Blauner if he didn't like it, he could get out of the car, which Blauner did. Blauner was amazed as he stood in his shoes on 186th Street and Behrke took off.

Blauner didn't hesitate to say that he thought Lord and Behrke were hangers-on, not friends, and if they were friends, then perhaps Bobby should get a better conductor than Behrke. Behrke says, "Blauner and I get along fine currently, but we have a long history of combat. Back then he would always say to me, 'Bobby can do better than you.' And I would say, 'He can do better than any of us.' Blauner always failed to mention that anyone else would charge money to be there. If you want someone to work for a year without being paid, you need an old friend."

From this picture it seems that none of these friends liked each other so much anymore, but they kept their arms loosely linked together around Bobby. There was uneasy comfort in this fraternity—and they were drawn to the flame. My dad was becoming rougher on people. And ruder. He pushed past fans clustered outside the Copa's doors. He didn't do encores, and he didn't entertain in his dressing room. And he took a lot out on Charlie. I wonder if he realized how much it hurt Charlie every time he said that if he could have picked a father, he would have picked George Burns.

My dad was very generous with some people and tight with others. For as long as Dick Behrke remembers, whenever he was asked when his birthday was, he said, "June twenty-fourth, a car." Bobby bought the Behrkes a new car and got the Lords a new car, too. Solid-gold lighters and watches went to managers and stars. Gold plate and souvenirs went to his family. Hesh Wasser had to pay Blauner for a gold charm of snapping fingers that he'd had made up as promotional gifts. Bobby gave Charlie a secondhand Caddy, which he prized. Then Bobby totaled the car, collected the insurance, and Charlie had nothing.

"Something happens that's unique to stars," says Steve Blauner.

125

☞ *That's why that flame was so bright and we are the moths that are attracted to it. Even though we get burned, we keep coming back for more. Bobby had the side that all people have but especially with performers who are asked to strip themselves naked in front of the world. As a manager, as a producer, as a businessman in any walk of life, we can hide behind other people. If we're not feeling well, we leave early or we don't go to the office. But in show business, for some dumb reason, the show must go on.*

When you get to the point of being the star and you are catered to from the minute you wake up in the morning to the minute you go to sleep at night, you have staff all around you and they're sucking up to you. Then you get into the car and people are crashing because they see you. They're waving and screaming "Can I have your autograph?" and everyone's fawning over you. And you forget that you go to the bathroom like everyone else, and you start to believe a lot of the publicity that someone creates for you.

And it's difficult to face or to remember what reality is. So Bobby had that side of him that would drive anyone up a wall. And a lot of that stems from fear. Probably all of it. Because if you're a performer, you have to go out. Show time. And you've got to get the people to love you.

Hesh Wasser had been doing Bobby and Steve's correspondence for a couple years, but as a practical matter it was necessary for Bobby to hire megapublicity outfit Rogers & Cowan. As Hesh made the switch, she found a new mission in life with Bob Crewe of Frankie Valli and the Four Seasons. She had no bitterness at leaving Bobby's employ, and I say this because Hesh feels emphatically that Steve Blauner, who arrived late on the scene, was responsible for driving a wedge between Bobby and his family. She says that Blauner didn't give a damn about Bobby's relations and encouraged Bobby to walk away from his past. I think she may have a point about Steve, but my dad was a strong-willed person. And I think Hesh is letting him off the hook. It's been well established that Bobby Cassotto wanted to get out of the ghetto. By the end of 1960 Bobby Darin had earned a quarter of a million dollars. He was good and out of the ghetto, but he had this family. They were uncultured, heavyset, and badly dressed, and they had voices that smacked of the Bronx.

Blauner says, "Opening night he'd have a table, and sometimes he'd put the table on the second level so Nina wasn't at ringside. Nina was big and fat and her daughters were heavy, and he was just embarrassed by the way they looked. Bobby was embarrassed by what he came from."

My dad's dark side wasn't lost on his sister, Vee. She remembers that Bobby liked to exercise control over the family, and he liked to do it with money.

Bobby always treated the family like shit. His attitude was always, "Oh, they're just family. I could do anything and they will always stand behind me." And that was the truth. If he'd been convicted of something, we would have shipped him off to South America where the law couldn't touch him. He was open and honest about his relationship with his family, and that gave him a lot of confidence to screw us royally with a smile on his face.

I remember in 1958 my mother and father finally had enough money to put a down payment on a little house in Lake Hiawatha, New Jersey. Then "Splish Splash" came out, and Bobby said, "Oh, we'll fix this up." My mother went a little crazy doing a lot of work on the house. Then Bobby says, "You need a bigger house. This is too small for you. Let's look for another house."

My mother found a house she liked for twenty-one thousand dollars, and Bobby said, "Okay, I'll buy it." But Bobby didn't buy it—he leased it. He put a few thousand dollars down and paid the rent for a few months. The rent was about a hundred and fifty a month. So my parents moved out of the Lake Hiawatha house into the new house.

Time passes. Now, because of tax reasons, because the sky is up, and the sky is blue, Bobby said to my mother, "I want the Lake Hiawatha house." So they turned the house over in his name, and I said, "Don't do it." My grandmother, before she died, said, "Don't do it." And Bobby's made it big by now, but my mother didn't listen. They put the house in Bobby's name. Two years later he sold it. He called up, said, "I finally made a profit." He made four thousand dollars on the little house, and he hadn't spent that much on the new house.

My parents were both working for him by that time. My dad was his driver and valet. My mother was doing all of his fan mail. He was paying them each one hundred and fifty dollars a week. I said to my mother, "Well, now you did it. Because when he fucks you, you're going to have no place to go." And he did. Within the year he fired my father, fired my mother, and stopped the house payments.

So Bobby and I got into a knock-down, drag-out fight in the kitchen about twelve o'clock at night. I went to his house, and we got into it. And Bobby said—and this is a quote: "I spent more money on your family in the last five years than your entire family has spent on me in my entire life."

And I stood up at the table, took both sides, and shook the table violently because I was trying to keep from hitting. And I said to him, "You motherfucker. My family gave you the very best they ever had. In all their life they gave you the very best they ever had. You never gave us the crumbs from your table. You're nothing but a cocksucker."

And I walked out. We had very much that kind of relationship.

I admit that when Vee told me this, I was holding the table myself to stop from hitting. I was defensive. This was my dad she was talking about! Two days later I realized that she was one of the few people who would deal with my father as a person, and whether he knew it or not, he was lucky to have her. She sounds angry when she talks about Bobby, and she is. But what she really is, is hurt. As she talks, she alternates between clenching her hands into fists and wiping the tears from her cheeks. She's fifty years old, and my dad's been dead since 1973. He still gets to her because she loved him, fiercely.

As for this story Vee tells, I could easily say to the Maffia family,

"If there had been no Bobby, what would your lives have been like? Do you think you would have been better off?" But that's not the point. Whether Bobby should have bought houses or leased them, should have hired Charlie and Nina or simply helped them out financially, the issue is this: The family that raised Bobby felt that their boy didn't respect them. And he didn't.

As for me, I realized that without checking it out, I had picked up my father's agenda and added it to my own. I was twelve when my dad died. Between then and now I had one occasion to meet with Nina before she passed away, and it wasn't pleasant. I rarely heard from Vee or from Charlie. Was it my place to call them? After twenty years of silence between me and my aunt Vee and me and Charlie Maffia, we made contact. For their part, they thought I'd been brainwashed, turned against them—that my mother didn't want me to know them. And that wasn't true. Now, because of this book, we touched. The warm feelings about being family obliterated the grudges and the pain. It felt good. I've made plans with Charlie to visit me in California. My mom spent two hours on the phone with Vee. I know that the big obstacles have been moved and that we will continue to talk from now on.

But now I want to return to the end of 1960. Bobby Darin was twenty-four years old. In two and a half years he'd gone from grubbing for jingle work to creating some of the biggest hits of the decade. People would lean out of cabs and yell, "Hi, Bobby!" He was that well known. He was practical in his relationships. If you didn't have a function, get out of his way. He had his good old friends tied up in knots, and he had new friends: a sweetheart in Peggy Lee, a dad in George Burns. He had a manager who would leave a trail of blood in Steve Blauner. Dick Behrke, Dick Lord, Dick Clark, and Don Kirshner were solid. Charlie, the man who put food on his plate as a child, was laying out his clothes and carrying his bags. Sammy Davis Jr. was his pal—even though Sammy said, "Let me know when you stop being a legend so we can be friends again." Frank Sinatra was on warning, and Jerry Lewis was quoted in *Life* as saying, "Do you realize you're alone in your generation? Sammy, Dean, and I are all ten years ahead of you. Unless you destroy yourself, no one else can touch you. If you louse it up, it's only going to be your fault. Because you have the talent, kid. You're alone. You're alone!"

My dad was quoted in an article in *Family Weekly* magazine. The date is October 1960, and he begins by quoting Polly as having told him that he is the most important person in the world, but that at the same time he is but a grain of sand on the beach and that everyone is as important as he is. My father concludes the article by saying:

> I saw a friend of mine in a nightclub in Las Vegas after his show. He was wasting his time sitting with a small army of people. He didn't know half of them, and they were only there because he was famous, and not Joe Blow from Hokokus.
>
> I walked over to him and said, "Whatdya need all these characters for?" He looked at me, surprised and hurt. I suddenly had the feeling that I had asked a painful question—and there was no reason for my doing it. That's the way he is. That's the way I am.
>
> I'm not like him or Sinatra or Como. I'm just Bobby Darin, but I can be friends with all of them.
>
> Sure, I've got my faults. I'm the egomaniac you read about. I'm an honest guy, but I can sometimes be cruel. I try to be completely objective about myself. But in the meantime, I'm a guy with some very definite ideas about just how my life should be lived. I think that I come first, but when I say "Jump," the fewer people that jump, the better I like it. I know I'm the most important person in the world. It would be a better world if you felt the same way about you.

So sayeth my dad. The days of wanting were over. The days of having were his. But there was a void. I find that "something missing" and a bit of prophesy in "Beyond the Sea," a song my dad made into a hit that year.

> *Somewhere, beyond the sea,*
> *Somewhere waiting for me,*
> *My lover stands on golden sands,*
> *And watches the ships that go sailing.*

DREAM LOVERS

Somewhere, beyond the sea
She's there watching for me.
If I could fly like birds on high,
Then straight to her arms,
I'd go sailing.

And so it happened that Bobby was cast in a motion picture to be shot in Italy. He would write the title song for the film *Come September* and would be featured opposite a young movie star. She was sweet sixteen, beautiful, and one of the top ten box office actors in America. And she'd never loved a man.

Her name was Sandra Dee.

6

Bobby and Sandy, 1960

Bachelor Darin's matrimonial eye is searching for a petite, blue-eyed blonde, but until the right one comes along, the 24-year old entertainer likes girls of all sizes and shapes.

—*The* Los Angeles Examiner, *September 1960*

———

The last man I'm going to marry is a man in show business. They're selfish, unreliable, and make lousy husbands. The Hollywood type of marriage is not for me. I want all my children to have the same father. I'm going to take a good long look before I get married. I'm not going to jump into it. Certainly not to a show-biz character.

—SANDRA DEE
Parade *magazine, June 1960*

———

We had been shooting for about a week when Bobby arrived. I was to do his makeup. He said, "You're with Sandra Dee, aren't you? What's she like?"

133

I said, "She's a wonderful girl. Why do you ask?"
He said, "I think I might marry her."
I laughed and thought, This guy's a little crazy.

—JACK FREEMAN
Sandra's makeup man and friend

No matter how much my father complained that he hadn't yet achieved what he ought to have achieved, he had to be excited boarding the plane to Italy that August day in 1960. Neither Steve Blauner nor Charlie Maffia, who were with him, remember what Bobby was feeling, but let's look at the facts. He had four gold records to his credit, he'd broken attendance records at the two most prestigious nightclubs in the country, he'd won two Grammys, and now the thing he'd wanted his whole life long was about to come true. He was going to do a movie. True, he'd done a cameo role as himself in a movie called *Pepe* a few months before, but this time he had a real part. His name would be in big letters in the opening credits, and he was going to play opposite a star. The movie *Come September* was perfect for him, a light comedy, and he'd written the title song. Come on, Dad, admit it. You were overjoyed.

Same time, same station, my mom was at the very height of her movie star life. She had seven films under her belt, and with *Come September* she was getting equal billing with two other stars of the brightest magnitude: Rock Hudson and Gina Lollobrigida. The studio publicist told Ross Hunter that all the requests from the media were for stories about Sandy. Sandy on location. Sandy playing opposite a new man—no longer John Saxon and Troy Donahue, but someone from a different world, and they wanted to know about it.

The film was being shot both in a huge studio in Rome and in the seaside town of Portofino. During the location segment, which was shot first, the cast and crew were staying in a large old resort hotel called the Excelsior in the neighboring town of Santa Margharita. My dad's part was not as big as my mom's, so filming was in progress when he arrived. It's probable that my mom had never heard of Bobby Darin, but it's impossible to think that Bobby had never heard of Sandra Dee. Everyone had heard of Sandra Dee. Even in little Santa

Margharita, the paparazzi were everywhere. And they were dazzled by Sandy and her pale yellow hair.

Fall was off season in Italy, and the hotel was hardly booked. Steve Blauner remembers the first time he saw my mother:

☞ *The guests of the hotel were all working on the movie, so there was no one to put on any airs for. I was walking down the hall and out came Sandra Dee, wearing a nice dress. I think now she was possibly overdressed for this resort in the middle of the day. She started to go down the hallway, and I heard a lady's voice yell, "Come back here! Put your belt on!"*
Sandy said, "Mom, I'm just going down to mail a letter."
"I don't care! Put the belt on for that dress."
That was my introduction to Sandra Dee.

My mom remembers the first time she saw my father. He was standing on the shore wearing a yellow suit, and she was in a boat just pulling in to dock. "Will you marry me?" he called out to her.

"Not today," she said.

So he asked her again, every day, until she finally said yes. It certainly sounds as though my dad knew he wanted my mother before he met her. She did fit his specifications. She was petite, blond, untouched, and a movie star, for God's sake! She was perfect. But it wasn't going to be as easy for my dad to score as it usually was, for a few reasons. One was the presence of the mother of all mothers, Her Chaperoneship Mary Douvan. The second was Sandy, who didn't go out on dates. And the third was my father himself. He was obnoxious, a jokey song-and-dance man from the wrong side of the tracks, an older man of twenty-four. Far from Sandy's ideal.

My mom says, "I know this. Bobby loved me. He was a calculating guy, but I don't think he arrived in Rome with a plan to *marry* this new little Mary Pickford of Hollywood. His reputation certainly wasn't spotless, and mine was. We weren't anyone's idea of a match. Aside from the fact that he was rude, brash, always trying to get a reaction, I didn't like this person. I just thought, This is a conniving SOB. I didn't want to have anything to do with him."

Conniving is right. Bobby did everything he could think of to get

135

to Sandy. He started by working on Mary, flattering her and sending her flowers every day. He spent so much time with Mary, people assumed they were an item. It wasn't such an outrageous notion. Bobby was fast, and Mary, in Ross Hunter's words, was a "hot number." And by the way, she was only thirty-three years old. By the time the production moved to Rome, Bobby was Mary's good friend. He'd work with Sandy during the day, and in the evening he'd come over to the Douvan suite in the Grand Hotel and spend his time.

My mom says that Bobby and Charlie Maffia and Kay Reid would sit in the living room at night, playing cards, and Bobby would talk nonstop for hours. Sandy knew he wanted her attention. She would be reading a book and Bobby would start to talk, and she would say, "Excuse me. Can I go?" And she would go to her room, leaving Bobby to talk to my grandmother all night. She says that she could hear him through the door, pontificating endlessly about God knew what.

On location Bobby didn't quite get movie protocol, and this irritated the hell out of my mom. If Bobby didn't think he was needed until a certain time, he didn't show up until then, or he'd show up late. He was used to having the party start when he got there. Problem was, waiting around the set all day for your few moments under the lights is part of the deal, and if the actor's not around when the director is ready for him, it's big bucks out the window. As if his lackadaisical attitude about time weren't bad enough, my dad was prone to stupid kid tricks. Once, as a prank, he doused Sandy with a bucket of water and ruined the entire scene. He probably didn't realize how much time and money it cost to dry the star off, dress her again, relight, etc. He'd wanted a reaction from the golden girl, and she wouldn't give him the satisfaction of a response. Bobby, genuinely perplexed, would say to Mary, "What's with her?"

In the end it was Mary who forced Sandy to go out with Bobby. I guess all the flowers Bobby sent did their work because Mary had become his spokeswoman. She told Sandy that her behavior toward Bobby was embarrassing, and she ought to be nice since she and Bobby were working on the picture together. Still, my mom says she wanted nothing to do with crass and nasty Bobby Darin.

Jack Freeman remembers the moment it all changed:

When we first went to Rome, it was almost impossible to get Sandra to go out and see this wonderful city. Go to the great restaurants and see the many sights. She would have dinner in her room, and we would go by and say, "Won't you come with us?" And she'd say, "No, no."

Sandy was very friendly with all the younger actors on the set, but she was very standoffish with Bobby. She thought he was maybe a little conceited, a little too grown up, a little too sophisticated, so she was always rather cool to him. And when he'd ask her to go out, she'd say, "No, I don't think so."

So Bobby began asking Mary out, and Mary found him charming. She'd say to Sandy, "You should go out with him." I remember it was a Sunday afternoon. Kay Reid was with Sandy, and she had just finished Sandy's hair. I dropped by just to say hello, and Bobby came by to see Mary, ostensibly. And he looked at Sandy and said, "Why don't we go for a carriage ride?" In those days it was the thing to do. And it was just wonderful to rent a horse and carriage and go driving through the streets, especially on a Sunday.

And for some reason, this time Sandy said, "All right," and they went. I saw her the next day, and she said, "Jack, he is amazing. He's so smart. He's brilliant!" She was absolutely entranced. And from then on it was love.

Then Mary came to me. She said, "Oh, Jack, this can't be serious."

I said, "Mary, they're just having fun."

She said, "But no. I think it's really serious."

I didn't agree, but of course, I was wrong. As soon as the picture was over, they got married.

Sandy remembers that something different happened when she went on this first date with Bobby. He had always acted so moronically young, had talked *at* her instead of *to* her. But on this occasion, as the horse and carriage rattled through the streets of Rome, Bobby told her he acted as he did because he was scared. He was out of his element.

He wasn't the main attraction. He was falling in love with her and was at a loss to get her to pay attention to him.

Bobby's honesty touched my mom. This time he wasn't loud, he wasn't flashy, and Sandy saw the real Bobby under the act he'd always put on for her. They didn't kiss on this date. There was no off-screen kissing between these two until they were engaged. My mom has told me that she wouldn't kiss Bobby because she was afraid that there was something wrong with her. Her stage kisses were fakes—colored as they were by her experiences with Eugene —and she feared that a real kiss would feel wooden, too. So she held hands with Bobby under an October moon, and she liked that, and she liked him, and that was absolutely all that happened that Sunday night in Rome.

So there was nothing for Mary to be concerned about. But she was alarmed. After pushing Sandy to go out with Bobby, she was pacing the hallway when her daughter got home from her date at 8:45 P.M. Normally, Sandy went to bed at 8:30, read her lines until 11:00, and then went to sleep so she'd be rested for her 5:00 A.M. call. So on the occasion of her first real date, she got in fifteen minutes late, and her mother tore into her. Really yelled and gave Sandy hell. In this respect, my mom was a typical teenager. When Mother says left, go right. Mary'd been saying "yes" to Bobby, and Sandy said "no." Then Mary said "no."

Bobby and Sandy started dating steadily.

He sent flowers to my mom instead of to Mary: eighteen yellow roses every day.

He told Mary that Sandy was going to marry someone someday, so she'd better get used to the idea that Sandy was going to marry him.

He told Mary that she had shown Sandy one side of life, now he was going to show her the other.

My grandmother must have been *choked* with fear and anger. And I have a sense that my mom was as exhilarated as Mary was infuriated. For the first time in years, she managed to slip the leash, sneak away for a lunch or a walk with a man who was focused on her. And what a man! Intense, experienced, my dad serenaded her in cafes. He made her laugh. It was the first time she'd experienced love and romance, and she glowed. My mom was a terrific actress, but she couldn't hide her feelings about Bobby, either on camera or off.

Before Bobby left for Rome, his friend Rona Barrett told him, "You're either going to fall in love with Sandra Dee, or you're going to fall in love with her mother. Or the two of you are going to wind up hating each other and there's going to be a murder on the set." Rona says now, "Bobby laughed at me. And the rumors started coming out of Rome that something was happening. And I remember calling him. 'It's very complicated,' he said. 'I love her. I love her.'

"And I said, 'Does that mean you're going to marry her?'

" 'I don't know. But I love her, and I'm not going to give her up.' "

My mother remembers a scene she was doing with my father-to-be. She was meant to come down a stairway, and when she got to where Bobby was standing, she was supposed to slap his face. My mom's not a hitter now and never was. But on this occasion, to compound her normal reticence, she was falling in love with Bobby. When she got to the slapping part of the scene, she couldn't do it. She walked down that staircase dozens of times, drew back her hand, launched it in the general direction of Bobby's cheek, and pulled her slap every time. The director was getting pissed off. The crew were exasperated. Even Bobby said, "For Christ's sake, San. It's getting late. Slap me." Take after take, Sandy did the scene perfectly up until the end, when she fizzled out.

Finally filming was stopped for the day without the completed scene. That evening my mom and dad had a spat. Next day, action. Film rolls. My mom walks down the staircase, draws back her hand, and clobbers Bobby good. First take. My dad didn't know what the hell hit him.

People say that Charlie Maffia is a simple man of simple tastes. If he gets his food, sex, and sleep, he's happy. He was a staunch bodyguard for Bobby; if you imagine him as a big old dog lying outside Bobby's door, you'd have it right. Charlie was one of those people who'd take a bullet for the kid, but I doubt anyone thought he was so perceptive. It was Charlie who was the first to know that Bobby was deeply in love with Sandy. Not that he was a mind-reader. As Bobby was going out with Sandy, Charlie was squiring Mary around Rome, so that meant they were together. A lot.

Charlie remembers:

☞ *In the beginning, Bobby used to tease her—"Sandra Dee has a flea," he'd shout across the room. And she'd get mad. She said, "I can't stand that Bobby Darin." And he'd always have his guitar, and he'd hang around with the Italian crew. He was very funny with them. He was with the poor men, and I'd be hanging around with the big shots, with Sandy, with Rock Hudson, with Gina Lollobrigida. I hung around with Gina because I was interested in her. When she heard my name, she said, "Oh, Italiano." I got lucky with her once. She was pretty high, too. We had a ball in Italy.*

But Bobby wasn't having any sex. The first week he looked at Mary and at Sandy, and he said to me, "I don't know. Sandy's beautiful, but I think the mother could give you one heck of a lay."

I said, "You take care of Sandy. I'll take care of the mother." And that was that. He was a good boy. He fell for Sandy, and he was true to her. Wanted to save it for her. And the two of them didn't do nothing.

At first he was never alone with her. Her mother was always there—all the time, day and night. If Bobby was there and they weren't shooting, the mother was there. And when they were shooting, everyone was there, so there was no chance. After a while it started to bug him a little. Not that he wasn't having sex, but he wanted to be alone with Sandy, just so he could talk to her.

Come September *was his first movie. He was a big star then in nightclubs. He lost money making that movie because in Vegas he was getting about twenty-five thousand dollars a week, and he was only getting sixty thousand for the movie, and he was there for a couple of months. But it was worth it. In the movie, he and Sandy have a fight, and so do Rock and Gina. Then Gina goes back to Rock, and Bobby goes back with Sandy. In the end, everything comes out happy.*

I remember when I knew Bobby was in love with Sandy. I rounded up two broads, really gorgeous, and he wouldn't have

*anything to do with them. He was in love with Sandy, and
he wanted to marry her.*

It would be hard to find anyone who endorsed the overnight engagement of innocent Sandra Dee to Bronx-bred playboy Bobby Darin—in fact, I can't find anyone. Mary was against it. Rock Hudson advised my mother not to marry him. Bobby called a famous diva girlfriend of his back in Las Vegas and asked her advice. She pulled at her platinum-blond hair and told him that marrying Sandy was a terrible idea. Ross Hunter says that when Sandy called from Rome to tell him the news, he was beside himself:

☞ *She said, "Oh, Ross. I've fallen in love, and I'm going to get married."*

I remember my reaction. I said, "To whom?"

And she said, "To Bobby Darin."

I said, "But, honey, you can't. You haven't even necked in cars yet. You don't know what it's all about. You've got to promise me that you will not get married to him until we meet." And I said, "You and Bobby fly in from Rome, and I'll fly in from Los Angeles, and we'll meet at the Drake Hotel in New York, and we'll talk this thing over. Because, look, I want you to get married someday and I have your best interests at heart, but this is certainly not the time. Go with him. Have a ball. Do anything you want to do, but don't marry yet."

So they flew into New York and I flew in, and we had a marvelous meeting, and when they got back to Rome they decided that they couldn't wait. And they called me and said, "We're getting married." What more could I do? I had done my job as a producer and as a friend. And Mary, she was the fence that Sandy didn't have the opportunity to climb over into womanhood.

Mary kept Sandy back. But Sandy was so in love with Bobby that not even Mary could stop her. I cannot honestly say that I thought the feelings between Bobby and Sandy were reciprocal. No one could help loving Sandy. She was such a doll. But for Bobby, I felt, it was very important to marry a movie star. He did not want a wife to be a wife. He wanted a movie star, and he always had.

Ross Hunter loves my mom and tends to see her in the best light, but Hesh Wasser, who loved Bobby, agrees with Ross. Bobby wanted to marry a movie star. He was reaching. In defense of my dad—and I feel like defending him in this—I think he truly loved my mom, if not in the passionate way he may have loved others. And I think his wanting to marry a movie star was not trophy hunting. He wasn't trying to show other people what he'd "bagged." I think my dad was attracted to glamour because it was the opposite of what he'd come from. And by marrying a glamorous woman, he confirmed to *himself* that he was no longer of the Bronx.

Ross qualifies his take on Bobby by adding, "No one really knows what's in another man's heart," so I'm giving my dad the benefit of the doubt. Today, my mother believes that Bobby arrived in Italy with the idea that he was going to make a move on her. When Bobby told Jack Freeman he thought he was going to marry Sandy, he wasn't joking. My mom says he had a plan, but "what shocked the hell out of him was that he fell in love."

I also think my dad was aching to be married, and he wanted to have kids. He was twenty-four and looking down that short road that ended in a drop-off to nowhere. He had proposed to Connie Francis. He had proposed to Jo-Ann Campbell. He proposed to my mom two months after he met her. He wasn't saying "Let's take our time and get to know each other." He didn't have the luxury of time. He may have believed that marrying Sandra Dee would give him credibility and class, but I believe he was also moved by the dictates of his heart.

My mom was lovable, and I believe my dad fell in love with her even without really knowing her. I don't know when she told him she was only sixteen. She didn't tell him about the sexual abuse until after they were divorced. She and Bobby didn't live together, or do the laundry, or take out the trash. When they had time together, it was in this "unreal" way; they were working on a picture. They stayed in a resort hotel on the Italian Riviera. Both had an entourage, and my mom had Mary. This was not an ordinary love story.

As for my mom, she was experiencing first love *requited*, a miracle so incredibly wondrous that if it ever happens to you, you never get over it. The question here is not "Why did she fall in love with Bobby?" but, rather, "How did she hold out for so long against the onslaught of his campaign?" He had a lot going for him: the moon, the yellow roses, the paparazzi, the carriage rides, the wine, the tunes he'd made up just for her, the sheer force of his personality. And to stoke the fire, there was the heady rush that comes with opposition to an antagonistic force. In this case the antagonistic force was the frankly terrified Mary Douvan.

The question was popped. The answer was given. My dad called Dick Lord and said, "I'm going to marry Sandra Dee. She's never kissed a man." And then Bobby had to go home. His shooting days were finished, and my mom had another week of work in Rome. She remembers standing outside the Grand Hotel, saying good-bye to Bobby, and Mary, predictably, was crying her eyes out: "I'll never go with my daughter on a picture again." And Sandy said, "Ma, I'm not going to be dead."

Rona Barrett says, "I believe to this day that Bobby began a flirtatious relationship with Mary in order to get to Sandra. Mary mistook what was happening, and when Sandy and Bobby fell in love, Mary was ready to kill."

Sandy stayed in Italy for another week, and Bobby went to New York, where he started to think about buying Sandy an engagement ring. He told Steve Blauner he wanted the diamond to be big and perfect.

My dad was good at earning money, but he wasn't as good at hanging on to it. Steve Blauner was now in charge of the checkbook. He remembers he used to "steal money from Bobby."

☞ *He would have money on him, and he'd put it on the dresser, and when he wasn't looking I'd take some. I had opened an account for Bobby that was different from the business account I maintained for him. This account was only for Bobby. It was in his name, and only he could take money out. And I never told him about it. I figured someday something was going to happen, and I would give him this little bonus that was his money to begin with, but he would have it.*

When the time came, he wanted to buy Sandra a ring, and he wanted a perfect stone. Because that's what he felt she was: perfect. I had an uncle in the diamond business, and they were the biggest diamond importers in the world. They got their diamonds right out of the mines, so I knew at least we'd get an honest deal and I wouldn't have to pay retail.

So I went to my uncle and said that Bobby wanted to buy a perfect stone, and he said, "Look, there isn't a person in the world who would know a perfect stone except a jeweler with a microscope." And he suggested getting a stone twice as big for the same money. I told Bobby.

He said, "I want a perfect stone."

I said, "How're you going to pay for it?"

He said, "I don't know."

So I handed him the bank book and there was over ten thousand dollars in that account. It was a lot of money in those days, and I had collected it just stealing off the dresser. To the day he died, Bobby always thought I might have another bank book lying around when things got tough. Anyway, I gave him the money, and that's how he bought the ring. It was six carats, and it was a perfect stone.

My mom finished the picture and left Rome. When she got off the plane in New York, my dad was waiting for her with a magnificent diamond engagement ring. My dad drove her straight to Dick Lord's apartment, but Dick wasn't home. Dick's wife, Ellen, was there, and she was very taken with Sandy. Bobby was hot then, and when Sandy went to the laundry room with Ellen, the women living in the building who were doing their laundry just freaked out to see Sandra Dee standing at the washer. Ellen Lord called Mickey Behrke, Dick Behrke's wife, and said, "She's lovely. She looks like a newborn lamb just opening its eyes."

My mother, wanting to tell someone who would be happy for her, called aunt Ollie at three in the morning, and Ollie gave her the support she wanted and needed. When she got home at last, she showed the ring to Mary. Mary just about passed out. Eventually she recovered and let Sandy wear the ring. This was Thanksgiving week, and Sandy and Bobby had set their wedding date for February. Mary viewed ninety days as time enough for anything to happen, so she and her daughter had a truce of sorts. Ross Hunter had asked Sandy to promise that she wouldn't marry until she'd finished her next film, and Sandy agreed.

My mom picks up the story from here:

We were planning on getting married in February, but Bobby was up to something, I just didn't know what. First of all, he'd rented a house in L.A. beginning in December for thousands of dollars a month. We were in New York for a few days, then one night we went to dinner with Bobby's friend Don Kirshner. Bobby said, "By the way, if you really love me, you'll have a blood test." And I thought, Why? We're not getting married for months. He said, "I don't want to lose you."

He wasn't going to lose me, but there was a doctor at Donny's house and he did the test on the spot. That night, after dinner with Bobby, I went upstairs to the room my mother and I had at the hotel. Bobby was downstairs saying good-bye to my mother. She was accepting our engagement a little bit at this point. I think she figured she'd get me back to California and the studio would get their hands on me, and things would change. She came upstairs, and without thinking, I undressed in front of her. She saw the bandage on my arm and figured out that it was from the blood test. She went crazy.

She leaned out the window and yelled at Bobby, "You dirty SOB!" This was the Regency Hotel on Park Avenue. And Bobby was yelling, "Just let me explain."

I don't know what he would have said by way of explanation, but my mom wasn't going to believe anything. She packed her clothes, took her dogs, and without saying a word left me in a three-bedroom suite alone. I had never been alone before.

So I just sat there for a while, listening to the blood pound in my ears. I was too young to have a checkbook. I had no money, no way to get anywhere. I didn't know what to do, so I called Bobby and asked him to come over to the hotel. This is how calculating he was. He said, "I can't go up there, San."

And he would not set foot in the hotel because I was a minor. And now I was really worried, because I had no way to get a plane and I had to be back at the studio when the weekend was over, and now Bobby wasn't going to come over. I said, "You're leaving me, too?"

And Bobby said, "I don't know what to do, San. How will your mother feel if I come over?"

I said, "Bob, help. I think we should do it." I was pleading with him to marry me. Meanwhile Bobby had rented this house, and we'd had our blood tests, and everybody thought this plan to marry was spontaneous. Somehow, in the confusion, I thought it was my idea to get married.

I called the studio. I said, "I don't know when I'll be out there." There was a flurry of phone calls back and forth, what to say, what to do. Obviously my mother had already called them.

Ross Hunter asked, "Is your mom going to be at your wedding? Jesus, how is it going to look if she's not? Think about it." In fact, my mother had gone home to her mother in Bayonne. Neither of us was talking to the other, and we wouldn't speak for months.

Then Bobby called and said he had everything worked out. We'd get married in a few days time, on December 2, at Nina's house in Lake Hiawatha. And he had a list of forty-five close friends, and the reception would be catered and everything. I told the studio the date, but somehow the story that we were getting married leaked out immediately, But Bobby didn't want the press or the hoopla. So he came up with a new idea.

When we were in Rome Bobby had said, "If you still want to marry me after you meet my family, then you must love me."

It was November 30, Nina's birthday, and Bobby decided

that instead of taking Nina and Charlie out to dinner, we'd go to Don Kirshner's house in Elizabeth, New Jersey, and get married there. He was on his way to New York from Washington when he made that wedding plan. Then his plane was delayed, so I ended up meeting the Maffias for the first time by myself. Suddenly I understood what Bobby meant. His family were the crudest people I had ever met. The first time they met me, they changed their clothes in front of me. They ordered from room service and tried to disrobe the waiter for laughs. I never saw any of them eat with forks. Strange as it sounds, I liked them all anyway. They were earthy, and they were real.

Eventually Bobby arrived. Then Bobby's friends Mickey and Dick Behrke showed up, and Mickey tried to find something for me to wear. I didn't have much to get married in on the spur of the minute, and besides, we were pretending we were going out to dinner with Nina and Charlie. I put on something memorable: a purple-and-lavender satin cocktail dress. It was winter, and Bobby had a polo coat sent over to me to wear instead of my fur so that I would look right when I left the hotel and still look right when I got off the plane the next day in California. Plane to California! Quite a spontaneous plan.

We set out on our trek to Elizabeth. Mickey Behrke took my Yorkshire terrier with her and got into a car with Dick. Charlie, Nina, Vee, and Vanna got into another car. Bobby and I got into a red Rolls-Royce—not what you'd call an invisible car—and of course the press were on our trail immediately. We drove out to the turnpike, squealing around corners, cutting off cars with reporters inside. Mickey said my dog peed all over her lap. She and Dick thought the whole thing exciting and adventurous, but to me, this was like a very bad movie. We finally arrived in New Jersey at Don Kirshner's house. The judge was waiting, but there was no license.

It was eleven o' clock at night. What to do now? Bobby fell asleep on the chair. I had no shoes on, the studio was going to release the story that I was getting married, and it didn't look as if it were going to happen.

Elizabeth was a small town. We got back into the car and found the county clerk. It was the middle of the night, but we plunged ahead, woke up the clerk, and begged him to give us a license. And he did it, waived the seventy-two hours we were supposed to wait.

Back into the car again, the press following the red Rolls, a Keystone Cops kind of thing. Bobby was yelling "Duck!" at me. Nina was in the car with us this time. She turned to me and said, "Don't laugh." Laugh? You fantasize your whole life about getting married, and now it was happening and it was the worst night of my life. It should have been the happiest, and it was a nightmare.

By the time we were standing in front of the judge it was dawn. My attitude was, "Do it already. Get it over with." Mickey Behrke said to me, "Don't you want shoes?" And I said, "No." We got married in a ten-minute ceremony, and at four A.M. we were pronounced man and wife. We had breakfast in a diner in Newark. I had a roast beef sandwich, and Bobby had lox and cream cheese on a bagel, I've been told. I don't remember.

Right after that, we caught a plane and flew out to the Coast. I was wearing the polo coat on the plane to cover my velvet cocktail dress, and I was sweating like a pig. The stewardesses kept bringing over champagne and flowers and asking to take my coat, which I wouldn't give up. Bobby put his head on my shoulder and went to sleep.

Steve Blauner picked us up at the airport in L.A. Dave Gershenson, Bobby's publicist, was with him, and the four of us went to the new house. Everybody was tired, of course. But I wouldn't let Steve and Dave leave the house. I wouldn't let them go home. It was my wedding night or wedding morning, and I wouldn't let them leave me alone with Bobby.

Eight or nine hours passed, and they were still there, and I was saying, "Can I make you some coffee? Is anyone hun-

gry?" I didn't even know how to make coffee, and by now everyone was aware that I was a little odd about food.

I can no longer remember what I said or did to keep these two men I didn't know from leaving our house, but I remember vividly that I was absolutely panicked at the idea of going to bed with Bobby. I was naive yet I'd been in bed with my father. It was sick. I was ashamed and I was afraid. Afraid to tell Bobby the truth because I didn't want him to look at me like I was dirty. And I was afraid that when I got into bed with my husband, I would shut off my feelings as I had with my father. Ten years later, I finally told Bobby about the abuse. I was drinking. I couldn't have told him when I was sober. I cried and he cried for me. He understood, but I couldn't tell him on our wedding night, so it's amazing how good he was about what must have seemed ridiculous. He said, "Good night," and he went to bed. I didn't leave the couch. My first day as a married woman, I didn't leave the couch, and my husband slept in the bedroom.

I suppose it was that night that we consummated our marriage. I can't say that it was wonderful. I don't think the first time is wonderful for most people. By all rights it shouldn't have been as easy as it was. But I was there with him, and I was conscious. And I didn't want to get up in the morning. Our bodies just fit, and that feeling, at least, was spontaneous. We woke up in the morning, and we were in the same position as when we went to bed the night before. Not that we hadn't moved, but we'd had a sound sleep, then started turning a bit in the morning, and then we were together.

Later our sex life was really good. And I thought I had made as good a marriage as I could have at the time. Anyone but Bobby might have expected me to be some sort of red-hot Hollywood babe. I was anything but. And I do remember my thoughts that first morning when I woke up in bed with my husband. I thought I had never felt so safe in my life as I felt with Bobby.

As for my dad, he slept well. He was married and looking forward to happiness. He said, "Now that I'm married, I care about living. I've finally found somebody who is more important to me than myself. All the running and searching and proving have come to a halt with Sandy."

As for me, I want to close the blinds, kiss them both, and tiptoe quietly out of their room.

7

My Mom and Me, 1993

My God, there should be a law against martinis. Yesterday I had my first one, and I didn't think it did anything, so when somebody said, "How about another?" I said, "Sure." And wow! I got looped.

I'm a big girl now. If I want to, I can say "hell" and "damn," and maybe even something more zingy. And if I want to, I can even have a booze or two in public. My goodness, I like to take a drink in the evening, and so what if people know it.

—SANDRA DEE, 1963

I interrupt this lovely picture of the scrappy kid from the Bronx and the girl next door spooning together in their marital bed to say this: My mother is an alcoholic. She has put me and everyone around me through such hell for the last three weeks that I have not been able to engage in this book or stomach one thought about how sweet she is, how badly she's been victimized, or anything else that smacks of apologizing for her.

As I write this, my mom is on a bender. The trigger this time may have been an important business appointment her manager made for her, or maybe it was because there's a woman in my life or because she woke up feeling hopeless. I don't know. What I know is that I came back from three days of vacation and my mother had drunk herself into such a state that she needed to be hospitalized. She had seizures, DTs, the works. I got her medical help. She stabilized. She got some therapy, then got drunk again. Then she wanted nurses around the clock, and I hired nurses. After four days she said she was okay, and I sent the nurses home. Then she went straight to the liquor store and plowed herself under again.

For the last three weeks I've been going to her house twice a day to make sure she's okay. She was too incapacitated to feed herself or her dogs or do anything responsible. And when she sensed that I was going for outside help from a rehab center, she took a drug that in concert with alcohol causes extreme nausea and vomiting. Thus she forestalled a crisis—my refusal to put up with this any longer—and we've both clawed our way up from the bottom of the barrel one more time.

But we haven't emerged unscathed.

Once again my mom has scared the hell out of me, and once again everything else in my life came to a halt. Finally, I'm mad enough to say she's fucked up and I've had enough.

And this is an area I want to get into, because I hope my contribution with this book will be more than recounting my parents careers. I want to talk about co-dependency and drinking and dysfunctional families.

The most important dispute I ever had with my mother and my grandmother was about my mom's treatment. At age fourteen I said to my grandmother, "You've got an alcoholic on your hands. What are we going to do about it?" Sadly, her response was denial. It was never time to talk about the problem when my mom was drinking, because when she was drunk, "nothing we say will sink in." It was never time to talk about it when my mom was sober, because "she's sober now, and let's enjoy the time, and let's be normal."

As I've said, my grandmother loved my mom, loved me, would do anything for either of us. My grandmother, at an age when her peers were cruising and partying and retiring, was working as a real estate broker and looking after my mom. She was sneaking into windows to make sure Sandy didn't burn down the house. She was intercepting deliveries from the liquor store. So she paid the price in the end.

However, if my mom had gone in for treatment in 1970, she might have had a much different life for the last twenty-five years. But my grandmother wouldn't go along with that, and I've come to realize why: she didn't want to face up to the ramifications of what my mom's problems meant about her. If Sandy was in trouble, what did that say about Sandy's mother?

Growing up, I didn't really reflect on that. It was years later and after some time in therapy that I realized that my grandmother wasn't so altruistic. She was concerned about her daughter but also concerned about what her friends would think. It seems clear that being able to preserve a fairy-tale image to the world was more important to her than admitting, "Yes, my daughter's an alcoholic and an anorectic and dysfunctional, and maybe I had something to do with it."

I remember when I was about sixteen saying to my grandmother, "Jesus Christ, Liz Taylor goes into Betty Ford, and it's like she's going to a golf tournament. She gets sympathy like you cannot believe! This isn't 1960. We're not talking about Sandy being a child molester. She has a problem. Get her into the hospital. And if she never works another day in her life, so what? Maybe she will have a life. And isn't that really, in the final analysis, what this is about?"

"No, no, no," was her answer. "She'll never work if she does that. The industry will blackball her. This is Sandra Dee." This line of thinking made me almost schizophrenic. My mom was suffering, and my grandmother was giving me bullshit answers. I wasn't the only one who wanted my mom to go into serious treatment. Dave Gershenson, who was my mom's manager, various people who loved her, and her medical doctor all said, "She needs to be in a treatment program." And her mother said, "No!"

I said to my grandmother, "What's your problem? Who cares if she never works again? Don't you want her to have a life? This is insane." And some of the most virulent, ugly, horrible fights I ever had with my grandmother were over this subject. I loved my grandmother dearly. She was the most important figure in my life. But she'd turn around and say, "You're a chip off the old block. Your old man wanted your mom to suffer. You're the same way."

I'd say, "Hey, fuck you! What are you talking about? I'm the one who's saying 'She deserves better.' Get her some help!"

On her deathbed, my grandmother finally realized what was happening. She said to me, flat out, "Don't be a victim as I was. Don't waste your life cleaning up after her." She didn't, however, take responsibility for her part in creating this mess, and I may not be taking responsibility for my part in perpetuating it. And that's an important lesson for me and for people like me. To anyone dealing with a similar problem I have this to say: If you have a wife, a son, or a daughter with this problem, you're not doing them any favors by denying it and thus enabling them to destroy themselves.

And I'm still an enabler to a certain extent. I'm not yet able to look at my mom and say "Sink or swim on your own. I'm not going to take care of any of your problems." Maybe that's my weakness. I had a lawyer who told me that by supporting my mom, I was blowing my funds, extinguishing my father's estate. He said to me, "You have a very tough situation. But ultimately you have to do what you can live with. It may be better for your mother if you said 'This is it. No more.' But if it's going to kill you and you can't live your life with that burden, don't do it. Do what you have to do to be comfortable." And that's what I've done. I've been trying to find the balance between being a loving son and helping my mom and yet not enabling her to continue her destructive patterns. It's not really working.

So here's my mother. The perception of her was as an innocent teenage screen star—a fluffy blonde, kind of a lightweight babe. In reality she's sensitive, very bright, a deep person who's had an abnormally tormented life. From the beginning she's had very little happiness. She's never meant to harm anyone, my mom. She's a sweet, loving person, and that's really the sad irony. She deserves better than what's happened to her. She was not a spendthrift who lived carelessly. This is someone who has had a hard life. She is in a business that is not forgiving to women of a certain age, and when she was working and a megastar, she wasn't cashing in the way stars of her magnitude do today. She has no friends; she became the emotional cripple her mother groomed her to be. And resorting to drinking and self-medicating and all the rest is her way of acting out shame and punishment.

I often say to her, "Hey, I love you. You're my mom. You're a good human being. I don't care that you're not a star. You shouldn't care. You have nothing to feel shameful about. Have some joy. Find something apart from acting that makes you happy. Because the nature of your business, unlike working in a bank, is sporadic at best." It's filling those hours that's a problem for her. Filling the hours.

To compound everything else, because my mom has no friends, she's without a support base. She has no one to call up and say, "Hey, you know, that politician is an asshole, and you know what my bank did to me? And my son, that rotten bastard . . ." The kinds of conversations we all take for granted. She has no one but me. And I'm her son, not a girlfriend, and there are certain things she should tell girlfriends, if she had them. The majority of people in my mom's life before 1970 were work related. The publicist was her friend. The makeup person. The hairdresser. The studio exec. After that my grandmother filled that role entirely: friend, confidante, adviser. And then she died.

When I was a kid, my mom would sometimes say to me, "I don't know how to relate to people if it's not work related." In other words, just being a person, a human being to someone else, is foreign to her and scary. It's almost as though she feels that if she's not working, she's not worthy of friendship. People have tried to reach out to her over the years, and she's been unable to respond.

Here's where my mom's problems get really close to mine. I have many of the same feelings of unworthiness in me. I can be withdrawn and have the same shame that somehow binds external success to internal self-worth. In order to be fair and honest, I have to tell my own part of this story, and I will. But at this point I just want to say, I've been affected by what I've been around and grown up with. I tend to be private and reclusive, almost to the point of being a problem. I have an inner circle of friends and acquaintances that I'm comfortable with, and anything outside that I'd rather not deal with. I don't like this about myself.

Now that all this has been said, let's return to our regularly scheduled program.

8

Bobby and Sandy, 1961-1963

SANDRA AND DARIN EXPECTING STORK

By Louella O. Parsons

Well, the news is out: Sandra Dee, who married singer Bobby Darin last December, is going to have a baby. Most everybody guessed that, but Sandra had firmly denied her impending motherhood. The baby will be born in December. Sandra's last picture was Tammy Tell Me True. *She was scheduled to make two other pictures in the fall for Ross Hunter at Universal International, but for the time being, her role will be that of mother.*

—Los Angeles Examiner, *May 25, 1961*

My child will be born Cassotto, and my wife is Mrs. Cassotto.

—BOBBY DARIN, *December 1961*

157

In 1961 my mom and dad were sixteen and twenty-four years old, respectively. They had gone from strangers to husband and wife in three months and had married while still transfixed by the bright light of romantic love. There was no reason to resist the primitive game of chase and run, capture and surrender, and if my parents examined their underlying needs and motives at all, I'm sure both believed that by getting married, they would lose nothing and gain everything. My mom believed she would escape Mary's oppressive ministrations and stand alone at the brilliant center of Bobby Darin's attention. For my dad, Sandra Dee was surely the gold ring, a symbol of refinement and excellence, and proof positive he was no longer a Bronx brat. They were both so happy and self-satisfied, I'm sure they were amazed when their "perfect" union became filled with misunderstanding and discord.

My mother was the first to be disappointed. Less than a month after their wedding, she flew to Vegas over the weekend to join her new husband. She reports that she went straight to his suite, "where I found Bobby playing poker with the guys."

He gave me a kiss on the forehead and then sat down and continued playing cards. I thought, This is it? This is what I made this whole trip for? We'd been married for three weeks. I was waiting for the yellow roses. I was waiting for the band. I was waiting for something more than "Hi, honey."

I went into the bedroom and didn't come out. He called in, "What do you want for dinner, San?"

"Nothing." He didn't even hear me.

Because we got married so fast, we didn't have a wedding band. Don Kirshner had given me his father's ring, and we'd put tape around it so it would fit me. So there I was, sitting on the bed, and when Bobby came in finally to see where I was, I threw the ring at him. I said, "I don't want any part of this marriage. I made a mistake. This is it." And I was dead serious.

It was only the first of the "I quit" fights my parents had—they had hundreds of them—but this time I'm sure my dad didn't know what the hell was going on. His career was and had always been the point of his life. Within days of their wedding, he had climbed out of his marriage bed and returned his "brilliant attention" to his work. He did an NBC special that January, and Steve Blauner had loaded up Bobby's calendar with club dates. There was a tour to do: return engagements at the Copa, the Moulin Rouge, and other clubs throughout the country. Blauner had also nailed down a three-year contract for Bobby with the Flamingo Hotel in Las Vegas.

My mother was not career driven. She was, in Ross Hunter's words, "a manufactured star" whose career had essentially pursued her. Now she was also a child bride, alone for the first time. Mary had disappeared the night Sandy admitted she was getting married, and Sandy didn't know where she was. Bobby had been instrumental in causing their separation, so it's understandable that Sandy needed him—or perhaps expected him—to pick up the slack left by my grandmother's absence.

Then my mom got pregnant the first month of her marriage. She miscarried. And then she had her first drink. My dad was opening at the Copa and his wife was expected to take on the role of hostess to the big shots, a role she was totally unprepared for. She was nervous and when she was offered a screwdriver, she downed it. It tasted like orange juice but had a different effect. The second drink followed, then the third. Before the end of the show, she was throwing up in the ladies' room and missed my dad's entire performance. My mom tells me that from what she's learned about alcoholism, she was addicted with that first drink. It was a wonder that she could stop at all, but she did stop drinking for a year. The month following her miscarriage, she became pregnant with me. At least she thought she was pregnant. She went to the doctor, who took some samples and said, "I'll call you tomorrow and let you know." My mom couldn't bear to hear the results either way, so she told the doctor to call Bobby. That way Bobby could be the one to break the news to her.

The following night my parents were having dinner at George Burns's house. This was my dad's version of bringing his wife home to meet his father. In fact, it was a dinner party, and many people were there, and the phone kept ringing for Bobby. My dad got five phone calls, and each time he left the table and returned, my mother would search his face with her huge brown eyes. Jack Benny, witnessing this look of utter adoration, turned to Danny Kaye and said,

"Isn't young love great?" But my mom just wanted to know one thing: Had the rabbit died or not?

My parents left the party and drove to Palm Springs, where they had planned to spend a few days of vacation together. In the car my dad told her, "You're gonna be a momma." Then he resumed his rapid-fire monologue as he always did. My mom was silent. After a while my dad asked, "You okay, San?" And she said she was, but she was trying to let the news sink in and it wouldn't. She was conflicted. She wasn't yet seventeen, and everything was happening very fast. My dad wasn't conflicted at all. He wanted a child, and he'd absorbed the news quickly. Then he was on to the next thing. He was recording new songs with a folksier sound than before. No hits here, nothing that compared with *That's All*, but he was experimenting, gathering momentum, moving forward. But even though he was eager to shake the old neighborhood, some of it was still attached to him.

This is what he said to *Seventeen* magazine in early 1961: "Where I grew up, when I said I wanted to be an entertainer, people laughed at me. They said, 'Around here? People who were born here, live here, get married here, and die here. They don't become successful or rich or famous or entertainers. Get that out of your head!' To be in show business is my obsession. It's my drive. If I wasn't as sophisticated and didn't know how to use words like that, I would just say I liked doing it. Or maybe I wouldn't say anything at all."

In March, my dad played his second engagement at the Copacabana. A *Time* magazine reporter wrote an article about Bobby, focusing on his upcoming twenty-fifth birthday. It was a fairly wicked story entitled "Two and a Half Months to Go," and the point of it was that my dad hadn't yet attained legendary status. The writer described Bobby as "an immodest boy with modest ability." But by the end of the article the writer grudgingly admitted that Bobby had made six LPs that sold more than 1.5 million copies, "Mack the Knife" had sold 2 million copies, and Bobby Darin "has all the bookings he can handle in America's major nightclub principalities from Las Vegas to Miami Beach." I love the way he describes how my dad "showed up for work one evening last week in a two-tone Rolls, slipped a sidewalk bum an easy fin, and led his wife inside." The Copa was far away from the Bronx indeed.

Meanwhile I can hardly imagine what my mom was feeling about her pregnancy. She and her body had always had a difficult relationship, and now there was this new thing to contend with. To start with, her skin broke out when she'd never before had as much as a blemish. The doctor said he thought that she had chicken pox, and it was lucky for me that he was right. Had she contracted German measles, I might not be here to tell the tale. My mom had to track down Mary to get her medical history (my grandmother didn't actually know if my mom had ever had chicken pox or measles), and in so doing, the two spoke for the first time in three months. Quite a hiatus for Mom and Mary, and the only time in their lives they had gone more than a day without speaking.

My mom spent a month in a darkened room because my father told her that light could blind her, and she almost went out of her mind from boredom. Then the spots were gone, and she got more activity than she bargained for. My dad wanted her to come with him back east, where he was playing some clubs between New York and Philadelphia. That meant my mom and *her* mom, with a hairdresser to whip the movie star's tresses into shape, would be with Bobby and his entire gang.

Dick Lord describes my mom as "shy, vulnerable, and I think a little bewildered."

She was surrounded by all these people she didn't know: me, Behrke, Blauner, Charlie, Tommy Culler, Bobby Ramsen, all of us knowing what the other one is thinking before he says it. I missed the wedding because I was on the road. My first meeting with Sandra Dee was unbelievable. Bobby was appearing at the Latin Casino in Cherry Hill, New Jersey. I met Sandy backstage in Bobby's dressing room. She was there with her mother and the hairdresser that the studio provided. She was sitting on a couch, and a man was sitting on the floor peeling an orange, handing her the slices.

Bobby introduced us. She was very nice. I was tongue-tied. I never saw anything like that before. I followed Bobby into the inner room. He explained, "The hairdresser goes everywhere. So does her mother. Don't worry about it," he said. "Don't feel ill at ease." I asked him who the man on the floor peeling the orange was. He said, "Some schmuck in the shoe business."

At this point a door burst open and a kid grabbed Bobby's arm and told him how great he was. Bobby removed the kid's hand and in a very low voice said, "Don't ever touch me. I don't like people to touch me." The kid almost fainted. He was about twenty-two. He apologized while backing out of the room. Bobby started to laugh, and then he said, "Let's get rid of the schmuck with the orange."

Quite a picture. There's Sandra Dee, accustomed to being the star, the center of attention, the one with the entourage. And here's Bobby Darin with his own entourage of a totally different breed—and all of these people are now traveling around together! My mother must have felt that she'd gone to bed one night and woken up on another planet. She'd been making movies for three and a half years, and her days had regular hours. She'd work on a movie for five or six weeks on the lot or on location, then she'd have a few months off between pictures. Suddenly she was thrust into this nightclub world. Her life became a crazy quilt of late night hours, overnight travel to different cities, and dressing rooms filled with men.

Then it was time for her to go back to work on a picture called *Tammy Tell Me True*. My mom remembers she had gotten used to waking up in the morning with a man in her bed. She and my dad had been married only a few months and were still living in a rented house in Stone Canyon. There was no one around, so the curtains were wide open and the house was surrounded by acres of green and a beautiful garden. My mom remembers basking in the sunlight that fell on her and my dad as she awoke and marveling at how good she felt. The grass was green, the sun was shining . . . Wait a minute. The sun was shining! She was working on a picture, and she was supposed to be at the studio at 5:30 A.M. She was used to waking up just before the alarm and having her mom tell her she could have five more minutes of sleep. But Bobby was not Mary. He had turned off the alarm and rolled over. The limo had been outside for hours waiting for Sandra, and the driver was an anxious wreck. This was the first and last time my mother was ever late on the job.

The newlywed Cassottos had been talking a lot about where to live. Up until that time, Bobby's family had kept a room available for him in Lake Hiawatha when he was on the East Coast, and he lived with Steve Blauner when he was in Los Angeles. Up until her marriage, Sandy had been living in the Benedict Canyon house with her mother. The Stone Canyon house was a short-term rental, so my parents needed a home of their own. Sandy was on the East Coast one weekend visiting family and Bobby was on the West Coast when he made an impulsive purchase. He'd gone to look at a house in Bel Air, fallen for it, and bought it on the spot. Abashed that he hadn't first checked with his wife, Bobby drove Sandy to their new home when she returned.

"I'll never forget this as long as I live," says Ross Hunter. "I had a house on Rising Glen. One rainy night, I was breaking down a script when the doorbell rang. And there was Sandy and Bobby at the door. They said, 'Oh, Ross, guess what? We bought the house next door.' And I thought, Oh, dear, do I need this? As close as I am, this may be too close."

In April my mom celebrated her seventeenth birthday, and in May she finished *Tammy Tell Me True* without telling anyone outside her immediate circle that she was pregnant. She remembers that for the first time since she was eight years old, she didn't worry about what she ate. It was a wonderful liberation for her: pints of pineapple-pecan ice cream daily and whatever else she fancied. She was starting to get the hang of pregnancy and looking forward to taking a break from working. It was six months into their marriage. My dad was off to Vegas to do that first month of the three-year contract Blauner had gotten him with the Flamingo, and he wanted his wife to come with him.

My mother could have written a book about Charlie by this time. She knew his habit of pouncing on room service leftovers as if stale toast were God sent, and when my dad gave him money to send out his sweat-soaked shirts to be dry-cleaned, she knew he pocketed the money and never sent out the shirts. She had witnessed his faux pas in front of the press, ranging from telling them the size of baby Bobby's genitals to announcing the birth of his own illegitimate child.

Mary, who had spent a lifetime telling her daughter that no one was good enough for her, felt sorry for Sandy. She rolled her eyes as if to say a UFO had landed and that Sandy had married into a family of aliens. This was not the life Mary envisioned for her Hollywood princess.

Some of Bobby's friends agreed that Sandy was a princess, but not all of them liked that about her. Sandy was used to having her own way, and Rona Barrett in particular was having a problem with Sandy's influence on her friend Bobby.

☞ *Bobby and I had a very bitter falling-out. When Bobby first came to Hollywood, I tried to protect him from the press. He was so brash and cocky and things like "I'm going to be a legend by the time I'm twenty-five," came from his wonderful mouth and got him in trouble. When his relationship to Sandra finally culminated in marriage, some people who knew them both were aghast. There was a reaction along these lines: How could Bobby marry this teenaged baby doll? He was a sex maniac. He was wild. He was a horrible person. He had seduced this virgin, and suddenly his life was being changed around. People kept saying, "Oh, look at the changes in Bobby Darin!"*

And I was sitting in his house, privy to what was really happening, and I was infuriated that Bobby was getting a bad rap. I saw that Sandy was far from being Bobby's victim. And having my little pen, I sat down and wrote an article about Sandra Dee who doesn't want her husband to go out on the road, who doesn't want her husband to be a musician, who would much prefer her husband become a major movie star, who prefers the life of moviedom as opposed to the music world, didn't understand why Bobby would be up 'til five, six o'clock in the morning, thrashing things out with the guys in the band. I then said that Sandra was a spoiled brat who'd had her way and that she was stripping the soul out of Bobby, stripping him of everything that was musical in his life.

When Bobby saw the piece, he was so mad at me. I didn't understand in those days what I had done. I was young and naive. My God! I was protecting my friend, and I was doing my job. I remember that Bobby said to me. "Rona, you seem to forget you were in my house. You were like my sister. You were my best friend. But she's my wife. I married her and I have to stand beside her and what you did was wrong. I know you love me! But you shouldn't have done it."

Rona was right: my father *was* turning his attention to the movie business. But I don't believe this was because of my mother's influence. My dad had wanted to be an actor since he'd known the meaning of the word. Blauner was scouring Hollywood, looking for a film project that would give Bobby a chance to spread his wings, and my dad was reading scripts by the score. Then he was cast in two films that were made in 1961: *Too Late Blues* and *Hell Is for Heros*, both dramas. Neither made much of an impression on the picture-going crowds. But my dad was growing as an actor. He was working with John Cassavetes and Steve McQueen. At the same time, my mom's life was turning ever inward. She spent the remainder of 1961 trying to deal with having a baby.

Mary hadn't explained the hows of childbirth to her daughter, and my mom had a million questions. First, How did you know when it was time to give birth? Her obstetrician told her not to worry, she'd know, but she honestly didn't have a clue. She asked him if her stomach would open up or what, and it fell to Dr. Goodwin to inform my mom about how the baby entered the outside world. My mother thought he was making it up, and I guess the good doctor had a pretty funny story to tell his wife when he got home that night. He gave my mom a book to read on pregnancy, and before she'd read the ink off the pages, she uncovered a slew of imagined things to be worried about.

Then there was an actual thing to be worried about. Before she got pregnant, my mom's doctor had given her penicillin for a cold. The penicillin caused a common infection, which could not be treated while she was pregnant and ultimately put my mom at risk of losing her baby.

She started seeing her doctor several times a week. Occasionally she went to his house after hours. He might be having a dinner party, for instance, and there would be Sandy at his door, saying, "I think something is wrong." In fact, the pregnancy marked a very healthy period for my mom. Cigarettes, yes, but no alcohol and a balanced diet for the first time since my grandmother had shoved all four food groups down her throat at once. And she spent a lot of time resting.

Dick Behrke and his wife, Mickey, were expecting a child at the same time, and Mickey remembers spending time with my mom: "Sandy was very big, and I was very big, and we were very uncomfortable. We were sitting around the pool, and Mary was running back and forth waiting on us. I didn't expect to be waited on, and I didn't like it, but no matter what we wanted, Mary would run to get it. I said, 'We're not ill. I can get up and move. And it would be better if I did move.'

"And Sandy said, 'That's my mother.' Sandy was angry because you could see that Mary was driving her crazy."

As her pregnancy progressed, ideas were springing into my parents' minds. My dad tried to sell Sandy on the idea of natural childbirth, and my mom was accessorizing. She had her hair washed daily and colored often, and she bought a new coat in preparation for the day she would enter motherhood.

The day never seemed to come. I understand it's not unusual for first-time mothers to deliver late, but waiting was especially hard for my mom. She had nothing to do, and she had a mother who had essentially become an all-purpose domestic servant. As a result, my mom made so many false "It's time to go to the hospital" announcements that everyone stopped listening to her. Somehow she convinced the endlessly selfless Dr. Goodwin to provide her with medication that would cause her labor pains to intensify if she was truly in labor and, he said, there would be no effect if she was just imagining things.

My mom remembers that she was at her mother's house and Bobby was watching television in the bedroom:

☞ *I wasn't very hungry, but I was cold. I put on some flannel bottoms and Bobby's sweatshirt and a pair of his socks, and then a contraction hit me. I said, "This is it, guys."*

Bobby was watching Route 66 *on television. He said, "I don't want to hear it. Have something to eat."*

I said, "Bobby. I'm really in labor. I think."

Nobody was listening. My mother called in from another

room. "Put your feet up," she said. Then she came in and
looked at me and she knew. After a month of lying over the
side of the bed to get my hair washed and dyed and buying a
new coat, I suddenly didn't care about any of it. "Take me
to the hospital," I said.

Which they did. My dad instantly rejected every thought he'd ever
had about natural childbirth. He yelled, "Give her something! I don't
want her to be in any pain!" They gave my mom sodium pentothal to
kill the pain for a few hours and put her in a private room. The nurse
asked for her autograph, and that's the last thing my mom remembers
that day. When she woke up the next morning, she was alone, in
pain, and wanting to use the bathroom. She tried to climb over the
handrails of the bed and was stopped by the nurse. "Where's Bobby?"
she asked. "Where's my mother?"

They'd all gone home, the nurse told her, and the baby was sleeping.
Baby? When did the baby happen? The doctors had knocked my
mother out and delivered me, and after I'd been viewed by my dad
and grandmother, they went home. My mom had me in two hours
while she was unconscious and so missed the entire event.

I was born on December 16, 1961, one year and two weeks from
the day my parents were married. My grandmother was elated that no
matter how you counted the months, I was clearly conceived in wed-
lock. My mom was just elated to have me. She says she wanted to stay
home with me and never go out. But after threats and inducements
from my father, she dressed me in cute clothes, put me in the baby
seat next to the dog, and drove over to her mother's house for a visit.
That kind of thing.

"Dodd" was my father's nickname when he was a child because of
the way he pronounced "Da-da." I inherited this nickname and was
christened Dodd Mitchell Cassotto. My aunt Ollie became my god-
mother, and Charlie Maffia became my godfather. Charlie says, "Bobby
was out of this world that he had this child, and he really wanted a
boy. He walked around with his chest puffed out, saying, 'That's
mine.' " I've been told I was very cute, but modesty forbids me from
quoting obviously biased friends and relatives. Nina, however, still
my dad's sister at this point in the story, constantly told my mom
that I was the *second* cutest baby in the world (the first cutest was my

father, who as we all know more closely resembled a naked mole rat than a human baby), which really ticked my mom off.

If Sandra Dee was a princess, I was getting the attention due a prince. My mom fired the baby nurse immediately and took care of me herself for the first months. She figured if she had a nurse, she'd never learn how to care for me herself. She and my dad made predictable mistakes of a minor kind: diaper rash took on the stature of the plague, for instance. And it took a while before my mom understood how much formula a growing child needed to thrive. My grandmother spoiled me so much, my mom and dad took me off with them to Palm Springs for four days just to get me out of her hands. Between my mom and dad and my grandmothers and aunts, I was in good hands.

Then a nanny joined the hairdresser and my grandmother in Sandra Dee's entourage, but it was my mom who sat in the front row of the club at every one of my dad's performances. My dad wanted her there, and my mom says if she didn't see him onstage, she'd never see him. He was a busy fellow, and when he wasn't performing, recording, or shooting, he was sleeping. It wouldn't surprise me to learn that my mom's drinking problems escalated when she was glued to a small chair one midnight after another. You sit at a nightclub table and the waiter says, "What can I get you to drink?" Eventually you say, "A black Russian, please." My mom says, "I was underage and I drank. I thought, big deal."

My mom also discovered gambling in a big way while in Vegas. Hairdressers to stars don't only do hair; they are there to provide companionship as well, and my mom ran through two hairdressers and was working on her third, a sweet woman named Emma, when this story takes place. Emma had been Marilyn Monroe's hairdresser, and she was used to working with stars. Aside from her gambling, Sandra Dee was a piece of cake to manage, but when she was gambling, my mother was out of control. So Emma would try to keep Sandy in her room for as long as possible, trying new hairstyles, turning back the hands on the clock, trying to forestall the moment when my mom turned herself loose in the casinos.

Emma had promised to go with Sandy to the casino when she was ready, and my mom said, "I cannot be more ready." Off the two went, one dragging the other along. Sandy loved blackjack. On this particular night she went to the tables, played three or four hands at a time, and within an hour—before 6:30 P.M.—blew thirty grand. This is roughly what my mother was earning annually at that time, so it cannot be dismissed as small change. My dad was getting his preshow sleep in his room while this blitz went on, but it was no problem for him. The studio picked up Sandy's gambling tab. After scrounging around in her handbag for more money for chips and coming up empty, my mom took Emma in the Rolls-Royce to a diner for a hamburger and fries. After this meal, they discovered that between them they didn't have three bucks. So my mom left her hairdresser as security while she went back to the hotel for change.

I asked my mom, "What was going on here? What were you trying to do?" She said, "I wanted Bobby's attention."

He had me sitting through the shows, and then he was with the guys every night. I never had to worry about another woman. It was just the guys. Every night, Steve and Dave and Charlie and the whole band. I had no life, and we had no life together. I wanted his attention, and he never got mad at my gambling because he knew he didn't have to pay for what I did. He was figuring I was a spoiled brat, but he wouldn't say no to me. I wanted him to say, "You damned little bitch. I'm going to hit you." Then I would figure out how to stop what I was doing. He never said it, so I went farther and farther.

I wanted to feel like a bride. In the first year I was married, a mother, and having a new life. I was a day person. I used to go to bed at eight o'clock. Suddenly my night didn't begin until ten. It was crazy, and I couldn't juggle it all. I'd be in the shower, and Charlie Maffia would be in the bathroom picking up dirty clothes, and I'd say, "Get out!"

And he'd say, "Oh, I'm just getting the laundry."

Jesus. I had enough firsts. First kiss, first date, first baby. I thought I'm going to live with these men for the rest of my life. It was really an unhappy atmosphere. I'll never forget, he would come in after his show and the band was in the cottage where we stayed. Bobby never went out anywhere. He

*would do his show and come back to the cottage. That's all
he did.*

My dad didn't approve of my mom's gambling binges and thought
he'd try to spend more time with her. He did two shows a night, one
at ten P.M., the other at midnight. Once, after a show, he told Sandy
he would call the Sands and order some food to take out, and Charlie
would pick it up for them. This was a Vegas-style dinner at home for
two, and my mom said, "That sounds nice." My dad said he needed
about twenty minutes to shower and change. My mom said "Okay,"
and at around one went to the casino for twenty minutes. Eight hours
passed. By design, there are no windows or clocks in a casino. My
mom said she lost track of the time, and I believe her, but I've had
enough encounters with psychotherapy to believe that this oversight
was no accident. She says, "This was really my fault this time. And
after that, we just never had dinner alone. Bob always had somebody
with him after the show, and I just never came back from the casino."

For his part, my dad seems to have been largely unconcerned about
what his teenage wife was going through. He was preoccupied. His
career was building, in fact Blauner projected a $1 million income for
Bobby in 1962. There was a certain gangster element in nightclub
life, but my dad was repulsed by the Mafia. He'd been told that the
mob had gotten their hooks into some young Italian singers, his peers,
and both helped them and owned them. My dad's attitude toward the
Mafia was "Where were you when we needed you?"—referring to the
fact that the Mafia had abandoned Sam Cassotto, the man Bobby
believed to be his father.

John Miller, the journalist friend of my father's throughout his life,
had close connections with the Mafia. Before he died, Miller told this
story:

☞ *I was a very intimate friend of {Mafia chief} Frank Costello.
I was with him the night he was shot, as a matter of fact. I
was a writer who was lousing up dozens and dozens of people,
and all kinds of people were out to get me. There was one
night when John Wayne and Robert Mitchum toured all of*

New York, going to every club in town to find me with the intention of beating me up. But the word was out that anyone who touched me would have to answer to Frank C. So that meant that all of the people who respected him, protected me.

Bobby knew of my association with Frank and that I was also close to Julie Podell, who ran the Copa. Bobby had a misconception about his father. He thought his father was a very important hit man with the Mafia, and he thought that when he went to prison, Sam took the rap for Frank C. And that wasn't the case at all. One day, knowing how close I was to Frank, Bobby said to me, "I want to get this straight. I'm working the Copa. Frank Costello is the man who abandoned me and abandoned my father. I think he's a real shit. And I'd like him to know that."

Well, it so happened I was having dinner with Frank C. not long after that, and I said, "Big Sam Curly's son says hello."

And Frank said, "Who's that?"

I said, "Bobby Darin."

Frank had been looking at the receipts, and he was very impressed with the money Bobby was bringing into the club, and he said he wanted to meet him. Now, what Bobby didn't know was that it was Frank who sent the piano to Polly when Sam was in prison, and this was the piano Bobby learned to play when he was growing up. And Frank remembered Sam very well. But Sam Cassotto was no hit man. He was on junk and a small-time guy, but Frank liked him very much. At one time he had literally kidnapped Sam off the streets of East Harlem, sent him down on the rum-running boats from Cuba, and kept him there for a cold turkey withdrawal, which didn't work.

Anyway, I explained to Frank what Bobby said, and Bobby was working at the Copa at the time.

Frank said, "Look. This is what the truth is. His father was a junkie, a bust-out, a creep in general. I liked him. I tried to save him. I couldn't save him, and he didn't take the rap for anybody. But you can't go to a guy and tell him that his father, whom he idolizes, was a creep."

Then Costello says, "You go to Bobby and tell him that I'm a creep. Tell him that everything he said about me was true. A lot of guys hate me. What difference does it make if one more guy hates me?" And then Costello arranged for two guys to come in from East Harlem to the Copa one night to sit down with Julie Podell and Bobby Darin and myself, and those two guys told him the most glowing reports about his father. They told Bobby, under Frank C.'s orders, that he was right. That Frank C. abandoned his father.

"The Copa had the biggest bar in the world," recalls Steve Blauner. "It was a circular bar on the second floor with a lounge and a little stage. Downstairs was the nightclub, and there was no stage. The bandstand was to one side, and the tables were all around. The performer was on the same level as the tables, so when Bobby was standing, the audience would be staring at his waist. The people were right up against him. There was nothing between him and them, so he got full intimacy with the audience like you cannot believe. If the audience was bad, it drained him because he was giving it everything. If it was good, the energy fed him. It was like putting gas in the tank. And he just went sky high."

Today, if you go to see a performer, even if the performance is in a club, it's a concert and the audience is there for the entertainment. When my dad was working clubs in the sixties, the setup was different. People went to clubs to eat, drink, come on to women. The performers were background, and the audience usually treated them accordingly. That's why the gifted entertainers were such standouts.

While my father was working at the Copa, Charlie Maffia acted the part of bodyguard, and Steve Blauner, weighing in at three hundred pounds, was doing some face smashing as well. It's been said that my dad sometimes liked to piss the audience off so he would have to work hard to get them back. I've been told that he liked the challenge. But often, without provocation, Bobby became the focus of hecklers' attention. Sometimes he walked off the stage as a rebuke, and sometimes he put the hecklers down so thoroughly that they would either have to return the favor or leave town in shame. My dad has said he'd rather talk his way out of a fight than be in one, but when he had Steve and Charlie around him, he found a way to start a fight and let someone else finish it.

I don't mean to give the impression that there were brawls every night, but there were plenty. Once a couple of professional hoods came in from Philly and passed the word through John Miller that Bobby was in line to be roughed up or worse. My dad, who at that moment was out of town, had insulted a mobster to his girlfriend, and the girlfriend had passed the insult along. Now these thugs came into the Copa intending to even things up with Bobby. They had guns, and if Bobby "accidentally" got killed, that would be okay. John Miller told Blauner what was going on, and Blauner fielded the threat and made some of his own. In the end it was Julie Podell, the club owner and probably on the Mafia payroll, who protected Bobby. It may have been strictly a business consideration. Bobby was a golden boy when it came to the cash box.

Sometimes the skirmishes involved overeager fans who wanted to come back to see Bobby after the show and wouldn't take no for an answer. A lot of my father's reputation for rudeness stemmed from the fact that he was in no condition to see people after he worked. He had oxygen backstage in his dressing room by this time, and he was using it between shows. Charlie would try turning people down politely, first. He'd say, "Bobby has this policy. He's not a strong guy. He rests between shows, has a little tea, then he lies down. . . ." But sometimes no wasn't good enough and that's when people were sent flying down stairs, mirrors were smashed, and booths were collapsed like houses of cards. John Miller says of my dad, "Bobby ignored it all. The more flak there was, the more arrogant he became. And it was sincere arrogance."

So how could Charlie know where to draw the line? He remembers this incident:

☞ *Peter Lawford came in with the president's sister.*
He got on the phone and said to me, "This is Peter Lawford. I'd like to talk to Bobby."

I said, "You'll have to talk to me first. What's your business?"

He said, "I'd like to invite Bobby to my table. I have my wife here and a crowd, and I'd like him to come down."

I said, "I'm sorry. Bobby does not come down for anybody."

And he started to get nasty. I said, "I don't care who the fuck you are, Peter Lawford. Bobby does not come down to tables. If you want to, you can come upstairs. He might see you."

Suddenly Carmine, who was in charge of the bar, came in and said to me, "Jesus, you can't do this to these guys. These are Kennedys."

And Bobby heard the commotion between me and Carmine and came into the room and said, "What's going on here?" And Carmine told him. And Bobby said to me, "Why didn't you tell me?"

I said, "Bobby, you gave me orders not to disturb you under any circumstances, and I don't give a damn if it is a Kennedy that's come in."

And Bobby said, "You stupid idiot."

I said, "Come on, Bobby, what's the matter with you? You need the rest." So he went down to the tables, and I went down, and he introduced me to Lawford, who said, "What a prick."

I said, "Yeah, when it comes to Bobby, I don't care who you are, and if I had my way, he still wouldn't come down."

John Miller said that when Bobby played the Copa, he frequently arranged parties for him at the Harwyn Club after the last show. "The Harwyn Club was a terrific place on Fifty-second Street between Park and Lexington, and Bobby liked the Harwyn very much. They had a trio that worked there, and there was a piano. And Bobby would play the piano for hours. I remember one night when he was very depressed, he got up there and he played from about two to five. He played all by himself, not talking to anyone, not singing, not doing anything but playing. There were three or four other people there, but the pub was closed at four. But he just played on. He told me that it was very therapeutic for his depression. That he needed escape valves, needed to let off steam."

Was my dad depressed because he was haunted by his death sentence? Or was it because of what he was going through with my mom? Bobby loved his friends, but he rarely confided his feelings. As for his friends, Dick Behrke was doing very well by this time. He was being paid good money, getting good notices, had a beautiful wife and child. Dave Gershenson, my dad's press agent, was green in every way when he started working on my dad's account, but he was thrown into the deep end immediately and formed a bond with my dad that lasted throughout my father's life. Bobby boosted Steve Blauner's earnings percentage from 15% to 20% as a birthday present. He told Charlie to have three or four new suits made up for *his* birthday, and Charlie never really forgave Bobby:

☞ *I said, "Bobby, I got a better idea. You tell Steve Blauner to have the suits made and you give me the five percent."*

Bobby got very insulted. He said, "I got eighty percent. It's all yours if you need it."

But it wasn't true. I was the lowest man on the totem pole. I wasn't mercenary. I was making one hundred and fifty dollars a week, and this was the first time I said "money" to him. I figured if I got five percent of Bobby, that would be nice. It wouldn't be for me, it would be for Nina, because I always sent money home. So I said, "This way it gives me a nice income."

He said, "Yeah, well, you know if you ever need it, it's all yours."

And he shut me up. He did that a few times. In fact, when he told me to go to work for him on the road, I said, "Bobby, I got a steady job. There's a pension there. God forbid anything happens." I didn't want to say "Your heart isn't too good." I was making one hundred and five bucks a week with the Sanitation Department. I wanted to go with him because this was something new, show business. But I had a family to worry about, and I wanted to make sure I took care of them. Bobby said, "Are you crazy? We're going to be millionaires."

175

And my father would become a millionaire that year, but nothing fell to Charlie beyond his $150 a week. My dad believed that it was wrong to help people when they were capable of helping themselves. And that went for Dick Lord, too. While my dad was playing the Copa, Dick was playing Chinese restaurants, doing stand-up for $75 a night less 10 percent for his agent plus a free bowl of rice on Saturday nights. My dad would take my mom to see Dick at these joints and would critique and encourage his friend. Dick was supporting a wife and child at this point, but my dad would not put him on the bill with him until he was ready. He bought Dick a car once to replace the death trap he was driving. He paid a writer several thousand dollars once to work with Dick on his act. And he sent him CARE packages, big baskets of food. In order to take the sting off what might have looked like charity, my dad would enclose a gold lighter or fountain pen with an inscription like "To pay your taxes in the future."

Dick recalls that "Bobby didn't shorten my apprenticeship at all."

In retrospect, he was smart to do what he did, but it was killing me. I remember working in this little bungalow colony in the Catskills. I was getting seventy-five dollars a show, and the audience didn't have much respect for the performers because they knew what level we were on. Sometimes you'd get lucky and have a good show. Sometimes it would be horrible. Their sport would be heckling the comedian, and I'd follow some guy who'd balance a lawn mower on his ear and it would go crashing down.

Then I'd get in the car and race to the next place I was going to work for fifty dollars, and I remember getting lost somewhere in Woodbridge, New York. It was a lonely road. There were no other cars. During the first show, I followed the lawn mower guy and the audience was screaming at him and my hands were shaking and I realized I was lost. I was going to be late, and there was no one to call and I didn't know what to do. I pulled over to the side of the road and I turned on my brights just so I could see something. And the headlights hit a poster of Bobby Darin that was tacked to a tree. I thought, My God. All the trees in the world, and it's that tree. And I know it sounds crazy, but that poster of Bobby calmed me down. I thought, I can do this. And I went to the second show, and I was fine."

My mother, however, was not fine. She was doing her best to adapt to a life for which she'd had no preparation, and she was falling apart under the stress. Her coping mechanism of choice was alcohol. Mickey Behrke says that "Sandy didn't want people around. She didn't have any real friends, and she didn't try to like Bobby's friends. And she could never understand when Bobby's friends treated him as anything less than a king. If Dick didn't like something Bobby said, he'd say, 'Bobby, are you crazy?' And that used to make Sandy really angry."

Beneath the sense of estrangement my mother was feeling around my father's crowd was a constant irritating hum of competitiveness. And this was something experienced between both my parents, I think. George Burns once said of my parents that he thought two careers in one family was great. I think it worked for him and Gracie Allen, but I know it didn't work for my mom and dad. My dad wanted to be a movie star. My mom *was* a movie star. My mom liked all the attention. When she was with my dad, there was a constant flow of people around him, a constant go. It was time-consuming, and it wasn't what she wanted.

My parents usually vented their anger indirectly. My mom would tell my dad his toupee was on crooked just before he went onstage. This remark would send him flying back to the dressing room as his musical cue was sounding. My dad would retaliate in kind, picking a fight with my mom just before they were ready to go out for the evening, which would send her to her room in a major sulk. On several occasions he provoked a fight just before she was due to appear on *What's My Line* as the mystery guest. Naturally, there would be a big scramble behind the scenes each time my mother failed to show up. Once my father was himself appearing on the show as one of the celebrities in the panel. He knew Sandy wasn't going to appear because he'd deliberately destroyed her morale moments before the car was to pick her up. He'd fired the worst shot of this kind just before John F. Kennedy's inauguration. He was to sing a song he'd written for the occasion, and my mom wanted to go with him. When my dad started in on her, she vanished into her bedroom in full dress and full makeup and stayed home alone in tears.

My dad made two films in 1962: *State Fair* with Pat Boone and *Pressure Point* with Sidney Poitier. Then Ross Hunter, out of friendship, put my parents in a movie together. It was a light comedy, a decent story, and it seemed like a good idea for my parents to work together. They would have the same hours, same weight in the film credits. And they were given a custom-designed pair of dressing rooms connected by a sitting room. His, hers, and theirs.

Ross Hunter remembers thinking it would be important for them to do a picture together because "Bobby was champing at the bit."

He couldn't believe that he wasn't as big a movie star as Sandy, which was ridiculous in a way because he was such a great, big, enormous chart singer. He had that great voice and that ability to bring people into his heart, and there was no reason for him to feel less than Sandy. But he wanted to make movies so badly, so I put them in a picture together called If a Man Answers, *and it became a big hit.*

I was never for the marriage, not because it was going to be a bad marriage or that I didn't feel that Bobby was good enough for Sandy. It was just that she was this innocent child. She never dated. She never knew what it was like to fall in love with a kid. And she never went out. She was more interested in her career than boys, and maybe that was Mary's influence. But Sandy was everybody's dream, and I had begged her to start dating. I tried to fix her up, but she didn't want to go out with boys. Maybe she was shy, maybe she didn't know what her future would bring as far as romance was concerned, and I'm sure that she felt she had plenty of time.

But then at sixteen, Sandy was so in love with Bobby. I liked Bobby, and the only reason I ever felt strange about him was because of the way he treated her. I was possessive of her and had no right to be. But all I wanted for her was the very best, and if she was going to have the guy, then nobody in the world could be happier than I, because she was breaking out of that womb of Mary's. Of course, I wanted a guy who just adored her and worshiped her, and Bobby was not that way. And Bobby knew that I disliked this about him, but we were friends and I decided finally that this was what Sandy wanted, so I shouldn't interfere.

I hope Bobby fell in love with her. I just found it hard to believe that anybody who loves someone would treat her the way he treated Sandy. Yet they were so darling together, you hoped that it was the real thing. I gave a party for Constance Bennett when we did Madame X *with Lana Turner. The world was there when Sandy came in with Bobby. And suddenly everybody stopped looking at Gypsy Rose Lee and Shirley Jones and Red Buttons and Ricardo Montalban. They turned to Bobby and Sandy and thought, Wow, that is some terrific couple. My heart just glowed. When Lana came in wearing three hundred and fifty thousand dollars' worth of diamonds and sapphires and God knows what, sure everyone looked at her. But I was so excited because there was a room full of these great big stars and everyone was talking about Sandy and Bobby. Sandy was wearing a marvelous gown. And Bobby was so darned attentive to her, it made my heart sing. I thought, Well, maybe it's happening. I wanted to think so. And I do believe Bobby loved Sandy in his way.*

If a Man Answers should have worked as marriage mender, but if anything, it made things harder for my mom. She worked all day on the film, and then stayed up all night with Bobby while he performed or did a recording session. She started arriving at the set looking like hell. She went to her doctor and told him she had no energy. He prescribed pills and my mom only remembers they were called "dexa-something." Now she had energy to burn and her weight was down. She felt great about both effects. She worked on the set all day, then was out with my dad all night. She was high, and the only thing that brought her down was a drink. Then she finished her movie and she kept taking the pills. She was too up to be interested in taking care of me or her husband and she didn't have a care in the world. Vegas again and more crazed gambling. Finally my dad had enough. He demanded to know what my mom was taking and grabbed her bottle of pills. My mom was defensive.

She said, "What does it matter what I'm taking?"

"It matters," my dad yelled, "because you've changed!"

My mom insisted she felt better and my dad gave her the bad news. He said, "You're not better to be around." He took the pills to the pharmacy and found out that they were speed. My mom says my dad was trying to help her, but she was out of control. She remembers he pitched out every pill she had and, as a last measure, kept me and the nanny in Vegas with him. Then he sent his wife home to Los Angeles with orders to put on weight or else.

Sanity was temporarily restored.

Then my dad decided to take on Universal in my mother's behalf. He told friends, "She's a beautiful girl. Got a wonderful feel for light comedy. She's a hard worker. They're exploiting her." Universal was making millions, and my dad just couldn't understand why he was making $25,000 a *week* and she was making $50,000 a *year*. My mom couldn't make him understand that the money was of no consequence to her. Every material need was satisfied. She had Kay and Jack and loved her Universal family. She didn't want to rock the boat. Steve Blauner sided with my dad, told my mom that in a few years' time, they wouldn't even remember her and that she ought to get paid now. Sandy acquiesced reluctantly, and Bobby bulled ahead. My mom's contract was renegotiated in her favor.

Around this time my dad had a car made for him that cost $150,000—that's about $500,000 in today's money. It was made for him by a dear old friend named Andy DiDia, who used to be my dad's driver when he was touring small clubs at the start of his career. Andy named it the "Bobby Darin Dream Car." It had fins, lots of lights, the works—and the first time Bobby drove it was to the Oscar presentations in 1962. My mom and dad pulled into line (Elizabeth Taylor was behind them), and the dream car started overheating, smoking, and then it stalled. My folks were in their formal attire, cameras were rolling, and their car was on fire. They had to get out and walk. Their relationship was kind of like that car: flashy, but not functioning very well.

I think in many ways my mom couldn't have been more disappointed in her married life. If her expectations for marriage matched those of the times, she must have imagined that she would be standing in a spanking clean kitchen cooking for her family, that her husband would come home after work and tell her about his day. When her expectations went unmet, she flailed out against Bobby. And he, like most men when faced with what seems to be a woman's unrealistic emotional demands, must have felt overwhelmed and clueless. "I'm faithful," he might have said. "I bring home a good paycheck. We have good sex. What more do you want?" The timeless, heartbreaking, universal question. But my mother could have enlightened him. "I want what we used to have," she might have said. "I want you to pursue me and make up songs and sing them to me, and I want one hundred percent of your incredible attention at least some of the time. It's why I married you."

My dad's sister, Vee, remembers that my mom had a terrible habit of promising to go somewhere and then backing out. It was especially bad when she'd say to Bobby's "nephew" Gary that they would go to the zoo, get his hopes up, then dash them when she changed her mind. But she would suddenly change her plans with adults, too, and night after night, evenings on the town would be canceled because Sandra didn't want to go. The big mystery to Vee is why people thought they wouldn't have a good time if Sandy wasn't there. Sandy was never a party girl. Ross Hunter tried to push her out into the world and failed. Bobby was having a similar problem.

Jack Freeman was very close to my mother, saw her many hours every day. He remembers that she was irritatingly capricious, and he has an opinion about what was going on in her marriage to my father. Jack feels that Sandy goaded my father intentionally—which she freely admits. A plan would be made to see a film with friends, and then, over dinner, my mother would say, "Bobby, I don't want to see the film."

And my dad would say, "But we've asked guests, the projectionist is coming."

My mother would shrug, say she wanted to go to a club on the strip. So, after dinner, they'd go to the Trocadero. Car pulls up to the curb. Everyone gets out. Bobby sees someone he knows outside the club and pauses a moment to chat. Mom says, "We're going in." Jack goes into the club with Sandy. Sandy orders a drink, waits a minute or two, then says, "Come on, we're leaving."

Jack says, "Bobby will be here in a moment."

Mom doesn't care. Flounces out. My dad hands the car keys to Jack, says, "Take her wherever she wants to go."

Jack says, "I'm driving you home. You have to be in makeup in four hours."

My mother says, "No."

Jack starts the car, asks, "Why do you do this?"

Mom says, "To stir things up. I'm bored."

Jack chides her, drives her home, leaves my mom standing in front of the house. He says now, "I love Sandy so much. When I say how willful she was, it's with sadness, not with criticism."

But it's not crazy to be critical of this behavior. My mom says over and over that she wanted someone to draw the line. She wanted the discipline to come from outside. I guess my dad didn't do it the way she wanted it. Or maybe he (rightly) didn't think that being her disciplinarian was his job. I know he was having a hard time with his wife. Mary's constant presence was a problem, the drinking was a problem, and that Sandy didn't want to play with his friends hurt him deeply. One time my dad ran into an acquaintance on the streets of New York. This fellow asked my dad what it was like being married to a movie star. It was uncharacteristic of my dad to talk about his private life, but he told this relative stranger that he was fed up with my mom.

Both of my parents were treating each other so brutally at this point, it's hard to have much sympathy for either of them, even harder to remember how sweet my mom was, what a good man my father was at heart. They were self-centered kids, each starving for attention. My mom was saying "Love me, and only me. You're the only one who can fill my bottomless need for love." And my dad was saying "Don'tcha get it? I'm going to die! I've got things to do, people to see, songs to sing. Look pretty and get off my back!" It's a classic example of women and men and their priorities. For her, the key thing was the relationship. For him, it was his work.

There came a time in 1963 when Dick Lord and my dad were finally working together at a nightclub and hotel in upstate New York. Dick remembers playing hearts with my mother, who always passed him the high cards because she didn't want to shoot the moon. He remembers her loaning him $20 and says he still owes it to her because he never saw her again after this engagement. Dick provides this even-handed, eyewitness account of the dynamics pulling at my parents' relationship:

☞ *We were at the Three Rivers Inn in Syracuse. The audience had a great time because they could see what was unfolding nightly in front of their eyes. Bobby ruined every show I did. He passed water guns out to the band. They drenched me while I was on. He yelled out the punch lines before I got to them in my stories. He had bras and panties lowered on a clothesline during my act. I decided to retaliate. I mopped the stage during his ballads. I repeated my punch lines into the backstage mike during his songs, and some of them fit in perfectly. The people went nuts. Bobby liked it too. The owner hated it, but the people loved it until the last night.*

By this time Bobby was very cocky. He also was a great ad-libber. He could bury Jackie Leonard, Don Rickles, the best. When Bobby got going, nobody would take him on. He could do impressions, and if he didn't get you with a joke, he'd get you with an impression of somebody. Bobby never started in first, yet people always wanted to put him to the test. During our last show, a drunk wouldn't let up. He was a local bigshot, and he knew management wasn't going to shut him up. So there was this drunk, and at first Bobby was funny. Humor didn't work. The guy was still saying, "Go fuck yourself." Then Bobby became sarcastic. This only got the drunk angry. Finally Bobby told him he was running everybody's evening and he was a schmuck. The guy shut up.

We were in the dressing room. There was a knock at the door. Charlie opened the door and the drunk slammed him in the face. Bam. Broke Charlie's glasses. Blauner saw that Charlie was bleeding. He belted the drunk, who fell down a flight of stairs. When the guy could talk, he demanded the owner call the state police. He was going to press charges against Bobby. The guy was one of the local hoods. The owner didn't want any trouble, so he talked the guy out of pressing charges and blamed it all on me. Bobby was the attraction.

I was the opening act. I was expendable. I never worked at that place again.

The first time I met Sandy, I was in awe of her. She was a star, and I was kind of shy. And then my wife, Ellen, and I and Sandy and Bobby would sometimes go out to dinner. And she was mostly quiet. She liked to laugh. And she had a sense of humor. I never saw her eat anything but salad with lemon on top. That's it. And most of the time she wouldn't finish it.

When Bobby and I worked the Three Rivers Inn, Sandy would come in to see the show, and the audience would go nuts. Not only did they get to see Darin, they got to see Sandra Dee. "She's right there. Myrna, that's her!" It was one of those. I'm not saying Bobby married her because she was Sandra Dee. He really loved her. But it was also to his advantage to be married to her. And she would sit in the audience. I don't know how many times you could watch the same show and be totally amused, because it gets boring. Sometimes when I'm doing my own show, I'm thinking, Oh, my God, I'm only up to this? I have to hear this again? How can these people stand it?

So I felt sorry for this girl who show after show would sit in the audience on display. And then after the show, Bobby would like to hang out. We wouldn't do bad things. We didn't inject heroin into our veins. We went to the diner, but once again, it's all guys—Barney the drummer, and Ronny and Behrke and me and Blauner and Charlie—and Sandy didn't like this. I don't blame her. But at that time, we were in our mid-twenties. "What do you mean she doesn't like it?" Bobby would say. He was like that.

We weren't toughs. We were educated kids, but show business is a tough business, and we all had so many mutual experiences and she was this beautiful young thing who was just plunked down in the midst of us all. And Bobby was a loyal friend. He loved his friends. He'd call us his "inner circle." He trusted us, was comfortable around us. Here was a man who really could afford to stay anywhere, and he'd come to my house and sleep in my son's bed, listening to his fish tank going all night. He would sleep on Behrke's couch. It was sad in a way. It was so touching that he wanted to be with us so much.

So we were at this same engagement in Syracuse, and there was a barbecue in the afternoon. Bobby was grilling hamburgers, and I was warming rolls on the grill. There was a girl in the chorus lineup who was sensational. Bobby Darin today would rise from the dead for a fine sexual hour. At the barbecue pit he says, "You know the girl in the line with the great . . ."

I said, "Yes."

He said, "She's upstairs. Nude. Begging to have sex with me. Please call her and tell her I can't make it."

I said, "Why? It's so unlike you."

He said, "I really love Sandy so much."

This was at three o'clock in the afternoon. After I did my spot, I always watched Bobby's show. Sometimes I had a suggestion or a line for Bobby, and he always listened to me. Not that he always agreed, but he trusted me. I went back to my room, took a shower. Bobby called and asked me to come back to his apartment, which I did. A lot of people were there, and Bobby was cooking spaghetti. And Sandy was really pissed. I felt awkward because she was yelling at him about hanging out with the guys, and even though I didn't want to be there, there I was. And she started in about his friends— who was more important, her or them. Then she mouthed off at Blauner. She said, "You know how many autographs I signed tonight?"

And Blauner got his dander up. He said, "What matters is how many autographs you sign five years from now."

So Sandy came back with a sarcastic accusation that Bobby was having sex with Blauner, which wasn't true at all. She was just being bitchy.

The room emptied: "Bobby, we're not hungry. See ya."

Blauner left, and it was just me and Bobby and Sandy and Charlie.

Then, boom. Bobby really slapped Sandy, and she went reeling back against the wall and crumpled to the floor. He said, "Don't you ever say anything like that to a friend of mine." It was four hours after he'd told me how much he loved her and told the girl in the hotel room to forget it. But that's how crazy their marriage was. He really tried, and she really tried.

They were trying, but they weren't communicating very well. At the end of March 1963 my dad began work on a film in which he would give the best performance in his career. It was called *Captain Newman, M.D.*, and Gregory Peck had the leading role. My dad's role was small but powerful, and Blauner, who had found this part for my dad, knew Bobby would knock everyone out with his acting. And he did. Since his marriage my dad had made five films, done major league club dates, cut a dozen and a half records, and had moved from specialized Atco to the giant, Capitol Records. He hadn't become a legend at twenty-five, but there are no living legends. And my dad—miraculously—was alive and well. In 1962 my dad told *Newsweek* that "the single biggest fallacy that had been built up is that I think the sun rises and sets on Frank Sinatra. I can tell you something. It rises and sets on my wife and my family." But less than a year after that article ran, his marriage was in trouble.

At the same time, March 1963, as my dad was working on *Captain Newman, M.D.* my mom finished *Tammy and the Doctor* for Universal. Jack Freeman remembers that she was enjoying her work: "She had been starring with young Peter Fonda. He played sort of a wild kind of guy. He would whisper rather provocative things to her, and she would say, 'Oh, Peter!' But it sort of titillated her, too. She thought it was fun, and she really enjoyed playing opposite Peter and being in this romantic role with him. And he had a great deal of charm, of course."

My mom was about to start a new picture on a loan-out to 20th Century–Fox. Her costar was to be Jimmy Stewart, and she was in a very happy frame of mind. She told Hedda Hopper, "If anyone had told me two years ago that I'd get up at five-thirty A.M. to cook for Bobby and the baby, I'd have thought them crazy. But I do it and I love it. My husband will eat anything I put on the table. . . . I was so in love with Bobby when we got married. Two years later I'd begun to feel that I couldn't possibly have loved him then because I love him so much more now."

She loved him so much that if my dad thought there were problems, Sandy was willing to do her best to make things work. At Bobby's suggestion she started seeing a shrink for her eating disorders, and once in therapy, the discussions turned to her marriage. According to my mom, the shrink said, "I'd like to talk to Bobby":

☞ *This was a Friday morning. And Bobby went in Saturday morning. I got a phone call Saturday night from Charlie. He said, "Bobby wants a divorce."*

I said, "What? Things are smooth. We're not fighting."

"He wants a divorce."

I said, "Where is he?"

"He won't talk to you."

I got this news through his brother-in-law. I was thinking, This is no joke, because Bobby didn't come home. Period. I didn't hear a word, so a couple of days later I went back to the therapist for my appointment. The doctor was beaming.

He said, "Well, your husband and I got a lot of things worked out. Things really went swimmingly."

I said, "He hasn't been home since he saw you."

He couldn't believe it. "But he was so encouraged by our conversation," he said. Then he said that he'd told Bobby that the problems weren't all my fault, and he'd explained what it was like for this teenager to have so much on her plate. He'd said to Bobby, "It's a little hard for her and quite understandable that she's having problems." But Bobby couldn't hear that. He couldn't accept that he might be at fault, too. So he left and I didn't see him for four months, which is the longest time we would ever be apart. I didn't think he would be back.

But here's something that Dick Lord told me recently:

☞ *Bobby said to me, "I think she's in love with someone at the studio."*
I said, "Are you crazy?"
He said, "No, no. I think so."
I said, "Well, if you think so, how can you say it so calmly?"
He said, "Well, what do you want me to do about it?"
I have no idea who he meant. The way he said it, "I think she's in love with someone at the studio." I was shocked for many reasons. First of all, I didn't think that. Second, that would never have occurred to me. Third, he said it so calmly. Fourth, he told me. And fifth, it was so ridiculous. And I remember then they started having their troubles, and she was drinking, and they separated. And I remember we were having dinner somewhere and he was just going to do Captain Newman, M.D. *And we were in the men's room and he said, "It's all over. I can't go on with this." And it was all over.*

My dad never confronted my mom with this Peter Fonda nightmare he'd invented. If he had, she would have been flabbergasted. My mom was happy. She felt light, and she was flirting. First time ever, and it meant nothing. But instead of telling my mom what he was afraid of, my dad went to see her shrink, Dr. Marmer. Then he had Charlie call my mom and tell her he wanted a divorce. He moved out and disappeared for long months without word. He didn't send Sandy a Mother's Day card, which she took to be significant. That told her it was over. Had my mom thought their marriage would resume, surely she would have had a different reaction when she realized three months later she was pregnant again.

9

Bobby and Sandy, 1963-1967

Bobby told me, "I'm going to mold the woman I marry into being the perfect wife. She's going to be the perfect person." And Sandy lived her life in Hollywood. She thought she was going to have a life like a movie script.

—RONA BARRETT

In February 1963 my dad picked up a new career. He bought New York–based Trinity Music from his former managers, Ed Burton and Joe Csida, for half a million dollars, and with this purchase Bobby Darin became a music publisher with a portfolio. In the mid-1960s commercial music was written and sold and recorded by a few dozen small, independent music companies. The way things worked, it was usual for these producers to hire writers on staff, rent a studio for a few hundred dollars when needed, lay down a track, take the demo out, and sell it to a singer or a group for a couple of thousand dollars. The tune could be out and on the radio in a week's time. With his own publishing company, my dad could publish and produce his own music and multiply his impact by having a stable of staff writers as well. My dad rented office space, put on a three-piece suit, hired some terrific writers, and went to work.

That was cool. But if I look at what was going on in my parents' marriage, I smell something fishy. My dad bought a business in New York, then a month later he suddenly wants a divorce? It was a shock to my mom, but this is where I come out: my dad knew he was going to leave my mother long before he did it. He had it planned.

Cut to Hollywood, California.

After Charlie Maffia called Sandy to tell her that Bobby wanted a divorce, after the word was more or less out in the world, my dad did finally get in touch with my mom by phone. He said, "I just don't want to be married anymore." That was the entire explanation.

My mom says, "Bobby was a really loving person when he wanted to be, and when he didn't want to be, he could be the coldest son of a bitch alive. Calculating, cold, and deliberately hurtful. I would do things to upset Bobby, but I would do things out of emotion. He never did anything out of emotion. That's why I didn't understand all these sudden separations. Suddenly he was gone, and I think you're supposed to know when someone is so upset that they're going to leave you. But I was always surprised."

My dad told columnist Sidney Skolsky that the separation "could go either way." But when the lonely weeks gathered into a month and Bobby had not returned, my mom understood which way it was going. When her anger wore off, she went into a state of shock. My parents owned the lot down the hill from the house where we lived, and they had had it paved over as a playground for me and my friends in the neighborhood. On the day reality struck, my mom went down the hill and sat on one of the kiddie swings. It was a damp day, drizzling a bit, and my nanny was alarmed at my mom's blank demeanor. She tried to summon her inside for a cup of tea, but my mom wasn't interested. The nanny was worried and called Dr. Marvin Goodwin. The good man came out in the rain, trudged down the hill, and brought my mom home. My mom only wanted to be by herself, but she was so depressed, people were afraid to leave her alone.

At around this time, the newpapers reported that when my mom showed up on the recording stage to sing a song for her film *Take Her, She's Mine*, she had a black eye under her sunglasses. I've asked her about it, and she says she walked into a door. What door? She was in a screening room with some unnamed studio person who made a move on her. Suddenly single-ish, my mom was an attractive target for wolves of all sizes and types. In this instance she said, "Excuse me," stood to leave, and walked into a door. I suspect she's protecting someone even at this late date, but I don't know why. The door did it. That's her story, and she's sticking to it.

There was also a bruise on her thigh that showed up at this point in the story. A different screening room accident; this time she bumped into the corner of the table while feeling for the light switch in the dark. My mom swears that with the exception of the slap Bobby gave her in Syracuse, my father never hit her. A former neighbor, who won't go on the record, hints at dark goings-on in my parents' house on Rising Glen but won't say more. So, all I can do is offer these explanations as my mother has given them to me. If she was drinking, walking into doors and tables doesn't seem so farfetched.

The story continues. The studio had offered my mom a vacation in Hawaii, and she decided she would take it. The luggage had been assembled. I was asleep in my nursery, and the nanny was on guard. There was a leaky faucet somewhere, and suddenly Sandy couldn't stand the sound. She decided to take one night to herself before her Hawaiian vacation. She called a hotel in Beverly Hills and booked a suite, took her cosmetic bag, and went to the hotel. She got a lovely room with a view, and for the first time in a long while she was alone. No baby. No nurse. No one saying "Are you all right?" She hadn't been sleeping well and fell fully clothed into bed.

Meanwhile Dr. Goodwin, who had been checking in on my mother regularly, called the nanny, who told him that Mom had gone to a hotel and had taken her medicine bag. Goodwin panicked, and the next thing my mother knew there was a house detective, hotel doctor, and Dr. Goodwin standing beside her, shaking her awake. They figured she'd taken an overdose and was dying or dead. My mother says she was mortified, and my heart does go out to her. Her small moment of solitude, crushed.

The vacation commenced, healed nothing. Newshounds noticed the bruises and reported that Sandy had been battered. This produced terse statements to the media from Betty, the PR lady who accompanied Sandy on the trip. All the newspapers could get out of Betty was that Sandy was on vacation and had no further comment. It was later, when she returned to Los Angeles, that my mom realized she was pregnant.

My mom loves kids, had had a few miscarriages by then, and if she and my dad had been solid, she would have been overjoyed to have another baby. But she was horrified at the idea of being with child and having her husband return to her because of that. So when once again she miscarried, there was relief mixed in with the sadness and disappointment.

Meanwhile, on the opposite coast, my dad had gotten himself a small studio apartment a few blocks away from the office. One of his first acts as a music mogul was to woo songwriter Rudy Clark to Trinity Music. Clark, still an unknown, played a demo record for Bobby, which Bobby said he would get produced in two months' time. He put Rudy under contract and got "The Shoop Shoop Song (It's in His Kiss)" produced on RCA. A couple of years later Clark and writer Artie Resnick wrote "Good Lovin'," which charted at number one for the Rascals. Terry Melcher, Bobby Scott, Van McCoy, and Kenny Young joined my dad's stable, and together, Kenny Young and Artie Resnick wrote the great hits "Under the Boardwalk" and "Sand in My Shoes." My dad had an ear for talent.

Steve Blauner was staying at his parents' apartment in New York when Bobby called and told him to meet him at the Copa at midnight. Steve was put out. It was late; he practically lived at the Copa, couldn't understand why he had to go there when Bobby wasn't playing. But he went and joined Bobby, who was sitting with Julie Podell.

Steve says he was bored. "I was watching this little trio in the lounge working, and with my peripheral vision I felt somebody was looking at me. It was Bobby, and I realized that the trio was why he wanted me there. After the show we went into the alley behind the club and waited for this trio to come out. One of them was Wayne Newton, and Bobby was excited about his talent. After that, they signed a recording contract.

The offices of T.M. were made up of a number of small writers' rooms and a huge conference room, which contained a big mahogany table, a piano, simple recording equipment, and dartboards on the wall. This is where my dad worked. Business hours were from nine A.M. until nine P.M., but after-work hours were until three or four in the morning. If my dad had an engagement at the Copa, he would leave T.M. at nine P.M. and return at two-thirty A.M. to go back to work. Today Rudy Clark lives in Florida. We had a long talk on the phone and Rudy was quite generous in sharing his memories. One of the times he remembers most is that my dad was so lonely, he would keep Clark trapped in this conference room with him during these impossible hours. The two would talk and play darts until wrung out, then Rudy would make his excuses and go home to his family. And Bobby would *still* beat him into the office the next morning. "His energy was unbelievable," says Rudy. "When I got in, Bobby was ready to roll. He'd have the lead sheets on the piano and the tape recorders set up." My dad wasn't about to sleep his life away.

Rudy Clark tells me that Bobby's emotional life was turbulent. If my dad spoke with my mother on the phone, which he did every couple of weeks, he'd clear the room before speaking and emerge from this conversation in such a terrible mood, the staff would just pack up and go home. If, however, the Reverend Dr. Martin Luther King called, which he did once or twice, my dad was in heaven—and that too would end songwriting for the day. The business between Dr. King and my dad had to do with entertainment. Dick Lord remembers that my dad introduced him once to Dr. King backstage after a performance by Harry Belafonte, but from what I've been able to gather, the reverend's relationship with my father was fairly slight. I asked Rudy why he thought King might have been calling my father, and he guessed that it was to arrange for my dad to attend a rally or an affair.

Nik Venet, a music producer and friend of my father's, accompanied my dad to Washington when two hundred thousand people gathered to hear Dr. King tell about his dream. Because they hadn't booked in advance and couldn't get seats on Washington-bound flights, Venet and my dad went to Washington by way of limousine. As a result, my dad took a licking from the press for being a "limousine liberal." In a letter my dad wrote to Harriet Wasser, he notes that the press said he'd demonstrated in Selma, Alabama, which he hadn't done, and that they had missed him at demonstrations he had attended. He said to Hesh, "It really doesn't matter, as I don't do these things for the publicity, but because I must do them."

Nik Venet remembers the time Dr. King came to see Bobby's second act at the Copa, came through the stage door and out on the floor where Bobby was performing. My dad stopped the show to introduce him. In Jeff Bleiel's *That's All: Bobby Darin on Record, Stage, and Screen*, Nik Venet says, "It was silent. Then two guys in the back, and I think they were waiters, started applauding, and then slowly the applause rode from the back to the front. They finally applauded, but Darin felt if he had introduced Sammy Davis, Jr., it would have been easier."

Bobby Darin's commitment to doing what he could to help end racial discord came from his heart. Rudy Clark, who is Black, says that he called my father "the vindicator" because he was out to champion the rights of Black Americans. "He was quite sincere," Rudy says, "and everyone knew that." Rudy adds that the two of them used to talk about what it meant to be poor, and my guess is that that was the common bond that led my father to empathize with the plight of the underprivileged. Throughout the years my dad was keeping Rudy in the studio at all hours, he was hanging out with other people as well.

Songwriter Artie Resnick also lives in Florida and in a phone conversation told me, "I was in awe of Bobby, and I used to hang out with him."

☞ *We went fishing a few times, and he felt comfortable enough with me to take his toupee off. I used to follow him around like a puppy. He would go into tie stores and snap his fingers and buy a couple of hundred dollars' worth of ties. He was cool. I remember once we went into Associated Recording, and some guy was using the phone near the door. And Bobby had that cocky kind of star thing, and the guy went, "Oooh, look who's here. The big man," and Bobby said, "Ooh, I love your office." The guy was sitting in the phone booth.*

Bobby was a lonely guy without Sandy around. After they got back together, Sandy came in now and then. It was fun when she came in. But when Sandy was involved, Bobby was a different person. He was like Mr. Star. He then had another position to maintain. My wife, Chris, and I were both signed writers at the time. I remember a session once when Wayne Newton was recording. Bobby had somebody there with him, and he was showing off. He said to my wife, "How'd you like that take?"

And she said, "I didn't like it."

And he said, "What do you mean you didn't like it?" He

turned very serious. And what began as an act turned ugly. Bobby berated Chris, and she burst into tears. Finally I just took her arm and said, "Let's go." The next day Bobby apologized to me. But that kind of thing was like a monkey wrench between us.

From talking with others who knew him at the time, I find the obnoxious side of my dad's personality coming up a lot in his behavior in mixed company. Several people have said that his personality changed when he was out for the evening, that he had to be the leader of the pack. My dad was with Rudy Clark and his wife, Bernice, and other friends one night when Bobby showed how big a jerk he could be. I've been told that Bernice Clark was a beautiful woman who had a sister and friends. For my dad, a social world that included Black women was exciting. Once at three in the morning, when everyone wanted to go home, my dad started working on Bernice. He wanted everyone to go with him to another club. Rudy tells me that his wife really looked up to Bobby, and she was in a spot. Rudy wanted to take her home, and my dad said to her about Rudy, "He doesn't deserve you." The last time my father told a woman that her man didn't deserve her, the man in question sent a couple of gunmen to the Copa to make my dad disappear, permanently. Rudy liked my dad, so he took his wife downstairs, went back up to the office, and had a shoving match with Bobby. Rudy made it clear that he was incensed that my father had been so audacious and so out of line. Bobby got the message and apologized.

I picture my father during this first half of 1963, struggling with anger and loneliness. I hear my aunt Vee's words: "Bobby was never truly happy. He was always trying to live up to his idea of what he was supposed to be," and that fits with what I see as his frustrations socially, professionally, and in the larger world outside himself. It was inevitable that he would try to make amends with my mother. He loved her and missed her and he missed me as well. But as different as they were, if they were going to make things work, changes would have to be made. Four months after my parents separated, my father called my mother and told her he wanted to put their marriage back together.

My mom says that Bobby was living in a studio apartment that was so small that when the bed was unfolded, you had to climb over it to get to the bathroom. There was another closet with a stove in it, and that was the kitchen. My mom left me in Los Angeles with a nanny and came to New York to try things out. She says she loved living in this one room with Bobby, and that his overtures toward her marked a dramatic change in him.

My mom says Bobby told her that maybe she'd been right, "that living with all of those people around us all the time was bad for our marriage."

☞ *I really didn't know if I wanted to go back with him. And Bobby would say, "You know, I think we can make it. I really do." We ate all our meals out and we brought home fresh fruit and we would lie in bed with the newspapers and eat nectarines. And we got to know each other better than we ever had before. We decided we were going to move to New York.*

It's funny how money is very important some of the time and sometimes it's not. We were having a glorious time in this one-room apartment, and now we're going to stay a little longer because we would be moving there. So the baby comes out with the nurse, and we went from one room to an enormous suite at the Regency, seven rooms connecting. And then Bobby was doing an album, and I had to be fit for a picture, which meant the studio flew people out with wardrobes. And then it was back: his entourage, my entourage. We were kind of walking on eggs, but we were never so happy.

One day Bobby says, "I've got a surprise." He went and bought a damn house on a lake in L.A.

I said, "You what? I thought we were moving to New York."

He said, "But you've got to see this." And he said the house was on Toluca Lake. It was three minutes from the studio, and my mother lived just over the hill, and I just looked at this man. I should have realized I had planned a life with somebody I really didn't know. He'd rented the house in Stone Canyon without telling me. He'd bought the house on Rising Glen next to Ross Hunter without telling me, and now he'd done it again. And that's how we came to live at Toluca Lake.

My dad now realized that if he wanted to resume his marriage, he'd have to give up nightclub performing in the interest of having a stable and more conventional married life, and—even more expensive emotionally—he would have to give up his beloved friends. My dad never did things halfway. Things came to a head for my dad and Dick Behrke when they played an open-air concert at an amusement park in the Bronx called Freedom Land. It was raining that night in July. The audience was soaked, and Bobby, declining an umbrella, was drenched along with his fans.

Dick Behrke tells this story:

☞ *By this time, everything had started to get very tense. Bobby was about to leave the road because Sandy didn't want him traveling anymore. She thought the whole atmosphere of the road was detrimental to their marriage, and there was a lot of unhappiness around. Sandy was a movie star, he wanted to become a movie star, and he hadn't had a hit record in a while, which may have had something to do with his mood. We were working at Freedom Land, and it was a rainy, cold, crummy day. Everyone was in a bad humor. And Bobby was particularly nasty in public to our drummer. And I was kind of like the leader of the rhythm section, kind of like the union boss. Even though I was hired by Bobby, I always felt that I was responsible for the guys we traveled with. These were our own guys, not people we picked up. Plus, I really hate people picking on underdogs. Every once in a while Bobby would snap at a waiter, and I hate that. And I would really call him down for that because it turned my stomach. I hate that from anyone. I hate that from stars worse than anyone.*

So, after the show I went to him, and I was yelling at him: "That was a really crummy, rotten thing to do." As I was yelling, he was lying there with his oxygen tank, which was not an unusual sight. It was business as usual. And he

197

got very mad at me for not caring that he was sick, that I only cared about the drummer. And I didn't even pick it up because we were all used to seeing Bobby in this condition. He obviously was feeling worse than usual, but not knowing that it was worse than usual, I was fulfilling my role.

After this incident, I settled in Brooklyn. Bobby was then living on the West Coast, and he had an office now on both coasts. And I didn't talk to him. I didn't call, but I never called anyone. He was always the one who would call. And then it filtered back through Dick Lord that Bobby was pissed at me. Lord had been to see him and told me that Bobby said, "I don't care what happens to Behrke. He can starve to death in Brooklyn for all I care." I didn't even know he was angry.

Bobby had promised all sorts of things when we were off the road: "Don't worry, I'll take care of you," which was meaningless. He didn't take care of me, nor could he. But as a result of his saying it, I think he was feeling some guilt that he was leaving the road, and I was out of a job, and anyone else involved with him was out of a job, too. Mostly he imagined this problem. I had accepted my new life in New York and had become an arranger. I hated L.A., left L.A., so I was fine. Bobby and I had had words before, and they always passed. Mickey somehow sensed that this one wasn't passing. Bobby sent birthday gifts to our son, Jay. And I kept sending them back. I'd say, "Talk to us before you send a gift to our son." When I found out he was mad, then I got mad. And we didn't talk for five years.

Dick Lord was often the go-between between Bobby and his friends. He recalls the same incident:

☞ *Behrke could be a pain, and every time something would happen between him and Bobby, both of them would call me. So after Freedom Land Bobby calls me and says, "You're not going to believe it. I'm lying there on a table getting oxygen. I feel like I'm going to die, and I have this thing over my mouth to get oxygen, and fucking Behrke is telling me that the musicians have to get ten cents a mile for the drive from New York to the Bronx. Do you believe this? This is my conductor? I'm his best friend. He's talking about ten cents a mile for the bass player."*

And two minutes later Behrke would call. "You're not going to believe it. You know, musicians are entitled to a certain travel expense, and I must fulfill the contract."

I thought Behrke was nuts sometimes. We'd be working somewhere, and after the show we'd have to get together the tons of stuff we'd brought with us. There was all the music and heavy instrument cases, and I remember once that Charlie was loading the station wagon. I didn't have anything to carry but my tuxedo, so I was helping Charlie and so was Bobby. So Bobby turned around and said, "Uh, Richie, you want to give us a hand?"

And Behrke said, "I don't do that. I'm the conductor."

There was always, always something like that. Behrke could ruin a sunset. I could understand Bobby's frustration. There was a singer named Julius LaRosa. He was the first star I was working with. I called up Behrke and said, "I'm working with Julius LaRosa." And he said, "Nothing like working with a star on his way down." I'm telling you, he could ruin a sunset.

I remember when we were all kids together, trying to make it. Now, 1650 is a show business building, and usually standing in front is a middle-aged maniac. He shrieks like a monkey, makes weird faces, curses at you, and nobody cares. After a while you don't even notice him. This building was my first acting class, my first theater. Every day Bobby and I used to hang around that building and make up improvisations and scenes.

Bobby's favorite magazines at the time were of the **True Detective** *type. We would use the basic plot from one of the stories, add our own imaginations, and do the scenes on the elevators and in the hallways. The elevator door would open* *and someone would come in, and Bobby would say, "Stand still, or you're dead." And the door would open again, and I'd run out, and Bobby would shoot me, and I would roll around in the hallway, dying. In another building one might register surprise when coming upon something like this, but not in 1650. I learned a lot from this playacting. I think we all did.*

Ten years later, in this same building, in Bobby's suite of offices, Bobby told me he would only spend time with Sandra Dee and wanted no part of friendship with me. He said, "Come back when you have eighty thousand dollars and we have something to talk about." He was actually hurting me to drive me away as he did with Behrke, whom he loved and about whom he said, "I don't care if he starves to death in Brooklyn." With me, he didn't quite carry it off. He started to cry. So did I, because I knew he couldn't really handle giving up all of his close friends because of a failing marriage.

He said, "I have to be with Sandy. I have to devote myself to Sandy. I can't have friends. She's upset. I just have to work it out with her, just be with her." And then he said, "Everyone I've ever tried to help has stabbed me in the back."

I asked if that included me, and he said, "No, but the innocent must suffer as well as the guilty."

And I said, "Okay." I was stunned. In spite of my sadness I realized at this point that the man was not playing with a full deck. He was missing at least two jacks and a nine. I started to leave, and I was crying. He said, "Wait, we'll leave together." As though nothing had happened. We descended in the same elevator we used to play cops and robbers in. He had just insulted me and humiliated me, and I had lost my best friend. When we reached the street, I stood on the sidewalk, not knowing what to say. He jumped into a cab, rolled down the window, and screamed, "Remember Pearl Harbor. Loose lips sink ships." All cheery.

It was the last I saw him for two years. I called Behrke

and said, "Behrke, you'll never believe what just happened . . ."

Harriet Wasser says that my father's decision to stop performing had as much to do with his health as it did with his marriage. She was at the Freedom Land concert, sitting with Sandy and Nina and Vee. She adds an interesting piece to the story. Apparently, while Bobby was performing he was in so much pain that the concert was called off in the middle. The audience grumbled and booed, and the doctor who saw my father afterward told him that if he continued to perform, he would die. A week later he went into the hospital for an overnight stay and canceled the rest of his planned tour. It's interesting that Behrke either doesn't remember this or didn't see what Hesh saw; interesting because people did not really believe that my dad was sick. He had this phenomenal energy, he didn't bitch about aches and pains, and he had acquired an abrasive star personality that made people say, "Oh, he's being a pain in the ass." It wasn't until six months before his death, when his color had gone green and he'd lost a third of his body weight, that people started to believe how sick my father was.

Whether it was because of his health or his desire to have a stable marriage, or both, my dad decided to stop performing. It was clear to Steve Blauner that he wasn't going to be needed anymore. Steve says he understood, perhaps better than Bobby, the strain his career was putting on the Darin marriage. Steve was still unmarried, and he used to go over to my parents' house every day. He liked to play with me, and he felt warmed by being around this family unit. He said, "Whenever business came up, Sandy's eyes would glaze over," and he says he made my father promise that when he came over, there would be no business talk.

Steve says, "It was around 1964 when we broke up our business arrangement. We'd had about five years together, and basically he wasn't going to work anymore in clubs. He was going to be a family man, and I had other things I wanted to do now. I got this job at Screen Gems, and I gave Bobby a private number to the phone line in my office. He was the only person who had it."

Steve went on to produce *Five Easy Pieces* and *Easy Rider*, and my dad made his friend and publicist, Dave Gershenson, his new manager.

My dad now had his new life as a combination family man and mover and shaker. He came across a song called "Danke Shoen," which had been put in his hands by a producer who meant for Bobby to sing it. But my dad had a better idea. He gave it to Wayne Newton, whose career took a sudden and unforgettable turn upward when he recorded that song. Wayne says, "Bobby was a big brother to me. I loved him and I always will."

Many people thought that "Danke Shoen" would have been Bobby's next "Mack the Knife," and that he'd made a mistake by giving it away. But Bobby was building his business, and he never looked back. Interestingly, even though he was reconciled with my mom, friends observed that he was still lonely. It seems to me that his loneliness was understandable. He was a gang leader, and he had no gang. He tried to group the people at T.M. into a gang of sorts, but most of these people had families, and they did what they had to to keep my dad happy—but they were on his payroll. He didn't talk to them about his wife, and he didn't tell them that he was going to die. As Hesh has said, "If you didn't know him from the beginning, you couldn't really know him."

The separation from his closest friends was not only shocking to my dad's sense of security, he was also missing the enormous charge he got from entertaining an audience. And where he wanted to feel close to my mother, he felt how different they were instead. The 1960s were marked by passion: social upheaval, the war in Vietnam, the assassination of a president. My father was powerfully affected by the times; he had demonstrated in Washington, accrued an FBI file ninety-six pages long, and put himself on the line for equal rights for all Americans. But as it was when he'd married her, Sandy's world was the studio and her family.

In 1963 the *Saturday Evening Post* painted this portrait of my mother:

THE ODD ODYSSEY OF SANDRA DEE

*The Former Alexandra Zuck Now Ranks as Queen
of the Screaming Teenies*

The mobile villa, sleek and baby blue, rumbled up the scraggy mountain from its home site, Universal Pictures. Snaking around the curves of the Hollywood Hills, it finally came to rest on the 20th Century–Fox lot in Beverly Hills. On Stage 8, where movies are made, it was unhitched.

Inside the mansion on wheels all was gold and glass, blue and beige, antique French and movie-star moderne. There were white rugs, paneled walls, custom-built furniture, a lavender French phone, some stereophonic gadgets, an air-conditioning unit, and a refrigerator. In short order a quaint parade filed inside: makeup men, hairdressers, assistant directors, reporters, photographers, publicity folk, assorted Pomeranians and poodles. And atwirl in the middle of it was the villa's tenant and sole reason for the extraordinary pother, a Tinkertoy named Sandra Dee. . . .

Sandra Dee ranks as a noblewoman of Hollywood, the only female to share every top-10 box-office poll with Liz Taylor and Doris Day. She is the chatelaine of a Sunset Boulevard pad with wall-to-wall furs, a Sargasso Sea of gowns, a soda fountain, projection room, three servants, four dogs, and electronic burlar controls. When she is too tired to pilot her red Thunderbird or black Lincoln Continental convertible, the studio provides her with a chauffeured limousine. She is, in short, A Big Star.

Since Sandra's acting skills might be equated roughly with those of Troy Donahue, the reason for her exalted station is not immediately apparent. But as Sandra explains, "It's glamour. I wear pretty clothes, have my hair done well, look clean. Older people see me as the daughter they would like to have—there's no scandal about me. With young people, maybe it's identifying with what they think they are or want to be, or—with boys—what they hope to have. . . ."

One could hardly trivialize my mother more than did the writer of this article, and superficially he wasn't far off the mark. My mom's world was as deep and as wide as her studio contract. It was as high as her love for her family. But I think she was doing pretty well under the circumstances. Sandy was nineteen, more or less keeping her shit together, and—while dealing with a suffocating mother, a mercurial husband, and a pretty big problem with alcohol—she was dutifully fulfilling the values of the people who employed her. Their idea of a social conscience was to present a glamorous, scandal-free dream girl as a model to the American public. Sandra Dee was in the glass bubble, and it was all that she knew.

My father had once thought he would mold my mom into the perfect person for him. It was arrogant of him and wrong to think that he could or should do that, and now, because he wanted to keep his wife, he would have to mold himself into a more conventional husband. Rona Barrett told me recently that Bobby always thought he was in control when he was involved with a woman. The truth, as Rona sees it, is that the women my dad got involved with were in control, not Bobby, but neither they nor he ever knew it.

My dad's movie career hit its highest point in 1964 when he was nominated for an Academy Award for his role in *Captain Newman, M.D.* His reviews were exceptional. This one in *The Hollywood Reporter* was typical: "Bobby Darin has a difficult part and one long trying scene that will undoubtedly put his name up for some of this year's acting honors." He was on the short list for best supporting actor, but the Oscar went to Melvyn Douglas for his part in *Hud*. To be so close and not win must have been a crushing disappointment. My dad once told "heartthrob" Jimmy Darren that if he looked like him, he could be the biggest thing in Hollywood. Darren laughed at him, of course. It was a ridiculous remark. But this is what my father was suffering from. Al Pacino, Robert De Niro, and Dustin Hoffman had not yet arrived. Character actors were not stars. Leading men were handsome then: Cary Grant, Rock Hudson, Warren Beatty.

Nevertheless, when my mom was chosen to star in a film entitled *That Funny Feeling* around this time, she suggested the studio cast Bobby as the romantic lead opposite her. Warren Beatty had already turned down the role, so she tried to convince the studio to pair her with her husband. My dad, I'm sure, felt threatened at the idea of taking on a role intended for Beatty and no doubt resented every bit of this negotiation. That Beatty had turned down the film, that his wife had gotten him the part—but how could he say no to a starring role? He told the press he'd take second billing to his wife any day, but I'm sure the episode stung his ego. The film was, in a word, forgettable. My father hadn't recorded a hit record since "You're the

Reason I'm Living" had reached number three eighteen months before. That dearth of hits, added to his Oscar miss and his withdrawal from live entertainment, undoubtedly made playing second fiddle to Sandra Dee depressing. And, as always, he took his anger out on those who loved him most.

My aunt Vee recalls visiting my mom at the house in Toluca Lake:

I liked her very much, more than I liked my brother. I loved my brother, but I liked Sandy better. With me and Bobby it was "Hello, put your hands up, we're about to do battle." Sandy's big mistake was that she became part of the family, so Bobby treated her the way he treated us.

Bobby was the love of Sandy's life, and he genuinely loved her. I'm saying that as straight as I can. He loved her, but there were parts of the relationship he couldn't handle. A big part of the problem was his need to be the center of the revolving universe. Sandy was a human being with her wants and needs, a star in her own right.

The two of them constantly fought for control in the relationship. Sandy generally used the baby. Five minutes before Bobby had to go onstage, she'd tell him his toupee looked like a rug. Or, "The baby's not well! Look, he's sweating, ooh!" But she had a sweater on him and a blanket on him, and she had the heat up to eighty-five degrees. And this was Las Vegas. And Bobby would drop everything and fly home. Or Bobby would say, "We were invited to George Burns's house for dinner."

She'd say, "I'd love to go. That's wonderful." A week later, when it was time to go, he'd have to go alone. "No, I don't really feel like it," she'd say. "I'm not in the mood." That was her way of controlling.

Bobby used the "If you love me" kind of controlling. If you love me, you'll take all the abuse I hand out only to the people who genuinely love me and you'll come back for more. And he got something from my father. Once everyone was at the dinner table, he would pick on something and run it into the ground.

One time Sandy had invited me to dinner. I was not much

for going over to their house. My adoration for Bobby was onstage, not one to one. Sandy said, "Come early. We'll sit, and we'll talk, and we'll swim." And we sat, and we laughed. We had a good time all day. And then Bobby came home. I remember we had steaks for dinner, the kind you could cut with a fork, and I was enjoying myself because I'm really into food, when in the middle of this lovely dinner Bobby started in on my friends. That he didn't like them. That my friends weren't worth my little finger. And I retaliated. I told him his friends were shit and why.

Sandy tried to cool things off. She said some innocuous little thing, and Bobby turned on her as I'd never seen him turn on anyone. She sat there, and the tears just started to pour. I jumped up and said some real nasty things to him that were all true. I told him what a miserable motherfucker he was. Then I said to Sandy, "Don't invite me when you know that the freak's going to be home. He's a low-life motherfucker, and I don't need to be around this kind of a person."

Sandy had nowhere to go. I felt so sorry for her. She was like a fly caught between two spiders.

One was Bobby. The other was her mother. Mary was warm and wonderful all the time, but she kept a very tight hold on Sandy. She never let Sandy go. I adored Mary. Everyone did. You couldn't help it. She was like Bobby, very lovable. And when it came to Sandy, Sandy was the center of the universe. Mary did the same thing to Sandy that our family had done to Bobby. The sun rose on Sandy when she got up in the morning. It set when she went to bed at night.

We'd all play cards together, and Mary would cheat for Sandy. She would cheat! She was so into that this was her kid and her only child, she would do all sorts of outrageous things. But the sin was that she never let Sandy become an adult. She fed Sandy's ego and covered up for Sandy so much, and she thought it worked to Sandy's benefit. It didn't. It worked against Sandy in the most destructive way.

Sandy could not admit she had a drinking problem as long

as Mary couldn't admit it, and Mary categorically couldn't admit it. Mary had a child who was a movie star. And Sandy was the most beautiful thing you ever saw. Sandy with no makeup, when she first woke up in the morning, with her hair going every which way, was enough to make a person get a gun and kill herself. She never photographed half as pretty as she really was. She was breathtaking. She was magnificent looking.

Mary wasn't a fool. She saw this child and decided that everything had to be geared toward Sandy's career. Everything. So it followed that if Sandy had a drinking problem, she might not get another movie. So Sandy didn't have a drinking problem. This was Mary's thinking and where her heart was—she was doing the very best for her child—even though her child was twenty and thirty—that she possibly could. There was no help for Sandy until Mary died, because as long as Mary was there to cover up, Sandy got all the reinforcement she needed. Her mother would take a drink out of her hand and say, "One drink is more than enough. You can't have a second drink." Second drink? That's the sixth or eighth drink that I had seen go down.

This book was meant to be a quest to realize my father as a man, and what I am finding is that the more I learn about him, the harder it is to hang a label on him. He was both cruel to my mother and protective of her. Some people found him arrogant and obnoxious. Others found a kindness in him that did not ask for credit or thanks. Dick Clark remembers that my dad helped him out of more than one emotional slump and that Bobby was there for him when he was going through a heartbreaking divorce.

Clark adds, "I was desperately trying to figure out how to get my career from one stage up to the next one, from Philadelphia to L.A."

☞ *I did a little pilot presentation of a show idea. And I did it on location in and around Philadelphia, partly in my own house. Bobby was the first guy I called. I said, "I need somebody of star value in this thing." And he came down and he sang and accompanied himself on the piano just so that I could have something more than the other silliness I had. He had to schlepp down from New York to do something that was obviously not top grade. He never hesitated.*

That was the Bobby Darin I knew. He was lavish in his love and praise. He'd give gifts to everyone in the world. I knew him intimately in my heart, but not on a day-to-day basis. We didn't have to touch base regularly. If he were alive today and I called him and said "Tomorrow, you've got to help build another floor on this building," he'd say "Wait, I'll get my hammer, and I'll be right over."

George Burns told me this:

☞ *When Gracie died, Bobby slept in my bedroom with me for three or four nights. He asked me to do that, I didn't ask him. He just came here and stayed. Bobby slept in Gracie's bed, and I slept in mine, and we talked. We talked about Gracie, about show business, about what I'm gonna do without her. He didn't give me advice because that kind of advice nobody has to give, because there was nothing I could do about her. Life must go on whether you want to or not. When you love someone, you cry, you keep crying. I couldn't stop. I couldn't sleep. When Bobby left me, he said, "Sleep in Gracie's bed. You'll feel better." I took his advice, and that did the trick. After that I could sleep.*

Songwriter Bobby Scott sometimes wanted to kill my abrasive father, but when Scott's wife was pregnant Bobby came through with concern and cash. Rudy Clark got into shoving matches with my dad and at the same time credits him with helping him learn to structure songs so that they would sell. Artie Resnick acknowledges the "monkey wrench" between them and says that he was a better writer just for being around Bobby.

One of the things I like best about my father was his political activism, which was uncommon for celebrities at that time. By 1965 African Americans were in a rage about discriminatory treatment at the hands of White people in this country. My dad was urgently impelled to help, but like most Whites, even the most enlightened, he missed one of the most critical points of the movement: although Black people were torn between the divergent philosophies of militant Malcolm X and pacifist Martin Luther King, they wanted Black leadership, not White.

Rudy Clark remembers when Watts, a Black section in Los Angeles, was a tinderbox.

Bobby saw the wrong that was being done to Black people, and he saw himself as some kind of leader who could go and speak to Black people. And we had a fight over this when the riots broke out in Watts. I had family out there, and I went out and saw that the mood was very ugly. When I came back I told Bobby about it and he became convinced that he should go out to Watts and get on a platform and speak because the people weren't listening to anybody. I tried to tell him it was bedlam out there. The people weren't listening to Martin Luther King, and they weren't going to listen to Bobby, but he insisted that he had to go. His mind was made up.

Our argument became heated. Bobby claimed that I was prejudiced and I just didn't want any White faces out there, and he had the whole thing wrong. I knew he would have gotten hurt if he went out there. One night he did a show at the Copa, and he was planning on leaving for California in the morning from the office. He had his baggage and tickets and briefcase and left them in the office while he went out to eat. While he was gone there was a phone call from Miss Dee or someone in her household, I'm not sure, but I told her what was going on and she said, "Stop him any way you can."

There was a way I could lock my door. Bobby didn't know there wasn't a key, so I took his luggage and tickets and briefcase and put them in my office and pulled the door to. I left a note on the door that I had gone out to get a bite, and I'd be back. When I came back, Bobby was standing in front of my door. He was so mad, his face was red. I told him I'd put his things in my office because there was no lock on the door to his conference room. He saw through this story and started screaming that I was trying to force him to miss his plane. We got into a big shoving match, and he hit me on the side of the face, not a bad lick, and it turned into a scuffle. It was a pushing thing, mostly. We wouldn't really hit one another. After it was over, I gave him his belongings. I was going out the door, and he came out behind me. And he just looked at me and we both started laughing, and we let it go at that.

If he had gone to Watts, he wanted to say that the Black people were going about things the wrong way. That their leaders had let them down, that there was no leadership and they needed to organize. And he would have said that they needed a representative to speak to the higher-ups in government. He knew he was one of the rare White entertainers selling in the Black market, and I suspect that in his mind he thought he could be a spokesman for social change, like Eldridge Cleaver or Rap Brown. But it would not have worked for Bobby.

I didn't go with Bobby when he went on the marches to Washington, but when he came back he always seemed surprised at what had happened. He had gauged the mood of the people wrong. The mood was "Black was beautiful," and we wanted our own leaders. We didn't want White spokesmen. That time had passed. And all of the Black leaders were saying the same thing: No matter how well-meaning a White person was, it wouldn't serve the purpose as would a Black person showing that the Blacks could lead themselves. And Bobby was always disappointed when he came back from rallies that they didn't give him any type of special treatment or allow him to take the grandstand. He would be bitter about that for a while, and I tried to explain to him not to take it personally.

Bobby had the seeds in him for some kind of greatness, and I guess he sensed this. I imagine had he lived longer and become the legend in the music field that he dreamed he would

*be, he would have wanted to expand and go farther. I believe
he saw the social crisis as a kind of vehicle to do bigger things
and greater things than being an entertainer and writer.*

But at this point in the story, my dad was a businessman. He looked
at the bottom line of his business and was pleased. In his first year,
T.M. had grossed over $300,000 and he'd brought in over $450,000
for fiscal 1964. He told the *Los Angeles Times* that he wasn't singing,
he was working a five-day week at the office—and that he hadn't done
a club date in almost a year. "I won't leave my wife and son for that.
And anyway, I want to be an actor, and if you want to act, you've got
to be in L.A."

My mother's career had slowed during the first years of her marriage
to my dad. She only made one film in 1964 and slipped from the top
ten box office listing that year. And then something happened that
shook whatever precarious hold my mother felt she had on her marriage. In 1965 Universal cast her in a film called *A Man Could Get
Killed*, which was to be shot in some fishing villages in Portugal and
in Rome. My mom did not want to do this film, which necessitated
spending months away from my father. My dad had a fear of flying,
traveled as often as possible by train or car, and she knew he wouldn't
be visiting her on the other side of the Atlantic. Combined with some
out-of-town business of my dad's, they would be separated for four or
five months. She loved him a lot, and I think she worried about what
my dad might get up to if she was gone for so long. She begged the
studio to use some other female lead in her place, but she was refused.
As she boarded the ocean liner with me and Mary and the nanny,
Irene, she felt disillusioned that her "Universal family" had let her
down.

From aboard the steamer, the *Leonardo da Vinci*, my mom wrote
this letter to my dad:

> Hello Angel—
> I love you—and feel so stupid writing to you. I feel like
> a stranger. Oh, well, maybe it just takes practice. I'm sure
> I'll get a lot of that this trip.
> After talking to you yesterday, Dodd and I got kind of

blue, but I'm trying so hard to be a "big lady" that I took him on deck and soon we both felt better. Honestly honey— I didn't think he'd take it so hard. The first night he woke up crying about you and asking me when we'll see you and believe me, that was a dilly to explain. But as the days go on, he's sort of accepting it. (You can bet your life, I'm not, though. I miss you more each day.) I know what you'd say to me now ("Sandush, you've got to be a big lady."). Bobby, I sure am trying to be. . . . The baby really has been a trouper. Today the weather is rotten—and your son is taking it like he was the captain of the ship. In fact, the way they treat him, you'd think he was. That kid sure wins people over.

Anyway darling—Mama and Irene send their best and you know you have all of Dodd's and my love.

All my love,
Sandush

My mom told the press this would be her last film abroad unless my dad was her costar. She said at the time, "I'm tired of being homesick. I'm appearing in a comedy, and all I want to do between scenes is cry. Sure, Bobby and I talk on the phone every night, but anybody who tells you a phone call can cure lonesomeness has rocks in his heart. I break into tears as soon as the receiver hits the hook."

While she was away, the movie magazines cooked up stories about my dad being out with other women. No names were ever mentioned, and no witnesses have verified this. I only know that when my mom returned with me, I went flying off the gangplank (we were docked, of course) into my father's open arms. As my parents were negotiating their marriage, the business of commercial music was changing.

Said Bruce Pollock, author of *When Rock Was Young*: "The arrival of the Beatles signalled the end to rock 'n' roll's age of innocence. The Beatles were sophisticated, hip. They brought with them visions of megabucks." The Stones followed the Beatles, then came the Beach Boys, and these groups not only captured the fevered hearts and souls of America, they transformed the nature of the recording business practically overnight. These groups were writing their own music, not buying songs from little guys. What used to be a business of writing songs and selling them for a few grand now became a jillion-dollar industry.

Publicist Connie DeNave noted in 1981 in Pollock's book that when my dad and Paul Anka did the Copa, they started a rush from teeny-bopper audiences to that of nightclubs. She adds, "The record business today is a total joke compared to what it was in the fifties. In the fifties the simplicity of the business was magnificent. It was a seat-of-the-pants operation; guts and gambling made the business. When you wanted to find talent you rode the subways. When the subway doors opened up, you'd listen to hear if anyone was practicing in the station. There were no showcases like today. Today the record industry is run by accountants, bookkeepers. In those days you spent thirty-seven thousand dollars on a record and it was life or death. Now they spend a million dollars and they don't blink an eye."

This seismic shift in the music business shook out many small publishers; they either sold out or went bust. T.M. was solvent, but I think that rather than stand on the sidelines, my dad decided to return to what he loved most, performing onstage. He said to the press, "I'm a singer of songs, and anything I do other than that is an offshoot." It had been ten years since his first record was produced by George Scheck on Decca and my dad decided to make the most of his return.

In January 1966 my folks and I traveled in a specially outfitted car of a Pullman train. The larder was full of champagne and caviar, various members of my parents' entourage were on board, and we set off on my dad's tenth-anniversary tour. The Deauville in Miami was first stop, then we headed out to Vegas. There my dad played at the Flamingo, where even after years of absence, he still held the attendance record. Spectacular reviews followed each of Bobby's performances, critics using phrases like "hot as a pistol," "explosive performance," and "the Compleat Entertainer." One paper said, "Bobby Darin gave the greatest performance of his short, spectacular career." But the big climax was to be at the Cocoanut Grove in Los Angeles.

Opening night at the Grove was attended by rafts of celebrities: Steve Lawrence and Eydie Gorme, Mia Farrow, Ben Gazzara, Eddie Fisher, Anthony Newley, Andy Williams, and Ryan O'Neal to name a few. I remember it was a very festive evening, a big deal for all. I was wearing a custom-made tuxedo, so I looked like a clone of my dad. My mom was regal in emerald green, her baby blond hair piled high on her head. And the two of us sat ringside.

My dad's performance was electrifying. Praise rolled off the presses, hailing my dad's triumphant return to the Grove. Said Belle Greenberg of the *Citizen News*: "Bobby's return to the Cocoanut Grove Tuesday night was a real smasheroo! He wowed the star-filled supper club with his talents, of which there are many. . . ." But for me, the highlight of the night was not the singing, quipping, or musical excellence. It came when my dad walked to the edge of the stage and lifted me into his arms. I asked him a riddle, and the audience laughed. I liked the attention so much, I thought I was going to do the show with him every night.

"Dodd was five and he was outgoing with the family, but when he was around strangers, he was really quiet," my mom remembers.

☞ *The night of the opening at the Grove, we put him in this little tuxedo, and he was really nervous. "Do I have to go on stage?" he asked. I assured him he didn't. The photographers took pictures of him, and he was very serious and very proud. We were at ringside, and when Bobby's performance was over, everyone started clapping. Bobby came out to take a bow, but Dodd thought he was coming to us. My son put his arms up, and Bobby leaned down and scooped him up.*

Bobby asked Dodd what he thought of the show, and Dodd said, "Good!" And then he told his dad a riddle, and the audience was laughing, and I was thinking, My God, this kid is really something.

Then Bobby said, "I think we've run out of material. Do you have anything to say to me?"

Dodd said, "Yes."

"What do you want to say to Dad?"

"I love you, Dad."

Not only did I cry, the whole damn place was in tears. You could hear a pin drop, and no one applauded until Bobby put the kid down. And for me, it was the first time I saw

Dodd as a person on his own. It was always "Take my hand when you cross the street" and "Watch out for the baby, the baby, the baby." Then suddenly the baby got up and took over. That wiped me out. It really did. Dodd became Dodd. And we were a family. Three separate people who all went together. It was a really happy time. The happiest time I ever had. It really was.

So naturally, almost predictably, if my mother was happy, she was about to get dumped. She was making a film called *Doctor, You've Got to Be Kidding.* She starred with George Hamilton and Bill Bixby, and she liked them both very much. The picture was going great, and once again my mother was unprepared for a phone call from a friend, telling her that my father wanted a divorce. This is all she can come up with by way of explanation:

We had so many separations. People would call us for dinner and say, "Are you two together or not?" Well, this particular evening we were doing great. Anthony Newley was married at the time to Joan Collins, and they invited us to their buffet Sunday night dinner. George Hamilton was there and other people I knew, and I was sitting with my agent, who was very friendly with Warren Beatty. I brought Bobby his dinner and was sitting at his feet, listening to the conversation, and Warren said, "How are you?" So I started to talk to him. My agent interrupted and suggested that Warren and I get together for lunch. I said, "Okay." Later Bobby and Warren and I went off on our own and had a conversation about the movie business. It was all very nothing, but Bobby was very quiet in the car on the way home. The next morning Bobby said something very strange. He said, "Do you know something I'm realizing?"

"What are you realizing, Bobby?"

He said, "When you finally grow up; you're going to be so much harder to live with than I am."

I still don't know what that means and yet I do know it

215

had to do with Warren Beatty. Bobby had always been my everything: husband, tutor, father. There was no women's lib in our house and I liked that. Now Bobby saw that I was having a business conversation with a good-looking man who had quite a reputation around town. Suddenly he saw me as a woman, and that scared the hell out of him. I think it made him feel insecure about me and about us. But I still didn't see it coming. I remember this time as one of the happiest periods of my life.

I went to work at Metro the next day, and when I returned home that evening, there wasn't a stitch of Bobby's clothes in the house. No clothes, no note, no message, and no phone call once again. Then Dr. Goodwin called—Bobby always got other people to do this dirty work for him—and told me that Bobby wanted a divorce.

My mom had started this picture as happy as she could be. The film was a comedy with lots of fun and dancing. She'd never danced before and was having a blast. My mom has often said that she is incapable of hiding her emotions off camera. If you found her smiling in a snapshot, she was happy, because if she was upset, she wouldn't stand for the picture. Suddenly a lighthearted Sandra Dee, dancing, clowning, and palling around with the crew, was monosyllabic and down. The press came out to take pictures and Sandra fled. No one could understand what had happened to her, and she was pressed to tell the director what was wrong. She said she was hiding from the press because she didn't want to tell them about the divorce she was going through.

There was a scene in this film that was similar to the scene in *Come September* where my mom had to slap my dad. In *Doctor, You've Got to Be Kidding* she had to slap Bill Bixby. My mom loved Bill Bixby, thought he was wonderful, and it was scripted that she had to hit him. Came time to shoot the scene, same thing happened as before: her hand froze in space.

My mom remembers that the director pleaded with her to slap Bixby:

I was trying to keep my emotions under control, and it was almost impossible. I thought I was going to have a nervous breakdown. I said, "If I break down now, I'm not going to stop crying."

The director said, "Don't even think that way." So I tried to do what would make everyone happy. I did the scene, but my acting was mechanical. Finally they decided just to keep the cameras rolling, and everyone had to be quiet because the red light was on. The director said, "You know, Sandy, I wish you'd leave your problems at home. The crew is tired. I'm tired. And because you have problems with your husband that I really don't care about, we're going into overtime."

Well, I did the scene. Not only did I break down, I slapped Bixby, and I walked off the set. I never stopped crying. I didn't drive home. I was driven home. It hurt so much because the whole crew heard everything. Six months later I learned that I gave Bill Bixby a concussion, and he was in the hospital, but nobody wanted to tell me. When I saw him again, Bill laughed and said, "Well, don't ever say you can't hit."

A calendar of events:

The tenth anniversary tour began in January 1966 at the Deauville.

In February Bobby played the Flamingo.

In March he had his triumphant return to the Cocoanut Grove.

In April my dad played the Copa.

In May the *New York Daily News* reported Sandy and Bobby's separation.

I smell that fish again. My dad got his business life on track first, then clapped his hands and made my mother disappear. For a little kid, divorce is horrible. As I sift through the clips and the evidence, I don't know any more than she does what went wrong. Was it her drinking that drove him away? Was it jealousy over an imagined flirtation, or that he saw she wasn't dependent anymore? Or was he jealous that her star was bigger than his?

Ross Hunter holds this view of my parents' relationship and its downfall:

When Bobby left Sandy, she was not only heartbroken but completely shattered by the way he did it. She loved him. She had never known another man, and Bobby treated her like nobody else, including me, ever did. Afterward we wanted her to go out with people like Troy Dohahue and Johnny Saxon, some of the other kids, but she didn't want to. She went into a shell. I do believe that Mary's relationship with some of the people around the house was not all that savory, and I think Bobby treated her very badly. I don't care what happened when she was younger, and I don't care what happened when she was alone with Mary. Nothing attacked her like her great love for Bobby.

Bobby probably loved her. Who am I to say what's in someone's heart? But I do believe that Bobby was her destructive point, too. I think that instead of being thrilled about her success, he was in competition constantly. But the most important thing for me was not what Bobby was doing to her, but the fact that she was in love with him. And this was her crutch for the world. The minute he left her, she was unable to walk, talk, eat, or do anything. She became like a fetus in a womb. She couldn't get out. And I do believe Bobby loved her in his way. But it wasn't my way. I know that he treated her badly. I resented it, and I would have killed him a couple of times if I had had the opportunity.

Sandy was the best mother. She was wonderful to Dodd. Her life became Dodd when there was no life with Bobby except for the intervals where he decided he was going to become a supplier with a little sex. Sandy was doing one picture after another, and it was working for her because she took the baby with her. And, of course, Mary was always there, which was not a good thing. When Sandy was in front of the camera, Mary was there to take the baby, even though they also had a nanny. Mary was always there. I told Sandy to go out and meet with a lot of people who were dying to invite her and take her out, and she wouldn't go. She was a social outcast, and it killed me. And her mother didn't help her.

Sandy did not know how to take care of herself. She always had her hairdresser, her makeup man, her mom, so there were no decisions for her to make. She became completely atrophied because she didn't have to do anything, and if she attempted to do anything, Mary stopped her. Mary said, "Honey, you don't have to. I'll do it. I'll take care of it. I'll do this." Sandra never even combed her hair. She never dressed herself. She never put on her own makeup. And that was my fault, too. I take a lot of the blame. But at least I tried to push her out. Sandra was not allowed to come out and be seen, to be heard, except as a movie star. And she sheltered herself. The minute she was finished with a scene, she'd go right back in her dressing room, and her mom okayed it.

I think Bobby Darin was a great big recording star. He had a voice that knocked everybody out, and I think that, too, was a mirror for Sandy. Sandy adored him for many reasons, but one of them also was that he really had made it. And she didn't have a jealous bone in her body. She never thought in those terms. But I think Bobby was frustrated. He wanted so badly to be an actor. He was really so good in Captain Newman. *I was thrilled that he was, and I thought maybe he could go on. But there was a conflict for him— whether he should be a singer or an actor, whether he should be Mr. Sandra Dee. Bobby finally realized that he just wasn't going to be a great big movie star. And I think that also had a lot to do with his feeling about Sandy. All of a sudden to wake up and say, "I don't want to be married anymore"? I think that's ridiculous.*

Whatever the reason or reasons my dad left my mother, one thing we know for sure: he was terrible at breakups. The first time, it was Charlie Maffia who told my mom she was getting a divorce. Three years later Dr. Goodwin gave her the news. Witness my dad's dismissal of Dick Lord and Dick Behrke. Other, similar stories abound. Dick Lord observed that Bobby was short two jacks and a nine. My mom, too, detects this flakiness:

☞ *If he had an affair, the divorce might have made sense. But this wasn't the case. He always left me just as I started a new picture and only when things were good between us. I loved him, and it's very hard to put into words how and why two people fit. It was an emotional thing. And there were external attractions, too. I loved the way he moved when he was performing. When he did a show, when he was on top of everything, no one could beat him. And yet he couldn't dance with a partner to save his soul. This is going to sound funny, because I do believe he may have been crazy, but what I loved most about Bobby was his mind. And his pride. Damn, I respected his pride.*

Bobby was the love of my life, but when he left the last time, I thought to myself, I can't do this anymore. It's like beating yourself on the head.

On March 7, 1967, a year after they separated, my mom got her divorce, custody of her son, and the Darin community property except for T.M. The courtroom was littered with press, and the judge thought the scene was disgraceful. The *Los Angeles Herald Examiner* ran this story:

SANDRA DEE DIVORCES DARIN

According to actress Sandra Dee, who got a divorce this morning, her marriage to singer Bobby Darin ended on a drab and sour note.

"He just woke up one morning and didn't want to be married anymore," she told Superior Judge William E. MacFaden.

Asked specifically if Darin said that in so many words, she said he did. Then he packed up all of his belongings and left their home.

"I was terribly nervous and upset," she concluded in her brief testimony at the default hearing.

Her attorneys filed with the court a property settlement signed last Feb. 16, under which Darin will pay $1,200 per month for the support of five-year-old son, Dodd.

DREAM LOVERS

Miss Dee and Darin were married in Elizabeth, N.J., Dec. 1, 1960. They separated last May.

I think I know why my parents were attracted to each other, but for the last twenty years I've blamed my mother for their divorce: her boozing, that she wasn't as intellectually inquisitive as my father, that she was capricious and argumentative. For the first time I think I see what my father was like as a husband. He wasn't a victim, and he wasn't a prize. He was complex and difficult, and like my mother, he was doing the best he could do. Last night I called my mom and thanked her for being a good mother to me, for being my mom, and she started to cry. I hope she knows that I was apologizing to her for all the years I silently took my father's side against her.

When a reporter asked my dad why he and my mom split, he said, "I don't know. Sandra doesn't know. Nobody knows." But there was forethought in this separation. As my mom says, "Bobby never did anything out of emotion." So I can't accept "Nobody knows." These are my thoughts. I think my dad grew and my mom didn't. I don't mean any disrespect toward my mom. They came to their places in the world from different paths. My dad looked around and saw the riots and the strife and Vietnam and was affected, and my mom, at least outwardly, was not. And he couldn't stand that. Maybe he didn't give her credit for being deep enough. Maybe cataclysmic events did move her, but she didn't seem to respond. She had her world of the studio and her films, her makeup man and her publicist. That's what she knew.

And there was something else that injured my dad, although I'm not sure he'd ever have admitted that it affected his relationship to my mother. Sometime in 1966 through 1967 he went into a shell for a while. He didn't want to go out socially. And my mom said, "This is silly. What is this all about?"

And he said, "I'm tired of people asking me what I'm doing. 'What's coming up next? What are you recording?'"

She told him he was being ridiculous, that he'd already done it, that he didn't have anything to prove. She said, "Just live your life and don't let other people's stuff get to you." She just couldn't understand how with all of his success, my father could feel embarrassed that he didn't have a hit or a movie or something in the works. Fifteen years later when my mom's most recent films were in the "Classics" section of the video stores, she said to me, "I understand what your father was dealing with. I understand it full well." But at the time my parents' marriage broke apart, my dad was a businessman. The Beatles and the Stones had made him—at the age of thirty, thirty-one—passé as a recording artist. And my mother was a big star.

I'm left wondering what my dad was afraid would happen if he actually told my mother why he no longer wanted to be married. He could talk the ears off anyone, so why couldn't he do that? Maybe he didn't want to hurt her, although he certainly did. Or perhaps it was because of that pride of his that my mom loved so much. I have an idea that my mother wasn't what my dad wanted her to be—and he didn't meet his own expectations for himself. He was disappointed in them both. Perhaps he couldn't address the failure of their marriage because it hurt his damned pride too much.

So he ran away.

10
Sandy, 1967-1972

Sometimes I feel like a has-been who never was.

—SANDRA DEE
Newark Evening News, *February 1967*

———

Never look back. Be aware of what's behind you, but don't look at it.

—BOBBY DARIN
New York Post, *September 1967*

———

When all is said and done, except for Dodd, they had nothing in common.

—HARRIET WASSER

My parents had fundamentally different views of their roles in their own lives. To put it simply, my father made his destiny. Destiny

223

made by mother. Sandra Dee was discovered for her beauty and made into a movie star. "I didn't plan it," she said. "It just happened." Then, because she was in the public eye, Bobby Darin found her and decided that she would be his wife. Without Universal, without Bobby Darin, one can imagine that some other studio and/or some other man would have appropriated Sandra Dee. It's harder to imagine that my mom would have forged a life of her own making. My dad, as has been amply discussed, planned everything. He used and pushed through his limitations, made more of himself than his natural gifts would have ordinarily allowed. It is understandable that my parents' divorce affected each of them in characteristic ways.

My mom couldn't imagine a future with any man but my father. "I'm not a dater," she told the *Newark Evening News* two months after the divorce became final. "I won't go out with a man just because I recognize his name over the telephone." Her escort of choice was Jack Freeman, whom my mother described as "a lovely older man, like a father." My mother made one more film for Universal, *Rosie*, starring Rosalind Russell, and arrived again in the top ten box office star category. Then, because she was forced to do a TV movie she didn't want to do, and because she felt Universal was generally ignoring her career interests as they cast her in one flimsy comedy after another, she refused to renew her contract with them. As a result, she shot her career right through the heart.

My mom was the last of the contract actors, and as she was leaving Universal, the entire business—the movies themselves—was changing. My mom had been making light comedies of the Doris Day type, and America loved them. Between 1967 and 1970 the public wanted a different kind of film: *Easy Rider*, *Carnal Knowledge*, pot-smoking guys on bikes, sex and counterculture. And my mom never made the transition. Part of her problem was one that sank the careers of other actors who got their start as teenagers.

My mom told the press: "If you started at 18 or 19 like Ann-Margret, it's easy to be accepted as an adult. I started at 14 and made a name at 16. It's hard now to play a 'Gidget' or a 'Tammy.' The fans I had at 15 are now 22. They're getting tired of seeing me on a houseboat. . . . I did the whole cotton candy sitting on a satin pillow routine. It's so hard to establish an image and you work damn hard to get it. But once you've got it, baby, just try to get rid of it."

In June 1968 my mom said her bitter farewells to Universal. The press noted that Sandra Dee's contract had been the very last one, and when it went unrenewed, it marked the end of an era. I think my mom understood what was at stake. She said at the time, "I've got to break out of the rut the studio put me in: I can't bubble my way through lightweight scripts anymore. I've got to go on and grow up or stop. I don't want to wake up at thirty and find I have no security." But I don't think she ever imagined that her career would just stop dead.

Sandra Dee had been the center of attention for so long, I'm sure she'd come to believe the fuss that was made over her was her birthright. She'd always been a hard worker, shown up on time, did her bit, never caused trouble. Six scripts a year were delivered to her door. Promotion, packaging, all of it was taken care of by the studio. Then there was no studio and no support. My mom was offered scripts but didn't know which to choose. She never learned about packaging and hustling and producing her own films, taking control of her career, which is what actresses do today. And she had nothing in the way of an alternate career or other resources to substitute for the yawning hole that would open in her life when there was no mother-studio.

My mom is a sweet person, never hurt a fly. She was also naive; she truly believed that the people who befriended her at the studio were her real friends. It came as a surprise to her that when it all ended, those people disappeared. She realized later on that the relationships she had were for the most part work relationships, and it was a painful realization. Most entertainers, because of the struggle they've had to get to the top, become callous from rejection. My dad was a perfect example of that. He'd experienced a lot of pain, doors slammed in his face before he made it. So when people did things to hurt him, he understood that that's the nature of business. My mom's career came so easily, modeling to screen test to movie star and everyone kissing her feet. Her rise had been relatively effortless, and later in life she had to learn the true nature of things: that she'd been a commodity. And she didn't have the skills or the confidence to make friends at the post office or the PTA.

My mom started in the movie business earning a few hundred dollars a week. By her seventh year with Universal, her salary had escalated to $2,000 a week. If she worked fifty weeks a year, which she didn't, she would have earned $100,000 in 1966. In 1967 her salary had jumped to $5,000 a week, and then in 1968 it was all over. She was off the payroll. My mother, who had never written a check, had never worried about bills, probably thought she was well fixed financially. My dad didn't pay her alimony, but he gave her the house and other property and child support. My mom invested in an oil well scheme that bankrupted many actors in the seventies, and it wiped her out.

At the age of twelve my mother was making an impressive wage. She never thought about money from that point on, and many would say she defined conspicuous consumption: Rolls-Royces, fur coats, small fluffy dogs, and a pink Tudor-style mansion on a lake that had belonged to Mary Astor and then Frank Sinatra before it became our home. In the seventies life would change dramatically for my mom. She was no longer a breadwinner. At the age of twenty-six, she was yesterday's news. It's shocking how quickly Sandra Dee disappeared from the public consciousness. Two years after leaving Universal, the *Los Angeles Times* asked: "Does anyone remember the Tammy movies or the Gidget flicks? Alas, an era has passed without many mourners except those who stay up late to see the re-re-re-runs. . . ."

Jack Freeman wrote to me with his thoughts about how the end of her relationship to Universal affected my mother:

☞ *In thinking back over the years we spent together, I would say that the studio was the key element that gave Sandra stability and form to her life. Her contract with Universal provided her with everything: work, money, celebrity, a huge loving family, all wanting one thing—to make her feel secure, loved, beautiful, and happy. And if anything was causing her worry or unhappiness, the studio was there to counsel, hire or fire, smooth the way, remove the obstacle, indulge the whim. Really do anything to please her, provided, of course, that her films continued to make money. And they always did.*

Whatever her so-called private life, the studio was a constant, always there for her. Then she ended her contract with Universal and was cut adrift. The Queen Mary *sailed on, and Sandy was in a small lifeboat, no pilot. No real destination.*

Nothing about her past prepared my mom for her present. Like those cartoon critters who run off a cliff, legs spinning in open air before plummeting, it would take a while before reality truly dawned on her. She had longed for time off from her work, which she had always seen as just that, work. And she loved being a mother. My dad, who had always been on the road a lot, continued to spend nights with her. He bought a house a few blocks from ours, and I saw him nearly as much as I had before. My mom was comfortable with this arrangement. She felt that she shouldn't tie my father down but undoubtedly believed that he would be back of his own accord when he was ready.

Enter Mary Douvan, who came back into my mother's life in full force, this time dropping a bomb she'd been carrying around for seven years. The story reads like a soap opera, but it's true—and tragic. Charlie Sinatra was an old school friend of my mother. He was also my grandmother's lover and had been since 1960—just about the time my parents made *Come September*. It was into Charlie's arms my grandmother had gone for comfort when she left the Drake Hotel with the dogs on the eve of her daughter's marriage. And she and Charlie had been living together ever since. The story Mary put out to the public was that Charlie was a tenant of sorts, and that she was helping him with his acting career. In order to maintain the illusion that Mary was his mentor, Charlie called her Mrs. Douvan.

It's not easy to hide a relationship of this sort; in fact, the only people who didn't know what was going on between Charlie Sinatra and Mary Douvan were Bobby Darin and Sandra Dee. But the platonic version was the official version, and Charlie hated the secrecy. He loved Mary and didn't want to be living a secret life in a house his friend Sandy was paying for. He wanted Mary to live with him on his salary, be seen together as a couple, and he begged my grandmother to go public with the truth, which she refused to do. After some violent episodes in which he both struck my grandmother, and threatened to kill himself, Charlie Sinatra disappeared. Weeks later his decomposing body was found in a motel room. The suicide note told of his sadness, love, depression, and, finally, resignation.

When my grandmother confessed the truth at last, my mother was shocked and horrified that Mary had lied over the course of seven years. She asked my grandmother why she'd kept this awful secret that had probably caused Charlie to take his life. Mary said, "I didn't want to hurt your career." True, Mary was seventeen years older than Charlie, and this kind of older woman—younger man romance wasn't trendy then. But my mother was horrified. She knew no one would have cared. Sadly, appearances were always more important to my grandmother than reality, and this type of denial would play a large role in her own death years later.

Since the first moment Bobby met Mary Douvan, there were rumors that they had had an affair. Mainly this was a result of the campaign my father waged in order to get to my mother in the first place. It's been conceded by all who knew the parties concerned that my audacious father would have had to win Mary over in order to get close to her precious child. But did the wooing stop there? Rona Barrett says that when my father called her from Rome and said that things were complicated, he was alluding to an involvement with Mary:

> ☞ *But, let's say they didn't have an affair. Bobby was capable of flirting to the point where you thought that maybe you were having an affair with him, that he was taking you out and wining and dining you and he kissed you on the cheek or he kissed you on the lips. And he hugged you, and he held you in a way that if there was no penetration, you almost felt there was penetration. I could see why Mary was furious when he started dating Sandy, whether they slept together or not. Bobby had a proclivity for older women, and Mary was cute, peppy, and only thirty-three. She was the perfect age for Bobby.*

If Mary and Bobby had been involved, it would explain my grandmother's three-month fit of fury when Sandy and Bobby announced their wedding plans. Some have suggested that my dad and my grandmother may have still had something going on while my mom and dad were married. This is hard to believe. But one fact won't go away: My dad and Charlie Sinatra disliked one another bitterly. Charlie was actually banned from our house. At one point Charlie was going to shoot my father, literally kill him, he was so pissed. Where did this anger come from? My mother feels that Charlie was attuned to some chemistry between my father and grandmother and was livid about it. She says if something had ever gone on between Bobby and Mary, she would never have known. She wasn't sensitive to subterfuge.

The story of Mary and Bobby ends inconclusively here. I tried to find out what I could, not out of prurient interest, believe me. The idea of my father and grandmother sleeping together is a horrible notion. But I followed it up because if the story were true, it would put a rather hard edge on both their characters. Fortunately, I'll never know. But it was a fact that in March 1967 my parents' marriage was officially over. My father started building a new life that included overnights with my mother and outings with me. My mom says that Bobby would show up and tell her that he wasn't feeling well and that he just wanted to sleep on the couch. Then the couch wouldn't be comfortable, so he'd move into the bedroom. My mom still loved my father with all her heart, and I've got to believe he still loved her. But what he said to the press was, "Sandy and I are divorced as husband and wife, but we are not divorced as parents."

My mother made a pretty awful film in 1969 called *The Dunwich Horrors*, and after that, she had no work. The effect of losing her career and getting a divorce meant that she had no support system except her mother, and while for most of her life she had tried to separate from her, now separation was virtually impossible. She depended on my grandmother for everything, and my grandmother rose to the occasion. She went to work selling real estate in Beverly Hills. She spent the rest of her time being with my mother or doing things for my mother. She was selfless. My mom would have probably made do on this meager sustenance: me, Mary's constant presence, my dad's overnight visits, and her belief that one day he would return for good.

Then, in 1970, my mom found she was pregnant again.

She had a reasonable hope that my dad would be pleased by the news and that everything would be all right. With a new baby, maybe the marriage would be renewed as well. But she miscarried, and when she lost the baby, she lost the illusion of my father's devotion. Of the miscarriage, my dad said, "It's just as well. It wasn't meant to be." That broke my mother's heart.

"I knew that Bobby loved me as best as he could," she says. "He just didn't love me well." Her desire for him ceased overnight. And although she would never again be with my father, she kept the door firmly locked between herself and other men.

My mother says that she *did* go out with other men, but that I rejected men she might have chosen, that I would say, "He's not my father." I remember doing this once when she was going out with a muscular TV star, but the relationship was very short-lived anyway. My mom says she didn't want to go out with men after my father, but she didn't want to go out with men *before* him, either. She didn't want to go out at all but claims if she had met someone she could have loved, she would have overridden my objections. Of the years when she wasn't working as an actress, my mom says that she had a job: being my mother. And this, she says, was all she wanted. When she's been drinking, she admits she loved being a movie star. By comparison to what she had when the lights went out, who could blame her?

In 1971 my mom sold the pink house on Toluca Lake and bought a more modest dwelling on Rexford Street in Beverly Hills. My father had a major operation that year and, after a first burst of energy, he became quite sick. Sometimes when he spent time with me, he asked to spend the night, and my mother refused him. Friends of his have said that my dad wanted to remarry my mother, but that she no longer wanted him. It's understandable that if she no longer loved Bobby, she couldn't allow him to use his illness as a way into her heart and home. It was during the last two years of my father's life that he handed my mom the tan valise and told her to keep it in the event something happened to him. Not knowing whether the suitcase contained securities, drugs, or dirty postcards, my mom put it on a shelf in the hall closet. And there it stayed until after he died.

11

Bobby, 1967 - 1969

Song for a Dollar
by Bobby Darin
(From his album, *Direction*)

How many steaks can you chew, boy?
How many cars can you drive?
How many moon-in-June type tunes can you write
before you're a lie?
. . . .

For 32 full seasons, you've been playing the game.
Part of the plan, you flim-flam man
to get some fortune and some fame.
But, how many times can you lie, boy?
How many games can you play
before you get down (to business)
and say what you've got to say.

As his divorce became final, my father found his feet, shook himself off, and then took stock. It was 1967. He'd acted in ten films, gotten two Grammys, and written seven top ten songs and title songs for five motion pictures. He'd won the Foreign Press Association Award for

231

Best Actor for his role in *Pressure Point* and had been nominated for an Academy Award. He'd sold two million albums and fifteen million singles. He owned a house in Beverly Hills with pool and tennis court, drove an Excalibur car, and had a successful music business with offices on both coasts and in Europe. "On top of all this," writer Sally Hammond reported in the *New York Post*, "Darin has recently begun cutting a figure socially on rarefied levels. Last August Princess Grace of Monaco invited him to headline the entertainment for her annual Red Cross gala in Monte Carlo."

My dad danced with Princess Grace and on this side of the pond was enjoying the sexual revolution. When I look at newspaper clippings from 1967, I find "Bobby Darin is just mad for Janice Branco." And "Didn't Susan Oliver have a date to go out with Bobby Darin in Reno?" And "Together again at Mark Goddard's house were Patty Foster and Bobby Darin." And "Bobby Darin's date after his ABC-TV special last night was Anjanette Comer." He was playing the field all right, but his most oft-noted partner was Diane Hartford, the gorgeous twenty-five-year-old wife of millionaire Huntington Hartford, and she and my dad had an affair that generated headlines from New York to Vegas to L.A. and back again. From the *Los Angeles Herald-Examiner*: "Didn't mean a thing that lovely Diane Hartford saw Bobby Darin a few times. I talked to her husband, Huntington Hartford, who said, 'Diane and I are very much together. I know she saw Bobby Darin. It was perfectly all right with me.'" Hmmm. Bobby and Diane could run, but they couldn't hide. The press was dogging my dad everywhere. He was, by any standard, famous. He'd come a long way from shining shoes, and he'd never had to get his face fixed after all.

Social life aside, Bobby Darin hadn't reached the goals he'd set for himself, and as a consequence, he reexamined his goals. He told *The Hollywood Reporter*, "I thought [*Captain Newman*] would open up a whole new career as a dramatic actor. Four years later I'm still waiting for another good role." But he wasn't really waiting, he was reconfiguring. Report upon report about my father at this time finds him— for lack of a better word—mellowing.

In November 1967 Ethel Kennedy invited journalist Barbara Howar to work on a fund-raising telethon to benefit the orphans of Washington's Junior Village. My dad was appearing at a theater nearby, and he volunteered his time. Howar had promised to take charge of one of the celebrities promoting the benefit. She chose my father, and the two formed a special friendship instantly. Later Howar joined my father on tour and wrote about her experiences with him in her book, *Laughing All the Way.*

This is an excerpt:

Bobby Darin and I became the best of friends. For all his show-biz flamboyance, he was a self-styled intellectual, a young man with a conscience and the Elmer Gantry ability to convert those who did not share his convictions. I know it would make better reading to report that I began thinking of the world's problems through an exposure to John Kenneth Galbraith or at least Paul Newman, but it was Mr. Darin, the teen-rage of the fifties, who led me through the maze of bigotry in which I lived and backed me down on every narrow-minded point, and made me care.

When I was not working on my Journal *article, I traipsed gypsy-like over the nightclub circuit where Bobby was performing. We ate greasy hamburgers and talked race in Philadelphia with Flip Wilson; discussed censorship with Tony Franciosa in Puerto Rico, before we started a brawl with a bar full of San Juan hookers; and talked life and times with Sugar Ray Robinson, Gore Vidal, and Liza Minnelli in a Copacabana dressing room. . . . Many times a day he would shout, "Open your eyes and look around." I did. . . . Bobby Darin did fine things for my soul. At the very least, he showed me I might have one. . . .*

Before he died, my father told me that the awards he'd been given during the course of his career were not important. Most he'd received for "just showing up," all of which were stored in boxes. But his mention in Howar's book meant a great deal to him. He gave me his copy of the book and inscribed it "Dear Dodd. Remember back to our discussion about awards. These pages are an award of which I am very proud and is of lasting value to me. Love, Dad."

My dad's image was changing inside and out. *The Hollywood Reporter* noted in December 1967: "Today's Darin is not the same young man whom the public saw as a somewhat brash, sometimes too-sure-of-himself performer. He has depth and thoughtfulness. 'I don't set goals anymore,' he says. 'I take things as they come. I have no complaints. I have a wonderful little boy, freedom, financial security and there's always some new area to explore. . . .' "

Feeling as good as he was feeling about his life, he could not have possibly been prepared for the bomb my other grandmother was about to drop that February in 1968. He was playing at the Latin Casino in Cherry Hill, New Jersey, as he had done many times before. But on this occasion Nina Maffia decided to tell Bobby that she was his mother. My aunt Vee was in on this decision. She and Nina drove two hours to the hotel my dad was staying in, and Vee was in the lobby when the news went down.

I've reconstructed the conversation between Bobby and Nina from an interview Nina gave on cable TV a year before she died and from what she told Vee:

> **Nina:** Sit down sweetheart, I have something to tell you.
> **BD:** (sits)
> **Nina:** Are you still going into politics?
> **BD:** Yes, I'm going back into politics in a few days.
> **Nina:** I don't think it's fair not to tell you. I'm not your sister. I'm your mother.
> **BD:** (a beat) You must be the strongest person in the world. That's why you always said to me when I was little, "If you do that again, I'll rap you, I don't care how big you get."
> **Nina:** (comments, "It was dawning.")
> **BD:** Who's my father? Not Charlie?
> **Nina:** I'm sorry, sweetheart, but that information will die with me. Your father never knew I was pregnant. The only person who knew who he was was Mama [Polly], and it's going to stay that way.
> **BD:** My whole life has been a lie.

I don't believe for a minute that this news was so crisply delivered, so well received, but let's say that it is essentially accurate. I try to imagine my dad's feelings as he processed this astounding announcement. One, he had spent a lifetime battling his sister; now he had to imagine that she'd carried him inside her body and given him life. Two, his beloved Polly, who had inspired him and had told him never to lie, wasn't his mother—and had lied. Three, he had formed his image of himself as the son of a beautiful vaudevillian and a Mafia hit man. Very romantic. So who was he now? Four, who was his father? He must have prayed it wasn't Charlie, whom he'd kicked around as his valet. Five, Why was he being told now? What was the real reason?

For a deeper explanation, I turn the page over to my aunt Vee.

☞ *I'd like to tell what I know about the mystery of Bobby's parents. My grandmother, Vivienne {Polly} Walden Cassotto, was one of the most wonderful people who ever lived. She was brilliant. She was beautiful and had a unique and genuine way with people. When she was with a person, she made them feel they were the most special person in the world. She inspired all of us. She inspired Bobby, but she was not his mother. My mother, Nina Maffia, was Bobby's mother, although she didn't tell Bobby until he was thirty-two years old.*

People say, "If Nina loved Bobby so much, why didn't she tell him sooner that she was his mother?" I never got a totally satisfying answer to that question, but I believe my mother was coping as best she could with what was a difficult problem. At the time Nina got pregnant with Bobby, it was a very bad thing to be an unwed mother and a very bad thing to be an illegitimate child. The kid would have been abused by everyone. They would have said, "You little bastard. Your mother wasn't married to your father. You're no good." My mother wasn't about to have that happen to her kid. Furthermore, once the lie was told that Polly was Bobby's mother, the two women made a pact never to tell Bobby the truth. "Bobby must never know." That's what they agreed.

Not being able to tell Bobby that she was his mother devastated Nina. She loved him and she was proud of him, and when he made it, oh, my God. She still had to keep it a secret. When Bobby decided to go into politics, I was the troublemaker. I sat down with my mother and said, "You've got to tell him the truth. You cannot let him find out that you're his mother and you didn't tell him." I told her the story would come out because the records would be searched thoroughly by professionals. My mother was very upset at the idea of breaking her pact with Polly. At the same time, she was dying to tell Bobby. She gave it a lot of thought, and in the end, she decided to tell him.

One day a month later, we drove to New Jersey where Bobby was playing at the Latin Casino. We went to his hotel room, and Nina took him aside. She said, "Sit down. I have something to tell you, and I think it might upset you." And then she told him how things were when she was young and why she had done what she did. And Bobby of course didn't understand. "My whole life has been a lie!" he said. And he wanted to know who his father was. I had advised my mother not to tell him, and she listened to me. She never told Bobby or anyone else, including me.

Vee tells me that Nina thought that Bobby had accepted the news, but Vee says he never did. And he never forgave Nina for keeping this secret from him for so long. But my father had no trouble believing this story. He never said, "You're a liar." Instead he asked, "Who was my father?" One can imagine he was desperate to know. When Charlie stepped forward, Bobby laughed him off. He told Charlie that he couldn't have been his father, that his father had to have been smarter, a doctor or a lawyer. One more kick in the ribs for Charlie.

After the secret was out, Nina told others that Bobby's father had been a college student when she met him and that she was in love with him. She said that she didn't want to derail the boy's college career, so she never told him she was pregnant. An interviewer suggested to Nina that most girls would have wanted to lay at least a little guilt on the responsible party, but Nina demurred. She said the boy would have quit college and gotten a "crap" job and that his life would have been hell. Interesting. Interesting that she would have protected this boy she was "in love with" and allowed poor Charlie to step into the traces. Also interesting because Charlie Maffia says he was dating Nina when she got pregnant. He says that when Nina first realized she was pregnant, she told Charlie that he'd "done the deed." She denied it ever since.

Charlie says that there came a time when Bobby started pumping him for information.

☞ *Bobby was asking me about Nina, who she went out with during that era. I said, "Bobby, I can't tell you. There are a lot of things I can't tell you, but if there is something you want to know, let Nina tell you."*

So then he came right out and said, "I know all about it."

"What do you mean you know all about it?"

"Nina told me. I know about her. Now I want to know about the other part of it."

I said, "Well, I can't tell you. You can figure it out for yourself."

Many times he had said, "Gee, if I had a father, I'd like it to be George Burns." Every time he said that and I was alone with him, I said, "Bob, you know you highly insult me. You put me down that bad. You pick George Burns as a father. Why? Because he's a big celebrity?"

So he'd grab me and kiss me and say, "You know it's you I love."

I'd say, "Yeah, but I don't like it. It bugs me."

Nina denied who I am, but I know who I am and so does everybody else. I did what she wanted me to do. I kept denying it to all my friends and relatives, denying it tooth and nail until right now. But they didn't believe me. They could see the resemblance. They'd say, "We can see Bobby, and we can see you. We can see Dodd, and we can see you." They saw me in Vee and Vanna. Nina kept saying, "Later on. Maybe when he gets a little older we'll tell him." To Bobby she said, "Charlie's nothing. He's just your brother-in-law." Well, that was a goddamned lie.

Nina died in 1983. The night before she died, she spoke to Mickey Behrke on the phone and the subject of Bobby's father came up. Nina swore to Mickey that Charlie was not Bobby's father. She said Bobby was the son of a boy she'd met at a party and slept with once or twice. Why would she insist on telling this story if it was a lie? To deny Charlie this pleasure? To insure Bobby's loyalty to her? To keep some part of her pact with Polly?

Mickey's thoughts are that the "boy" was married and that he was indeed a mafioso. If Charlie isn't my dad's father, that's the most plausible reason I've heard for keeping the real father's identity a secret. The man was married. And he was with the Mafia. But Charlie is right when he says that some see the resemblance between Bobby and Charlie. My mother is one of those people. And Rona Barrett, having witnessed Charlie's undying devotion toward Bobby, says that Charlie's love was a true father's love.

Vee doesn't dispute the love, but she says her father is lying and that he won't claim he's Bobby's father to her face. She says he "might say that he *could* have been Bobby's father, that he *should* have been Bobby's father, but he won't stand before me and say that he *is* Bobby's father."

She adds: "If Charlie is Bobby's father, he behaved in a strange way. Imagine it's 1937. Bobby is a year old and my father moves in with my mother and takes on the support of Bobby, a sickly child. He also takes on the support of my mother and my grandmother, who was also sickly and had a very large drug habit. My grandfather, Sam Cassotto, who Polly said was Bobby's father, was dead before Bobby was born. And now my parents get married. If Bobby had been my father's child, why didn't he and my mother adopt him? They didn't do it."

When Nina told my dad that she was his mother, he was angry, hurt, disoriented. He took great pride in being an honest man, and because he'd been lied to, he'd misrepresented himself to others. When he said, "My whole life has been a lie," it was a howl of bewilderment and pain. The Maffia family creed had always been "Tell the truth." And as Bobby would later say to Nina, she had told the "biggest lie of all by denying her own child." I doubt he completely believed

Nina's reason for making her delinquent confession. While there may have been some truth in her concern for his political aspirations, he detected underlying motives—a need for recognition, obviously, but there was also an implicit slap across the face. My dad told his therapist in later years that he felt Nina's hostility, and surely it was there. Bobby could be brutal at times and had often hurt Nina. Now he was paid back in full.

This long held secret of Nina's affected everyone in the family. Charlie might tell people that Bobby Darin was his son, but his wife and children called him a liar. The children themselves had a sense of something not right. Vee remembers that she never felt like the oldest child, that she often asked why the world always revolved around her uncle Bobby. She had a suspicion of the truth when she was a teenager, but she could never bring herself to ask the question outright. She was afraid of what Nina would tell her.

Vee adds this:

I saw Bobby's father once. Nina and I went to an oculist in Harlem, where we used to go as kids. We were sitting there waiting for the glasses to be ready, and my mother got a funny look on her face. I said, "What is it?"

She said, "Nothing. I'm not feeling too good." I followed her gaze and saw a man picking up his glasses. When I asked her later about it, she said, "Well, he was a friend."

I said, "Uh-huh."

She said, "He was a friend of Bobby's father." And she could tell I didn't believe her. She gave me a look that said "I know that you know. That's the one." So I got to see Bobby's father once. I have no idea what his name is, and if I did, I wouldn't tell.

My mother was smart not to tell him who his father was. I believed then and believe now that if Nina had named Bobby's father, whatever small emotional investment he had in his family would have come to a dead halt and he would have lavished it all on his real daddy, a person who didn't even know him. Didn't raise him. Didn't have to crawl across the floor because he was in agony if you walked. To have told him would have been a big mistake, and at this point in history I couldn't have cared less about Bobby and his hurt. I cared about my mother's hurt. My mother was a very foolish woman in many ways. But she was very loving. She loved her kids.

My mother said a very wrong thing to me, and this is it. We called my mother "Nina" all of our lives. All of us: me, my sister, my youngest brother, Gary. When we were kids people would say, "That's not nice, little girl. That's your mommy. You call her 'Mommy.' " It became an issue, and I took it to my mother. She said, "Nina is my name, and I want to be called Nina." It is amazing how your mother can hurt you even when you are a grown adult. Bobby had been dead many years when I spoke to Nina about this again. My mother looked at me and said, "If my son didn't call me Mama, no one's going to call me Mama." Oh.

I know my grandmother must have hoped for some profound display of affection from my father, but knowing Bobby as she did, she might have guessed better. Said Nina before she died, "He didn't stop loving me, and he didn't love me more. He loved as he always had. He didn't accept me as his mother, yet he told his closest friends. So he obviously wasn't ashamed. But he never acknowledged it publicly. He never sent flowers on Mother's Day as he did with Polly."

Recently I came across a notebook my father used as a scratch pad while hospitalized during the very last days of his life. Some of his scribbles were gibberish, but one line was absolutely clear. He wrote: "She robbed me of my dream to always show 'Mama,' wherever she was, what I could do."

It's sad that with all of the sacrifices Nina made for Bobby he couldn't find any tender feelings for her. Couldn't forgive her for a lie that surely had caused her unimaginable pain throughout the years. Nina Maffia was his mother, and she'd done well by him. Similarly, I realize that the only two people who should care about who Bobby's father really was are me and Charlie Maffia. Nina is listed as "mother" on my father's birth certificate. Beside "father" is the bleak word:

"Unknown." I've had a long time to think about my father's family and have concluded that whether or not Charlie is my dad's biological father, he was with my father throughout his life. He sacrificed for him, raised him, loved him. That makes him his father as far as I'm concerned, and when I'm asked who Charlie Maffia is to me, I say he's my grandfather. And I'm proud to say it. Case closed.

My dad told very few people about Nina's disclosure when it happened, choosing instead to reveal it selectively over the years. Blauner says the news crushed him emotionally and physically. That his heart went out of rhythm then and would continue to go out of time until he died. John Miller recalls my father's reaction: "Bobby took it very badly, yet he took it resolutely at the same time. He felt the family deception as kind of typical of the corruption of the system. It was a blow to him, but at the same time, hey, why not? The whole world is corrupt, the whole world sucks, so why not? It was just another verification of what he was saying about the system in general."

A month after receiving Nina's news, in March 1968, my dad told columnist Earl Wilson, "My goals have been changed, and what I aspire to now is to make a more meaningful contribution. To be called the greatest entertainer may mean being paid more than anybody or having four limousines. Those are not essentials to me anymore. Being accepted universally as an entertainer and human being are." Wilson reported that my dad went to Indiana with comedian Jimmy Durante to emcee a rally for Democratic senator Birch Bayh and that he was making plans to campaign for Bobby Kennedy for president.

On April 4 Dr. Martin Luther King was shot down as he stood on a second-floor balcony of a motel in Memphis. Devastated, my dad canceled his engagement in Syracuse, New York, and in May he joined Robert Kennedy's presidential campaign. I've been told that he did fund-raising, soliciting contributions from movie people and businesspeople alike. At rallies he would "open" for his candidate with a song and a joke before Kennedy would be introduced. He met RFK a few times and spent a few hours sitting with him and fifty other people on a plane trip from Portland to Los Angeles. Of that trip, he told Estelle Changas of the *Los Angeles Times*, "Everything about the man was confirmed. All the pieces of the puzzle were put into place for me, and I said, 'This is the man I believe in.' "

Then on June 4, 1968, the man he believed in, a man many hoped would have made a difference as president, was mortally wounded. The next day he died. My dad went to the memorial service in New York and attended Kennedy's funeral at Arlington Cemetery. He stood at the gravesite long after the other mourners went home. It's been said that the gravediggers left the coffin aboveground for the next shift to bury, and that my dad, alone, stayed with Kennedy's body throughout the night. Dick and Mickey Behrke remember that Bobby told them the candle that he held at the vigil, among all the candles around him, was the only one that did not blow out. And he said he had had a revelation as he stood by the grave.

My father expressed his revelation to columnist Earl Wilson: "It was as though all my hostilities, anxieties, and conflicts were in one ball that had been flying away into space, farther and farther from me all the time, leaving me finally content with myself."

What I take from that quote is that his ambitions to be a legend, for instance, or a box office star were quelled. Perhaps he was coming out of the shock of Nina's startling revelation. But my dad never got over the death of Robert Kennedy. Four year's after Kennedy's assassination, my father told reporter Estelle Changas about the depth of his feelings: "What I did was I stepped out really meaningfully for a man I thought could and would help to redirect the system. Not make tremendous changes, no single man can do that. But I thought Bobby could really begin a new beginning. And indeed, if he were able to do it, succeeding presidents would have no choice but to put us all together and make it all viable so that the little Black kid in Alabama would have the same shot as the little White kid in Forest Hills.

"Now, when I pledged myself to that one human being, I also pledged a certain amount of responsibility for anything that happened. By holding Bobby Kennedy up to be a savior in the immediate sense, the moment he's killed, I'm responsible for the assassination. Because I'm one of the people who said, 'Yes, I think he's right. Yes, I'm going to work for him.' And I did. So the moment he gets his head blown off, by making him vulnerable, I helped to pull the trigger."

My dad's journalist friend John Miller reported that Kennedy's death marked the beginning of many changes in my father. Before the assassination my dad told Miller that he was going to run for office himself, that he would be Bobby Kennedy's protégé and that one day he might be vice president. After Kennedy's death, my father was emotionally gutted. His regard for Robert Kennedy was so enormous that he would not support another candidate. There can be no doubt of the effect the issues of the times had upon my father. His changing ideals and aspirations were reflected in his music.

In July 1968 my dad formed his own label, Direction Records, for the sole purpose of seeking out "statement makers." *Billboard* magazine reported: "Darin's decision to launch the label is based on a desire for artistic freedom. He says events of the past months have affected him and it is through his music that he feels compelled to express himself. . . . His first LP is controversial in the sense that it establishes a new image. . . . The songs are built on Darin's feelings for people and his concern for a troubled society."

A month after founding Direction, my dad sold T.M. to a conglomerate called Commonwealth United for $1.3 million. He was given $300,000 as a cash payment that largely went for administrative and legal fees—and my father received $1 million in Commonwealth United stock. It's important to understand that T.M. owned the copyrights to all of my father's music.

Rona Barrett remembers when my father made the decision to sell T.M.: "Bobby thought that he was going to become really, really rich. He was one of the first entertainers to sell his publishing catalog. His whole future and his desire to protect everybody he cared about was tied up in Commonwealth United stock. This was the equity that was going to take care of his mother, his sister, Charlie, Sandra, Dodd—they were all going to be taken care of. Absolutely. He said to me, 'This will take care of everyone.' "

The company started trading at eighteen dollars a share and rose briefly. Blauner remembers my father calling to tell him how much more his million was worth. "Sell" said Steve, but what my father hadn't told him was that there was a clause in the deal that prevented him from selling the stock for two years. A few months later the stock found its floor at fifty cents a share. Commonwealth United bellied up, and my dad lost T.M., a catalog some say would be worth somewhere between twenty-five and fifty million dollars today. Rona Barrett told me that my father took this as a "crippling blow," but I am heartened by the revelation that his intentions were to provide financial security for his family.

My dad was down after the loss of his bankroll, but he wasn't out. He had his voice, he had a fledgling recording company, and he had his name. In 1966 he had recorded "If I Were a Carpenter," a folksy ballad written by Tim Hardin that became part of his repertoire. Now he added protest songs to his act. He wrote "Long Line Rider," which was about the discovery of inmates' bodies at an Arkansas prison camp, and debuted it at the Cocoanut Grove in October 1968. His presentation there was unusual. He walked off the stage in his tuxedo in the middle of the show and returned in denim jeans and jacket to sing this song and conclude his act. There was more than a ripple of consternation as the audience tried to reconcile the two versions of Bobby Darin.

But soon my dad would go all the way. Photos of him in November 1968 show that he had let his sideburns grow, added a mustache, and abandoned the tux, replacing it with blue denim. He explained his new appearance by telling the press that images no longer appealed to him. He said his life had changed because of Kennedy's death. He was making $40,000 a week and dividing it up between Uncle Sam, his agents, his managers, and his flacks. He got rid of everyone but the federal government and a four-piece band. He said: "I don't have a press agent anymore. I want to get back to basic reality. My work has changed because I prefer to sing to express my beliefs and convictions rather than to entertain." He started signing his correspondence "Peace, Bobby." But instead of peace, my father was about to experience another devastating blow.

Since his first TV performance bomb, when he lost his place in a song he'd sung a hundred times, my father had found confirmation and renown on the stage. With his heartfelt convictions firmly placed in his onstage act, my father put on his denims—with tie—and performed at the Copa in January 1969. The audience was in no way prepared for this Bobby Darin. And they hated him.

John Miller says, "I suffered through those nights when Bobby worked the Copa. I was there every night, and I suffered. He was doing guitars and a four-piece rock band and protest songs and he just died."

George Scheck told him his act stunk. Dick Clark said, "You're Bobby Darin, not Bob Dylan. You're a different kind of dog." Musicians and friends pleaded with him to give up the protest genre, but he shook them

off. Steve Blauner said my father's music at this time was amazing, the
best of his career, but the audience wasn't ready for it.

One of the songs my dad sang at the Copa was "Long Line Rider,"
and he was scheduled to sing it on the nationally broadcast *Jackie
Gleason Show*. Just before taping, producers telegrammed my father
and told him that he would have to cut this stanza from the song:

> *That's the tale the warden tells*
> *as he counts his empty shells.*
> *By the day, by the day.*
> *This kind of thing can't happen here.*
> *'Specially not in an election year.*

My father had sung this song on the other two networks and had
gotten prior clearance to sing it intact for the Gleason show. Rather
than cut his song, my father walked out of the studio and subsequently
sued Gleason and CBS for nearly a quarter million dollars. He was
warned that this could have an ill effect on his career, but my dad
didn't hesitate a beat. He said, "I don't care if I never do another
television show in my life; they are not going to interfere with my
right to express myself."

At the end of January my dad played the El San Juan in Puerto
Rico. He went onstage without his hairpieces and with his mustache.
He called himself "Bob" Darin. He sang "Mack the Knife" and other
hits and filled out his show with what a local paper called "a bit of
Bob Dylan–type songs thrown in." Same songs, same reaction as at
the Copa. The crowd was unhappy. The press tried to give him a good
review, blaming the sound system for some of my father's failure to
win approval. But my father was not fooled. He told the *New York
Post*'s Al Aronowitz: "As I walked out on the floor, they walked out
of the audience. That's the key thing I remember, the total feeling of
rejection, like I had come down with the plague. . . . When I put on
my denim I was divesting myself of the slick and the sharp and the
styled and the tailored. When Bobby Kennedy was killed I thought,
'If a man like that could die, then what can I do for this world?' I only
knew him a short time, but in my relationship with him, I was seeking
my own identity through someone of courage and conviction. When

he died that void that I was trying to fill in committing myself to him was even greater."

But although his commitment was sincere, he had still to learn that the audience was paying to see "the slick and the sharp, the styled and the tailored." When they saw the workclothes, they heard pinko, commie, protest music, no matter what he actually sang. My dad called it right. He told Aronowitz, "They hear what they see."

During the summer of 1969 my dad found some acceptance at the Troubadour, a club that showcased folk singers, but he was already discouraged. George Burns saw him at the Troubadour and "was heartbroken."

☞ *He was still in the jeans and playing with five or six guys, and all the things they were playing were all amplified. I went backstage and said to Bobby, "You're doing it all wrong, kid. In the first place, you're not gonna bring back Bobby Kennedy. He's gone. People exit different ways. That was his finish. When the time comes for you to go, they'll probably give you back your pictures and take you." That's how they do it in show business. They give you back your pictures and say, "You're closed." I said, "But if you want to do something for Bobby Kennedy, put on your toupee and your tuxedo and get rid of these musicians. Play Vegas and all the great nightclubs and make as much money as you possibly can and give it to the Kennedy charities. Then you're doing something. You're doing nothing for Kennedy now." He did it eventually. I don't say he did it the next week, 'cause he had a mind of his own. And I loved him very, very much.*

My dad explained his act to a reporter from the *Los Angeles Herald Examiner:* "It wasn't that the people hated me. The audiences liked it, but they were too small. I thought I could present myself differently and by this change in appearance I would be close to making my personal statement. I took off my tuxedo and my hairpiece and grew a mustache and went into New York with the very show I had played in Las Vegas. But I turned off so many people they didn't hear me— and those whom I've known for years swore to me that I had tried to be a hippie. If I had gone into the Troubadour in a tuxudo and sung the songs I had sung in Las Vegas in New York, they would have said, 'Look at this Establishment nightclub artist trying to tell us he knows where it's at.' They wouldn't have heard my lyrics any more than the people at the Copa heard them. People hear what they see."

But even hearing wasn't working. My dad produced two albums under his Direction label, both full of quality material, especially lyrically. The first album was called *Bobby Darin Born Walden Robert Cassotto*. The second was called *Commitment*. They were like nothing my father had ever done before. No big band. No nightclub tricks. The songs were of the protest genre, each meaningful, many poignant. Critics approved; one claimed to be so stunned by the quality of the first that he couldn't write a word about it for three weeks. He said that he had a need to write a really scathing review of someone else's work just so he could feel his power as a critic. My dad's music took his words away. He wasn't alone. Many critics thought the *Commitment* album a true tour de force.

But the albums were commercial bombs.

Robert Hillburn reviewed both albums in one article, citing several songs that he called well structured and original. Here is a condensed version of Hillburn's review in the *L.A. Times*:

DARIN TOUCHES ALL THE MUSICAL BASES

Will the real Bobby Darin please stand up? During Darin's colorful 12 years of stardom, he's gone through rock, traditional pop, folk, country and other trends with a speed that has led many to question his sincerity as a singer and songwriter. Last year Darin formed his own label, Direction, and the word was out that he was making a big change. His appearance went from nightclub singer to coffee house protester. But his first Direction album made some of the skeptical take a second look. Darin's second album, *Commitment*, continues the creative work.

One of the points to remember about Darin is that beneath the huge ego and artistic hopscotching has rested a large talent. After years of stardom and success, disappointment and doubt, praise and put-down, Darin seems to be involved in a painful search for identity. It's a search that holds promise of rich rewards. Maybe the real Bobby Darin is beginning to stand. I hope so.

That summer my dad rented a house in Malibu and had the Maffia family as his guests for the summer. He told Nina, "There are going to be changes. Soon there won't be any money." Dick Lord remembers a call he got from my father at around this time.

☞ *Bobby called me up and said, "I just talked to Bobby Kennedy."*

I said, "Bobby Kennedy is dead."

He said, "I know that. I went to his grave and he told me what to do."

When someone that close to you talks like this, you don't hang up on them. I said, "What did he tell you to do?"

Bobby said, "Kennedy told me that all of this is bullshit. 'Mack the Knife,' shiny suits, nightclubs, it's all bullshit."

I said, "What are you going to do now?"

He said, "I'm going to live in a trailer. I don't need things. I'm going to write message songs because I don't have long to be here and I want to leave a message."

My father had an idea that he needed to take himself away from everything in order to sort out his thoughts, so he decided to strip down to bare essentials. He packed some workclothes, some books, and some albums. He brought his guitar. His friends watched in amazement as he gave away all of his possessions, including his clothes. He gave his projectors to Steve Blauner, his portable phone to Wayne Newton. Everyone who walked into his house walked out with a chandelier, a coffee table, something. He drove up the California coast to a remarkably beautiful area called Big Sur and rented an eighteen-foot-long trailer parked in the middle of an apple orchard. There he stayed alone for nine months.

In 1967 my dad said, "It's not true you only live once. You only die once. You live lots of times if you know how." No question, by giving away his material goods and sending himself on retreat, Bobby Darin was attempting to transform his life yet once again.

12

Bobby, 1969 - 1971

There is the calmness of the lake when there is not a breath of wind; there is the calmness of a stagnant ditch. So it is with us. Sometimes we are clarified and calmed healthily, as we never were before in our lives, not by an opiate, but by some unconscious obedience to the all-just laws, so that we become like a still lake of purest crystal. . . .

—HENRY DAVID THOREAU
A Writer's Journal

Life to me is struggles, successes, and failures. Living is what goes on between those things. I have life, but whether or not I am living is something else.

—BOBBY DARIN, *1971*

My father once said he'd been called cocky, brash, and arrogant so many times, he felt like a three-man vaudeville act. If so, effective 1969, the vaudeville act went into retirement.

After he separated from my mother in 1966, my dad experienced a series of stunning blows, each causing him to reexamine who he was, what he stood for, where to draw the line, and where to cross it. The first blow was the finalization of his divorce, which made him feel he had failed as husband and father. When Nina disclosed her awful truth, his deep-rooted understanding of his identity was ripped from him and overturned in the space of minutes. Within the next four months, two idols—who were also his friends—were shot down in their prime. Then he lost his business and, with it, rights to all of the songs he'd written since the beginning of his career. His business partner and friend, Ed Burton, died not long afterward, a reconciliation with my mom failed, and he was booed at his home base, the Copacabana. His best work bombed at the cash register, he was broke, and his heart, which had always been shaky, was racing like that of a hare with the hounds close behind. At thirty-three my dad had outlived the outside estimate of his life expectancy by three years, and now he was up to his eyeballs in what could be described as midlife crisis. No wonder he decided to get away from it all.

My dad described his retreat to a simpler life this way:

For the better part of 1969, I lived in Big Sur in an eighteen-foot trailer. A friend of mine had some land there, and he was kind enough to let me live on his orchard, and I did that. I took with me a few pairs of dungarees and a couple of shirts and a pair of desert boots. I really divested myself of the material things that I hadn't even realized had accumulated so heavily over the years of trying to make up for an early poverty. And without going into hearts and flowers, particularly, I did divest myself of those things that were totally superfluous and unnecessary. . . . What I was trying to do was more or less deeply triggered by the death of Robert Kennedy. I tried to take the philosophy that I had really been living with all my life and apply it to my extrinsic self—be the person I philosophically believed I should be. And I believe to a degree I was successful with that.

When my dad shucked off the trappings of his glamorous life, gave away his houses, his cameras, his games and toys, he explained, "If they don't own me, I don't know what does." He reduced his monthly expenses from $28,000 to under $300. "Big Sur," he explained, "is symbolic of Walden Pond. No pun intended, but Walden is my first name. Big Sur is a place that's existed for millions of years, and pieces of millions of years were still around. During my time there I didn't have to answer to a series of conflicting and confusing energies that can only occur to you when you live in the city. Big Sur offered me a place to sit for hours and hours and just pick my guitar. I played it and enjoyed playing it without having to worry about auditioning, testing, being on. And with this goes a certain kind of escapism that citified sophisticates always insist is a way of running away from yourself. And I don't doubt it. Except, so what if it doesn't hurt anybody? It didn't hurt me."

Before leaving for Big Sur, my dad had done a small part in a film called *The Happy Ending*, which was written, directed, and produced by director Richard Brooks. My dad was thoroughly inspired by Brooks, and while he was on retreat he worked on a film of his own. He called the film *The Vendors*, and he worked on the script every day. My dad would write, direct, produce, and score this film about a folk singer with a drug habit who gets involved with an over-the-hill hooker. My dad described the film as "a small picture, a crude story, told crudely about people. There was a certain adrenaline about the screenplay. It was going to be done despite being turned down for money, by actors, et cetera. I haven't applied this type of attack to anything in years. My friends hate it. And since I couldn't get any backing, I put my own money into it."

And that left him with lint in his pockets. When the Sahara Hotel in Vegas offered my father a two-week engagement in December 1969 at $40,000 a week, he said yes. Wanting to forewarn his audience, he had a life-size cutout of himself in costume posted at the entrance to the Congo Room. There he was in denims, cowboy hat, and mustache. The audience filled the room. My dad went on with his four-piece group, sang his protest songs, and did a running commentary on political issues, taking a few pokes at Richard Nixon and Spiro Agnew. Disregarding the clamor for "Bobby" Darin, he turned down a request for "Mack the Knife." Grumbling followed. Some rude noises were heard. No disrespect intended, my dad wasn't into "Mack" anymore.

It was costing the Sahara a bundle to stage this debacle, and my dad appreciated it. He said from the stage at the time, "It took a lot of guts on the Hotel Sahara's part to try me out doing what I'm doing now. They pay me a lot of money for what I would have done for nothing." But when the crowds walked out, Bobby couldn't pretend it didn't hurt. The shame of it was, he was really good.

Steve Blauner, in his capacity as friend, went to Vegas:

☞ *I saw him at the Sahara. There he was, with the jeans, with four pieces behind him. It was the smallest band in the history of Vegas. And this was not a lounge. This was the main room. And Bobby was brilliant. I never thought he could be better than when I was with him, but he was brilliant doing Dylan kind of music—and people were walking out.*

Now, when he started this protest mode, I sat with him and said, "Bobby, you can make it this way, but it's going to take you a long time 'til people know you're for real. People are going to resent what you're doing at first, but if you have staying power, talent will out. And part of that means that you've got to go with the album under your arm and see the disk jockeys with the FMs. You're going to have to work at it. And prove that you're sincere. And eventually, when you don't go away, it'll take. Your performance is breathtaking. Incredible. As good as I've ever seen you, and I never thought I could say that about you doing this kind of material."

My dad must have been pleased with Blauner's support. Blauner had never lied to him, and he trusted his judgment. Still, he knew that the Sahara gig had been a bust. He told the press: "I doubt they'll invite me back. They wouldn't accept what I was doing, but I truly believe it must be done." When he left Vegas, he returned to his trailer and picked up on his film where he'd left off.

Dick Lord remembers Bobby's call:

☞ *"You want to be a movie star?"*
I said, "I'm up for that. Absolutely."

He said, "Okay, you're in a movie. You're playing a part of the folk singer's manager."

Now when Bobby did the movie with Richard Brooks, he'd fallen in love with Richard Brooks's wife, Jean Simmons. Bobby said to me, "I'm suicidal over her." This is the same man who says, "I'm dying, I'm not going to live till Thursday." Now he tells me he's suicidal over her? I didn't know what to say. I heard that he'd been to Brooks's house and told Brooks that he was in love with his wife, and Brooks and Jean Simmons let Bobby make a fool of himself. Anyway, Richard Brooks seemed to have a way of directing where nobody got to see the entire script. The actor would just see his own part and the pages he was working on that day. The theory was that in real life, we don't know what's going to happen two hours from now, so if you could put that element of the unknown into the acting, the acting would be better. But Bobby Darin, as a director, was not Richard Brooks. Maybe he could have been, but at that time I don't think he was.

So, I went to Nancy Sinatra Jr.'s house, where they were shooting the film. Bobby gave me my pages, then he said, "Let's have lunch." We went to lunch, and after we ate, he took a twenty-dollar bill out of his pocket, threw it on the table, and said, "That's the last twenty dollars I have."

I said, "Well, I have some money."

He said, "No, no. You don't understand. Have in the world. In the world, that's the last twenty I have."

I said, "Naw, that can't be."

He said, "It is. Everything I've got I put into the movie."

That was true. When my dad got rid of his material goods, he'd given his projectors to Steve Blauner. Blauner recalls that now that Bobby was trying to raise money to make the movie, he asked for his projectors back. Blauner tells me he may have gasped, but he gave my dad back the projectors and waited to see the film. And it was terrible. The acting was poor, the camerawork was bad, the colors on the film didn't match, the story didn't work, and the only sympathetic character (played by Mariette Hartley) wasn't the starring role. The musical score, of course, was great. Blauner gave my dad some advice on how to recut the film, which my dad ignored.

When my father came out of his trailer in May 1970, he was holding a few pounds of film that would die, unreleased, in the can. I'm one of the few people who have seen *The Vendors*, and it is bad. My father was convinced of this when he couldn't line up a distributor for the film, but he seems not to have been scarred by the disappointment. He never complained about it, never cursed the loss of the $350,000 he put into it. He just let it drop. And he felt his time in Big Sur had been quite valuable.

He told the press: "I feel that what I've been able to do is return to that love which is really the most compelling. Performing to me is just about all that my life wants to wake up to every day with the exception of my son. He takes priority over everything. But I have found I can live far more simply than I thought I could. . . ."

Then he turned on his television—and freaked out. Reporters wanted to talk to my dad about his film, but he only wanted to talk about the war in Vietnam. He said to the *Citizen News*, "I was watching TV, and suddenly I hear President Nixon say he was going to send troops into Cambodia. Cambodia! Why, he promised me and everyone else he was going to end this war. What was he doing to me! To us! I decided I had been asleep, and nothing was going to happen to stop the war unless I personally got my tail out of the eleventh century and woke up. I decided I wasn't going to let him, president or not, do this without my having a say in the matter."

My dad was seething: about the war, about what kids were being taught in school about equality, which was untrue, and about what he'd believed about democracy that turned out to be power in the hands of the few over the many. He took out full-page ads to announce that he refused to be taken in anymore by all the promises from the government and that he was organizing a march on Washington in June to let the Pentagon know what he and his friends thought of what he saw as hypocrisy. He made speeches and came up with a call-in plan to jam the switchboard at the White House with antiwar messages. But while he was standing up and being counted, he also needed to eat.

He got an offer from the Landmark Hotel in Vegas and took it. He compromised on his dress code—still wore the denims, but they were tailored; he cut his hair and shaved off his mustache. He found a way to compromise on his music, too. He had more horns and different arrangements.

He talked to Frank Lieberman of the *Los Angeles Herald Examiner*, who asked why he was changing his image again:

☞ *It has nothing to do with imagery. It's just that I'm an entertainer, and I'll go out to entertain in more than one direction. I've spent a couple of years in a strong self-involving, self-questioning period. Just in the last few weeks have I started to see myself start to come out of it.*

In the midst, I got the call for the Landmark. It was just at the right time. And I'm doing what you have to do as an entertainer for the people who want to be entertained by that, but I'll do the other thing at the Troubadour as well.

It's no rank thing to do both. I did myself a disservice by thinking it was a rank thing. I got to the point where I wasn't answering the questions I was asking. I've been taking stock. The disservice I did was in thinking I was not able to function while I was asking myself the questions. To some people it was hibernation. It was quite necessary, but what I'm saying is that in doing that, I just shut out all people.

Also, you can't argue with the prices in the state of Nevada. It's a luxury. Here you can work ten weeks a year and do whatever you want with the remainder. I guess the past two years I could have taken advantage of that kind of formula, but I just couldn't get up to do it.

I hadn't arrived at the way it would be pleasurable for me to do it and, at the same time, profitable. I had come to the point it wasn't pleasurable to face those audiences. Though, it wasn't the audience. Obviously, it was me. A constant reflection that I was working mechanically on stage. Now it's exciting all over again. New songs to sing and new things to do.

While my dad was at the Landmark, his old pal Wayne Newton came to see the show. Newton asked him what hotel he would be playing next in Vegas, and my dad said he didn't have a booking. Newton was shocked; he was working twenty to thirty weeks a year, and it was unbelievable that his "big brother" couldn't get work on the strip. Wayne saw a chance to pay Bobby back for giving him his big break. He went to Walter Kane, who was the talent booker for the Hughes Hotels, and said to him, "You've got to do me a favor." He asked Kane to give Bobby ten to twelve weeks at his usual rates. Kane was nervous about "Bob" Darin, but he did this favor for Wayne. Bobby was given three bookings at the Desert Inn. The first was in 1971, from January 8 through February 8. Wayne never made a big deal about doing this for my dad. That's the kind of guy he is. The truth is, without Wayne's help my father might not have had a comeback. For this act of kindness and for his friendship, I will be forever grateful.

Steve Blauner remembers that "Bobby came to me and said, 'I'm going back into the tuxedo.' I was sort of disappointed. I wanted him to make it this way. So I said, 'Why?' And he said to me, 'I don't want to stand in line for medical treatment.' "

Bobby Darin was happy to be booked at the Desert Inn. He had endured the hard, cold slap of reality. But with his world more or less restored to working order, my dad could foresee better times ahead. He'd settled his identity crisis; he could be Bob Darin on the street and get applause and make a living as Bobby Darin on the stage. But now he had to deal with the fibrillations he'd suffered for a couple of years. Sometimes for eight or nine hours at a time his heart would beat out of time, and it would race at 140–160 beats a minute instead of a normal 80.

In October 1970 my dad was taping a show in Toronto when Harriet Wasser came backstage to see him between songs. She found him slumped in a corner, pale, shaken, for the moment unable to stand. My dad told her that he felt as though he'd been running around the block, and he was sitting still. He said a doctor was coming and that he was really scared. Hesh had known about Bobby's heart since she'd first met him. She put her arms around him, and he cried. My dad thought that he was going to die that day. Then he told her not to tell anyone what he was going through. "If my family finds out about this," he said, "I'll know who told them."

My dad's heart kept going out of sync, and Dr. Josh Fields, a pioneer in electric cardioversion, proposed using mechanical means to return my dad's heart to a normal rhythm. I've read an interview in which Dr. Fields discussed my father's heart condition, and I've translated it into layman's terms:

My father had heart murmurs and "atrialfibrillation." Many things can cause this condition, but in my dad's case his mitral valve as well as his aortic valve were malfunctioning. Instead of contracting, as they were supposed to, the atria would speed up uncontrollably, go out of rhythm, and just quiver. When my dad's valves were injured by his bouts with rheumatic fever, scar tissue formed over the leaflets, or "doors," to the valves. Later, calcium deposits adhered to the scar tissue. The leaflets are made of a very thin, pliable substance normally, but with scarring and calcium deposits, they become more rigid. The calcium also plugs the opening the blood is supposed to go through, so instead of having an opening the size of a garden hose, the diameter narrows dangerously. The opening scars so there is hardly any movement at all.

My father had mitral stenosis, which encompasses two conditions. One, as just described, the opening in the valve gets smaller and limits the amount of flow. Two, in a degeneration called "insufficiency," the valve grows so weak that it cannot move the blood flow out efficiently, allowing some of it back in.

If you have a damaged heart, your heart can, up to a point, compensate for the damage. It tries hard to maintain the blood flow. Normally, when you run, the heart speeds up because you're using more energy. You need more oxygen, so you have to pump more blood for that period to supply the body. When you stop and rest, your pulse rate goes back down. If you have a block, instead of a big pipe to send the blood through, you just have a little hole, and the pressure builds up behind it as the heart struggles to push enough blood through that little hole. Second, the heart will speed up to get more blood through per beat. Later, in a last-ditch effort to compensate, the heart can stretch and increase its size.

In my dad's case, his heart was enlarging and pumping harder to get the blood through. And because he suffered from insufficiency, perhaps half of the pumped-out blood ran back in. Thus the heart stretched its size so it could pump more blood out and give the body more of what it needed. But when the heart can no longer compensate, it "decompensates," and when Hesh found my father on the floor in Toronto, his heart had reached the point of decompensation.

My dad's heart condition was advanced by the time he saw Dr. Fields for the first time. In the interview I read, Dr. Fields explained that in a sense the body is like a little boat with multiple holes in it. The boat is in the water, and the heart is bailing the water out. The boat stays virtually dry because the pump bails as fast as the water comes in. And the heart is able to bail out that amount plus maybe five times more because it has a lot of reserve. The term *decompensation* is used when the heart fails to pump out blood as fast as it's coming in. When the heart fails in this way, water accumulates in the lungs, feet, and liver, and everything swells up. The person also experiences a shortness of breath because the lungs get kind of wettish and heavy, and water is taking up the space that air should occupy. When my dad wanted to dance and sing, he needed to take deep breaths and blow the air out past his vocal chords. But he was having tremendous trouble getting a full deep breath.

Once this atrialfibrillation started, his heart would fibrillate for several days continuously. He didn't know at first what was going on; he only knew he was getting short of breath and feeling tired. There's also a good chance he wasn't getting as much oxygen to the brain as he would normally have gotten. My dad's cardiologist, Dr. Marvin Levy, was considered an excellent doctor, and he used all of the drugs available to help my father's condition. When the drugs no longer worked, Dr. Levy talked to Dr. Fields about cardioversion, a relatively new technique using a specialized synchronized defibrillator that Dr. Fields had coinvented. The machine essentially stops the heart, then shocks it into the proper rhythm. The doctors agreed that the procedure could benefit my father.

Before converting the heart, it's important for the patient to take anticoagulants. When the valves just stand there and quiver, blood that is not flowing at a good rate tends to clot up a little bit. When the heart gets converted, suddenly the valves start contracting and these little clots get sent out into the bloodstream. If clots go to the brain, the effect could be devastating, so anticoagulants are used not to dissolve the clots, but to prevent them from forming.

Dr. Fields recalls that my father "was a little apprehensive."

He was fearful of dying. He was afraid of going to sleep, that he might not wake up. I said, "First of all, I have never had anyone die after doing this, but it's possible." I spelled out some of the possibilities, but not all. Normally the doctor will do surgery or a procedure without fully enlightening the patient and getting "informed consent." This time I took a risk. I didn't give him a fully informed consent because he would never have consented. I did not paint as dismal a picture as I would have for my full protection—explaining that he might be totally paralyzed or go blind, for example, or that I might not be able to start his heart again. I said, "Things can happen, and they can be serious, but they're not common, and I don't think it will happen to you." And we had long discussions about that.

When Dr. Levy and I talked about the technical aspects and preparations, Bobby would say, "Gentlemen, don't do that. You're making me very upset. You bring out my paranoia. Please don't talk about me when I can't hear everything loud and clear." So we agreed not to do it, but we would do it every now and then because we wouldn't always remember to keep our voices loud. That became a pattern. I had to learn not to do that. I performed the first conversion on Bobby at Midway Hospital in October 1970. It worked very well.

Some of the details involved with this patient's cardioversion give insight into his character. Many people who do the procedure use an anesthesiologist to give a drug like Pentathol to put a person to sleep. The shock we apply on the chest takes two milliseconds, which is a very short time, but the muscles contract and it hurts. It's as if a mule kicked you. I didn't use Pentathol in Bobby's case. Some new medication had come along called Valium, which people took by mouth. When you give it intravenously, it puts you out almost immediately. It's like Pentathol but only lasts a few seconds. After the first effect, say, a minute of deep sleep, it has a sedative, mild tranquilizing effect, as if you've taken it by mouth. Five milligrams would put most people out. It comes in a ten-milligram vial for that use and has become a standard form of therapy, because right after it, the patient is wide awake except for being a little tranquilized.

Bobby got the five and we waited for the circulation to run it through, twenty or thirty seconds, and he was still talking away at us, jabbering all the time. He didn't even blink with the five. I finished the syringe to ten. He was talking about his son and about a hike they'd gone on together, how he'd shown the boy mushrooms that were growing on trees and some other ones. I gave him the ten, which has always worked before, and Bobby just kept rattling on, maybe a slight slurring in his speech. And I turned to the nurse and asked for a repeat ten of Valium. I gave him a little of it because I was worried that he was still conscious. But finally I gave the whole ten, and he still didn't go out. Then Bobby started to get a little worried because he couldn't hear. I now had to be careful because he said, "Don't whisper to the nurse." And I said, "Fine," and I worried. I had never used two vials before. I had used more than one occasionally, but very infrequently, and I had never used two.

So now I had to consult with Dr. Levy, who was there, but I'm getting in an area I'm a little unprepared for. I didn't like it, but Levy was aware of what was going on. Still, I wanted him to know how unusual this was and I had to be careful because Darin would hear me. Whatever I said, Darin would hear me; it had to be said loud and clear. So I said to Dr. Levy that I needed to go to the full dosage. I said for Bobby, "because he has heightened anxiety, don't you, Bobby?"

He said, "No. I guess I'll just accept it."

I said, "Well, you're using up the stuff we're giving you. Do you have trouble falling asleep?"

He said, "Yeah, sometimes."

Obviously his anxiety level was high, and he was fighting the medication, or he had a very high tolerance. I asked if he drank, and he said no. And he didn't, because on occasion I would offer him liquor, and he would never touch it. So I gave him a third vial, which even the nurses had never seen. Now, we're at thirty milligrams of Valium, and he was barely going out. I was just waiting for him to close his eyes and relax. Momentarily I would assume that he had amnesia from that, just enough. With that, I took the paddles and shocked him, and he woke right up. But he didn't really remember the shock. He was wide awake seemingly and went on to mumble, "What the hell?" and then he relaxed again, but he kept his eyes open. Anyway, he converted. Usually the patient converts in one beat. But Bobby's heart took it, rumble, rumble, and then converted about ten seconds later.

After we did the cardioversion, the treatment was drug therapy. We used quinidine, which bothered him. The side effects were diarrhea, nausea, ringing in the ears, dizziness, and a feeling of uneasiness. It's a very toxic drug, and you have to give it in high doses.

There were other subsequent conversions in other hospitals. I availed myself of the anesthesia departments because I wanted extra help and to utilize more potent agents, such as Pentathol. Bobby would do well when he was converted, but he needed a lot of medication, which he didn't want. But he was a good sport about it. He did take the medication even though he was having side effects; he tried to tolerate it.

What was triggering him into more frequent persistent fibrillations was his valve, which was progressively closing to the final point where we could not convert him or where it wouldn't stay.

Four months after this first conversion, and having had several others in between, the Desert Inn engagement was upon my dad. Success there would wipe out the stain of the Sahara fiasco and would be important to his future nightclub career. By this time his doctors told him he needed open heart surgery to replace his damaged valves, but my dad didn't think he could put off the Desert Inn and still get work again.

My dad told *New York Post* reporter Alfred G. Aronowitz, "Having lived with a damaged heart for 26 years, I didn't think there was anything heroic about going in for surgery. I also always felt I was going to kick off by the time I was 30 anyway. The only reason it was time for the operation was that my valves had deteriorated to a point where if it was not now, then it would have to be next year, and in the meantime I'd have to curtail my activities.

"Because I'm fearless and insane, it was no risk. I told the doctor, 'You give me these six weeks to work—the first six weeks in 1971—somehow you keep me alive by remote control, and the moment I close I'll go home, spend four hours with my son, and then I'll check into a hospital and give myself to you.' "

Blauner recalls my dad's Desert Inn show: "Bobby went back to work in a tuxedo, and the hairpiece, and he now augmented the rhythm section with eight brass. I started to count the number of pieces in everyone else's band. I knew that Bobby would eventually see them and decide if this guy had twenty, he would want twenty-one. And if he had twenty-one, Tony Bennett would want twenty-three, and then Frank Sinatra would want twenty-five, Sammy Davis twenty-eight. It got to the point where one time Tony Bennett brought in a symphony orchestra! You couldn't hear him. But it was that kind of thing with performers. Who had the biggest orchestra. Bobby had the smallest, maybe eleven people—the same number as Laura Nyro, Dylan, James Taylor, Neil Diamond. Contemporary singers. And the audiences were now giving Bobby standing ovations because he was in a tuxedo and had eleven pieces. But it was essentially the same show they'd walked out on before."

Dick Lord was opening for my father at the Desert Inn. His act was getting good reviews, he was enjoying Bobby, and he was completely unprepared when my dad told him he was going into the hospital for open heart surgery after they closed at the Desert Inn:

☞ *I was surprised, and I tried not to look shocked. I said, "Well, what are you worried about, Bobby? You know you have no heart. You're all plastic. You're a plastic person."*

He said, "Nine out of ten survive. I called the hospital, and the last nine guys lived. I'm number ten." He told me this near the beginning of the engagement.

Bobby slept every day until 6:30 P.M. He came to the dressing room, then did the shows. We always had dinner in the dressing room. In four weeks he never left the hotel, never saw sunshine. After the second show we would go to his room and talk about old times until five in the morning. The highlight of his night was an ice-cream sundae. Then the show was going to close that night, and Bobby didn't want to fly to Los Angeles. Jim O'Neil, his road manager, had everything ready for the trip to the hospital. We had a station wagon fixed up with pillows and a mattress, a blanket, a few books, and a reading lamp. Watching Bobby's last show, I thought this might be it. I called Dick Behrke, who came to Vegas to say good-bye. We really didn't know how long Bobby would live.

Watching the show with the audience completely electrified, I couldn't believe that this dynamic performer was going right into our homemade ambulance for heart surgery. After the show, Bobby asked me to come into the dressing room while he was getting dressed. He hugged me and kissed me, and he said good-bye. Then I watched this small, underweight, exhausted man lie down in the station wagon. Jim handed him his hot-fudge sundae, and he waved, and they drove off into the desert, very possibly on his way to death. And I remember the station wagon driving away and the little light was on and Bobby waved to me and my tears were coming down. He looked so small and he'd lost so much weight. He was eating his ice cream like a little kid. And meanwhile the people are banging on the stage door, wanting autographs. They didn't know anything that was going on. I opened the door and said, "Bobby's gone."

My dad told Al Aronowitz, "I closed in Vegas at the Desert Inn on February 8. I spent a few hours with my son, who was nine years old. I explained to him I was sure everything was going to be okay, but it was very possible I would never see him again, and I told him, 'Wherever I am, you know I love you.' And he looked up at me and said, 'Don't worry about it, Dad, everything's going to be fine.' And I checked into the hospital."

I told my dad everything would be fine. And it was. The operation was a success. He was in intensive care for five days, then he recuperated in the hospital for six weeks. He felt better and better, and when he was ready he had a thirty-fifth birthday celebration for himself. It was a huge carnival-type party for his friends: tents, hot dogs, the works. All just to show them he was his old self. When asked what he was thinking about while he was recovering, my dad said that he was thinking about getting back to finishing what he'd started out doing years ago.

In November 1971 my dad expounded on his new self-awareness to reporter Estelle Changas.

☞ *I've found out a great deal out about myself in the last six months or so. I am a nightclub animal. I do not drink, and I am not a head. I am stoned twice a night when I'm working with audiences, by the contemplation and the anticipation in the audiences, by the contemplation and anticipation of what it is I can do to them, with them, through them, and therefore in turn what they can do for me.*

The knowledge at 35 years of age that this is what I do best, of all of the things that I do, is very recent knowledge. And there is the fact that I may possibly wind up being able to do it as well as or better than anybody else has ever done it. I've touched base with film. Some people think I'm a fine actor, and I'm very happy about that. I have touched base as a songwriter. Some people feel I'm very equipped in that area, and I'm glad about that. But the thing that really is a super charging, super energetic source for me is doing nightclub performances.

I haven't given up social protest. I haven't stopped breathing. But when it comes to control, the only kind of control that I really enjoy is exercising that control over audiences. Power makes pagans of us all. And I really believe that.

That's why I can look at the political spectrum and just want to vomit. Whereas with performing, it's give and take. When I leave the audience, I don't owe them anything. They don't owe me anything. If you work together during that hour and a half, dynamite. I hope they all walk out pleased as they can be. That's my function. And I can hold it and keep working on it, sharpen it.

I don't give a goddamn about records anymore. I don't care about pictures anymore. When I say don't care, it doesn't mean that I wouldn't do more. It doesn't mean that I wouldn't love to be accepted as a motion picture personality, as a recording artist, and have my albums in everybody's home and theater ticket stubs in pockets of people—but that's yesterday's news. That's not going to be. What's going to be is my polishing my club act and all of the immediate ancillaries of it.

When I worked on The Vendors, *I worked 17 and 18 hours a day with no sleep and no food, and never thought two good goddamns about it. And we were off Sunday, and I couldn't wait until Monday when the crew and cast came back. I wasn't off on Sunday. I was scouting locations and running around filing things and setting up shop, working things out on paper. I was consumed totally by the film. I'm a person obsessed of perfecting whatever it is that I can do. And really I don't want to waste my time doing a bunch of things that just give me immediate satisfaction, but are not sustained. Performing has a sustaining feeling to me. A feeling that something of me has gone out into the casino, out into the cold air with the audience. That feeling is dynamite.*

So saying, Bobby Darin played Harrah's in Reno, then did ten days at a club in Ohio. He did some television dates, then played another four weeks at the Desert Inn in February 1972. It had been a year since his last performance there, and once again he broke the house record.

Columnist Robert Hilburn of the *Los Angeles Times* wrote a rave review about my dad. The headline was BOBBY'S BACK AND LAS VEGAS

HAS HIM. In the article Hillburn reiterated the ups and downs of my father's career, then summarized:

> Onstage at the Desert Inn, Darin opened with some tradi-
> tional songs, the kind that Las Vegas nightclub audiences
> would easily recognize: "For Once in My Life," "You've
> Lost That Lovin' Feelin'," "Help Me Through The Night,"
> and "Mack the Knife."
>
> Then he shifted smoothly to tunes that are less predict-
> able. Taking off his tuxedo jacket and tie, he went through
> a long folk-blues treatment of "Midnight Special," sang
> Tim Hardin's "If I was a Carpenter," did his own "Simple
> Song of Freedom," moved to a blues version of "You Are
> My Sunshine," and finished with "Splish Splash." It was a
> bit of something for everyone, and it was all done with the
> excellent vocal stying and arrangement precision that has
> marked Darin's best works.
>
> At the end of the hour show, Darin got a standing ova-
> tion. And he deserved it. Darin is back, and since he is
> using his full range of skills and styles, he is better than
> ever. As a songwriter and performer, he deserves the respect
> he has so long sought. Darin, the boy from the Bronx, has
> always wanted to be something special. And he is.

But my dad still had one more hurdle to clear before he felt truly back to where he'd been. Specifically, he wanted to make good on his flop at the Copa three years before. He told Al Aronowitz, "The Copa is the most important engagement. I told Julie I wanted to play it and settle the situation. I did a bad thing there last time. One thing I now know is that I'm a saloon singer. There's a certain frame of mind in a saloon that's perfect for me. I'm a saloon singer, and that's what I'm going to major in."

By all accounts, Bobby's engagement at the Copa was a smash. Don Hecker, entertainment critic for *The New York Times*, wrote: "Darin is still a first-class performer. He sang, played the guitar, drums, and piano, tied things together with a virtually nonstop and often quite witty patter, and managed to pull a lackadaisical first-night audience out of its lethargy."

The crowds were elated, and so was Julie Podell, who booked my dad for a return engagement seven months later in October of that year. "Comeback" complete, my dad would go on to do a weekly television series.

And for a short time, he would be married again.

13

Bobby, 1972

Age is the enemy of progress, because we fondle what is easiest for us to embrace, which is our memories. What can an old man fondle? He can't even fondle his genitals successfully anymore. He fondles his memories. What he retained. What he remembers. And the memory is like moonbeams. You do with it what you want to do with it. I am always concerned about anyone who spends too much time fondling and embracing yesterdays. That's not a particular desire of mine. It's a very today universe for me, and it's pleasant.

—BOBBY DARIN, *1972*

After my dad's triumphant return to the Copa, good things continued to happen. NBC hired my dad as the summer replacement for *The Dean Martin Show. The Bobby Darin Amusement Company* was a variety show made up of equal parts guest stars, comedy skits, and music. It debuted in July 1972 with guests George Burns, singer Bobbie Gentry, and Burt Reynolds, who had just done a news-breaking nude centerfold for *Cosmopolitan* magazine. It was a great kick-off, and the show got pretty good reviews, which got better and better as the summer unfolded.

My dad had a steady relationship with a woman he'd been seeing for a couple of years. Her name was Andrea Yeager, a divorcée, a legal secretary, who was quite beautiful and very kind. They had spontaneous chemistry, and for the three years they went together, my dad referred to Andrea as Mrs. Darin. I spent a lot of time with Andrea, whom I loved, and her two sons, Armin and Alex.

Andrea recalls the first time she met my father:

I was working for a law firm in Long Beach when I met Bobby in 1970. He was waiting in the reception room, and we said hello. He was very charming, did his number, and I didn't recognize him. The last time I had seen him perform, he had a chip on his shoulder and he was wearing a tuxedo. Then he dropped out of sight. When he came into the office, he had long hair, Levi's, cowboy boots, and cowboy hat, and I didn't know who he was. The next day I got a little piece of stationery from him, and it said, "Peace, Bobby Darin."

And I answered it! He was at the Landmark, right after his Big Sur trip, and I flew in to see him. I stayed for the weekend, and we hit it off right from the get-go. Bobby was the first man I had encountered who made me feel as if I were worth something. He liked my sense of humor and my ditsiness. I remember we were on a plane with some friends of his. I'd had something to drink on the plane and something before that at dinner, and it didn't take much to make me silly. This was the first time I'd worn false fingernails that you put on with glue, and I put them on in the bathroom on the plane. When I came back I said, "Oh, I've lost my fingernail." Well, one of them was stuck in my panty hose. Bobby fell on the floor, laughing. And he pointed out the fingernail to everybody. That was our first weekend together.

I started spending every weekend with him in Vegas, and then I'd drive back to L.A. on Sunday night. He was doing two shows a night in Vegas, and we'd go out to dinner between shows. If someone would come up to him and said, "Are you Bobby Darin?" he would say, "No." Offstage he could look like a bum, just a down-and-outer, no problem. Without his hairpiece, wearing his glasses, he didn't look anything like

*he did onstage. I noticed right away that he was a very earthy
person. He drove a Renault, and he enjoyed spending time on
a lake, if he had a boat, or camping out. He was very warm,
easy to be with, just good vibrations from the very beginning.*

*Bobby had Dodd with him every other weekend. One week-
end he'd gone to take Dodd home, and it was a long ride
back, and he said, "I've decided that you should move in with
me," because he didn't like me to have to leave abruptly on
Sunday. One weekend I went home and started to cry because
I was so happy. Falling in love had never happened to me like
that before. And from that point on, it just mushroomed to
my moving in with him, with the kids, my cat, quitting the
job that I had. I had a house in Long Beach and a mother and
furniture and all that stuff, and I just got rid of everything.*

Andrea also accompanied my dad to New York. John Miller remembers being with my dad and Andrea one night during one of my
father's Copa engagements. They all got into a limousine and went on
one of my dad's tours of his life in New York. But when my dad and
John Miller hung out alone, they would cruise together for girls.

"It was always fantasy time," Miller reminisces. "We would pick
up girls, and Bobby would say that he was my chauffeur. He'd say
that I was a very important person in from Los Angeles, and he couldn't
explain what I did because I was a mystery man. But if they knew
what was good for them, they would pay attention to me. We would
pick them up on the street or in clubs or anywhere. Bobby would have
been a great con man. He could sail into pitches at a drop of the hat.
Once he said he was an airline pilot. We did a thing one night where
he said that he was a jade importer from Hong Kong who got into
New York twice a year. Believe it or not, people would believe him.
He loved the idea that he was putting somebody on who didn't know
that he was the star. But I think if he ever thought for a minute that
he wasn't the star, it would have crushed him."

My dad enjoyed a couple of obsessions during this last good period
of his life. He bought a tugboat, converted it into a houseboat, and
spent his free time there with Andrea. He also discovered chess. Bobby
Fisher and Boris Spassky trained a glamorous spotlight on the game

in 1972, and my dad caught the bug. He read everything he could find on the subject and bought chess boards for all his friends so that when he went to visit he could pick up on games he'd started with them the time before. He organized a chess tournament, and, incredibly, he talked NBC into letting him put a chess problem on his TV program for a minute or two every week.

Obviously, watching Bobby solving a chess problem was dull stuff in the middle of the variety show, and the bit was short-lived. But my dad played a number of characters that were highly entertaining and became regular fixtures every week. The skit everyone loved was called "Angie and Carmine." My dad played Angie and Carmine was played by Dick Bakalyan. The comedy piece featured two guys from the neighborhood who talked about life from a front stoop made to look like the one in front of my dad's old apartment in the Bronx. The skits were scripted but open to improvisation, and they were warm and quite funny. There were a number of writers on the show, and in addition to them, my dad called on a real pal from his actual neighborhood.

Dick Lord recalls how "Bobby asked me to come out and audition for his show, and after I told one of my jokes, the producer asked, 'How would you like to be the creative consultant on the show?' I said, 'Okay.' "

☞ *The first week there I found this guy to open the show. He was about four feet, seven inches, very small. And he was a one-man band. He wore a Tyrolean hat and lederhosen. And he had a big bass drum and cymbals and had a harmonica strapped to his chin. He took himself very seriously, which is what was so humorous. The opening of the show became this little man walking across the stage hitting the drum and playing "Mack the Knife," and written on the side of the drum was the name of the show, "The Bobby Darin Amusement Company."*

So I did that for starters, but I wasn't performing, and that's all I wanted to do. I didn't want to be a creative consultant. I'm a comedian. But I did what I did for Bobby, I swear to God, totally for him.

It was so sad, during the summer show. We would sometimes go to the studio together. I didn't want to complain to him how much I hated it, so I didn't. But he complained to me a lot. And some of his complaints were out of control. One day he said, "The soap. The soap. I want Charlie to put the soap over here. I don't want to have to reach over there." And I said, "You're talking about a bar of soap." And he started to laugh. He realized himself then that he was nuts. But he was becoming more irritable because his life was so terrible.

He would go the studio every day. He would certainly work a lot harder than I did because he was in every segment. I was just killing time, but Bobby really worked hard, and he would come home at five o'clock and get into bed. Andrea would turn the phones off and she would take a chair and sit by the door and read in case he needed anything.

When Bobby finished the summer show, it was being considered as a winter show. I met Bobby at the airport and he said, "I'm not gonna do the show. I'm tired of auditioning."

I said, "What do you mean, auditioning?"

He said, "I can make more money in Vegas."

I said, "Don't be an idiot. How many people get a chance for their own television show? So it's four thousand a week less. What does it matter to you? You're not gonna get any more chances. You've blown it on every fucking network you've been on."

And this is an example. He was on Dick Cavett's show. Lucille Ball's daughter was on, talking about cruelty to animals. Bobby's like my brother. I can see him sitting there, and I knew it was just a matter of moments before the shit hit the fan. All of a sudden he says to her, "How can you talk about cruelty to pussycats when people are dying in the streets in India? People are eating dog vomit, starving to death in the Appalachian Mountains, and you're talking about pussycats? Where are your priorities?" After that, Lucille Ball apparently called people at CBS, and that finished him there.

I'm not saying he stayed with his NBC show because I told him to. But he did go on with the winter show.

That season NBC canceled *Banyon* and *The Bold Ones* but announced in November that they were picking up *The Bobby Darin Show* in January 1973. The press reported, "*The Bobby Darin Show* was the only summer show to be picked up midseason this year, and the reason is that Bobby's bright, lively musical-variety hour racked up very respectable ratings last summer." Between the end of the summer show in September and the beginning of the winter show in January, my dad made his last film, *Happy Mother's Day, Love George*, with Ron Howard and Cloris Leachman. He recorded his last record for Motown. And he went on a nightclub tour that would be the pinnacle of his performing career.

From coast to coast he was incredible. Bobby wasn't only back, he was better than before. Critics who didn't want to like him couldn't help themselves. A reviewer from the *New Orleans Picayune* said, "This is a class nightclub show you do yourself a favor by seeing. I never particularly cared for Darin before, but Thursday night made me a believer. He is GOOD!" Apparently my dad had never gone over well in Louisiana because another New Orleans reviewer said, "Bobby Darin surprised me. I wasn't sure I'd like him. He's great. Great is an adjective I use sparingly to describe entertainers, but no other word will do for the show Bobby Darin puts on in the Blue Room."

Praise was given unreservedly elsewhere. The *Chicago Tribune* said he was "every inch a consummate entertainer who knocks the customers out of their chairs." The *Chicago Daily News* said his renditions of "Splish Splash" and "Mack the Knife" "brought rafter-shaking applause." The *Dallas Times Herald* called Bobby's show "one of the fastest, funniest shows to be seen in a long time. He loosens up and goes into one of the funniest, thigh-slapping routines I have ever heard." The *Dallas Record* said, "Bobby Darin is one of the greatest vocalists and entertainers of today."

My dad played the Copa in October and, astonishingly, forgot the lyrics to "Mack the Knife." He cracked to the *New York Post*, "It's like Moses forgetting the Ten Commandments." The *Daily News* said, "If there were no Bobby Darin, they would have to design, mold, and program one to be the perfect entertainer for the Copacabana. . . .

Fortunately, there is very much a Bobby Darin, and he's back where he belongs. Darin has absolute command of what he's doing. He has a timing, both comedically and musically, that is impeccable and, above all, a fantastic contact with his audience." Joe Delaney of the *Las Vegas Sun* said, "Bobby Darin is just a sixteenth note away from breaking through in all media as the next authentic superstar. The sum total of the man is a joy to behold. . . ."

My dad was in love with his career all over again, and since it was wholehearted, not a stepping-stone to other things, it may have felt like love for the first time. But he was exhausted. There was always oxygen present backstage, and sometimes he gulped some in between songs. In December 1972 my dad made a call to his great friend Steve Blauner. They arranged to get together.

Steve remembers that Bobby came into his office one day and said:

☞ *"Look, Steve. I made a million dollars last year, which was more than I made when I was hot. But I didn't sell any records, and I need you. It will only take you ten minutes a day to manage me from your office."*

I was making films. I didn't want to manage Bobby anymore, but I didn't want to say no to him, either. So I put him off for as long as I could, and when I couldn't do that any longer, I concocted a deal that I knew he couldn't live with. That way he had to say no to me.

I sat him down and I said, "You want me? Fine. You can have me, but these are the terms. One, you've got to give me a million dollars whether you ever work another day in your life. Not up front, but guaranteed with my normal twenty percent, even if you get sick tomorrow and never work again. And this time I want a contract in writing, and I won't travel, and you can't call me after six o'clock at night and not at all on weekends. You're not number one anymore. You're not even number two. I have a wife and kids. And if your lawyer lets you accept this deal, we've got to fire your lawyer. So now let's figure out who to get to manage you instead of me."

Bobby looked at me and said, "You've got it."

I went home to my wife and said, "Kevin, I'm sorry, but we are now managing Bobby because I couldn't tell him that I was kidding about this deal."

My dad was restructuring his life, and everything was coming together for him. He told the press he'd learned he could live without the glossier trappings of show business, but that he wasn't living in the "Hotel Shambles," either. He bought a house on Rodeo Drive and showed it to his friend Rona Barrett, who remembers that Bobby was never happier than when he was planning to renovate this house.

Just when things couldn't be better, my dad made a tragic mistake. He went to the dentist to have his teeth cleaned. Heart patients are supposed to take antibiotics when having dental work done, as a preventive against bacteria invading the bloodstream. They are supposed to do this for as long as they live because infected blood can screw up the valves and prove fatal. For reasons known only to my father, he didn't take the antibiotics. And he went off his anticoagulants as well.

When Bobby met Sandy, he was twenty-four and she was sixteen. They were married three months later. This photo was taken the day after their wedding as they got off the plane in L.A. *(Photo by Allan Grant/LIFE magazine © Time Warner Inc.)*

A proud mother; Nina and Bobby at the premier nightclub, the Copacabana, 1961.

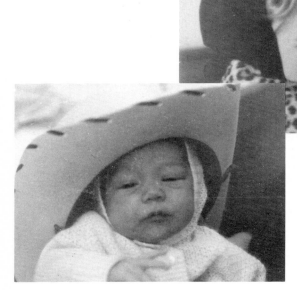

Another proud mother, mine.
Sandy and her newborn son.

I was named Dodd Mitchell
Cassotto.

My Dad celebrating his twenty-sixth birthday at the Cloisters, 1962.

A still photo from my parents' second film together, *If a Man Answers*, 1962. *(Copyright © 1962 by Universal City Studios, Inc. Courtesy of MCA Publishing Rights, a division of MCA, Inc.)*

Dream Lovers. My dad's song by that name reached #2 on the charts in 1962. This picture of Bobby and Sandy was taken at about that time.

Me and my dad at his triumphant
return to the Cocoanut Grove in L.A.
I had a tuxedo like my dad's and I
went on stage!

My mom's twenty-first
birthday. Behind my dad are
George Hamilton (*left*) and
Bill Bixby (*right*).

Publicity shot from the third
and last film my parents made
together: *That Funny Feeling.*
*(Copyright © 1965 by Universal
City Studios, Inc. Courtesy of
MCA Publishing Rights, a
division of MCA, Inc.)*

A happy moment with my
mom. I was seven years old.

My dad in his "hippie" phase, 1969. The tux and the hairpiece were gone and he sang protest songs. His new image didn't fly with the major clubs and his career took a hit. But he stood up for what he believed in.

Thanks in good part to a helping hand from Wayne Newton, my dad made his comeback at the Desert Inn in 1971. When the show closed, my dad went into the hospital for major heart surgery. (*Photo by Las Vegas News Bureau*)

My dad and his loyal fans, who became like family: the Masterantonio sisters back stage. From left to right, Lucille, Antoinette, my dad, and Rose.

My mom in 1983. Still a living doll. (*Photo by Harry Langdon*)

In 1991, John Saxon called my
mom and asked her to be in a
play with him, called *Love
Letters*. When the curtain parted,
they got a standing ovation that
went on for five minutes. I was so
proud of my mom. This picture of
us was taken at that time.
(© 1991, Smeal/Ron Galella, Ltd.)

Audrey Tannenbaum and I were
married on June 5, 1993. I was a
nervous wreck before the
wedding. It was the happiest day
of my life.

14

Bobby's Wives, Family, and Friends, 1973

The Curtain Falls

Off comes the greasepaint,
Off comes the clown's disguise.
The curtain's falling
The music softly dies.

I hope you're smiling
As you're filing out the door.
They say in show biz, that's all there is.
There isn't anymore.

. . . .

People say I was made for this,
Nothing else I would trade for this,
And to think I get paid for this.
But now the curtain falls.

—(Music and lyrics written for Bobby Darin
by Sol Weinstein)

The last year of my father's life was, predictably, a very full year. *The Bobby Darin Show*, amended somewhat from the summer replacement show, debuted in January. At my dad's insistence, the new show would have more music, fewer skits, and less comedy. Four months later, with ratings that would make a network executive gloat today, NBC canceled *The Bobby Darin Show*. On April 27 my father filmed the last show of his series, and although he didn't feel good about it at the time, history records it as a superb finish.

Said TV and radio critic Don Freeman, "Watching the finale unfold, well paced and brightly tuneful, I wonder why *The Bobby Darin Show* fell flat in the ratings. . . . From the onset, the Darin show was blessed with solid production and very good guests and a number of funny bits. . . . In the final show the atmosphere was virtually all night-club—Bobby and the band, pouring it on, and then Bobby and his only guest, Peggy Lee, with her artlessly meticulous phrasing and her honest and delicately pure approach to a song that knocks me into tiny pieces of, I guess, putty. Brash Bobby and Peggy with the richly sensuous, smoky tones—it was a good way to go."

By the time *The Bobby Darin Show* wound down that April, my father was really ill—but no one knew what was wrong. He went into the hospital for six weeks, and doctors discovered that he had septicemia, blood poisoning, the result of bacteria shooting through his system after his dental work months before. He spent six weeks in the hospital, May through early June, then in July Bobby and Andrea Yeager were married. Four months later, because of a gross misunderstanding, my dad divorced her. (Rather than give the details here, I'll let Andrea explain later in the chapter.) In between, he slept and worked and slept. Steve Blauner was true to form as a manager who "left a trail of blood." Scant days before my dad's show was canceled, Steve got him an extraordinary deal with the MGM Grand Hotel in Vegas and booked my dad into a tour of sixty clubs in ninety days. There was no way my father could do any of this. He was dying. And the same gross misunderstanding that broke up Andrea and Bobby's marriage also caused my dad's relationship with Steve Blauner to end.

Plenty of people felt that my dad was simply hypochondriacal and was creating his own illness. Medical doctors couldn't find anything physically wrong with him. Internists, cardiologists, infection specialists, all shrugged their shoulders, and his friends didn't know what to do for him. Unbeknownst to anyone, the septicemia had penetrated the lining of his heart. That was what was causing the tiredness and the sluggishness. At the same time, when my dad stopped the anticoagulants, he developed blood clots, or embolisms, on the brain. It's probable that these embolisms caused the erratic behavior he was exhibiting. He became forgetful and irrational. He was in pain and struck out at people he loved.

My dad checked into L.A.'s Cedars-Sinai Hospital in October for congestive heart failure. He seemed to recover briefly, then his health spiraled downward. He made a one-day trip to New York to see old friends, then was wheeled into Cedars for the last time on December 10, 1973. Along with feeling truly horrible, my dad was very frightened. I remember my mom telling me he would call and tell her that he was changing room numbers at the hospital. He'd say, "I'm in room 28A now, but tomorrow they're moving me to 38B. Write that down. Remember now, I'm going to 38B." He was afraid we'd lose track of him.

And this was upsetting to my mom. She'd say, "Of course we're not going to lose you. We know you're in the hospital. We'll find you."

I hadn't seen my father for several months prior to his death. He didn't want people to see him really ill, and not seeing him was painful to me. I just couldn't understand it. I had seen him ill before. I knew he was in and out of hospitals, but this time my mom and I were barred along with everyone else except my aunt Vee. I guess my dad knew how really ill he was and didn't want us to remember him suffering. Apparently his body weight dropped drastically. He had never been big, but he always had a solid build, with good muscle definition. Suddenly he looked wasted.

A heart specialist to the stars had reportedly told Bobby that there was "nothing wrong with him from the neck down." It was such a quotable quote that my dad repeated it to many of his friends, all of whom remember him saying it. It only added to their consternation, but Dave Gershenson felt that my father was dying. He told me that my dad was having long, horrible spells of hiccuping, which may have been the result of not getting enough oxygen. These spells could last several weeks and, combined with the rapid heartbeat, were just murderous. He could hardly take a simple breath of air, and the spasms were a strain on his heart. At one point my dad decided that if he picked an age he wanted to live to and chanted that age, he would cheat death. He picked the number 64, but death had another number in mind.

I remember clearly the last conversation I had with my dad. He called from the hospital on my birthday, December 16, three days before he died. When I heard his voice, I almost couldn't tell who it was. He was part hysterical, part sobbing, almost unintelligible. I eventually understood that he was calling to wish me a happy birthday. He told me that he loved me and that he was very sorry he couldn't be with me, but his manner distressed me so much, I cut the conversation short. I gave the phone to my mom, and she realized that my dad was falling apart, both from his illness and from all the medication he was taking. After my mom talked to him and he talked some to my grandmother, the phone was handed over to my aunt Vee. He told her that he was breathing his last, and she tried to calm him down. But we were all just in shock by his tone. I wrote my dad a note telling him I loved him, too, which Vee took to him in the hospital. I'm glad that at the age of twelve I had the presence of mind to do that.

My father had a terror of a painful procedure called an arteriogram, in which a catheter is threaded through an artery into the heart. Whether it was the pain that scared him or whether he was more afraid of what he might find out, we'll never know. But we do know that my dad had rejected his doctor's entreaties to do the procedure. It was another mistake he made. When he fell into a coma just before the end, his doctors got Vee's permission to use this diagnostic tool, and it cleared up the mystery of Bobby's worsening state. Belatedly, they learned that one of his artificial valves had been malfunctioning. When the doctors opened up my dad's chest to repair the damage, they found that the whole heart muscle had deteriorated from the infection. During the first surgery in 1971, much of the left side of my dad's heart had been cut away, and now the doctors had very little to work with. They cleaned out the infection as best they could and closed up his chest.

One of the most difficult aspects of open heart surgery is getting the patient off the life support machinery. My dad made the switch, and the doctors were on their way out the door when his heart massively failed. Because there was brain damage and every probability that he would survive the crisis only in a vegetative state, Vee agreed to let the doctors pull the plug. My dad had requested that his body be given to science. When he died, his remains were transferred to UCLA Medical Center.

During the last year of his life, my father was in pain, bewildered, and half out of his mind. His friends were frightened for him, but he managed to keep most of them at bay. Rather than paraphrase, I'll let the people who loved my father the most tell about their last days with Bobby.

Andrea Yaeger Darin Burton

Bobby got septicemia during the winter show and went into the hospital when the show was over. It was near the end of his hospital stay when he asked me to marry him. I said I would when he got out of the hospital, and he gave me a little ring and said, "Let's get married this month." I remember pointing out to him that I was hearing desperation in his voice and felt that I was being cornered, but in the end I agreed. From the time Bobby came out of the hospital in May, it was all downhill. He was on death row, unbeknownst to me.

Everything was super until June, but right after he came out of the hospital his heart went out again. He put up with it, but it would go in and out. When his heart was out, he was cranky and everything was distorted. Nothing could please him. He just hurt. His frustration and anger just ran rampant in his whole being and made an old man of him. But when he was feeling good, he was like a kid.

We started our summer vacation with the kids in June of 1973. We rented a houseboat and went by river up to the Sacramento delta. The day we arrived, we pulled the boat in and told the kids we were going to the store. Then we ran off and got married in our Levi's and blue workshirts. I remember feeling how happy Bobby was as we stood in the judge's chambers. He was practically giddy. When we came back and told the kids that we had gotten married, they didn't believe us. They were mad at us anyway because it was hot and they didn't have anything to drink or eat, and they felt abandoned.

After the vacation, Bobby took Dodd and went north to Big Sur, and I took my boys to San Diego. Then Bobby and I met in La Jolla because we were thinking of buying a house there. We were there for a few days, but we didn't look at houses because Bobby couldn't get out of bed. Then we went to Vegas and he worked. His heart was out again, but I had no idea that it was much more serious than it had been. We were in Vegas for five weeks. From there I came back home and he went on to Tahoe to do a date. Then he came home and went to bed for a month. Again, he was so depressed he wouldn't get out of bed.

I remember there was no fight left in Bobby. He was just mush. He was gray and he was staggering, and he'd get in the car to go someplace and forget where he was going and get lost and stagger around and fall down. All this time he should have been in the hospital. He was going to doctors, but nobody was saying "He should be in the hospital. This is what's happening. This is what you should expect. This is what you should do."

Then he started seeing a heart surgeon. Dr. Corday was what you'd call a celebrity's doctor. Bobby heard about him and went in hoping for miracles. The doctor made some changes in his pill prescription, and Bobby quit him in the middle of the program. So he was going without his blood thinner for a while. Finally, one day near the end of August, I said, "You're gonna get out of this bed. We're gonna see Dr. Pearlmutter and get some answers." Jonah Pearlmutter was a shrink Bobby had seen for a short while some months before and had quit seeing. Suddenly he wanted to go again. His attitude was like "Gee, somebody cares."

Bobby asked Steve to come with us, and the three of us went to see Dr. Pearlmutter. I had talked to Pearlmutter and told him that Bobby was in pretty bad shape, but when he saw what Bobby looked like, he was flabbergasted. Jonah said, "You have a choice. But what I think you should do is check in at UCLA and have a thorough, thorough checkup: physical, mental, everything." Bobby didn't hear it that way. All he could see were these monsters closing in on him, trying to lock him up, trying to commit him, trying to put him away.

After the meeting, we walked outside. Bobby went across the street to Dr. Corday's office. Corday saw him for a while, but Bobby was unhappy with what he had to say. So we left. The next day I was talking to Bobby's lawyer's office, and the switchboard operator says to me, "I read in the trade papers that you and Bobby are getting a divorce." And it *was* in the papers. I called [Hollywood Reporter columnist] Army Archerd and asked him where he got the item, and he told me that Bobby called him. I have never been so mad in all my life. It was a pretty shitty way to find out that I was getting a divorce. The way the marriage came out of the blue, so did the divorce.

Bobby disappeared about a week after that. He was supposed to check into a convalescent home and nobody was to know where he was. All he did was go to the house in Vegas, and he didn't answer the phone. He didn't do what he was supposed to do. By this time, whatever he did would have been futile. I don't think anything would have helped. When he came back to L.A., I called him a punk. He hated that word. Better to call him a motherfucker than a punk, but I couldn't stop myself from saying it. What he had done to me was shitty, and everything about it was cruel.

A short while later, we reached a settlement. I got twelve thousand dollars plus the Toyota to replace the car I'd had when I married Bobby. I know he was thinking, "I'll give her X amount of dollars to live on for the next year. If I make it, then we'll live together the way we were before we were married. If I don't make it, she'll have enough to live on for a year and she'll get on her feet." I wasn't hurt by this settlement, because Bobby was demented by this time. But I asked his lawyer to tell Bobby not to call me for a while. I needed time to get things together, and I just didn't want to hear Bobby's bullshit.

After Bobby came back from Vegas, everything was fine. We were like dating again. The divorce didn't mean anything to him. The divorce was just Bobby. He wanted me to fix him Thanksgiving dinner, but I wasn't in the mood. Instead we went out to a little French place and then went back to his hotel. It was a nice evening, but Bobby looked really bad to me because I hadn't seen him in a week. We made love, and I woke up crying the next morning because the whole situation was just so sad. I was up before Bobby was, and I just left. I had to get out. Bobby didn't like it when he woke up and I was gone and I hadn't left him a note or anything. But I had to go home.

After Thanksgiving, he rented a little house on Rexford near the fire station. He had an idea that his friends would drop by with their hobbies and keep him company. "Bring your knitting, your sewing; if you make model planes, paint them here." And I was supposed to make enough food, not just for him and me, but for a gang of people, just in case. I went to see him every day. I couldn't stay with him because it was just too painful to watch. He was in the house by himself, and he shouldn't have been. He only took his medication sporadically. He'd be good for a while, then he'd have some trouble and he'd say, "What the fuck am I taking this shit for? It's not helping me." And then he wouldn't take anything at all. Then something would happen and he'd go see a doctor, who would put him back on medication.

Bobby had a temper and would blow up at people, but the people who loved him the most and would do anything for him usually got the worst treatment. It was like "They love me, and I can't do anything wrong, and I know they'll be there no matter what." And then he'd kiss the ass of people who would shit on him in a moment. He had severed his relationship with Steve, so I told him, "Call me. Just call me anytime you need to call." And it was a very funny thing because it was like two friends talking. "I really appreciate it," he'd say. He was getting worse and worse. And he was so skinny.

Finally, one Monday I said to him I wanted him to see a doctor. He couldn't walk from the bedroom to the bathroom without falling down. So he went to the doctor, and the doctor put him in the hospital, and he never came out. I saw him once after that. The nurse told me to bring Bobby a radio, and I didn't know which one he wanted. I brought him the wrong one and he became very angry and I got put out and started to cry. He said to me, "If you can't keep your emotions out of the hospital, don't come back."

So I didn't. Meanwhile I was in touch with the doctors, who kept saying, "He's going to be all right." I don't know if they were lying to me or if they believed that they could help him, but I don't like the way the whole thing was handled. I could have given him more support if I'd had somebody supporting me. When he knew he was going into surgery that last time, he called Dodd and he called me. He said to me, "I love you very much," And then he said, "I ain't gonna make it this time, kid."

I said, "Yes, you are. Everything's gonna be fine. I'm going to New York, and I'll see you when I get back." He died while I was in New York. To be honest, I was relieved when he died. He was out of pain and misery for the first time in his life. But I didn't believe he was gone at first. For at least a couple of months after his death, it felt to me as though he were away on the road. He was going to be back. Then that passed.

I remember when his heart was off and he'd sleep through the whole day. When he got up, he'd still be dragged out, but he'd go out and do a show. And you'd never guess in a million years that the man even had a hangnail. Those who knew how sick he was would think, What's the guy trying to do? Kill himself? And he was. He did say to me "I'd like to die onstage." He was very dramatic, and that would be something he would have liked to do. To die at the end of his performance.

John Miller

The last few years, Bobby was utterly obsessed with chess. That was all he did in the dressing room, between shows, after shows. He had things going with people on the phone where he was playing chess long distance. And it bothered him enormously when I didn't want to learn to play chess. I watched his last Copa engagement with Andrea just about every night. I thought Andrea was just a sensational girl, and her sister, Terry, was his valet. His "valette," Bobby used to call her. Terry was an absolutely gorgeous girl, and she obviously had a great deal of affection for Bobby. She handled everything for him, everything. There was genuine caring, yet there was nothing going on between the two of them. And I would go downstairs after leaving them and sit with Andrea and watch the show.

In the last days I spoke with him several times, and he had deteriorated because every conversation with him was strange. It wasn't Bobby at all. Ordinarily he would call me more than I would call him because he was hard to find. Then all of a sudden I called him several times on the phone and didn't get a call back. It was the first time in twenty years I didn't get a call back. My last conversation with Bobby was unfortunate.

I finally got him on the phone, and I said, "Bobby, what the hell's going on? I called you five times. I didn't get a call back."

He said, "I didn't call you back because I didn't call you back. That's all there is to it, John."

And that was not Bobby. I could have been talking to a stranger. I spoke to Andrea once after the divorce had been announced, and she was as confused as hell about what was going on, and so was I. I just couldn't understand what had happened to my dear friend. Things changed a lot at the end.

When we last really talked, he talked a lot about family stuff. Bobby's feelings for his son just defied description. He wanted Dodd to have a much better life than he'd had. And we got into long conversations about what Bobby's purpose was here on earth. He felt that it had to be something very meaningful, very important, and yet he felt in spite of his hit records, his show, he hadn't really achieved what his purpose was. He spoke often of touching the lives of people in different sections of the community. He wanted to do that, and he didn't fully understand the whys, hows, and ramifications of doing it. He spent hours just trying to figure it out. He spent hours and hours trying to figure out zillions of things there really weren't any answers to.

Bobby talked about death all the time, but I thought that we both were going to live forever. I just thought Bobby was a hypochondriac. And if he had paid attention, he could still be alive today. That's the shame of it. I remember his last engagement at the Copa. He complained about being sluggish. I saw every single show. There were shows where he took his medicine and shows where he didn't. And there wasn't any difference between shows. There really wasn't. But Bobby insisted that he was falling apart onstage.

My last *fun* night with Bobby, we went to Nathan's Coney Island Hot Dogs on Broadway and Forty-third just to goof off. There were a couple of girls in the lobby of the Copa, and we took them with us to Nathan's. A lot of the characters who hung out in there recognized Bobby, and he wound up buying hot dogs for fifty-five people, at least. It was like saying "The drinks are on the house." The whole thing came to about twenty-three dollars. It wasn't that much, but he had such a good time in there. He loved talking to all these people. He did impressions, he danced, he really put on a show, and we had a sensational time.

Bobby was a very special person to me. I would have great difficulty writing about him. When he died all I wrote in my column was that I would think of him every day for the rest of my life.

Dick Lord

One day Bobby said to me, "I want you to do me a favor. I want you and Andrea and Steve Blauner to go with me to a psychiatrist. And I want you to tell them if you think that I have changed."

And I said, "Not me. Maybe the others will do it. You're not getting me to do that."

He said, "Why not?"

I said, "Because you're my best friend, and I know you. You will turn on me."

He said, "How can you say that? I'm asking for your help."

I didn't go. Then NBC picked up Bobby's show for the winter, and in between Bobby stayed at my house. We were working together at the Concord Hotel, and he was bugging me. "You're going to come back to my show, right?"

I said, "I don't know."

I went on stage, did my act, and I did great. Bobby cleared backstage because he didn't want anyone back there. He threw his arms around me and said, "Magnificent show. That was a magnificent show."

I said, "Thank you." I left. I had another show to do. The next day he starts in again. "When are you going to come back?"

And I said, "Okay. I'll come back on one condition. I'm a comedian. You never put me on the show. I don't want to be a hog. I'm not asking for anything special, but you're asking me to give up my career to work on your show. It's not helping my career. When I'm gone that amount of time, it's like I'm out of business. So, here's the deal. Why don't you say, every once in a while, 'Here's another guy from the old neighborhood. He's a really funny comedian,' and I'll do my five minutes. I'm not saying every week. Just enough to keep me alive, so that when I come back anywhere to get a job, they'll say, 'Oh, yeah, I saw him on the Darin show.'"

And he says to me, "Hey, you're not Alan King. How's it going to look in the paper? Today's guest on the Darin show, Dick Lord or Alan King. Who are they gonna pick? You know, we've got to get the ratings."

I was dumbfounded. We went back to my house. I had a job that night. He did not. Like a little kid, he says, "I'm leaving. Who's going to take me to the airport?"

I said, "Get a limo."

My wife, Ellen, says, "I'll take you." I wanted to choke her. Whose side are you on?

He said, "I don't like to take a limo. I don't like that."

I said, "I've got to go now." I was so angry. Still am. And the phone would ring in the house after that, and I would say, "If it's Bobby, I don't want to talk to him." And he'd talk to Ellen. I would finish dinner. I would go upstairs. I would take a shower. I would put my tuxedo in the bag. And every once in a while Ellen would say to me, "Don't you want to say something?"

I would say, "I don't want to talk to him."

Now, the winter show goes on without me. He can't really believe that I'm not going to come back. One day I'm working in Buffalo. I'm in the hotel room at night after the show. The phone rings. It's Ellen. She says, "Bobby's here. He's very bad."

I said, "What do you mean, 'bad'?"

She said, "Well, he came to talk again about Nina being his mother. The Behrkes are here and we've called California, and he's going to go directly to the hospital. They have an ambulance to meet him at the plane. And Bobby wants to talk to you."

I didn't know what to say. I was stunned. And I remember what Bobby said when I took the phone. He said, "I can't think of anything funny to say."

And I just said, stupidly, "How do you feel?"

And he said, "Very bad. Very weak. This is really it."

I would always panic when Bobby would say "This is really it," because the thought of his not being here was so awful. Even though I'd be so angry. And this time it *was* really it. It was the last time I ever spoke with Bobby.

I was appearing somewhere in Pennsylvania. For some reason, I didn't want to stay over. I wanted to go home. Ellen was with me, and it was a long drive. We got home, and at about six o'clock in the morning the phone rang. A voice said, "I'm calling because your friend Bobby Darin died."

I said, "God. He died? When?"

"Two forty-three this morning." Something like that. She wanted to know who to invite to the funeral. I gave her five or six names, hung up. There was no funeral.

My friend Steve Karmen once asked me what I'd say to Bobby if he came back. I told him I'd say, "You're my best friend. I love you and think of you every day, but I'm mad at you for a couple of things, and if you don't apologize, I'm not going to talk to you." I really have so many emotions about Bobby. I was happy to be so close to him. I loved him, and it was always exciting when I was with him. And I always felt empty when he left. It was like brief moments of togetherness, and then he'd be off, boom, to here or there. And I would feel so lonely.

Sometimes when I do a great show now, I swear I wish Bobby could see this. I was pretty good when he died. I'm terrific now. It's too late for me to be Jerry Seinfeld, but that's okay. I'm a terrific comedian, and I'm sorry he missed it, and I like to tell myself, "Well, maybe he sees it." I wish that. More than my parents, more than anybody, I wish Bobby could see me now.

Steve Blauner

It was early 1973, and I was managing Bobby again. They had already shot four shows of *The Bobby Darin Show* and were on hiatus. I had gone out to NBC, and I had seen the four shows. Now they were going to go back the next day to do the other nine shows, and Bobby had me come to the Beverly Wilshire, where he was staying. And he said to me, "Steve, doing this show is dishonest. This is not creative. I want to walk."

I was stunned by this, but had I known he was going to die, I would have gone along with him. I understood what he was saying. The show wasn't creative. But the first thing I thought was, Oh, my God, I haven't made his insurance policy yet. I hadn't made the deal in Vegas that I knew I had to make for him, because with his exposure on television, I knew I could make him such a good deal, it would be like an insurance policy for the next few years. And out of my mouth came the following. I said, "Look, Bobby. All your life you've thrown your tantrums. You've gotten away with it since you were a kid. Everybody's catered to you." Then, and this is one of the only times I lied to him, I said, "This has nothing to do with business. But for once in your life, see something through to the end, and it will be more constructive than anything else you can do, from the standpoint of making you a man, my son."

And I left, waiting to see what would happen.

The next day he drives through the gate at NBC, so he's going to stay on the show. But he's ill. And I say to myself, Look at this son of a bitch. He's going to make us suffer. And it was unbearable. In the beginning I thought he was doing a number on us. Then I thought, He ain't this good an actor to do this number this long. There is definitely something wrong. So, I start to call doctors and shrinks and screaming that I'm the only person in the world who can stop him from working. And I have this on my head, and I need some help. "Tell me, am I killing him?" And they had done CAT scans, and no one could figure out what was wrong with him. I can see he can hardly move, and it freaks me out, but I'm going to live with it because I've got to make a deal for him in Vegas before anybody knows that the show will not be renewed.

We knew the show was going to be canceled when he did the last show of the television series. Up until that point I'd only been there trying to get Bobby through it. Now, I made waves. I said, "I want Bobby to do a one-man show."

The producer's attitude was, "NBC won't accept it."

I said, "This is the last show. Don't worry about NBC because they're not going to pick you up again anyhow." So we agreed on one act. We got Peggy Lee, and she and Bobby were very good friends. The producers said, "Peggy Lee's going to do a hunk. Bobby's going to do a hunk, and they're going to do a hunk together. That's the show." Peggy was out on the stage rehearsing. She was always very well rehearsed and conscientious, and I figured the producers have got this under control. Well, Peggy Lee gets through, and they give the orchestra the dinner break, and there's no rehearsal for Bobby. I'll never forget this because it was my responsibility. I should not have assumed that people knew what they were doing. Bobby came out in his bathrobe, and when he found out he wasn't going to rehearse, he slammed his fist on top of the piano.

Bobby and I had a routine that developed over the years. After the show I would come into his dressing room. I never said anything. But if I was there and didn't address anything, he knew that my attitude was that he bombed. If I shook his hand, that meant he was okay. If I hugged him and picked him up off the ground, that was, "Oooh. He did everything great." And he would wait for my critique. If it got to be something that was really necessary to discuss openly, I was relentless because I felt if he was going out there, he owed people a performance. To the best of his ability.

Bobby was sick all during the last nine shows. I knew he was only up to seventy percent of himself. He would sit around all day, slumped. His hand was a claw. He wasn't getting circulation. Now it's the last show, and he gets no reheasal. We don't know how much time he's going to do. So he gets up there and he starts to sing and he gives a show—even though he was only seventy percent—that was once in a lifetime. When he got off the stage an hour and ten minutes later, he got a standing ovation. I'd never seen in that day and age a standing ovation in a television studio.

Bobby has left the stage and the musicians are on a break, and when they come back they are going to do Peggy's segment. And then Bobby and Peggy still have to do something together. I went looking for Bobby to hug him, and I couldn't find him. Finally, in the deepest bowels of NBC, I found him standing alone, sobbing like a child. I think he felt this was his last performance, and it was incredible, and Sandy had not let his son come to see it. And in the front row was Andrea with her two sons, but Dodd wasn't there.

Now, he's supposed to come back and do his bit with Peggy Lee. She's looking daggers at him. He has no idea why, but what had happened was while he was performing for an hour and ten minutes she was standing up the whole time in her dressing room completely dressed, not knowing when she was going on. But it wasn't Bobby's fault.

Finally, he was all through with his show. It was over. He was sitting in the dressing room, dealing with "We're never coming back on the air" and the rejection by the mass audience. And he was sick.

After the show was over, he found out that he had this blood disease that is common with people who've had rheumatic fever. He went into the hospital for six weeks, and they gave him antibiotics intravenously, and I had the greatest time in the world with him. Every afternoon I'd go down there, and we would just sit there rapping, and he would be talking about Andrea, and he would be crying, and it was just incredible.

During this time, I went to Vegas one day at eight o'clock in the morning and stayed until eight o'clock at night. Before Bobby got sick again, we had gotten maybe thirty-five thousand dollars a week. Now I went around to everyone, every hotel, saw every guy who was in charge of making the deals. I went in and gave these people ultimatums as though I had Frank Sinatra, the biggest star in the world. Some people laughed at me. Finally, I made a deal. The MGM Grand was being built. It was a new hotel and they needed talent, and I ended up making a deal that was hard to believe. Even I couldn't believe it. It was twenty-seven weeks over three years, seventy-five thousand dollars a week, plus they paid for his backup singers, musicians, power of the pencil, which means we could sign for anything we wanted. It was food, beverages, dozens of rooms, suites for friends, everything. A two-million-dollar contract. Bobby never got to play the MGM Grand because he died before it opened, but in the interim I booked him into the Hilton for the same price.

When Bobby left the hospital, his heart went out of rhythm again. He let everybody go, including his musicians. We were in Bobby's lawyer's office, and Bobby said, "Well, Steve, everything is timing. Too bad." And I was going to be cut off. Which was all right because I had made the deal for him in Vegas, and my contract with him didn't even need to be signed. But he was getting so ill, he wouldn't get out of bed. And Andrea asked me to go over to the apartment and read the riot act to him. I went. The shades were drawn. I said to him, "What's the worst thing that could happen? You could never go onstage again. With most performers that would be the end of their life, but for you, you can write. You're a record producer. You don't need to be onstage."

And Bobby looked at me, took it all in, and then he said, "Thanks, Steve. When you leave, please close the blinds after you."

Bobby was starting to go in and out of what I thought of as senility. For example, he'd call me up and say, "Steve, I want you to meet me at Friday noon in Westwood. Now that I can't sing anymore, I'm going to open up a little sixteen-millimeter movie house where you can lie on the floor." Or some other bizarre kind of idea he had. So I would agree to meet him. Two hours later he'd call and say, "Listen, on Friday, noon . . ." Same thing all over again. He'd be walking down the street, and he would walk into a wall as though he were drunk. I didn't know at the time he wasn't getting enough oxygen to the brain.

One day Bobby called me up and said, "Steve, I want you to meet me in Beverly Hills at the shrink's office. You and Andrea will come. She'll tell her thing, then you'll go in and you'll tell your thing, and then I'll go in and tell my thing, so the doctor can know not only from me, but from people who love me exactly what's going on."

I agreed to this. The day comes, and we were sitting in the outer office. Pearlmutter opened the door and asked Andrea go in alone. Bobby and I went for a little walk, came back, then the shrink asked us all to come in. I'd never seen the shrink alone, but the three of us now go into the shrink's office. And he said, "Bobby, I want you to go into the UCLA psychiatric ward. We're going to register you as a heart patient, though, so you don't have to worry that word will get out." Then he turned to Andrea and said, "Do you agree?" And she said, "Yes." Then he turned to me and said, "Do you agree?" And I choked, but I said, "Yes."

And I think the way the shrink confronted Bobby was wrong. He hadn't seen him in months, he didn't know me, and most people who are performers have too much ego to stand still for being talked to this way in front of people no matter how close the people are. So, Bobby got up, ended everything, and we all walked out. At the elevator he said to me, "This is very interesting." He was now under the impression that we were all plotting against him.

I said, "Bobby, this was your idea. I didn't ask to see the shrink." He left me and Andrea at the curb. He went across the street to see Corday, who was also Frank Sinatra's heart doctor, and Corday made the mistake of somehow comparing Bobby to Frank. So that was a disaster, too. Bobby left the doctor and called Andrea's sister, who picked him up. Bobby was burning up with anger. He got in the car to drive, which was frightening by itself. And the next day, in Army Archerd's column, Andrea found out she was getting divorced.

A few days later I was at home. It was about dinnertime, and Bobby appeared in the living room. He looked like death warmed over. He then proceeded to inform me that "this is a wrap."

I said, "What's a wrap?"

He said, "The relationship." I had done this horrible thing, and now the relationship was over.

I said, "Bobby, you can't legislate love." I walked him to the car, I leaned in, and I kissed him on the cheek. I said, "You do what you have to do. I will always love you whether we ever see each other again."

One day a few weeks later, Bobby called me. He was coming in from Vegas to see Dodd, and he came to my office. It was his way of apologizing. The minute he walked in, I grabbed him, I hugged him, I kissed him. And we had this nice time. Then I said, "Listen, one thing we should do now is clean up our business."

"Fine."

I said, "There are two things in question here. One, you erroneously thought I was paid up, but there is an eighteen thousand dollars payment that is due me, and I'd like that. And two, it wouldn't matter if I was single, but I have a family, and I'd like a piece of paper saying that no matter what happens in the future, if you honor the engagement in Vegas, I'll get my commission. I want that in writing."

And he said, "I'll think about it and talk to my lawyer." The next day the lawyer called and said that Bobby didn't want to put anything in writing and that his attitude was, "How could Steve think I wouldn't do the right thing?" My attitude was that I wasn't about to leave this unsigned agreement to the whim of a guy who was sick who didn't know what day was up.

I said, "This means a lawsuit. I'm going to sue him."

The lawyer called me the next day and in a moment of rational passion said, "Steve, do me a favor. You're a hundred percent right. You're entitled to the eighteen thousand. You're entitled to the commission. Let's wait and see if he gets better."

I said, "What if he dies?"

The lawyer said, "I guarantee you'll get the money." So I didn't sue. And I never talked to Bobby again.

Bobby went into the hospital for the open heart surgery. I sent him a note so he would know I still loved him and hoped everything went all right. I was asleep when I got a call from Dave Gershenson saying that Bobby had died. I went into my office and put the radio on and kept going up and down the dial, infuriated that they weren't playing Bobby's music. That's how irrational I was. I was still the manager even in death.

But I have lived ever since with the fact that I was going to sue this person I loved, this person who believed in me before I believed in myself, this person who gave me the balls to become a success and who was more of a brother to me than my own brother. He died without my talking to him.

I was in the lawyer's office sometime after Bobby's death. When I walk in, he shoots a piece of paper across the desk, and it's a check for eighteen thousand dollars. So Bobby made good on our deal. He wasn't trying to get away with anything. It wasn't even in his mind.

The last time I was in New York, I took my little seven-year-old daughter with me because I wanted her to experience the subway ride. We took a subway to FAO Schwarz on Fifty-seventh Street. When we get out of the subway, we walk down the street to Fifth Avenue, and I didn't realize it beforehand, but there was the Copa right in front of me. And I just got all crazy.

My daughter said, "What's the matter?"

"It's the Copacabana!"

She said, "Yeah?" And she was looking at me, like "What is with this crazy guy?" I walked up the few steps to the door and went inside. The lounge was a little different from years before, and there were people there cleaning. As there always was, there was a riser, like a stage, and on it was a portable radio playing music. I stood in the middle of this floor, and I was telling my daughter, "This is the Copa." She wanted to leave, but I couldn't go yet. I was just tripping out.

All of a sudden, Bobby's voice comes on this radio. It was a Christmas song I'd never heard before, but it was Bobby. I said to my daughter, "Thank goodness you're with me so nobody thinks I made this up." And my knees started to buckle. I had to sit down on this riser, and I was starting to sweat. Finally I said to my daughter, "Let's get out of here. This is spooky." She said, "Right."

But it was cold out. We walked around the corner, and the wind blasted into us. We hit Fifth Avenue, and we were a block or two from FAO Schwarz. I reached into my pocket to change from my sunglasses to the regular ones, but I didn't have them. So we had to go back to the Copa. When we got there, I still couldn't find my glasses. Not only that, but the radio wasn't on anymore. I asked who turned off the radio. I figured whoever turned the radio off might have found my glasses. They were prescription glasses, useless to anybody but me. The cleaning people swore that no one turned off the radio. And we never found the glasses.

Outside, I retraced my steps. If I'd dropped them on the street in those three, four minutes, then I should have been able to find them. But they were nowhere. I said out loud, "I'll be a son of a bitch. He's getting me. That's Bobby letting me know he was there."

Peggy Lee

Bobby knew that he was not going to be long for this world. I remember once giving a party not long before he died. There were a ton of people there, and everything was all decorated. There were helium balloons everywhere, and the garden was tented in case of rain. After everyone had seen how beautiful it was, Cary Grant and I went off into another room, and we were just sitting there talking. I was kidding him and saying, "Now take this helium balloon and inhale it and say 'Judy, Judy, Judy.' "

And he said, "Oh, that doesn't work."

I said, "Yes, it does. I'll show you." And I did it. Came out little high-pitched "Judy, Judy, Judy." So finally Cary took the balloon and did it, and he said, "Ju-dy, Ju-dy, Ju-dy." He was screaming with laughter when Bobby came in.

I said, "Bobby, do this. It's fun."

He said, "No, I wouldn't dare. Not with my heart."

And I said, "Well, there are four doctors here." And he didn't know what to say to explain to me, so I said, "Well, you don't have to do it. But it isn't anything like drugs or pot or anything. It's just helium. And it just paralyzes the vocal chords for a minute. And it is so funny when you do that."

However, I hurt his feelings. I could see it. And I felt terrible about it. Of course, he got over it in a matter of minutes, but I think he was a little annoyed with me. I never got over upsetting Bobby that way. And to tell the truth, I don't know whether I'd try helium now myself. I'd certainly ask my cardiologist before I'd try it. But it is fun. One of these days Bobby and I can try helium on another plane.

George Scheck

Bobby was a clever man. Here's an example. I went to see him at a show he was doing in Miami. I went in style. I took thirty-one people, but I was sitting in the second or third row. Bobby was performing, and he saw me. And he dropped the microphone on the floor in the second number. And he said, "Ladies and gentlemen, I never do this, I shouldn't do this because this is a performance, but there's the man who is responsible for my career." And he did a number on me for about ten minutes to the audience. Then he sent a note that I should come up to his dressing room, "with your entourage." So I went back and started to introduce him to thirty-one people! I taught him this. Forty minutes later, when they all left, he said good-bye and thank you for coming, and he used each of their names. They never stopped talking about this. Bobby charmed everyone. He was the greatest charmer in the world.

Bobby used to call me periodically throughout his life because I had had two heart attacks and we used to compare notes. He called me when he was doing the winter show, and he was depressed because it was a short run and the network wasn't going to renew. His ratings weren't that bad, but the network said they were. And Bobby was a little bit difficult to work with as usual. I said, "Bobby, I think you're going to come out good. I like the show, but you're a little tough to work with." He said, "You know me. They're all crazy, but I'm all right." But he really wasn't all right. He told me he wasn't feeling well.

I talked to him not long before he went to the hospital. We met on Seventy-ninth Street at Tony's, an Italian place. Bobby was raving about how great he felt. I looked at him. He didn't look good, but he was very happy, very easy. And I felt, looking into his eyes, that he was taking medication for his heart and they were giving him something else to keep him in twilight. I whispered to him, "What are you on, Bobby? What pills are you taking?"

He said, "Absolutely nothing."

I said, "Yeah, but what pills are you taking? Tell me so I can tell you what I think."

So he said to me, "I don't know what they are, but they're just things to calm me. Look at my hand. It's steady."

Bobby had a couple of people with him, and he said to the group, "Mr. S. thinks I'm on something." He was trying to show me up. He said, "Hey, I'm all right now. I'm very normal. Very good." I never saw Bobby again.

Charlie Maffia

The last time Bobby was in New York. I took him and Dodd all through the neighborhood, and we reminisced. I took him every place from the time he was born to the places in Staten Island and in the Bronx. I took him to all the public schools and to Science, and we spent an entire day just driving around to different areas, different buildings. I had a hunch he felt he was going to die when he went on this reminiscent trip with his son. He didn't say so, but why, all of a sudden, was this so critically important that he show his son everything from the time he was a baby until the time he'd left New York?

After his first operation he said, "I feel like a newborn man. I first feel like I'm gonna live." When that infection affected his heart, he should have gone into the hospital right away. But he waited until he was almost dying to go in for the second operation. He was too weak. He was down to bones. My daughter said, "You wouldn't recognize Bobby if you saw him."

Vee spent a lot of time up there with Bobby. She was with him when he died. So I wanted to get a plane to go out there even though there was a plane strike at the time. But Vee said, "Don't come up. You're gonna get sick. Don't come out. He's not too comfortable. By the time you get here, he'll be gone."

I said, "I want to see him. If he's dying, I want to see him."

She said, "He may not even be alive by the time you get here. Why go through all that expense? Besides, he don't want to see nobody. He don't even want to see his own son, with what he looks like." I don't know how he looked when he died. But that's what Vee told me, so I didn't go. I figured he didn't want to see me, and if I was there, he would get more sick. But he died. He died within a few days after I talked last time to Vee. The doctors tried to operate on him. He never came out of it.

Harriet (Hesh) Wasser

The last time I saw Bobby was in New York at a recording session in January of 1973. I had always wanted my friend Bob Crewe, who was a record producer, to make a record with Bobby. Bob had a contract with Motown, so did Bobby, and both were in New York at the same time. Bobby was playing the Copa, and Motown wanted very much to get a Bobby Darin rendition of "Happy," the theme from Lady Sings the Blues, on their label. Bob Crewe suggested a session. Within twenty-four hours they recorded live. Bobby went in and sang with the orchestra, with no overdubs. The recording had to be completed in one session because he was leaving town right after his Copa closing. The record came across very emotional and very beautiful, I thought. And it was his last chart record.

I was at the session, and I thought that although Bobby seemed to come through fine, he didn't look so good. He looked a little weary and his face was drawn, but he had been doing the shows at the Copa, so I marked it off to that. Bob and Bobby talked about doing another session together when they both got back to L.A., but Bobby got very ill and went into the hospital, so that session was never done. I felt very bad because Bobby was in such terrible shape. And I remember Bob Crewe saying, "You can't expect him to make the record under the circumstances." For about two months Bob Crewe talked about "When Bobby is better. When Bobby is better." Bobby came out of the hospital, did one more session with Bob, but because of his poor health, an album was never finished.

A friend called me at about four in the morning to tell me that Bobby had died. I wasn't surprised, but I think I went into shock. I had known about his illness since we first met. And since we first met, I knew that my life was changed by meeting him. I think most people would say that Bobby Darin was one of a kind and that you truly felt you were gaining a new experience by being a part of his life.

Naturally, when he died, it was a tremendous loss. But Bobby has really not died totally. Even though he did physically die, I can still feel his presence. I can't talk to him. I can't tell him off. I can't scream and yell and hang up on him. But I have photographs. I have records. I have letters. I have things around that are reminders of his being alive. I can put on the radio and hear his music and hear people talking about him and the fact of this book, and there's going to be a movie—all those things help to keep the person alive.

When I think of Bobby, I don't think of him as someone who's not around. I think of him as a real live person because I last saw him in a very live situation. I didn't see him in a casket. I saw him in a recording session, and that's how I picture him. I'm glad I did. And it was almost like a miracle in one way. I had wanted Bob Crewe and Bobby to work together, and for twelve years they weren't able to do it. So it just seems so strange that at this particular moment in time this opportunity would come up. And the fact that I played a part in getting the thing together made me feel that maybe that was the way it had to be. That Bobby just had to do one of his last record sessions in New York.

It's been so many years since Bobby died, yet I don't feel it, because his presence was so incredibly strong. After Steve finally broke with Bobby, it seems he never really did anything with his life. I don't mean he's not making money, and I don't mean that he couldn't be doing things that I'm not aware of. But it seemed to me that his life ended with Bobby Darin's death. I get that same feeling with Dave Gershenson. And with Sandy. I get the feeling that Bobby was so strong a personality that they just stayed with him in order to keep the feeling alive. To keep the dream.

Dick Behrke

Mickey and I had seen Bobby three months before he died, when he came to New York. I had to get a wheelchair for him because he couldn't breathe. He was turning blue. It was a horrible feeling. And he said, "You know, the one thing I will always regret in my life is not having a home life like you and Mickey." And at that time he spoke very sadly about Sandy. He said, "What kind of a mother is she? Dodd finds her drunk at her dressing table at night, and she burned holes in the dressing table because of her smoking. And then when I'm there, I come in and I yell at him and I scream at him because I've got to play the father role." He said he would always regret that he wasn't more of a father and that he'd never had a real family life.

We tried to take him to a New York hospital, and he got hysterical. He said, "No, I'm dying, and I know it." He screamed it. He wasn't supposed to have come to New York. His doctor warned him not to leave. He started to feel bad, and he felt so guilty, he had to get back to L.A. I was going to go with him, but there was only one seat left on the plane, so we called up Dave Gershenson, who said he'd meet him at the other end. And he was afraid to tell the doctor that he'd been here.

We called up the doctor from here, and he was cold as ice. We described Bobby's condition to him. I asked him, "What should we do?"

"Tell him to come back. I'll see him when he comes back. I told him not to go."

We were incensed with this guy. Was that all he could say? "I told him not to go, so I wash my hands"? I asked him, "Should we send a nurse? What should we do? Help us." The doctor showed no sign of compassion. The next day we put Bobby on the airplane, and he really, physically, was not well. And that was the last time Bobby and I talked, three months before he died.

When Bobby went back to L.A., he got a little better, then he got worse. He was living in a rented house that was totally devoid of furniture except for two hospital beds. I know this because the night Bobby died I stayed with Vee in this totally empty house. That's where Bobby spent his last weeks. It was the most depressing thing I had ever seen. It was terrible. Just about everyone had given up trying to work with him. As difficult as he was, it seems amazing that Andrea would give up. We thought she should understand. He was an invalid. He was crazy, but still an invalid. There should have been some caretaking by someone. But Andrea had left, which I guess we never forgave her for. Andrea had another relationship going by this time. She wasn't an awful person. She was a very kind lady, until the end. Anyone who met her would just be bowled over with her beauty and her gentleness. But she was passive.

The big problem seemed to us to be that everyone on the West Coast started to believe that Bobby's problem was more psychological than physical. Not being there constantly, Mickey and I found it easy to say, "Well, you should've been able to see through his madness. You should have been strong. You should have been more attentive. You shouldn't have left him at a time like this." It's easy for us to say that because we weren't burdened with him every day. But it seemed clear that people were just so tired of him acting erratically that they kind of faded away.

I called Bobby when he first went into the hospital in December and asked if I could see him. I was told, "No, it would just upset him if you come out." The classic thing. The doctors said they didn't want people coming out because that would make him think he was dying and he wasn't. And they said he'd get over it, but he'd get depressed if you came. That's what Vee said the doctors said.

Vee finally circumvented everything and said, "Come out." But it was too late, and I didn't see him while he was alive. So you learn a lesson from that. If you have any doubts, go see someone. Don't worry that they'll be upset to see you, because that's bullshit. You'll have seen someone before they die. Otherwise you'll always regret that you let them go without saying good-bye.

Vee Walden

In the fall, Bobby called to speak with my mother, who wasn't home. He and I talked for a few minutes, enough for me to know something bad was going to happen. He had gone to a psychiatrist whom he hadn't seen in months, and the psychiatrist decided that Bobby was a mental case and needed to be hospitalized. Bobby and Andrea were still married, so all you needed was a wife and a doctor saying he needed to be put away and it would be done.

My mother came home the next day, which was a Saturday, and because we couldn't get into the bank on the weekend, we went to every bar, every grocery store, and we made out checks. We got enough money together, and we started driving. We drove continuously. We flew that car. My mother was a diabetic with a heart condition, but she did all the driving. We drove from New York to Las Vegas, and when I saw Bobby I could understand where the doctor was coming from. Bobby was fucked up. His weight had dropped drastically, and he was very sick.

I got my mother and Bobby both seated and got a tranquilizer for myself and sodas for both of them, and Bobby went into his fears as a child. It was terrifying to hear him. Now he had the opportunity finally of telling my mother everything she'd ever done wrong in his thirty-seven years. The big accusation was, "How could you not let me know? Everybody knew and I didn't. The gangsters knew I wasn't Big Sam Curly's kid." And so on. I had to get them away from each other because I had the feeling I was going to bury them both at the same funeral. I sent my mother home. Bobby went back to California for a few days, and my younger brother flew out and drove my mother back east. I stayed to take care of Bobby because there was something bad the matter with him.

I told my mother I thought he had a brain embolism because he had no short-term memory and his long-term memory was fine. It's important to understand that Bobby had a phenomenal memory. If Bobby met you at the Flamingo backstage in July and you talked about wanting to be a writer when you grew up and your name was Mary Jones, ten years later in his dressing room at the Copacabana you might say to him, "Gee, I know you won't remember me, but . . ." And that's as far as you'd get. He'd say, "Your name is Mary Jones. I met you almost ten years ago. I remember it was very hot. It must have been July or August. And you wanted to be a writer. How's the writing coming along? Can I see something?"

How could you not love this man? Thousands and thousands of people, and he remembers you. You were somebody special. He had that effect on total strangers, and when he listened to what you had to say, he listened with both ears, which is a nice quality.

Bobby's got this phenomenal memory, and now he calls up fifteen times to tell you the same thing in a half hour? It made people who knew him crazy. And I could understand where Andrea would get him to a doctor because something bad was happening. His short-term memory loss worked to his advantage in this re-spect, because his heart was so bad at this point, he wouldn't eat. I would make him breakfast, and he would eat two or three mouthfuls and be done. And I'd take the breakfast away, and I'd fix it all over on a clean plate, and I'd get two or three more mouthfuls down him. I would do this at lunchtime and I would do it dinner. All told, I'd get one meal down him a day, but it would be a job. And what was heartbreaking was that Bobby kept trying to get me to go out to clubs because he was afraid I'd get bored and leave him. He couldn't do anything but pretty much lie in bed, and I'd have to help him to the bathroom. And he was afraid I would get irritated and leave him and he'd have nobody except someone who didn't care. A nurse or someone. And his worrying about me was totally against his character. It was very upsetting.

And I couldn't be upset anymore. One of us had to be totally in control.

Bobby stayed in Vegas long enough to get his divorce from Andrea, and then we drove back to California. On the drive back, we talked about his will. We were driving in the desert, and Bobby told me he'd set up a fund for Dodd so that Dodd could go into business someday, and we talked about how Dodd shouldn't get a lot of money when he was still young. When he got back to California, he went directly into the hospital and I went home.

A couple of months later, I got a call from Bobby's lawyer: "We needed you yesterday." Bobby was very sick, and he kept telling the doctors he was dying. There was something wrong with his heart, but he wouldn't let them perform an arteriogram. So I went back out to California. And Bobby looked very sick. He weighed a hundred and fifteen pounds. He looked sixty-five to seventy years old. He walked little, like a very old man, and he was hooked up to every kind of machine imaginable. We talked a lot. And he said, "Honestly, I resent people who are in good health. I don't want to see anybody." And I handled him because he needed to be handled. I would put my arm behind his back and take him by the wrist and lift him up. And if the machine broke down, I watched where the doctors banged it. And I banged it until it was working again. Stupid stuff like that. And I wouldn't leave the hospital at all.

Dodd's birthday was on December 16, and Bobby had written something to him. He wouldn't let Dodd come to the hospital. He didn't want Dodd to see him looking as he did. So I went to visit Dodd and give him the note from Bobby, and while I was there, Bobby called to talk to Dodd. And he wasn't making any sense. He was hysterical on the phone. Normally I'm a very slow driver, but when I hung up the phone, I got into my car and put the pedal to the metal.

When I got to Bobby's room, they were doing all kinds of heroics, the stuff you see on television. He had gone into cardiac arrest out of the blue. I knew the doctors didn't want me in there, and to be honest, I didn't want to be in there. So I went outside, and I could hear him yelling. After that, he was all right for a while. I tried to find things that would interest him. He would lie in bed propped up on pillows, and every two hours when he was strong enough, he'd sit up and shake his fist at God and say, "You prick! I'm thirty-seven years old. How could you do this to me?"

While he was in the hospital, Bobby and I discussed Dodd. Fifty minutes out of sixty, we discussed Dodd. "Promise that you'll look out for my son. Dodd's got to know his father loves him. He's got to know that I didn't want to leave him, that I really cared, that he was the world to me. That I did a lot of wrong things, but that I didn't know they were wrong." He was worried that Sandy had problems and that Dodd would need someone to talk to. He wanted me to take care of Dodd, and I was not financially able to. In the end I could not help Dodd, and I could not let him go. You cannot make the amount of promises I made and not feel guilty if you don't keep them. To this day I have a problem with what Bobby made me promise.

From Dodd's birthday on, I never left the hospital until Bobby died. The doctors and nurses tried to get me to leave, but I refused. I would go in and check on him, and I took up residence in the waiting room. I remember the last thing Bobby said to me; he opened his eyes and said, "Cypress 2–6725." It was our old phone number from the first phone we got in the Bronx. He was very excited when we got that phone.

I said, "Bobby, do you know what you're saying?"

He repeated the number, then he smiled and put his finger to his lips and said, "Shhh." Then he went into a coma.

Now the doctors wanted me to sign to do the catheterization that Bobby was so afraid of. They wanted to do it because they now believed one of his valves was malfunctioning. So I gave them permission. It took me a while to accept the inevitable, that he wasn't going to make it. I thought, No way. He's got all the money in the world. He's got the best doctors, and they love him. There's no way he's going to die. I finally called Dick Behrke. We were never close, but I called him and said, "If you want to see him alive, you're going to have to come now."

Dick pulled a lot of strings to get to L.A. because there was an airline strike. But he got there the day before the operation, so I had someone for support. Dave Gershenson came, too, but neither Dave nor Dick saw Bobby conscious. We sat and waited as Bobby went into surgery. Then doctors kept coming out and telling me there wasn't much hope. I kept saying, "Until Josh Fields comes out, I'm not hearing anybody." I had never even met the man. But Bobby had put his faith in Josh. He loved Josh. Then Josh came out at last and told me what the situation was, that there had been brain damage.

When Bobby was sick, he cried a lot, and he got me crying a lot. He resented that he couldn't do physical things. And I tried to explain to him that he had a brilliant mind. "So you can't get up and run and play football with your kid. Okay. So what? At least you'll be here. You can talk to him. There's a whole lot of things you can tell him, things that he wants to know. It doesn't have to be getting up and playing frigging football with your kid." So when they said brain damage, that's when I finally let go. Bobby died at around midnight on December nineteenth. Technically it could have been the twentieth. It was right on the line.

Dave Gershenson wanted to get to the news media immediately, and I stopped him. I grabbed him and I said, "No." Dickie Behrke's eyes were the color of taillights, they were so red. There were just these glowing red eyes. Dave Gershenson had tears running down his face, and he kept talking about how he had to call the wire services. He was literally rushing to the phone. I grabbed his arm and I said, "No. No! You will not. There are other people who need to know about this first."

I called my mother, and as soon as she heard my voice, that was it. She just folded. And then I started calling Sandy. I let the phone ring twenty, thirty times. There was no answer, so I had the operator try again. I put the phone call through to her six, seven, eight times, and nobody answered the phone. Dave was getting very anxious. He was a PR man, and he had to make his phone calls. I came out of the phone booth and said, "I can't reach Sandy. We need to go to the house." At that point, Dave got on the phone.

We left the hospital, and a third of the way home I got sick. When I get upset and I can't hit somebody, I throw up. We stopped at a gas station, and I threw up. We stopped at another gas station and I had nothing left, but I kept trying to throw up. I was so sick that when we got to Bobby's house, I said, 'I can't go to Sandy's. I'm sick. I can't."

So Dick and Dave went to tell Sandy, because she only lived two blocks up the street. And all these years, I've regretted that I didn't go. Thanks to Dave, Mary heard the news on the radio. Mary called Sandy and couldn't get through. Then she went to the house and started beating on the door, and nobody answered. Finally she broke into the house and crawled through a little window in the garage. Sandy was lying on the floor, passed out, the phone right next to her.

Sandy and Dodd and I spent that Christmas together. We had Kentucky Fried Chicken. All the time I was out there I never saw Sandy in anything but a peignoir. She never stepped foot outside the door. And Mary was telling her that she didn't have a problem. I was having one of my own. A year later I had a nervous breakdown.

In the final analysis I think it's fine that Bobby didn't leave a dime to anyone in the family. But while he was alive, he should have taken care of them. My mother died an old lady on Social Security. Before that, she was on disability. When my mother died, her kids chipped in to bury her—and I'm not talking about the prick she gave birth to first. Me; my sister, Vanna; and my brother Gary. Bobby set it up that way. He didn't want us to have anything. That was Bobby's will.

I was asked once what my life would have been like if Bobby hadn't been a star. My guess is that Charlie would have kept his job with the sanitation department and he'd have a pension now. My parents wouldn't have gotten divorced—not that they loved each other so much, but my mother was very practical. My sister and Gary and I would have lived with our parents in the little house in Lake Hiawatha, New Jersey. We would have followed the same careers we eventually had, but we wouldn't have been known as Bobby Darin's family. It would have been better. I loved Bobby more than words can say, but being related to him is the biggest cross I've ever had to carry. And whether my family realizes it or not, it was for all of us.

Sandra Dee

After the marriage to Bobby was over things were hard for me, then it was okay. The last time he left, I was pregnant and I told him, "This is it. Don't tell me you're sick and you want to come back." I really didn't want to see him. I had the suitcase he had pushed into my hands, and I said, "Robert, go." But he always used his sickness to come back. He would come to the door with his vitamins and say, "I have nowhere to go." And I would let him in and things would start again.

The last year I said, "No," and I meant it. When he said he had no place to go, I cared, but I didn't believe him. He had cried wolf so many times before. But I didn't understand then that his mind was getting really bad, even though he would do very strange things.

For example, one day he called and wanted to pick Dodd up. We never had any rules about visitation. Any time Bobby wanted to see Dodd, he came and got him. Well, he hadn't seen him for a while and he said, "Have him ready!"

I said, "He'll be ready."

And Dodd was all excited. It was Saturday, and from experience, I knew Bob's pattern. So I didn't go near the front door because if Bobby saw me, he'd want to come in and have coffee. There was no way I was going to allow that because I knew that if I did that, I'd feel sorry for him and that would be it again.

So on this occasion, I said, "Dodd, it's five of ten, wait outside." Out he went. I got on the phone, then into the shower, and when I got out it was probably noon. I was in my part of the house, but I was ready to go out. I went to pull the car out of the garage, and I saw the kid on the stoop. I said, "Dodd! Are you back?"

He said, "I never left."

Bobby hadn't called, and I couldn't reach him. And I didn't know what to do. I was thinking, This is a trick. I figured Bobby was setting up an argument, and if you argue, then you have to talk. You have to come in the house in order to talk, so I was suspicious of him.

Bobby called that night. I asked him what happened. He said, "Oh, my God. Are you sure I really said that I would pick him up?"

"Yeah, Bobby, I'm really sure about that. You want to talk to Dodd? He's the one who waited."

"No, no. I don't know how I did that."

"I don't either."

"Oh, God," he said. "I've got to make it up to him. Does he want anything special?"

"Yeah, he really needs a new bike." Dodd wasn't spoiled. He really did need a new bike, and I didn't want him to wait until his birthday.

Another Saturday arrived. Bobby came to get Dodd so he could "get my son a bike." I was cooking, keeping busy, when the phone rang. It was Dodd.

"Hi, Ma."

"Hi, honey."

"Can I come home?"

"Well, what do you mean? You're with Daddy. Aren't you with Daddy?"

"Well, yeah."

"Did you get the bike?"

"No. Dad did."

His father took him to the bike shop, bought himself a bike, and forgot why he was there with Dodd. Then he left Dodd on the corner. He didn't come back. The kid was standing in Westwood, and I was thinking, Well, Jesus. What's going on? I didn't believe Bobby was that sick. I really didn't.

Around this time, Bobby started to call Dodd at ungodly hours. He would say, "I want to talk to Dodd." And it could be one in the morning. Again I thought, He's trying to provoke an argument. I'd say, "Dodd is sleeping," but Bobby would insist, and I'd have to put Dodd on the phone.

My room was on one side of the house, and Dodd's room was on the other side. An hour or two would go by since Bobby had called, and suddenly I'd notice that the button would still be lit on the phone line. I'd think, Well, Dodd didn't hang up. And I would go down the hall and look into Dodd's room, and he'd be sleeping on the bed with the phone next to his ear. And I could hear his father just talking. Talking. That's when I thought for the first time, Bobby can't be putting on an act. I'd pick up the phone and say, "Bob, why don't you call back?" Because I knew he'd forget.

Dodd didn't see his father for two months before he died. Bobby was living on the same block as we were, but he didn't want Dodd to see him. I didn't understand why. He kept saying, "I don't want him to see me like this."

"Bobby, like what? Isn't there someone with you?"

He said, "No, there's no one. The doctor says I have to fend for myself."

And I said, "You're telling me that you can't get out of bed, and you're there by yourself?" What doctor in his right mind would give this kind of advice? I didn't believe Bobby. Now I think about his being all alone, and it must have been a horrible way for him to die.

Bobby called on Dodd's birthday. We didn't have a big party because Bobby was in the hospital. When he called, I said, "Oh, good."

He said, "Oh, you're glad to hear from me?"

I said, "Yeah. You want to talk to your child?"

He said, "Oh, in a little bit. Why?"

I said, "Well, you called to wish him a happy birthday." He forgot. He absolutely forgot. And he was rambling, talking strange. There would be long pauses. I'd say, "Bob?" And then I'd hear a breath. It wasn't so much what he was saying that was scary as what he wasn't saying. There was just this silence. And the nurse got on the phone at his end and said, "He was doing so well. It only took him forty minutes to call." Forty minutes to dial! He was thirty-seven years old, and she was talking as though he were ninety-seven and an imbecile.

The night of the operation, Dodd went to the Gables' house. I got a call from my doctor. He said, "He's got to have open heart surgery."

I said, "When?"

He said, "He's going down now." Then he called me back and said, "We found the problem." They finally did the catheter. It was late at night, and Dodd was already long gone. I called my mother, and I called Kay Gable and told her what was happening. Kay told me to call her with any news.

At two in the morning, I heard that Bobby died. I called Kay and said, "Miss Gable, I think I'd better come and get Dodd."

And she said, "Why? Believe me, he'll know for the rest of his life what happened. But he won't hear it on the radio. My daughter and I will go through the house and get all the radios. Let him have his breakfast in the morning. I'll bring him home after breakfast."

In the morning, a lot of people were at the house. Kay Gable walked in with Dodd, and I didn't know how to tell him. Honest to God, it was so weird. Kay sat with my mom in the other room, and she told Dodd to come into my room. I was lying on the bed; I told him his Dad had died, and then he said, "Ma?" I figured, Here it comes. He said, "Can I go skateboarding now?" I thought he was a sociopath. I was waiting for anything, and Bobby's son comes out with "Can I go skateboarding now?"

When my mother died, it all caught up with Dodd. He grieved for four years, and he grieved for everybody. He grieved for the world. Watching him in so much pain really got to me. But at the time when Bobby died, I hardly know what he said or I said. I was gone. I was in far worse shape than Dodd was.

Dr. Philip Oderberg, Psychiatrist

It was hard getting together with Bobby because he was so sick. The first time he came to see me, he came by cab from the Beverly Wilshire Hotel. He was wearing pajamas and a bathrobe. He was weak. Wasn't walking too well. Suspicious. Not very open. Wary. And feeling pretty desperate. Like feelings that have to do with being on the last leg of something. Feeling pretty bad about it. There just wasn't a lot of life in him at that point.

We started to get into a discussion of what could we do together. And I told Bobby that I didn't know if I could help him or what I could do for him, but he didn't have a whole lot to lose at this point. He felt very tight. Had a lot of hostile feelings. We began to talk about his family, about his sister who was his mother. How hurt he felt. How he carried it and how it weighed on him. And how mad he felt about living his life as a lie. Jeez, if that wasn't true, then how can he know what was true?

I don't think he was self-destructive in any conscious sense. Unconsciously, I guess you'd have to say on some level if a person lives the way he lived, then there's some self-destructive implication to it, but I don't think his aim was to destroy himself. I think he was so driven by having to make it, and having to make it his way, and by the ghosts that he experienced in his life in the last few years, that he did himself some serious damage.

I had about ten sessions with him, including some long ones at the hospital when we talked for a couple of hours. We talked about what he wanted out of life. I think he needed trust in relationships. Somebody he could trust and be trusted by. Admired and appreciated, but loved, too. I think he desperately wanted a sense of peace. He wanted to be able to relax, and he absolutely couldn't relax. It was just so hard for him to find even a tentative kind of peace. He was always on guard. Always watching. We talked about meditation, other means of approaching relaxation, but he never got to a place where he could do it.

I think he saw his life as being hard. He was very taken with what he could do and very upset when he couldn't do it. That last television series that he did just really wiped him out. Not just physically, but because he couldn't get himself to do what he needed to do. He was a tremendously talented guy who couldn't do what he could do physically. That really hurt him a lot. We talked how it could be. How he could be a talent and still be able to live a life where he could feel within a relationship. Not always have to have an issue of opposition. Of having to fight for what he wanted and struggle all the time. How to be able to feel good about yourself. Not to be always testing yourself. Not to feel that he had to do everything himself. And we talked about his dreams.

Bobby had dreams in three categories. He had a lot of anxiety dreams. Anxiety dreams are characterized by being chased, not being able to move your feet, that kind of thing. Generally he was being chased. Somebody was in one car and he was in another. Usually it was men. Usually it was a city kind of thing. Sometimes he was on foot. Sometimes it had to do with guns or knives, sometimes with neither. He was terribly afraid of dying. He was even more afraid that he'd make it and be crippled. He found it very difficult to imagine any kind of life other than a stage life.

He also had what I call compensatory dreams. This is where you might have a certain conscious attitude about something that is not constructive or growth oriented or a healthy position for you. Someplace that's skewed in some way. So very often a dream will compensate for your conscious attitude by giving you the other side. Bobby had a lot of dreams like that. And he found that very interesting. The concept of unconscious compensation. He was really taken with the idea that he had something going for him that wasn't in his head, because he really worked very hard on a head basis. And what I tried to do with him was bring in the other side, the feeling side.

Wishes were the third kind of dream. Mostly wishes for his kid. Wanting very much to provide for the kid. Wanting to know how things would go with him. And still not wanting the relationship to be one based on his providing. He was always concerned about being taken. He wanted a connection and to be able to have an influence on his kid, to be able to affect him.

He didn't talk much about Sandra. He talked more about Andrea. Had a lot of negative feelings, some of which were really screwy, but some of which seemed quite valid. The screwy part, I'd say, was that he was extremely sensitive to her. She could really affect him very strongly, and their life-style was kind of an odd one in any case. On some level it was as if he were saying she could do anything she wanted with anybody she wanted. It was okay with him. And I didn't believe it for a minute. I'm not talking about who she actually is. I'm just talking about his perception, or my perception of his perception. He talked about how her need to be independent was so strong that if he was going to have relations with her, he would have to accept that. But someplace in the process he was acting like a guy who had gotten dumped on. He felt he was one down in the relationship with her, and it bugged the shit out of him. The guy was so flaked out by the time I saw him that I don't think sex was very strong on his mind. It felt to me that he felt out of control and control was very important. It was one of the central issues in his life.

Bobby needed to be in control even more than he wanted to be in control. I think that's the part of what really bugged him in that situation with his mother/sister. His security system was tied up in knowing and controlling. And all of a sudden he didn't know a goddamned thing. I think he felt that there was some hostility in Nina's tone of voice. That she was getting to him. Hurting him. When he talked about the brother-in-law, it was like not having a lot of respect for him. Nice guy. Not very strong, but he had treated Bobby kindly. Had shown him warmth. He didn't have the same feelings toward him that he had toward his sister: "Why does he tell me now?" He felt the sister was by far the stronger element in the relationship—so much so that anything negative he would attribute to her.

He had difficulty talking to me about Steve because Steve sent Bobby to me and because I knew Steve. We had talked about the experience at the doctor's office in relation to Steve. That he steamed out of the office. That he was really pissed. He was obviously a very intense person. He was under a lot of pressure in a lot of different directions, and for whatever reason the previous shrink had zeroed in on his pathology and maybe the kinds of things we're all prone to do under pressure. A disposition. Which is not the way you can deal with Bobby. He just wasn't that kind of person. He wanted to make a connection.

Steve was one of the things on his agenda. The business with the lawsuits, and the vindictiveness and the anger. Steve was very attached to Bobby. Had been for a long time. Really had been very hurt by what had taken place between them. Not in the sense that Bobby had done anything bad, but in what they'd done to each other. I think it's one of those things when each one is sure the other is fucking up. The question of who did what to whom. Who deserved how many slaps with a wet noodle. Steve had been very hurt by what he had experienced as Bobby's rejection. But I don't think it affected his basic feeling for him. And the other way around, too. I think that Bobby really wanted to have the connection, the relationship, and he talked about being able to get back together.

Bobby was very weak and awfully afraid he wouldn't make it. He could hardly get his energy up and had trouble breathing. He was very much into his condition. From a medical point of view, he knew what the hell was going on. I think he probably knew more of the whole picture than almost anybody except his doctor, Josh Fields. He loved Fields. He told me they'd played chess together a few times. That he really admired his brain. One of the times I was at the hospital, the three of us talked together about Bobby's condition. About what would be helpful to him. About the way he was relating to his condition. We talked about the decision to have the arteriogram. What he should do. Whether he should go ahead and do it or not. And Bobby was having doubts. Going back over the history of his medical treatment and surgery in great detail. He could tell you the day and the week and the month. And he looked for things that didn't fit, the enigmas, the paradoxes, and so on.

We talked about his fear of dying, or of making it and being incapacitated, or of staying the way he was. He couldn't stand that idea. He really wanted to work out some of his emotional issues. During a session, after I'd been with him a while, he began to relax. After the first twenty minutes or so he kind of calmed down, and we talked quietly for a while. We shared some ideas, and then we'd get into some dreams. Usually by the time the session was over, he felt better. He'd always say that he got a lot out of it and wanted to meet again. I'd have to say I experienced him as a warm person who was very capable of trusting. But by the time I saw him, he was very careful. And he was cynical in terms of people's motives. That they were out for themselves. That they didn't really care. And when it came down to it, it was still dog eat dog.

The last time I talked to him, I just called to say good-bye and say I'd get back to him. I didn't know he was having the operation. I told him to take it easy, and we talked about all the things he could do to try to make his decision and relax. During the time I saw Bobby, I just wished to Christ that I'd been able to see him a few years before. Before all that shit started and before all the heart surgery and all that stuff got laid on him. I thought he was a very bright guy. When he began to trust me, he was very open, very related, and really willing to share himself in a very direct way. I really liked him. I thought he was an interesting guy. Very nice, and he obviously had, as we all do, a lot of shit, too. But I liked him and felt I could work with him. Maybe it's just an inflated wish, but I wish I'd been able to see him three to four years earlier. I don't think he would have had to die the way he did.

Jackie Cooper

We had the only celebration of Bobby's passing. My wife, Barbara, said a day or two after he died, "Somebody's got to do something.

Let's just sit around and have a drink, and invite some of Bobby's friends to the house." We did that, and it was so depressing. I just very quickly got smashed. But everyone sat around the bar and on the floor, most of these people I'd never seen in my life. And Steve came and Bobby's wife was here, and I met her for the first time. And we played the tape of Bobby's last NBC show, which no one had ever seen. And everybody cried, and the show was fantastic. Sometimes it was so good, we'd forget to cry and start laughing and yelling and snapping our fingers. And that was the only thing that was held for Bob.

George Burns

Bobby had everything going for him and was moving the right way before he died. He was getting bigger all the time. I didn't think of Bobby Darin dying at that age. I don't think it's right. I don't think people should die at that age, and I don't think they should die at all if they're booked. The guy who booked Bobby up there was bigger than Sammy Weismuller. Bigger than Abe Lastfogel. When you're booked that way, you move in that direction, there's nothing you can do about it. What can you do? You gotta go, you gotta go. I tried to call him in the hospital a few times, but I couldn't get through. Bobby left me his love. That was good enough for me.

15

My Dad and Me

My goal is to be remembered as a human being and as a great performer. Probably epitaph time will come and strike me square between the eyes and I will not have achieved it.

—BOBBY DARIN

My way of dealing with my father's death when I was twelve was to deny that I was in pain. Teachers and friends tried to console me, but I brushed them off. My dad's dead. I expected it. No big deal. But I was plenty aware that he was gone. The day after my father died, Steve Blauner drove by our house on Rexford Drive. I was hanging out in the front yard, saw his car, and flagged him down. I said, "Come inside. I want you to talk to my mom." Steve had had a strained relationship with my mother over the years and was reluctant to see her. But I insisted, and he did what I asked him to do. Later Steve told me that in his head I had already taken over the role of the man of the family. I know that by bringing Steve in to comfort my mom, I was hoping to make peace and to start the process of healing. Healing was not that easy, but by turning over the stones I've left undisturbed for so long, I'm attempting now to complete what I started doing that December afternoon in 1973.

When I try to gather all my memories of my father, my most

accessible recollections are of being in Las Vegas. I remember sitting in the showrooms, watching him onstage, and feeling enormous pride in him. It was really something fantastic to see the way people responded to him, the standing ovations he got and the autograph seekers crowding around him. I remember beaming as I read his reviews. And I remember there used to be a Hollywood all-star game each year where celebrities would play at Dodger Stadium. He was always into that, and I was just as proud as could be to be Bobby Darin's son.

I remember the first time I was struck by a wave of grieving for my dad. I was around fifteen or sixteen. I was listening to his music, and I started to appreciate just how special he really was. Not just special because he was my dad who was famous, but special as a musical entity as compared with other artists of the times. I remember my dad once told me that you can't be all things to all people. But despite that, he ranged over a wide musical spectrum. He could do country music, folk music, and rock. He could do Ray Charles. He could do Sinatra. And the frightening part was he was great at all of it. Some people resented his changing images and styles. They said, "This man is a chameleon and a rip-off artist," but they had him wrong. They didn't understand that he was exploring, constantly pushing out his own boundries. My dad was influenced by other artists, yes, but he was not a copycat. I'd like to know who else could do "Mack the Knife" and then go into a James Taylor song and do it well. "The public won't let you be all things to all people," he said. But go into a record store today and you can find my dad's music in rock 'n' roll oldies. You can find it in pop vocals. You can find it in easy listening. The man defied categorization.

When I think of how my dad presented himself, I think of a showman, an entertainer, a cocksure, streetwise guy. The truth was that underneath the bravado was a man who thought he was funny looking and short and didn't think he had a great voice, even with all that he could do with it. He knew he wasn't a Sinatra or a Presley or a Johnny Mathis. For proof of his insecurity, one has only to listen to how self-conscious he was in his use of words. He was always overcorrect gramatically. A journalist once asked my dad about what she called his "fussiness in grammar." She wondered if he was really into words or if this was a side effect of his perfectionism. Her question struck a nerve.

It took my father 250 words to respond, and this was the heart of his answer: "I believe that if you do know something, if you do know how to phrase a sentence, if you are aware of grammar and you have the option, then indeed you should opt to use it correctly, if you have that available to yourself. Unfortunately, there are times when I'm around corners and over the head and I don't mean to do that. It's not a desire to circuitously get to some point. It's just a natural bent. . . ."

I think that my dad's manner of speech was a mask he wore to disguise his lack of higher education, to convince people that he was not from the poor side of town. I suppose that it's hard even for me to really believe that inside brash and cocky Bobby Darin was a scared little fellow, but I know it's true. He was insecure about his looks, his height, his hair, his background, and who knows what else. I don't think he was ever really happy. I don't think he ever experienced tranquillity. He had money and a family and adulation, but I don't think he ever had peace of mind. And it's sad because I could see that he was on the road to contentment before he got sick for the last time. He knew he could be the slick singer and nightclub performer everyone wanted and paid big money to see and yet at the end of the day could take off his toupee, throw on his sailor hat, go to the market for some doughnuts, and be a regular person. He was close to feeling that he didn't have to be on twenty-four hours a day. That he didn't have to be a star.

People have referred to my dad as a "man's man"—not in the macho sense, but in terms of honesty and loyalty. Those qualities were very important to him. Many entertainers are so competitive, they can't be happy for other people's success because they feel it somehow diminishes their own. One of the things I really admired about my dad was that he didn't have that pettiness. He didn't like gossip. If someone came to him with a story knocking someone else, my dad would say, "I don't want to hear it." And he wasn't a guy to listen to his own music at home or play it for guests. His insecurity didn't strike him in that way.

If my dad had a vice, it was women. At heart, I've always been proud of his conquests. It seems sexist of me to wink at his womanizing, and I know that if he'd cheated on my mom, I would have felt differently.

But I've been told he was true to her, although both before and after her, he fully indulged himself. I imagine that because my dad knew his life would be short, he wanted to do it all before he died. And I think one of the reasons he divorced my mom had to do with her unwillingness to experiment sexually. Maybe I'm wrong, but I cannot imagine her watching pornography or having sex with a woman. Apparently this was something he wanted to do. And it's interesting because Andrea was the complete opposite of my mom. She was a very real, down-to-earth, unpretentious person who didn't care if her man was Bobby Darin or Joe Blow. And she was open-minded in the area of sexuality. Whether she engaged in activities with him or just tolerated my dad's sexual behavior, I don't know.

My dad didn't gamble, didn't drink, didn't do drugs. In fact, he had a fear of drugs. Part of his fear was seeing Polly, who was addicted, and knowing that Sam Cassotto had died from drug withdrawal. Partly he was afraid for his heart. But he'd also witnessed enough drug use to be appalled by what it can do to a person's mind. He tried pot a couple of times. Once he smoked some with some of his musicians in Vegas. Afterward he went to the market and on the way back got lost for three hours. That just blew his mind. When I was about ten he said to me, "We don't have to have a long talk about drugs. If you do them, they're going to fuck up your life."

As a child of divorced parents, I can honestly say that I was always told by each that the other was a great parent. It was always "Hey, we love you. We don't work well as a team, and you gotta understand that." But there was no using the kid to bash one another, so in that sense I was lucky. I do, however, remember lots of fighting. My dad was, I can say with assurance, jealous and hurt that I was with my mom all the time. I know that was a problem for him later when he was with Andrea and she had two boys roughly my age. They all lived together, and I was not with him. I can sympathize with his feelings. I was his one and only son, and we weren't together a lot. We saw each other every other weekend, but that's not the same as living under the same roof. I harbored my own pain and resentment at his being with Andrea's kids. I liked both of them, and we got along when we were all together, but it hurt to leave my dad with them when I went home to my mother.

Sometimes the fighting between my parents had its comical side. I remember huge fights where my mom would call my grandmother and say, "Come over and pick me up. I'm getting out of the house for a while." An hour or so later my grandmother would arrive, and by that time my parents had made up. I remember a few times seeing my grandmother circling the house in her car, my mom having forgotten that she'd called her. I don't know what my parents fought about, but I imagine sometimes they fought about me. My dad wanted to be able to visit at will, and I'd be surprised if my mom didn't occasionally use the power of her custody against him. She was the smarting, hurting, divorced woman, and it would be a human response to make him suffer once in a while.

This seems like the right place to address the accusation that my mom didn't let me attend my father's last television show. I don't remember the details, but I did talk to my mom about it later because Steve Blauner and I discussed it. To the suggestion that she kept me from going to the studio, her answer was, "That's preposterous. I don't remember saying no, and I don't know why I would say no to him." The fact was, the show was done, it was the last show, Andrea and the other kids were there, and if asked, I would certainly have wanted to be there. But no one knew it was my dad's last show. We all knew it was the last show of his NBC series, but no one understood how ill my dad really was. So I don't think my mother deliberately prevented me from going to this event. I don't deny that it was painful to my father that his two stepkids were there and I was not. In his heart he knew how sick he was, that's for sure.

I remember one incident where a blowup started innocuously. It was the summer of 1970, and I was at my dad's beach house. And a lot of his friends were around, and they were smoking pot. When I got home I told my mother I had a headache, and she wanted to know why. I was always taught "Never lie. No matter what you've done or what you're responsible for, admit it." My mom asked me, "Were you around marijuana?" I said, "Yeah, at Dad's house." And she freaked. She got her lawyers on the phone and threatened my dad by saying that he would not be allowed to see me. He just went ballistic. And I remember as if it were yesterday what happened next.

My dad came over to the house with a tape recorder and started grilling me. "State your name. Your address. Where we are discussing this?" Most of the grilling was about the marijuana, but he went into another area that was real sensitive to me. As I've said, I was in awe of my dad, and he could easily intimidate me. In truth, it was harder to be candid with him than with my mom, and for whatever reasons, my mom told him, "The kid isn't honest with you. Sometimes you'll call him and say 'Let's do something,' and he'll agree out of guilt or fear, and you ought to know that." So on this occasion, my dad turned into Perry Mason and really put the screws to me. "Is it true what your mama said about you being afraid of me?" I managed to squeak, "Not anymore." This half-hour interrogation was just scary as hell to me. In retrospect, I know my dad was only trying to protect himself and our relationship because my mom was threatening to make a stink. His questions were pressing, but there was nothing harsh in his tone of voice. Even so, at the time I felt brutalized. Here's a condensation of the tape recording, minus most of my dad's ums and ahs as he tried to phrase his questions. My part is delivered in the falsetto voice of a very nervous nine-year-old.

BOBBY: Now. Tell me exactly what happened.

DODD: Well, I was chewing a piece of Dentyne gum, and after I was finished I saw the wrapper. And I said to my mom, "Whoever smokes pot could roll it in this piece of Dentyne wrapper." And Mom said, "You ever seen anybody smoke marijuana?" And I said, "Yeah. At Dad's," because I couldn't tell a lie.

BOBBY: Okay. And then what did your mom say?

DODD: Well, she just said, "How did you know about marijuana?" And I said, "Well, one time we smelled some of it."

BOBBY: Well, do you know the smell of marijuana?

DODD: See, one time at school we had a drug report, and they gave us the distilled smell of it, you know?

BOBBY: What does it smell like? Can you describe it?

DODD: No.

BOBBY: Does it smell like burned oregano?

DODD: I don't know what oregano is.

BOBBY: Uh. It's a seasoning. In other words, how do they give you a smell of it without using the real thing?

DODD: I don't know.

BOBBY: Oh. Okay, could it be what you smelled in the house was something other than marijuana, too?

DODD: Maybe.

BOBBY: Isn't that possible?

DODD: Yeah.

BOBBY: Right. Okay. Now, have I ever told you to keep anything from your mama?

DODD: No.

BOBBY: Have I ever told you that we have any secrets against your mama?

DODD: No.

BOBBY: Have I, uh, ever said anything in any way in front of you or to you that would indicate to anybody that I thought that your mama was not a good person?

DODD: No.

BOBBY: Well, what have I said when I talk about her as a mama?

DODD: Well, you just said she's a good mama, that maybe she's not a good wife.

BOBBY: Ah, okay. There's a big difference between a wife and a mama, isn't there?

DODD: Hm-hmm.

BOBBY: Okay. Let me explain something to you, at least the way I feel about it. Maybe I'm wrong. Your mama is, um, under some pressure. Whatever it is, I don't know. Your mama seems to want to go to court. She wants to get the attorneys involved, okay?

DODD: Hm-hmm.

BOBBY: She's on the phone now with her attorney, as if I were committing some criminal act. That's what she has an attorney for. I don't have an attorney to represent me in those things anymore. I may have to if she indeed wants to bring it to court. I want to avoid that. So, I'll ask the question again. At any time at Daddy's house, did anybody even come near you with what you think was pot or marijuana?

DODD: No.

BOBBY: Um. Would you want to see your daddy get into trouble?

DODD: No.

BOBBY: You wouldn't want to see your mama get in any trouble?

DODD: No.

BOBBY: Okay. This conversation is being taped in front of Dodd's house, Monday, August, I think twenty-fourth, 1970, as a result of a heated phone call that came a couple of hours ago to my house out at the beach, in which Dodd's mama, Sandy, said that she would go to court or call an attorney if anybody ever smoked anyplace near where Dodd was if he was at my house. Now the facts are obvious that Dodd does not know for sure whether it was pot being smoked at my house and that it is a very unfair position to put him in the middle of this thing. However, if I don't put it on tape exactly, my memory sometimes slips and it wouldn't be exact. I'm having this conversation in front of my son, who will be nine in December, and will just testify to the fact that he's standing here. Have you heard everything that I just said?

DODD: Hm-hmm. Yes.

BOBBY: Just tell me your name, please?

DODD: Dodd Darin.

BOBBY: How old are you?

DODD: Eight and a half.

BOBBY: And where do you live?

DODD: One oh five one Valley Spring Lane.

BOBBY: And are you my son?

DODD: Yes.

BOBBY: You love me?

DODD: Yes.

BOBBY: I love you, too.

And I did. Scared or not, I loved him fiercely. I remember being in a Little League game. I had hit four home runs in one game, which was quite impressive. My dad was yelling at me to run the bases faster. He thought I was hotdogging. Of course I was hotdogging! That's part of the fun of playing baseball. But that was his caustic side coming out, and it was formidable.

When I was eleven, not too long before my father died, he did something that for me was unbelievably traumatic. I had been going to a private school called Buckley since I was about five. It was a very conservative place. The uniform was oxford shoes, a blazer, and ties. The girls wore skirts. It was like a Harvard prep school. One day in the middle of fifth grade, there was an announcement that certain kids whose hair was too long would have to have haircuts before returning to school on Monday. I was on the list.

So I went home and told my dad about the hair rule, and this piece of news punched all his buttons. He was livid. He made an appointment for the following Monday to talk to Dr. Isabel Buckley, who looked exactly like Margaret Thatcher and had her demeanor as well. Day comes, he sat in front of Dr. Buckley and went into his pitch, which was basically, "I'm paying X amount of money a year. My kid's obviously bright and should be here. How dare you say his hair has anything to do with learning or his contribution to this school? I refuse to cut his hair. Will you reconsider the policy?"

To which Dr. Buckley calmly responded, "Thank you, Mr. Darin. No, we will not."

I never went another day to school there. The next day I was yanked out of Buckley and put into a public school on my block in Beverly Hills, on Rexford. I've talked about my being in awe and intimidated by my father, and here's a graphic example of my not standing up to him. My dad did ask me, "Do you mind?" But from whatever I was feeling about him, love, fear, God knows, I said, "No, I don't mind." I should have spoken up and said, "Dad, this is wrong. My friends are here. They're important to me. I'll cut my hair." But I was afraid.

On the other hand, I remember standing with him in front of a hotel somewhere. Again, I must have been ten or eleven, and I guess he was observing me. I had taken out some gum, and I was chewing it, and I had put the wrapper neatly back in my pocket. And he said, "That was unbelievable."

I said, "What are you talking about?"

He said, "Nine out of ten kids would have tossed that on the ground. Just littered without thinking twice." I was so proud of myself and of him when he praised me that way. Put all together, this package was my dad. It's very hard to describe the feeling of "He's my dad." But it was just very special.

I've been asked if I'm angry at my father. That it would be understandable if I were. He divorced my mother and, in doing so, left me. Then he died and left me again. If I'm angry, I've never been in touch with it. Maybe it's almost a sick fascination with him, more than what the normal son feels for his father, that's caused me to block it. I've dealt with him making me feel lousy and his cruelty at times and his celebrity, all of which has contributed to the baggage I carry. But angry? No.

My dad, I think, realized that his powerful personality could have an adverse affect on me, and he was way ahead of the game. When I was ten, he had me go to a shrink, and those sessions were really a joke at the time. My doctor was a very respected therapist, and she used to fall asleep in the sessions. God bless her, I guess I didn't have too many problems. But my dad was looking out for me. I remember many times he would be on the road and he'd call and say, "How ya doin' in school?"

"I'm doing pretty good."

"Who you doing it for?"

And at first, and this was the true answer, I'd say, "For you and Mom."

And he'd say, "No, no, wrong. You're doing it for yourself. Not for me, not for your mother, but for yourself. Remember that. This is for you."

Naturally, I wonder what my relationship with my dad would have been like if he were alive today. I know he would have cracked the whip when I was going through my hellacious teenage years. My theory has been that I would have become more aware of him as a flawed human being as I got older, and as a result, I would be less burdened with his mythic proportions as an adult. As I've been getting to understand him better through the process of researching and writing this book, I wonder if knowing that he was flawed would have released me from the weight of his celebrity.

I've asked my dad's friends how they thought my dad's career would have gone if he had lived, and not surprisingly, all have said he would have been what he always was: huge. He would have pushed at the boundaries of his abilities, taken risks. Some have said he would have done what Paul Simon has done, changed in advance of the times. Or maybe he'd be performing and recording in his area of greatest strength, as Sinatra is doing. Some think he would have gotten involved in producing films or broken through as an actor at last. That he would have been successful at whatever he chose to do.

As for his personality, we all know Bobby was a control freak and tough on people who didn't excel. If I've measured myself against my father throughout my life, it's been mostly a private matter. If he were alive, I have a feeling I would have been accountable to him on a constant basis, and instead of feeling better about myself as I solve my problems on my own, I might have been standing before him with my head bowed, trying, unsuccessfully, to please him.

Today, as I assemble my thoughts and memories and suppositions, as I both applaud my father and expose his faults, one fact is unwavering and absolutely true. My father loved me. He could be a jerk, but he loved me. He could be cruel, but he loved me. He could make mistakes, but he loved me. I have been blessed with an abundance of love.

There was very little by way of ceremony for my father's death on December 20, 1973. There were some obits in the papers citing his achievements, some stopping to consider whether or not he'd become the legend his brash, twenty-three-year-old self had wanted to be. The Coopers had friends over for a drink and a screening. And there are three wonderful ladies living in Colorado, named Rose, Lucille, and Antoinette. I call them "aunts," but these sisters are actually fans who met my dad in 1960 in Las Vegas. They've had a lifelong devotion to him. They've kept scrapbooks, gone to see all of his shows, and have never missed a birthday of mine or my mom's or a let a holiday pass without sending us a card. They are the most loving ladies in the world, and they asked us if they could put a stone for my father in their local cemetery. My mom agreed.

My mom and I had our own somber ceremony. We opened the tan vinyl suitcase together. For years it was a joke around the house. What does this man have in there? Stolen bonds? Gambling loot? But my dad was very serious about this suitcase. "I'm entrusting it to you and your mom, but don't open it unless something happens to me," he said. The actual moment of the opening is lost to me, but I have the suitcase now and have looked over the contents many times in the last twenty years. Inside that case are many precious mementos: my dad's baptismal certificate, pictures of him and various family members in the early 1940s, a swimming badge, a program from a play my dad was in in high school. Then there are souvenirs of my dad's life with me and my mom, letters I'd written to my dad from the time I was quite young to those I wrote to him when he was hospitalized in 1971. He had kept my mom's first magazine cover from her modeling days at the age of eight and her diary from that first movie she made in Paris. He had saved a lock of her hair and letters she'd written to him when they were separated by work. And there were dozens of photos and clippings of articles about the two of them together.

I know my mom was very touched, because my dad's love for her was in that suitcase. It was important for her to see that, because she had been hurt by him and had gone through so much with him, and this was confirmation that he loved her as much as he could. This was evidence that his love was real.

Whatever money my father had—and there wasn't much after his medical expenses—was left for me in trust. Although residuals come to me now and are a very decent stipend, I will not have access to the body of this trust until I am sixty-five years old. When people hear that number, they are appalled. Twenty-one is customary. Forty might be stretching it, but sixty-five?

Different things were on my father's mind when he made this decision. He was very concerned about my mom and my grandmother and their potential for extinguishing his estate. My mom had some money problems before he died, and he saw that. And I think he also saw that I might be put in a position where I'd have to say "no" to my own family if they asked for money, or else I'd have to give in. That would have been tough. More important, my dad wanted me to have to work for a living, make my own way, and he believed that I would be handicapped by having access to the bulk of his estate when I was young. I think he was right. He started life without advantages. He made his destiny. He planned it all and struggled to get where he got, and I have tremendous respect for him for doing it the hard way. "Bobby left me his love," said George Burns, "and that is good enough for me." I agree.

As for my dad's epitaph, I don't think it's prejudice on my part to say that Bobby Darin was a remarkable talent and that his death was a major loss to the world of music and entertainment. He was certainly known as a great performer. Countless thousands were dazzled by him in Vegas showrooms, nightclubs in New York. For a few hours they lost themselves in the magic that was my father's talent, and when they walked outside into "the cold air," they knew they had been entertained by a world-class performer.

And I think he made his mark as a human being, too. True, not many people remember the protests he made against the war in Vietnam or the stands he took for equal rights for all people. But he did it because he acted on his beliefs, whether people knew it or liked it. My dad's personality was such that people loved him or hated him. The ones who hated him have not stepped forward to talk to me, but the ones who loved him say that he was a unique individual, a brother, an irreplaceable soul. Many are overwhelmed by tears when they speak of him twenty years after his death—even if they were furious with him when he died.

In 1990 my dad was inducted into the Rock and Roll Hall of Fame, an epitaph of sorts and definitely an award that you didn't get, as my father would say, "simply for showing up." But what would please my father the most, if only he could know it, is that his music has endured. Anyone who can sing along with him when "Dream Lover," "Mack the Knife," or "Beyond the Sea" comes on the radio can feel an essential part of my father's life.

I've had a recurring dream where my dad comes back. He tells me he's hidden himself away for the last twenty years and now he's well. In the dream we walk down the street together, and it's great because we have a strong similarity in appearance and the people on the street say, "Oh, they look so much alike!" I think Dr. Oderberg would say that this dream falls into the "wish" category. I *wish* he were here. I would like to be able to have a little more time with him. And I would hope he would be proud of the way I turned out, because I've done the best I can do. Since there is no gravesite, no carved tombstone, anyone who knew Bobby Darin or knew of him is free to create his or her own epitaph for him. My personal choice is "Beloved Father. Deeply missed."

16

My Mom, My Grandmother, and Me,
1973 - 1991

Every step forward is made at the cost of mental and physical pain to someone.

—FRIEDRICH NIETZSCHE

So far I've talked about my mom and her troubles and my dad and his. It's time to own up to mine.

My dad died a few days after my twelfth birthday. By the time I was fourteen I had turned myself into the typical Hollywood fucked-up kid. I was in trouble academically, I was experimenting with drugs, doing my best to be the casebook example of a rebellious teenager. I was clearly unhappy. I was in denial of my dad's death. I was, I guess, afraid. There were no other men around. No boyfriends of my mom's. No uncles. Nobody. So to some extent the absence of male figures must have played on my fears. A psychologist said to my mom at one point, "He'll either be in jail or dead by the time he's twenty."

I remember teachers saying to me, "It's not that you're not bright and can't do the work. What's the problem?" And I'd just laugh. What did I care about grades? Throughout high school I was into surfing and girls and drugs. My mom and I had the typical relationship that went with the problem teenager. She tried to exert control, and I was uncontrollable. She was scared. She was thirty-something, alone, with no experience raising kids or of even being one. And she went through hell with me. She says now that she would have given me to Martians if they'd only asked. I feel for her and think she did a great job as a parent. I wonder if I could have done as good a job as she did if I'd been in her situation.

Case in point. One time when I was about seventeen, I'd been drinking with a buddy of mine. I was driving my car and pulled up to a red light. I told this guy, "I'm going to race that policeman up ahead and cut him off." That's what I did, and sure enough, five minutes later I was arrested. Here's my mom as a loving parent. This is the genius of her. The cops called her and said, "Your son is here. He's stoned and he's an asshole. What say we let him stay here overnight and cool off?"

My mom said, "I agree."

My grandma's response was, "You're out of your mind. I'm going down to get him. You don't leave him in jail! Whatever he did, the cops are wrong. To leave him there is criminal. How could you? He's not stoned."

My mom said, "He *is* stoned. Let him sleep there."

So I stayed in jail with handcuffs around my wrists all night. I was a loudmouth and a snotnose the first few hours, and I had a good old time. But eventually I sobered up. The handcuffs hurt, and no one would take them off. I asked to use the phone, and I was ignored. Sobering up was scary and intimidating. I learned a lesson, no question about it. At one point the police wanted to transfer me to a place with adults, and my mom said, "That's wrong," and I wasn't transferred. In her heart she wanted to get me out of jail, as my grandmother did, but she was going to let me suffer because it was important for me to understand what I'd done.

But I hadn't grown up yet. I was still smoking and drinking, daring trouble to get me. Once I almost killed myself and four of my friends. I was driving a jeep, a vehicle with a short, high wheel base that tends to tip over without much provocation. The five of us had been out drinking and carousing, and I took a turn too fast. The car flipped over twice, and it's a miracle we weren't all squashed like bugs. In flipping, the car righted itself against the curb. It was mangled as all hell, but it essentially parked itself facing in the right direction. The five of us acted as one. We hid the beer bottles in the ivy growing alongside the road and scampered off into the night, leaving the car in the street. None of us were hurt.

I went home, and the next morning I dealt with the wreck and the consequences. I told my mom and my grandmother, then got the car towed to the shop. The cops were never involved. I had the car fixed and sold it, and although the accident didn't make a dent on me physically, it impressed me psychologically. It was a turning point. I imagined the headlines that could have been in the paper the next day about a whole group of kids getting wiped out because they were drunk. I could see all our little smiling head shots from the yearbook right above the tragic story. And it would have been all my fault. I told myself, You are a lucky asshole. This is a warning. You'd better get with it.

While my mom was dealing with my problems, she was wrestling with demons of her own. And none too successfully. I want to comment on a normal kitchen situation in the house, circa 1977 or 1978, when I was about sixteen. My mom had one section of the kitchen that was all hers. She had her vinegar, salt substitute, and her own special ingredients, and she kept her area totally sterile, covered with plastic. No one could go near it. She also had a section of the refrigerator that was just hers. My grandmother's stuff, my stuff, the maid's stuff, none of it could go near hers. The way she prepared her food and ate it was an ordeal for everyone. I understand that my mom's way of dealing with food is fairly typical for people with anorexia. Controlling what they put into their bodies is the only way they feel in control.

Obviously I'm speaking as an observer here, not a professional. But what my mother communicated to me was that if a grain of sugar got near her chicken, for instance, that could contaminate it. I believe her behavior is less extreme now. She lives by herself, so she doesn't have to worry about alien cookies or potato chips getting near her food. I have seen her eat in her own home, but other than fruit, she hasn't eaten a bite of food in a restaurant in twelve to fifteen years. The results of Mary's force-feeding my mom when she was five are readily apparent today. You can track from the big bowls of everything, to the enlightening first cup of consommé, to the head-of-lettuce diet, to the five-foot-six, ninety-five-pound woman my mother is today.

Along with her problems with food, my mom was trying to deal with her addiction to alcohol. Both her father and her father's brother died of alcohol-related problems, so if indeed alcoholism has a genetic component, she never had a chance. She drank throughout her marriage, and when my dad died, she drank even more. I watched my mother try to limit her drinking, and there was a time when she could actually start and stop at will. She used to plan her drinking to the hour. She'd make sure she had no appointments. She would get real food: ice cream, spaghetti, chili dogs, the great stuff all of us eat occasionally or regularly. And then she would eat and drink and enjoy herself. My grandmother and I used to sneak in and watch her with amazement. I suppose it sounds sick, but we used to love seeing her eat. It made us believe that it was possible for her to lead a happy and normal life. Eat ice cream, Mom. Enjoy it! Two days later she'd be downing milk of magnesia and detoxing and saying, "Everybody's food away from me." And she'd deny that she ever ate a chili dog, ice cream, any of it.

During the ten years following my father's death, my mother worked so little, it hardly bears mentioning. She says that being my mother was her job and that it was all she wanted. When she's sober, she says that she didn't want to act anymore. She explains that she felt a rush of excitement at the very beginning of her career, but after she made her first movie, acting was just a job. But I think she shares her truest feelings with me when she's been drinking. Then she says how sorry she is that her career ended. That she misses it. That acting is the only work she knows. My mom is fifty years old and has a very able mind, but without work or hobbies or real friendships, she's in a bad way. So that's where the booze comes in.

My mom recalls an interview with Rex Reed in which he described her as a pink powderpuff and told his readers that butter wouldn't melt in her mouth. She says the whole powderpuff image was an act. Since she was old enough to understand, she knew what was expected of her and she'd trained herself to be perfect.

She told me, "In public, I *was* perfect. I'd have a glass of wine at a party, but no one ever saw me drunk. I never even said, 'Oh, darn.' I was a lady through and through. But by the late seventies and early eighties I was anything but what the public thought I was. I was miserable, and so I drank scotch and wine by myself; anything to forget my misery."

My mom admits she should have gotten help, but that wasn't the way she'd been trained. She had good reason to believe that her mother would have preferred her to sit in the house and destroy herself rather than go public with her problem; the easiest thing was to go along with her. But the two did have a classic case of mutual manipulation. My grandmother would hide my mom's bottles and my mom would figure out a way to get Mary to give them back. There was one notable incident where Mary hid the scotch and my mom staggered out to her Rolls saying she was going to the liquor store to get more. As she expected, my grandmother went tearing out into the yard trying to stop her daughter from driving. My mom quite deliberately backed the car into a tree. As she puts it, "Everyone in Beverly Hills was watching" and both of them knew it. Mary gave in to the blackmail, told Sandy she would give her the bottle and then, as if the whole scene had been rehearsed, my grandmother said loudly to the lookers-on, "She hasn't been feeling well." "Yeah," said my mom. "I hope I get rid of this fever soon." What a pair.

My mom's drinking escalated even more later on, but at this time, things hadn't gotten critical. I was worried and I vocalized my concerns, but I didn't get through.

In 1980 when I was about eighteen years old, I started to get some healthy fears about where I was going to fit into the world. My friends were getting ready for college and making plans, and because my reputation as a hell-raiser was feeding itself, I decided that the best thing I could do was move out of Beverly Hills. A girl I'd been seeing in high school had similar problems, and together we wound up in San Diego. I loved it there instantly. I got a little money through my dad's Social Security, got some help from his estate, and enrolled in school. Until this point I'd thought academics were a joke. Now I had something to prove to myself.

I did very well both in school and personally. People I'd known for a long time said the change in me was so rapid, it was almost scary. I've heard it's fairly common for people who've had drug problems or drinking in the family to suddenly go totally the other way. They used to be a wreck, and then overnight, they're like Mormons. That's what happened to me. I couldn't be around anyone who smoked pot. I couldn't have a drink. I was hitting the books as though my life depended on it, and in a way it did. I was scared because time was passing by, and I never touched drugs again. Ever. I was a zombie on drugs and obsessive when I start using them. I can't drink moderately, either, so drink and drugs are and were totally out for me. The girl I was going with decided to move back to Beverly Hills, but I was happy in San Diego. I made new friends and got away from the problem people in my past. In 1983 I was accepted into USC and moved back to Los Angeles. I majored in political science and economics. I was living on my own, and I was growing up.

From the time I was nineteen until I was twenty-five, my relationship with my mother changed for the better. I got closer to her and started to try to be a friend to her and do things with her rather than rolling my eyes as I had done before, thinking, Oh, brother, she's my mom, and I gotta listen to her shit. I started evolving as an adult, and that was a good, healthy period for us. The closest we've ever come.

By the time I was twenty-six, I'd been out of the house for quite a few years. I was involved in buying and selling real estate, and I'd had a number of serious relationships with women. By and large, the women I got involved with were dependent on me, which was the only way I knew how to relate to women. I got satisfaction from being the hero, and I gave a lot of financial and emotional support as my part of the deal. Sooner or later I would come to resent being the strong one and the giver all the time, but usually it was later. I wasn't programmed like my father when it came to women. Generally I would be in a relationship that lasted for years, then it would be interrupted by another long-term relationship. I've been described as a serial committer.

Came 1987, I had been on retreat in Arizona for the summer with a young lady, and I phoned in to talk to my mom and my grandma. My mother said something that should have alarmed me, but it didn't. She said that my grandmother wasn't feeling well. My grandmother never got sick, prided herself on never having been to a doctor in her life. This time my mom said, "Come home, because I need you." I told my mom I'd be home soon, and I'd deal with the problem when I got there.

I arrived home a few days later. When I opened the front door of my mother's house and saw my grandmother, I knew that she was gone. She was gray, emaciated, looked like an old lady. It was horrifying. My grandmother was only sixty-five, a woman full of piss and vinegar. She had more energy than I have today or ever had. When we went to Vegas together, she'd be the one who stayed up all night, playing the machines. She was go, go, go, just a pistol. Now all of that unbelievable energy was gone. Apparently she'd been telling my mom that she couldn't sleep, had been throwing up, just wasn't feeling well at all. There was an unspoken pact that my mom and grandma had lived by since the dawn of time: Don't acknowledge it and it won't be true. So for my grandmother to be saying she was sick was as terrifying to me as flashing lights and sirens. I said to her, "You're going right into the doctor for testing." And what was upsetting beyond belief is that she didn't argue with me.

To provide a little context on my grandmother's illness, she was a smoker. Whenever I saw her, I would say, "You know, you're gonna do yourself in." I loved her. I would just do whatever I could to get her to stop smoking. And she either wouldn't or couldn't stop. Same time frame, my mother had noticed a lump under my grandmother's arm. She pointed it out to my grandmother, who said, "It's just a fat pocket."

My mom said, "Why would you get a fat pocket there?" But this line of questioning wasn't pursued. To my grandmother's general complaints of sleeplessness or nausea, the two of them would make up explanations of what it could be. My mother would read an article about, say, Epstein-Barr syndrome, call Mary, and the two of them would say, "Oh, it must be that." But until I said "You're going to see the doctor," there was no movement toward getting professional medical help. Again, you can look at my mother's history and see the chain of events leading up to this crisis. Mary never called the doctor unless her daughter was either dying or completely recovered from whatever ailed her. I have no clue where my grandmother's aversion to medical help came from.

Dr. Louis Fishman was an intern during my dad's final illness. While growing up, I used to play racquetball with him and tell him my troubles, and he'd been a friend as well as our family doctor for a long time. My grandmother and I went to see him on a Monday, three days after I'd come home. My grandmother's relationship with Dr. Fishman had been strained over the years because Fishman had given her unwanted advice regarding my mom. He'd said, "Look, you've got to get Sandy into an alcohol rehab program. You've got to get her some help." And since my grandma couldn't deal with that, she had nothing but negative feelings toward Dr. Fishman.

Now that she was going to be seeing him, they joked to relieve the situation. Fishman said, "I'll be your doctor. You don't have to be my patient."

My grandmother described her symptoms to Dr. Fishman. He examined her and then sent her down to radiology for X rays. I went with her to the radiologist, who was on a different floor in the same building, and waited for her in the waiting room. I sat there for at least a half hour. I could see through the receptionist's window as my grandmother left the radiologist. Then I heard her say in a very squeaky voice, "Are you done with me?" It was the voice of fear. I couldn't see the doctor from where I sat, but I heard him say, "No, we just need a few more pictures." I'll never forget my grandmother's voice, the matriarch of our family, saying, "Are you done with me?" The sound and image are emblazoned on my mind.

A few minutes later we walked upstairs to Fishman's office. He called her into one of the offices, and I sat again in the waiting room. She asked him some questions: "Why am I coughing? Why can't I keep fluids down?"

And he said, "After seeing the X ray, I'm not quite sure. Looks like some kind of ulcer." Which is what her hope was all along. When she started to feel lousy, she was thinking, "Oh, I have an ulcer."

After talking to my grandmother, Fishman took her out to the waiting room and brought me into his office. He shut the door. I looked at his face and saw written on it exactly what I'd known from the moment I first saw my grandmother three days before. Fishman said, "We've got a big problem."

I said, "No, come on."

He pressed on. "We've got a big problem," he said again. "She's got a tumor the size of a grapefruit in her lung." He flicked on the light behind the X ray and said, "You see, this is all supposed to be clear," and where he was pointing was a huge black cloud.

I said, "Oh, my God. What are you telling me?"

"This is a very serious medical condition," he said. "What are we going to do?"

I said, "What do you mean?"

And he said, "Well, you know your mom and your grandma. Your mom will kill herself. Your granny can't handle this."

I said, "Well, what would you do if we were dealing with two stable people?"

"I'd put your grandmother in the hospital immediately. Right now. This moment."

I said, "Give me a day to think." He said okay. He didn't have to go into details about time. I got the whole picture. I left him and went outside with my grandmother, and the first thing she said to me is, "Is it cancer?"

She knew. With all her bullshit denial, she knew.

"Absolutely not," I said to her. "Absolutely not."

My grandmother was staying at my mom's house. I dropped her off. I couldn't tell my mother the truth right then. I said to her, "It looks like an ulcer, but they're not sure. I think she may have to go in the hospital for some more tests."

I called the woman I was seeing at the time and told her the whole story. I really gave in to all of my emotions as I tried to figure out what to do. It was hard to be rational. I was so filled with pain that I was going to lose my grandmother, sorrow that things had gone so far and were probably hopeless, and I was deeply frightened for my mother. My grandmother was her lifeline, and neither she nor my mother really had anyone else. I felt helpless and heartsick and just plain wretched.

My mom had always said over the years, "If anything ever happens to my mother, I'll kill myself. Respect it and understand. I'll have to do myself in. It would have nothing to do with my not loving you, Dodd. I'm just telling you, that's what she means to me." That was their relationship. It was weird, but they were as close as people can be. I knew I had to tell my mother the truth, and two days later, when I had gotten something resembling a grip, I told her just how serious the situation was. She went to pieces. It was awful; the two of us were just fearful and lost and on the verge of breaking down.

Afterward Louis Fishman talked to me and my mom, and we asked all the questions. "What about surgery?"

"No point. Too invasive."

"What about chemo?"

"I'm telling you, there's no point."

My grandmother had always said, "Nobody's going to cut me open. If I ever get sick, that'll be that." She had a fear of doctors, the truth, surgery, everything. Early on, it was apparent that my grandmother was in the last stages of dying. In theory, I question whether hiding the truth is ever the right or kind thing to do, but I had to look at the specifics of this unusual situation. All three of us agreed to keep her disease a secret. It was a tough decision.

I said to my mom, "You've got to be an actress with this. You can't let her know." Meaning no disrespect to my mom, my grandmother was the strongest personality in my life from the time I was twelve. She was a very bright, sharp woman, the "go to" person for me. If I had practical problems, she'd have the answers. She was the head of the family. And now my mom and I decided that my grandmother couldn't handle the truth, so we weren't going to tell her.

A day or two later it was time to take Grandma to the hospital, ostensibly for more tests. We brought her to Cedars-Sinai. She could barely sit through the check-in process, she was so tired. She checked in and remained in the hospital for about forty days. Up until her last week there, she did not formally know what she had.

My mom, God bless her, was doing as well as she could. She came to the hospital each day. And it was rough. My grandmother was hot when she always used to be cold. You could see your breath in her room, the temperature was down so low, but she was sweltering. She asked for bizarre foods and couldn't eat them. Most heartbreaking of all, she said to my mother, "I want them just to open me up and zap this thing out." She must have been carrying around the cancer for five years. The lump under her arm was as large as a golf ball. Had she been less in denial of her illness and gone in for a checkup when she'd first experienced symptoms, maybe she could have been treated successfully.

I started sleeping on a cot on the floor of my grandmother's room at night. I wanted to be there for my grandma, and I wanted to give something back. We talked all night. But as the disease progressed, the doctors put her under heavier and heavier sedation. After three weeks of sleeping there, Dr. Fishman said to me, "You've got to go home and sleep," and finally I did.

I'll never forget a day when I was standing outside the door to my grandmother's hospital room and Fishman was inside talking with her.

The door was mostly closed, but I could hear as her doctor told her, "You have cancer."

Her response was a shrieking, agonized "Oh, my God!"

I gave way to full-blown crying right outside the door. I went in after the doctor left and gave my grandmother a huge hug. She was inconsolable. She wasn't herself. And she wasn't responding to a word I said. All of us will have our day to be introduced to death and will deal with it in our own ways. My grandmother went inward.

I cried and then I left her room. Her illness was harder for me than my dad's illness, by far. I was much closer to my grandmother. I had known her much longer, shared a lot more with her in terms of life experiences. The jail, the drugs, my mom, now this. When she got over the initial shock, it seemed to me that she was embarrassed at having cancer. Once she knew, no one else was allowed to know. We weren't to tell her clients or staff. "Mary has an ulcer," was what we were supposed to say. I don't want to judge, but it's a sin that she denied herself the comfort of telling the truth to friends she'd known for twenty years.

Physically, my grandmother was having trouble breathing. She was on six liters of oxygen, which is essentially forcing oxygen, and still she was suffering. The doctor said, "We're almost at the point where we want to give her morphine." My mom and I asked what that meant and were told, "Basically, this is the end. We'll give her morphine and she'll be in a state that is almost vegetative." All along she was being loaded up with heavy tranquilizers, and she was still hurting. We said okay to the morphine, and the effect of that drug was frightening. She became vegetative, to the point where she wouldn't come to even when we shook her and wanted her to wake up. I thought she was dead. We had been told that she would drift in and out of consciousness, but instead she was just gone. We reversed the morphine decision because we couldn't live with it.

My grandmother was in the hospital for about a month when the doctors told us they'd done all that they could do for her. In truth, we had dragged out her stay at Cedars for as long as we could, because honestly, I couldn't see taking care of her at home. She had a feeding tube, and it was comforting to know that trained people in the hospital were looking after her. Finally, for practical, financial reasons, we had to check her out of the hospital. And she didn't want to go home. I guess she knew the jig was up.

The last day in the hospital, she made herself up in the room, and it was really the last time I saw her being "normal." She had a little smirk: "Look at me. I've still got my hair." Getting her from the street into a cab took a great deal of effort. It was heartrending to watch someone who had been so incredibly vibrant deteriorate to this degree.

We took my grandmother to my mom's house. I had a knock-down fight with the estate lawyer in order to get money for a nurse, and fortunately I was able to get someone to help us. My grandmother had a friend named Eileen, who was also her assistant in her real estate business. The two of them had a strange relationship. Eileen was overpossessive and perhaps insensitive, but she was also dependable and very close to my grandmother. She'd been with her a lot while she was in the hospital and was also aware of her condition. In the final weeks of my grandmother's life, Eileen moved into the house so she could tend to her friend.

Suddenly there was this strange domestic complication, where Eileen was changing the linens, feeding Mary, doing all the little housekeeping things around the house. She'd become the daughter, and my mother was on the outside looking in. Her reaction to that was, "I'm totally offended. I can do all this. I want to change the bed. I want to be the daughter." But the fact was, my grandmother felt more comfortable having Eileen doing the household and caretaking tasks.

Originally, Eileen and my mother had been good friends. Then, on an occasion when my mom was drunk, Eileen made a comment and my mom never spoke to her again. So now this ugly, weird, tense atmosphere was happening around my grandmother's bedside, and my mom started drinking. I could see my mom's side totally, yet my grandmother was fighting for her life. Whatever would make her feel better, she should have had. She was two weeks away from death, suffering, and my mom and Eileen were fighting in front of her. At one point my grandmother literally lifted herself out of bed, used everything she had in her, and yelled at my mom, "You're a murderer! You're a murderer!" What she was saying to my mom was, "I can't even get any peace now. You can't make peace with Eileen. You're in

my face with the drinking. Even at the end, you are so fucking selfish."
And my mom was devastated. I understood her pain and her take on
the situation, but coming into my grandmother's room with a scotch
in her hand was like pissing on the Vatican.

A day or two before my grandmother died, she and I were talking
about my mom. She said to me, "I now understand how sick your
mom is. Don't be a victim. Get her in for help. Don't let happen to
you what happened to me." Ironically, my grandmother had dedicated
the previous five years to cleaning up after my mom. But she had to
be on her deathbed before she could see how sick and selfish my mother
really was. When my grandmother told me that she finally saw reality,
it touched me. But she never admitted to her role in my mother's
problem. She never said, "I should have done something for her. I
contributed to this mess." Out of my grandmother's presence, I'd say
to my mom, "You've got to get help. You don't want to drink like
this, do you?" And she was more honest about it than my grandmother
was. She'd say, "You're right. I should get help. I have a problem."
But thanks to my grandmother's influence, getting help seemed
shameful to her.

My grandmother was home for two weeks, and then she passed
away. My mom and I had had ample time to prepare ourselves for my
father's passing, but with my grandmother, it was so unexpected that
it sent my mother into shock. She describes her immediate reaction as
similar to mine when my dad passed away: denial. She was very anxious
to get all the medical equipment out of her house. She couldn't
understand why anyone wanted to know what to bury my grandmother
in. She finally said, "Pink. She likes pink." But her tone was, "Why
do you ask?"

When my grandmother knew she was dying, she mentioned to
Eileen that she wanted to be cremated. She wanted to spare my mom
the pain of going to her funeral. Later in the illness, she recanted her
decision, thinking that for religious reasons she should be buried. My
mom and I both knew that my grandmother had a fear of being alone.
She used to leave the bathroom door open so she could talk to my
mother; she didn't even like to be alone then. She also had a horror of
bugs and worms in the ground. I came up with the idea of a wall crypt
as a final resting place, and that felt good to my mom and me. It was

a good solution. My grandma's not cremated and she's not in the ground.

When my grandmother died, my mom wanted to die herself. Her parents, grandparents, and Bobby were all dead. With her mother's death, her support structure was totally gone, and she had nothing to replace it. I suddenly felt that I was responsible for her. In the past, I had been able to duck her problems with alcohol. When my mom was drunk, that was my grandmother's job. When she had to detox in a hospital, that was my grandmother's job again. I was affected by what went on. I loved them both and suffered what any child of an alcoholic goes through. But my mother wasn't my responsibility. I was still able to be a kid.

Then everything changed. I realized at the age of twenty-five or twenty-six that I was now my mother's everything. That my grand-mother was no longer going to be climbing in the window of her house to see if she was alive. That my grandmother wouldn't be there to intercept the liquor store deliveries or check to see that all the cigarette butts were out. With my grandmother gone, there was only me. Leaving my mother on her own was unthinkable. She had no means of support, and I could not in any kind of conscience leave her to her own devices. She would have died, and anyone who advocates tough love in a case like this can do it with their own mother. I couldn't abandon her and live with myself.

Needless to say, becoming my mother's keeper created a weird dynamic between us. I resented her because she was the parent. I was going through my own problems and wanted to look to her and lean on her for support and love and comfort. But that was impossible. Our roles were almost reversed. I became the parent. I love her, but she was a pain in the ass. I couldn't be the carefree twenty-five-year-old. And she didn't want me telling her what to do. On an emotional level, she was right to feel this way. There is nothing wrong with my mother's mind. She's more than smart, she has an acute intelligence. She's a proud woman. And she has reason to be proud. She had supported herself and her mother from the age of nine until her "retirement." Now, to be thirty-five or thirty-six years old and feel that her life was behind her had to be devastating.

Money became our biggest issue. My grandmother had been bring-ing home a paycheck, and now the only money around came from what I earned and the residue of my father's estate. I started paying my mother's bills, and to be honest, that's one of the most painful things that my mom has had to deal with. It's one thing to say, "I was an alcoholic, I was anorectic, I was a fuck-up." It's another to say, "I have money problems and I need help." And that complicated things for us, and our relationship soured. I started to resent her. She didn't want to spend time with me. She felt shameful about money and the overall situation, and we grew apart. It's been awkward for both of us, and we've had horrific fights where she's accused me of trying to make her suffer as my father had. Obviously this hurts me a lot.

While her mother was sick, my mom went from her pattern weekend bingeing followed by a week of sobriety, to a total week of drinking and then a week of sobriety. After her mother died, she didn't leave the house for four months. She'd been so sheltered, she didn't know how to balance a checkbook or pay the phone bill. She had no resources to marshal, no means of getting on her feet. She was angry, and she missed her mother more than words can describe.

Taking in food is what keeps many alcoholics alive. My mom subsisted on soup and crackers and a quart and a half of straight booze daily for weeks on end. Her weight dropped to eighty pounds, and she couldn't get out of bed. When she started throwing up blood, I knew she would die if I didn't get her into a hospital, and I practically carried her in. She didn't like the way her hair looked, and I remember jamming a hat on her head and getting her checked into Cedars. By that time, early 1990, she was hovering between life and death. She stayed in the hospital for a good two weeks. She was given blood transfusions and had to be fed and hydrated intravenously because her system could no longer handle real food.

I cursed my grandmother for letting her daughter become such a basket case and for dying and leaving me in charge of this disaster. I love my grandmother to this day and believe in my heart that she was pure in her love. But she fucked my mom up. In her attempt to protect my mom and shield her from the realities of this ugly world, she made her an invalid. Totally crippled her. She could have prepared her for the future by saying to her, "Hey, this is gonna end. It does for everybody. And you'd better not rely on me and your accountants. There's more to life than being Sandra Dee and raising your son. Get a life." By sparing her everything, by force-feeding her unreality, my mother found herself on her own at forty years of age instead of eighteen to twenty, which is what's normal for most of us. Which is why she drank herself into the hospital and why I had every reason to expect that she would die.

My mom had been systematically destroying her body since she was a child, and there's only so much a human body can take. It was virtually a miracle that she lived through this crisis. While in the hospital, Dr. Fishman introduced her to a psychiatrist, Ronald Gershman, who is a specialist in addiction and substance abuse. My mom had tried therapy before, but either because she didn't stick with it or because she had the wrong doctor, therapy had done little for her. Now she had finally reached the point where she wanted help, and Dr. Gershman became an important part of her life. Within a few months she was a better and happier Sandra Dee. She stopped drinking, and she was eating, driving her car, shopping, going to the gym. Her certain decline into death had been halted.

During this time, my mom got a call from *People* magazine. It had been quite a while since the public had expressed any interest in Sandra Dee, but Todd Gold, the reporter who interviewed her, liked my mother and thought her story interesting and worthwhile. My mom was seeing Dr. Gershman as the five-day interview with *People* was going on, and suddenly she had these two people focusing on her life. While Gershman was making observations and suggesting what my mom's childhood had been like, Gold was asking pointed questions. My mom tried her old game of denial, denial, denial, but the spotlight was on her and she found herself talking about her childhood abuse. And even though she was afraid of what her former fans might think of her now, she talked to the press about her anorexia and alcoholism for the first time.

The *People* article ran in the fall of 1991. My mom was a cover girl again, and the results were heartwarming in the extreme. Women in the supermarket came up to her and told her how touched they were by the magazine piece. And she was touched by them in return. Her fans were no longer little girls grabbing at her coat, trying to touch her hair. They were women her own age. They'd grown up and had had problems like hers. They wanted to tell that to my mom and congratulate her on her bravery. Wonderful, supportive letters poured in from all over the country, and she got calls from TV magazines and talk show hosts.

Sally Jessy Raphaël called my mom and asked her to appear on her show with her former costars, actors Jimmy Darren and John Saxon. She said she would. Late that year, with the cameras trained on her, my mom walked down a long, long set of stairs from the top of an amphitheater to the stage below. And the audience went crazy when they saw her. She walked onto the stage, and although she had been absent for so many years, she was as natural and as graceful as though she'd never been gone. She *owned* that stage. She handled the questions, the applause, like the star she had been—and she was a star again! She simply glowed.

Meanwhile John Saxon had a big idea. A two-person play called *Love Letters* had been getting a great deal of attention in many theaters across the country. Generally, two well-known actors would team up and do the play for a week, and then another couple would replace them. John had just seen Ben Gazzara and Gena Rowlands do *Love Letters*, and he was intrigued by the idea of doing it with my mom. (The play is about a man and a woman who had become friends as children, then communicate by letter throughout their lives. The two characters have a strong emotional connection that is never consummated. When the man is available, the woman is not, and vice versa. Missed opportunities mount up, until at last, when he is free and she is, too, the woman tells her dear friend not to come to her. And then she dies.)

John Saxon contacted my mom's agent, and within a short time the two of them signed on to do this show. There was a brief rehearsal, and then my mom and John Saxon, who had first starred together in 1958, opened at the Canon Theater in Beverly Hills. When my mom walked onto the stage to take her place, the audience rose and burst into spontaneous, heartfelt applause. I am not exaggerating when I say the applause went on for a solid five minutes. It just wouldn't stop. My mom had been absent for so long and her fans had been so moved by her true story, their emotions just overflowed. John tells me that he knew the public had seen him "knocking around over the years," but they had missed Sandra. He knew that this was really her moment. He jokingly whispered to her, "It's never going to be better than this. Let's leave while we're ahead." But the best was yet to come. My mom says, "Doing *Love Letters* was the best high ever."

☞ *John and I walked out onstage and people started clapping, and I'm not used to that. When you make a movie, someone says, "Quiet on the set!" This was completely different. John Saxon was standing beside me, and Dodd and Steve Blauner were in the audience, and the audience was so responsive. I loved doing the show. It was different every night. Some nights it was a comedy. Some nights there was a sad tone. It depended on the audience. I had no worry about missing my mark or forgetting a line. If I made a mistake, I'd take my pencil, say "Whoops," and erase what I was pretending to write. It was just the best experience. It was like coming home every night, the best of both worlds. There was no five A.M. call, and yet I'd see people who would come backstage. And by the way, there was a show to do.*

Afterward we'd all go out to a restaurant. And Steve had arranged something that was really sweet. Outside the theater were klieg lights sweeping the sky. It was just like a fifties premiere. I had been too young for this kind of thing in the fifties. It was something I'd read about that was now coming true.

My mother had done her last film when I was about nine years old. Her stardom and her big days were pretty much over when I was old enough to remember. So for me to be able to see her performance and the audience's reaction was just wonderful. She was so radiant, so alive, so much in her element. I was so proud of her, I couldn't believe it. The producer came up to me and said, "You know, a hundred and fifty million people have done *Love Letters* over the years. But your mom really gets it." I was so happy for her, I got a high myself. I had seen her struggle for so long, and I know how proud she was that I could see her in her glory. But there was still more.

John Saxon remarked to me recently that "the most important moments never happen in public." And he was so right. *Love Letters* provided my mother with an infusion of self-worth, but it didn't happen onstage. It didn't come from me mopping my eyes in the front row or her five-minute standing ovation. Something happened that was bigger than all of that, and nobody noticed except my mom.

She says, "If my mother had been alive, she would have wanted to be backstage dressing me. Before I went to the theater, I said, 'Jesus, Dodd. I've never done this for myself.' If my fly had been open or my makeup was wrong, it would have been my fault. I actually cried in the car before the opening because I was so afraid. But you know what a great girl I was? I did it myself, and that gave me an enormous sense of accomplishment. It was another step. It seems so stupid. You dressed yourself? Big deal. But it was a big deal. I dressed myself. It was the proudest moment of my life."

If life was a movie script, I could bring up the music about now, roll the credits, and write those magical words *The End* across the screen. But life, as we all know, isn't tidy and rarely has Hollywood endings. When my mom had that sudden flurry of attention, she felt she had things together. But being an actress often means waiting for the phone to ring.

My mom closed in *Love Letters* and waited. The phone didn't ring, and there was no tennis tournament, no trip to Palm Springs, no sailing lessons, to fill the void. And the waiting was brutal. When she had been active in her career, everything had been scheduled for her. She didn't have to fill her day. The studio filled it for her, and she never missed a beat. If movies were still like that, she would love it. "Show me where to show up and I'll be a pro, I'll be great." But that's not how it is.

I would love my mom to be able to feel good about what she accomplished in the past, for it to have given her a foundation of self-worth. If she had been an accountant or a lawyer and had achieved in that field what she achieved in film, she could take great pride in that, as most people would. But the nature of her business is so fleeting that there are really no good feelings left outside of her for what she did. When the applause ends, and it ends for everybody, you've got to have something to fall back on. Something to feel good about. She didn't have that, is still searching for some meaning beyond work.

If my mom had continued to get work after *Love Letters*, I know she would have stayed sober. But she didn't. After *Love Letters* she had a major relapse, which resulted in hospitalization again. Following the hospital stay, she went into an alcohol rehabilitation center and made progress. Another step: she ate lunch with women in her therapy group. A very big deal to eat an egg, truly. She resumed therapy with Dr. Gershman, slid back, and pulled herself together, and today she's more stable than she's been since my grandmother got sick. She's not out of danger, but she's not drinking. She's auditioning, working on her emotional problems, and doing things many people consider so routine that they might not understand what a triumph it is for her to go to exercise class with a new friend.

My dad once said to my grandmother, "Sandra's only seen one side of life, and I'm going to show her the other." What he meant was was, "There's another world out there. It's filled with people struggling and it's ugly and it's painful, and if you work at it, you can sometimes get by." That's what he came from. And he wanted my mom to at least acknowledge the dark side of the moon. Ironically, she never saw this dark side during their marriage, but she's stood entirely in its shadow during the last fifteen years. I love my mom dearly and can fully understand why she feels helpless in the absence of what she used to rely on. Being Sandra Dee, movie star, worked for her once, and nothing else has since. My mom's not lazy. She's not sinister. She's a product of what she was and what she grew up with. I feel now that with luck, courage, and a little help from her friends, she's going to do well for herself again. She's determined to do so, and the path may not always be straight up. But I believe she'll get there. It's just a matter of time.

17

Audrey and Me, 1993

Dream Lover

Every night, I hope and pray
A dream lover will come my way.
A girl to hold in my arms,
And know the magic of her charms.

'Cause I want
A girl
To call
My own.
I want a dream lover
So I don't have to dream alone.

Dream lover, where are you?
With a love, oh so true.
And a hand I can hold,
Feel you near as I grow old.
. . . .

Some day, I don't know how
I hope she'll hear my plea.
Some way, I don't know how
She'll bring her love to me.

Dodd Darin

> *'Cause I want*
> *A girl*
> *To call*
> *My own.*
> *I want a dream lover*
> *So I don't have to dream alone.*

—Words and music by
BOBBY DARIN, *1960*

I met my wife when I was eleven years old. She was an older woman of eleven and a half, and we both went to the school where I was enrolled against my will after my dad yanked me out of Buckley. At Buckley I had always been the joker, the class clown. I was always in trouble, but I made the teacher laugh. She'd discipline me and I'd get her to crack up and I'd get away with murder. I had excess testosterone at an early age, was the first to notice girls, and so had friends of both sexes. Then, in the middle of the fifth grade, the ground dropped out from under me, and I was in a whole new world. The Buckley uniform of blazers and ties was gone. I wore jeans to class, and I was just another fish in a big pond, not *the* fish anymore. Even though I was extroverted in a certain way, I was also very shy. After the change of schools, my mom said, "Go to the schoolground and play around. Make some friends."

I said, "No, my friends are at Buckley, and I refuse to know these other kids."

She tried to bribe me. "I'll give you a few bucks. I'll give you a new baseball glove."

I spent twenty minutes of every day for weeks saying, "No, no, no." But the first time I went to the playground after the three o'clock bell, I was there for four hours. My mom could hardly get me into the house after that. I had broken the ice. Suddenly I had a whole new life, new friends. And one of my friends was a girl named Audrey Tannenbaum.

I had a major crush on Audrey from minute one. She was the first girl I ever had that special feeling for. Not just hormones. Love. Audrey let me kiss her and put my prepubescent paws on her, and our "relationship" lasted until we were about thirteen. Then she got interested in older boys and I got interested in hell-raising, and we went our separate ways. After high school I didn't see her for ten years. When the *People* magazine story on my mom came out, Audrey saw it, and she decided to look me up. When we spoke on the phone, her voice sounded wonderful, exactly as it had when we were in junior high.

Strange as it seems, I had thought of Audrey often throughout the years. I had gone out with other girls longer than I went out with Audrey, had done more things with them, but they had all just passed into the darkness of memory. People always say, "When you find the right person, you'll know she's the one." That's how I felt about Audrey. I often wondered what she was doing, even thought, Wouldn't it be great to see her. And what makes the story almost fictionlike is that she called me.

Naturally we agreed to get together, but I had something to do before seeing Audrey again for the first time. I said, "Let's meet at RJ's restaurant in two weeks."

She said, "Do you want to talk between now and then?"

I said, "No, let's just set it up now. Two weeks from Wednesday. We'll meet at RJ's."

"Sure you don't want to confirm beforehand?"

"I'm sure."

Audrey thought I was going to break the date, but the truth was that I'd gained some weight and needed time to work it off. I hung up the phone and went on a powder diet. I became a maniac on the treadmill. On the day of our lunch date I was twelve pounds lighter. I felt pretty good, but I was nervous. My anxiety was completely uncalled for because from the moment I saw her, everything was wonderful. I liked her tremendously, and I was attracted to her all over again. She had great auburn hair, expressive eyes, terrific skin, and an easy, off-center smile, and the rest of her was just unbelievable. We spent four hours at lunch talking about everything. I was amazed at what I found myself saying on this first date, and she was as surprised at herself for the same reason. We picked up from where we'd left off in junior high and just had a terrific time. When we left the restaurant, Audrey realized that she had parked in a half-hour parking zone. The cops are vultures in Beverly Hills. They'll zap you if the parking meter has expired by a minute, but Audrey didn't get a ticket. We interpreted that as a sign that we were meant to be. That's love for you.

After our lunch at RJ's, I didn't see Audrey for over a week. She had planned a trip out of town before we made our date, and the whole time she was gone, I obsessed about her. We had both been at the tail end of bad relationships when we became reacquainted, and when she returned from her trip, we came together for good. Not to say that we didn't hit a few slippery patches in the road, bump into some potholes. After we'd been dating for a while, I got frightened because Audrey is different from anyone I had ever been with. She's independent, strong-minded, wasn't looking to me for emotional or financial strength, she didn't need anything from me. She just loved me for me. What could possibly be better than that? Or, if you look at it another way, what could be more frightening?

Audrey comes from a show-biz family, so my being a celebrity kid didn't impress her at all. While that was a revelation, it was hard for me to adjust to. She also had a career and was earning really good money. Instead of saying to myself, This is great—the woman can stand on her own feet and maybe carry me a few blocks if I need her to, I found myself wondering what she saw in me. As in, Jeez, I don't know if I can handle this. I'm not paying all the bills and I'm not being a hero, so where do I fit in here?

And something else was producing anxiety for me. Audrey has a family: father, mother, sister, brother. I have no history of sitting down to dinner with family members and conversing about the events of the last seven days, and I found having dinner with the Tannenbaums somewhat uncomfortable. Audrey came by her independent nature honestly, and there's a certain competitive dynamic that exists within her family. I put the pressure on myself. I was measuring and analyzing way too much, and as a result I was preventing myself from experiencing new things and people in an open way. I dreaded every Tannenbaum family occasion. It was strange, because I liked each family member individually, but their collective interaction brought out my insecurity. And there were times during the first year and a half with Audrey when I wanted to flee. I told Audrey what I was feeling, and she was understanding as I worked out the difficulties I was having with myself. I've grown tremendously because of Audrey.

And those aren't just words. They are fact. I love her. And I feel very fortunate that she's in my life.

After dating for a year and a half, I asked Audrey to marry me, and she said yes. Left to my own devices, I would have taken her to Las Vegas and gotten married by a JP. No pressure, no ceremony, just in and out. But Audrey wanted her special day, and I realized that my wanting to get married in a wedding chapel in Vegas was a response to my own fear. We decided to have a pretty big outdoor wedding a couple of hours up the coast from Los Angeles, at a ranch in the town of Santa Barbara. We told her parents our plans, and then I told my mom. My mom liked Audrey a lot, was happy for us, but given my role in her life, I imagined that she might be frightened that my marriage would cost her some of my attention.

I even thought there was a chance that my mom wouldn't come to the wedding. She hadn't done any real socializing since she'd left Hollywood, and I knew a public outing would be a trial for her. But I truly wanted her to be there, and she said she'd come. She suggested that I invite my aunt Ollie. She said, "Send an invitation to your aunt. Let her know that she's invited. She'll never come all the way from Bayonne, but do it anyway." As luck would have it, Aunt Ollie accepted the invitation and also wanted to bring her daughter and two grandchildren. I called her, said, "Great!" Then, a month before the wedding, my mom said that she was feeling tormented and asked me to please understand if she didn't go. Two weeks later she said to me, "I'm not going." I tried to convince her that it wasn't going to be a horrible day. I said, "It won't be an ordeal for you. Once you're there, you'll be glad about it. And more important, after it's over, you won't feel the guilt and anxiety that I think you will feel if you miss this."

I got nowhere with her. Not only was she going to skip the wedding, but her relatives were coming out to California. She would be obliged to see them, spend time with them and entertain them. She couldn't imagine getting together with people who, because they were her family, would accept her whoever she was. Her fear was, "I can't take them to Chasen's anymore. I can't bring them up to Warren Beatty's house. I can't entertain them the way I used to." Now, on a practical level, she probably couldn't afford to take them out to dinner. But that wasn't the real issue. The issue was that her life had changed in the twenty years since her mother's sister had been to see her in Los Angeles.

Rather than brave the discomfort, my mom did something that was really foolish, and she suffered immensely over it. She decided to disinvite her family. She actually called them and said, "You know what, Ollie? I have hepatitis A and it's infectious. I can't go to the wedding, so I don't know if you should come out."

This was the height of lunacy, and I got angry. I said to my mother, "How can you do that to someone? I've talked to them. I've invited them. They're coming. If you don't go, that's your business, but don't make these people feel unwanted."

Three days before the wedding, my mom had something like a nervous breakdown. She was sobbing hysterically and couldn't complete her sentences. The essence of what she was saying was that she was unbelievably sorry at how she was behaving and feeling. She understood the importance of this day to me, and she felt awful that she couldn't be there. She knew I wanted her to go. She knew she should go. She wanted to go. But she just couldn't go. I was scared for her. I said, "You've got to calm down. The wedding is a done deal. You're not going. It's fine. Don't have a heart attack over this, because nothing is that important. I'll cover for you at the wedding. Look beyond this because now you're compounding it, and I don't want to worry about your health while I'm getting married."

My mom took some medication, calmed down, and was basically all right. Three days before the wedding, it finally sank in for me that my mother wasn't going to be there. I felt bad for Audrey and her family as well as for me and mine. I started to react to the social significance of her absence. What did it say about our relationship if my mother couldn't manage to sit in the front row and dab at her eyes for a few minutes as I said "I do"? Where was her loyalty? Her respect for me and Audrey? I said to my mom, "Look, we'll just drive you up to Santa Barbara. You can sit through the vows and we'll drive you straight home afterward. You don't have to talk to anyone." No way. All kinds of family friends offered her transportation and insulation, but I told them, "You don't understand. Respectfully, Saint Peter could come down and offer to drive her to the wedding and she still wouldn't come. It's not the issue. But thank you."

My mom simply couldn't face people and the emotion of the moment. That's what she said. I was angry for a minute and a half when I finally got it, but I didn't have any real deep-seated anger toward her. How could I? I'm so much like her. I understood that it was easier for her to do *Love Letters* after having been hospitalized near death than it was for her to have dinner with her aunt Olga. She could go on *Sally Jessy Raphaël* and appear before millions of people without panicking because that was work. She didn't have to get intimate with anyone. But go to a family gathering and have someone say, "So, what are you doing now?" Here comes the nineteenth nervous breakdown. I understood this well because the apple doesn't fall far from the tree. And indeed, I have the same insecurities.

My mom was only one part of what I was coping with as D day drew near. I hadn't seen Charlie Maffia since he drove my dad and me around New York in 1972. We had tried to get together in 1990 when my dad was inducted into the Rock and Roll Hall of Fame, but at the last minute Charlie ducked out. He made a reasonable excuse, but when I heard him say that he'd gotten fat I figured out that he was embarrassed to see me. Afraid he wouldn't live up to my expectations. This time I was going to make sure we connected. I called him, made some plans, sent him an airplane ticket, and looked forward to his arrival. I told friends that after all the years of murkiness and controversy, I was going to introduce the people I loved to my grandfather.

One of the people I told was Steve Blauner. Steve and I lost track of each other after my father died, but seven years ago we got together and have had a meaningful friendship ever since. I love Steve. I know he thinks of me as an adopted son, and I grew up calling him "Uncle Steve." I not only care about him as a person, but if we're at a ball game or we're playing a game of chess, we imagine that my dad can see us together and that he digs it. So I told Steve what I planned to do by introducing Charlie. Steve has some great human qualities, and he can also be acerbic and overly tough. About my formally adopting Charlie, he said, "How could you do that to your father's memory?" In other words, "Charlie's the antithesis of what your dad was. Not only could he not be the biological father, but how embarrassing even to mention him." And my reaction to that was, "Respectfully, fuck you. That's your opinion, but the fact of the matter is, Charlie was there. He was changing my dad's diapers, paying for his dental work, christening him. He was the father."

So this was the general drift of my emotions a few days before the wedding. My mom was out of it. Audrey was upset. And I had my own fears that had nothing to do with my mom. There was the general pressure that went with having a wedding, plus a little extra having to do with Charlie, Aunt Ollie, getting the "aunts" in from Colorado, Wayne Newton dropping in between shows, reuniting friends of my father's who didn't like one another, seeing relatives I hadn't seen since I was twelve—and God forbid, what if it rains? Up until the night before, I thought our wedding day was going to be awful. I said to Audrey, "I wish it were over." But once it started and I saw all the people who were there, truly people that I cared about, I enjoyed myself thoroughly.

And it was a beautiful day for a wedding. The sun was out. The garden was glistening. We asked for people to think about my mom and dad for a moment, bring them to the service mentally, and to understand that they both would have been there if they could have been. And everyone did understand. Audrey looked gorgeous. Her dad gave her away. Her sister, Madelyn, was the matron of honor, and her mom, Barbara Tannenbaum, cried from happiness. As Audrey and I exchanged vows, a pair of hummingbirds did their mating dance in the air above us. Now, that's a sign!

Afterward we had a sensational dinner for our guests. My best man and great friend, Rick Ward, gave a rousing toast, which was followed by many more goodwill wishes. Audrey and I had given a lot of thought to who would sit where and why. I looked around the room and saw people genuinely having a good time. I was beyond happy. It all went better than I had ever expected. And Audrey and I toasted our friends in return. We went from table to table, just basking in the warm feelings surrounding us. Then I made my little speech introducing Charlie as my grandfather. It meant a lot to me to do that, and I really hope that it was as significant to Charlie. He deserved the acknowledgment, and he had never had it in my dad's lifetime. He didn't hear it from me until that day, some twenty years after my dad's death. I don't know what took me so long. It sounds strange because I hardly know him, but I love the guy. I made a firm commitment at my wedding that this was the beginning of things for us. Not the beginning and end. The beginning of my relationship with Charlie.

I was sorry when the wedding was over. In fact, Audrey and I stayed an extra night in Santa Barbara. The next day she drove home and I went to Charlie's hotel to spend more time with him. I knew before I saw him that I was kind of raw. We were sitting at the bar, and I felt all these enormous emotions just welling up. Before they could spill over, I abruptly got up and paid the bill. Then Charlie walked me to my car, and as we hugged good-bye, I lost it outside in the parking lot. It was a touching moment, and when combined with the emotions of getting married and having a new sense of family, I was overwhelmed. Moments later, as I was driving out of the lot, I saw Charlie, this lonely, older man, walking back into his hotel. And this picture of him was framed in my mind.

Since Audrey had gone back in her own car, I started driving to Los Angeles by myself. In the car, I thought about my aunt Vee. She hadn't wanted to come to the wedding, but I thought of her every time I looked at Charlie. When I first spoke with Vee while researching this book, she told me a lot of things about my father that scraped my nerves raw. My first reaction was to defend him. It's okay for me to say whatever I want to about my dad, but if someone else does, it feels like murder. Before talking with her, I had heard from different people that my dad looked after Charlie, Nina, and their kids. To this day, my mom says that she knows my dad was sending them money while he was alive because they shared the same checking account.

Now, based on learning new things through writing this book, I understood that my dad was very inconsistent. He could be a real prick when it came to money, doling it out in exchange for labor, and even then it depended on his frame of mind. When I first heard from Vee, my reaction was, "Why did my father owe Charlie, Nina, and their kids anything? They have their own fingers, toes, brain, and talents." Now I thought, Family is family. And I'm sure that had my dad lived longer, he would have regretted some of the things he had done.

But to take this whole issue of money and support a layer deeper, I suddenly understood that Vee wasn't really complaining about insufficient financial support. Strip away all the talk about the leased houses and cars, and I find a woman hurting because she was shortchanged emotionally. She was also carrying her mother's pain and that of her siblings, and Charlie had been injured, too. As a kid, my dad got the lion's share of everything: money, education, and most of all, attention. And he never acknowledged the sacrifice his entire family made for him. I think if he had said "Thanks, guys. I did get the best you had," that would have sufficed for all of them. But he didn't have the humility to thank them, and they were all offended. Anyone would have been. I was glad that I reached out to Vee. I could tell from speaking to her on the phone what an impressive woman she is, and I hope we'll be seeing each other soon. I want to tell her, "What you've heard about me may or may not be true, but you're seeing me now in the flesh." And I'd like to get to know her on our own terms.

It was a three-hour drive from Santa Barbara to Los Angeles, a lot of time to be driving with a million thoughts and feelings churning around in my head. I thought about what had changed for me during the year I've been engaged in writing this book. When I began this project, I was concerned primarily about separating myself from my parents' fame. In many ways I wanted to be like my parents. I wanted to have the respect and the recognition they had, but at heart I knew if I didn't find my own path, I'd never be happy with myself. What my parents did with their lives was inspirational and I'm proud of them, but their lives and mine are different. I don't want to be strictly defined by them or be a prisoner of what they were. I'm not a songwriter, entertainer, or actor, nor do I want to be. I run a book publishing company and am getting into film production, and I want to be the best book publisher, producer, whatever I'm doing, for me. Their looming shadows have always made it hard for me to evaluate my own abilities or to appreciate them.

When I started this book, I decided that in order to separate from my father, I had to examine him wart by wart until I could bring his image down to human size. To a large extent, I've done that. I no longer see Bobby Darin as an impossible, mythic being. He was a man all right, and interestingly, I love him as much as I always did. Maybe more, because in revealing his darker, coarser sides, I saw his love for me come shining through in a thousand ways. I found this humbling and ennobling, and no amount of chipping away at his feet of clay can weaken my memories of our feelings for each other. But the process of digging around in his friends' memories was cathartic, and through it I did manage to dislodge my boyish awe of my father. This has been good.

I have a lot more anger toward my mom, and it goes back a long time. I was a six-year-old boy who worshiped his father, and because of something I couldn't really understand, my father left home. In my heart, I blamed my mother. I decided that somehow she made him feel lousy about himself and gave him reasons to leave. I pictured her as a spoiled, prissy bitch, the kind of woman that men just can't stand. At times she has said to me, "Your dad is a giant figure to you, but let me tell you what he was really like." And I'm sure she felt terrible that I sided with him in arguments between them. I think my mom got labeled the villain in certain ways, and it wasn't fair. Again, examining the evidence as I wrote this book, I addressed this lopsided view of my mother, and I certainly have more sympathy for her in the role of my dad's wife than I ever did before.

But I can't help but be affected by the last fifteen years of knowing her as an adult. This part is between me and my mom and has nothing to do with her relationship to my father. I've dealt firsthand with her manipulation and her selfishness. And I hate these qualities in her. But, boy, I've also seen what she has struggled with and how far down she had to reach to find the qualities that enabled her to be an excellent mother. It was no contrivance when I called her to say thank you. She earned my thanks and my devotion, and thanking her was long over-due. She was there for me always. She watched out for me, and like my dad, she loved me totally.

I said at the beginning of this book that I felt I had taken on the responsibility for my mother's happiness. Things have shifted in that regard. To begin with, my mom tells me that she has to be happy for herself in her own way. She can't be a happy housewife on Long Island, married to a building contractor just because that's her son's idea of what would make her happy. Okay. But I would love for her to be able to feel good about herself and to take some pride in what she has accomplished. Because she really doesn't.

And that's the key to why she has suffered so. She couldn't go to my wedding and just be a human being, because in her mind unless she was Sandra Dee, who had a major career and had things going, she was a nothing, an absolute nobody. That's how she feels about herself. It doesn't matter that she raised a son, survived a dysfunctional

363

childhood, had a wonderful career. And I say, if she never works again, the career she's already had is magnificent. She brought a lot of laughs and joy to people and was a very respected professional. And if it never happens again, that should be enough to give her some self-esteem. But she's only affected by external stuff: "You're a pretty girl. You're a star." If the wedding had come at a time when she had professional things going on, she would have been absolutely at ease with showing up. But because it came in the context of what her life is now, she couldn't face it. And the sad thing about that is that she could have taken pride in being the mother of the groom. I arrived at this stage of my life as a pretty healthy individual, joining my life to that of an extraordinary woman. My mom could have taken some credit for that, shared the pleasure of a happy occasion that in a large way she produced. She'd done something really monumental, and it was as if she didn't show up to accept her award.

So what caused this system breakdown? The finger points at my grandmother, and to be honest, getting to know Mary Douvan has been the most tormenting element for me in all of this. At heart I didn't believe my mother's story about Eugene Douvan when I started writing this book. Not that I thought she was lying, but I loved my grandmother so much that it seemed impossible she could have been culpable. It's still hard to reconcile my feelings for my grandmother, but I can see the trail of deceit and denial that ruined my mother's life and impacted mine.

No single thing convinced me of my grandmother's true nature; it was the compilation of testimony and my reexamination of my own experiences with her when she was alive. Through writing this book, I heard my mother's terrible story in its entirety. I listened to Ross Hunter and my aunt Ollie as they described my grandmother's style of mothering. I remembered again that Charlie Sinatra took his own life because my grandmother wouldn't acknowledge him publicly. I revisited the scenes I'd had with my grandmother when she refused to get help for my mother. And I saw clearly that her denial was due mostly to her fear of what her friends would think of her if she had an alcoholic daughter. But if there was one factor that tipped the balance for me between believing my mom's story and writing it off, it was this: If my mother wasn't molested, wasn't sacrificed, what did happen to her? What crippled this sweet, pretty, intelligent woman who by all rights ought to be coping with life at least as well as her peers? What caused her destruction? What cost her the last twenty years of her life?

I believe my mother was molested. I believe my grandmother knew. I believe my grandmother came from a place of love—she may have been blinded by her desire to make sure her daughter survived—but there was also an evil aspect to her behavior that I cannot deny. If my grandmother stood before me now, I'd still love her. I'd hug her. I'd kiss her. But I'd ask better questions now, and I wouldn't let her get away with murder.

When I signed on to do this book, I had a number of conflicting feelings. I wanted to tell my parents' story, but I knew if I did, I would have to tell all, and I'd be exploiting their fame. I swallowed my guilty feelings with a promise that in doing this book about their lives, I would be as honest about myself as I was about them. So in that light I want to say that I am still not satisfied with my contribution in this world.

I sometimes think of a song my father wrote, one that I quoted earlier in this book. My dad was thirty-two when he wrote "A Song for a Dollar," the same age I am now. Many believe, and I would agree, that the song is autobiographical. The narrator of the song is a reformed "film-flam" man who is recounting a career spent grabbing off some fortune and fame. Having done that, he now wants to stand up and truly say what he has to say. There are very few among us who don't have to sing for our supper, and if sing we must, it behooves us to sing as well as we can. My dad sang his songs for a dollar. My mom sang hers. This book is my song for a dollar. The wedding coalesced the threads of this story, made it into an event. But without the book, I wouldn't have reached out to Charlie or Vee, wouldn't have known my father, mother, and grandmother as I do now. My mom has told me that working with me on this book has been illuminating in a positive way. She says that some issues have been clarified for her and other issues have been brought to light that she never knew or understood before. My aunt Vee told me that this book has built bridges for our family, and that's made me feel very warm indeed. And I've learned a hell a lot about myself. I see now that the only way I can become my own person, Dodd Darin, without the "son of Bobby

Darin and Sandra Dee" suffix, is to step out of my parents' shadows and say what I have to say.

All of this was in my mind as I drove back from the scene of my marriage to Audrey. I got off the freeway in Los Angeles, and when I got to Beverly Glen, I went directly to a flower shop, where I picked out eighteen yellow roses. My dad had once written a song by this name for my mom, and it became a hit in 1963 during the height of the Beatles invasion. But this bit of musical trivia aside, I got the roses and wrote out a card that said, "Dear Mother, you will never lose your son. You have only gained a daughter-in-law. Love, Dodd." And I went over to see her.

During the whole drive down from Santa Barbara, I was carrying around the feelings about the wedding, sorting through my new revelations. But as soon as I entered my mom's house, the emotions just drained out of me. I gave her the flowers. I gave her the card, and she was very composed. I was very much expecting—hoping, really—that she would be emotional and interested in what had gone on. And she wasn't. I was in her house for three or four minutes, and then I got out. It was a weird, deflating experience. But I meant what I said on the card. And although she seemed cool to me, my mom was feeling more than I guessed.

Later she said:

☞ *I thought marrying Audrey was the best thing that ever happened to Dodd. I was so happy, so truly happy, I was more disappointed than he was at how I was reacting. Dodd said, "I love you. You don't have to come. I'm not making you do this." He was worried that I was going to jump off the balcony. The way I was acting wasn't like me. I think I had a minibreakdown. I didn't leave the house for two and a half weeks. I locked myself up in my room and cried.*

Somehow I got through the day of the wedding. I was loaded with guilt and feeling that I was going to suffer for the rest of my life because I missed it, but I got through Saturday because Dodd had called and said he was coming to see me. I was so relieved that he was at least talking to me! He could surely be forgiven if he never talked to me again.

When he called, he told me he would be coming home on Monday. He said. "I'm going to go straight home. I'll call you when I get there."

I said, "Okay." By Monday my eyes were puffy from crying and I looked a wreck. I hated being this way, and I remember that I talked to myself, literally said out loud, "You are not going to fall apart in front of Dodd." I washed up, got myself all together, and I was waiting for my son to call. I figured when he called, I would go to his house and see him. And all of a sudden I heard the key in the door downstairs.

"Mom? You home?"

"Yes, Dodd!"

"Don't come down. I'll come up. I've got a little something for you."

He walked into my bedroom. He sat on the bed and gave me the roses. I thought it was so sweet. So really sweet. Dodd often brings me flowers for no reason. This time he brought me eighteen yellow roses, and they were just perfect. Every one of them opened perfectly. They were so beautiful, I just wanted to bronze them.

When I left my mother, I drove four miles to my own house. I let the dog inside, then I went upstairs and got into bed with Audrey Tannenbaum Darin. My wife. She was wearing a white T-shirt and a pair of socks, and she smelled really good. I took her in my arms and told her that it felt as though it had taken me half my life to drive from Santa Barbara to Los Angeles. And in a way, it had. I was exhausted, but I knew that at last I was home.

AFTERWORD

Writing this book was quite simply the most difficult thing I have ever done. To be honest, if I had known how difficult it was going to be, I would not have undertaken it. Many times during the year of working on it, I was ready to give it up. Not only did I have to unearth and acknowledge painful aspects of my parents' lives and of my own, but I had to do so without the insights of my grandmothers and my father, who were no longer with us to tell their side of the story.

Another psychological impediment was that I detested the notion of the "celebrity kid cashing in on his parents." These issues combined with the fact that I am a very private person made the decision to do this project very difficult. After much soul-searching, I decided to go ahead with the book for three reasons.

First, someone else would inevitably have attempted to do this book. Two books have already been published about my father, and with a major motion picture being developed about him, commercial concerns probably would have led to the publication of a third. No doubt that one would have been out of my hands, and it certainly would not have been written with the care and concern we have put into ours.

Second, I am so very proud of my parents. I wanted their contributions and their lives to be chronicled and retained forever. Excuse my arrogance, but the book you now hold is my small and humble attempt to immortalize them.

The third and most decisive reason I undertook this book was that I had the full blessing of my mother and her direct cooperation. This was critical to me, in that I knew she would have to face the painful aspects presented on these pages and still go on with her life. Every emotion and problem I have had with my mother I have expressed to her before, but that is a far cry from seeing the same items on the printed page and disseminated to the world. My mother takes some harsh criticism in this book, and I know how hurt she is by some of the things I've written. I want her to know, and I pray that deep down she does know, how much I truly love, respect, and admire her. I am so proud to be able to say that she has been sober for over a year and has committed herself to resuming her career. A big part of the credit for her sobriety goes to her caring therapist, Dr. Ronald Gershman; our good friend and family doctor, Dr. Louis Fishman; and our friend Barbara Friedman. My mom has a tremendous amount to offer, and I know she will succeed at what she does. My hope is that she enjoys her career the second time around.

My biggest regret, of course, is that my father is not here with us. It is my hope that the man I so loved and looked up to would be proud of this book and, more important, of the man I have become.

Who says dreams don't come true? I have now been married to my junior high school sweetheart for over one year! I feel very blessed to have Audrey Claudine Darin in my life. She has been the best thing that has ever happened to me, and without question she is the finest, most loving person I have ever known. She has helped me to become a happier and better human being, and it is with her love and strength that we hope to bring the next generation of Darins into this world.

ABOUT THE COLLABORATOR

Maxine Paetro is the author of three novels: *Manshare*, *Babydreams*, and *Windfall*. Her nonfiction book, *How to Put Your Book Together and Get a Job in Advertising*, has gone into its fourteenth printing. *Dream Lovers* is her first collaboration.